Contemporary Neurology Series:

Additional volumes in preparation

CASES

OF

APOPLEXY AND LETHARGY:

WITH

Observations

UPON

THE COMATOSE DISEASES.

By J. CHEYNE, M.D.

FELLOW OF THE ROYAL COLLEGE OF PHYSICIANS, EDINBURGH;
LICENTIATE OF THE KING AND QUEEN'S COLLEGE OF
PHYSICIANS IN IRELAND; ONE OF THE PHYSICIANS
TO THE MEATH HOSPITAL, AND COUNTY
OF DUBLIN INFIRMARY, &c.

LONDON:

PRINTED FOR THOMAS UNDERWOOD, MEDICAL BOOKSELLER
40, WEST SMITHFIELD; ADAM BLACK, EDINBURGH;
WALTER DUNCAN, GLASGOW; AND
GILBERT AND HODGES, DUBLIN.

1812.

I HAVE every wish to avoid unnecessary distinctions in medicine, and to see simplicity in the nosological arrangement; yet, at the expense of restoring another genus to the table of diseases, I conceived it right again to draw the line between apoplexy and lethargy. I found great confusion arising from the attempt which had been made to identify these two affections of the brain; and those who best understand the nature of apoplexy, will be the most ready to admit, that it is a disease which requires an undivided attention. If in describing the morbid appearances which are connected with apoplexy, I shall be thought tedious, I beg to remind the reader, that, independent of the practical tendency of such a detail, the anatomy of apoplexy is connected with a forensic question of great importance. Being aware of many defects in the following pages, I beg leave to say, that, until lately, I have not had the benefit of leisure to make the proper use of my opportunities of observation; and that in a work compiled under the disadvantages of the fatigue and hurry of professional employment of the most laborious kind, neither deep research into the writings of medical authors, nor the most orderly disposition of materials, can reasonably be expected.

The Diagnosis of Stupor and Coma

Second Edition

Fred Plum, M.D.

Anne Parrish Titzell Professor of Neurology
Cornell University Medical College
Neurologist-in-Chief, The New York Hospital

Jerome B. Posner, M.D.

Professor of Neurology
Cornell University Medical College
Chief, Neuropsychiatric Service
Memorial Hospital for Cancer and Allied Diseases, New York

 F. A. DAVIS COMPANY, PHILADELPHIA

Preface to the Second Edition

Since the last edition of this monograph, medicine and society have increasingly concerned themselves with the importance of the brain's integrity in human individuality. Consequently, all parts of the text and bibliography have been brought up to date to give account to advances reported in the medical literature, and the text has been modified to take advantage of new experiences gained in our laboratories and on our clinical services at The New York Hospital and Memorial Hospital during the past 5 years.

Several figures and diagrams have been replaced or introduced in an effort to clarify points in physiology, particularly in the changes induced by tentorial herniation. Many of the illustrative case studies have been replaced with better-studied material. New sections dealing with the physiology and pathology of coma and ocular motility have been included, and the older ones have been considerably revised. We have added descriptions of several metabolic diseases causing coma as well as a short chapter that explicitly considers the diagnosis of psychogenic unresponsiveness.

Inasmuch as physicians are ever more often being asked to predict the neurological outcome of serious brain injuries, and particularly the moment when brain death occurs, we have considered these matters in a new chapter dealing with prognosis in coma and the definition of death.

Any oversights or errors are our own. However, no matter how many the reader finds, they are fewer than when we started only because many friends, students, and colleagues have offered criticisms and helpful suggestions. We are particularly indebted to Prof. Bryan Jennett, who read and discussed with us the entire text; Dr. Robert Brennan, who supplied the tabular material on cerebellar hemorrhage; and Dr. Norman Chernik, who helped with the new illustrations. Mrs. Carol D'Anella has again cheerfully and accurately prepared the many manuscript drafts, correcting spelling and syntax, and proofreading galleys and page proofs. Finally, with eight volumes of the Contemporary Neurology series separating the two editions of *Stupor and Coma,* it is a pleasure to tell Robert H. Craven and the F. A. Davis Company how much we appreciate the patience, care, and quality efforts they have put into publishing these volumes.

FRED PLUM, M.D.

JEROME B. POSNER, M.D.

Preface to the First Edition

Stupor and coma are such common clinical states that it is unusual for a busy hospital emergency room to pass a day without facing a diagnostic problem involving one or the other. Despite this ubiquity of the problem, however, no current volume has directed itself at the clinical approach to diagnosis of states of impaired consciousness, and Cheyne's monograph of 150 years ago, from which we have appropriated the charming frontispiece, is now medically somewhat out of date. It has been our good fortune to be associated with hospitals and colleagues serving wide segments of the community and receiving many diagnostic problems from other physicians. The demands of patients for care forced us to develop for ourselves a systematic approach in diagnosing coma, and the lively interest among our associates in the whys and hows of unconsciousness prompted us to explain our approach and summarize some of the lessons learned. This book is the result.

The clinical material came from the King County Hospital and University of Washington Hospital, Seattle, between 1953 and 1963, and from the Cornell University services at The New York Hospital and Bellevue Hospital since 1963. We are indebted to many medical and nursing associates at these institutions for their help and personal contributions. Certain colleagues deserve particular mention and thanks. Drs. August G. Swanson, Harold W. Brown, Gian E. Chatrian, Henry Leffman, Richard M. Torack, Raymond F. Hain, and Ellsworth C. Alvord contributed many of the ideas and some of the studies included here. Misses Helen Goodell and Carol Manning provided particular assistance in manuscript preparation and we give them thanks. Before he died in 1961, Dr. Donald E. McNealy was a valued and stimulating co-worker who left many of his ideas and the stamp of his enthusiasm and energy on these pages.

FRED PLUM, M.D.
JEROME B. POSNER, M.D.

Contents

Chapter 1

The Pathological Physiology of Signs and Symptoms of Coma

ALTERED STATES OF CONSCIOUSNESS

And men should know that from nothing else but from the brain came joys, delights, laughter and jests, and sorrows, griefs, despondency and lamentations. And by this, in an especial manner, we acquire wisdom and knowledge, and see and hear and know what are foul, and what are fair, what sweet and what unsavory . . . —The Hippocratic writings

Since the Greeks, men have known that normal conscious behavior depends on intact brain function and that disorders of consciousness are a sign of cerebral insufficiency. However, the range of normal human conscious behavior is so rich and variable that its medical aberrance is difficult to test except when it undergoes a very great change from normal. Impaired, reduced, or absent conscious behavior implies that severe brain dysfunction has already occurred and demands urgent attention from the physician if potential recovery is to be provided for. Nervous tissue can tolerate only a limited amount of physical or metabolic injury without undergoing irreparable harm. Stupor and coma mean brain failure, just as the uremic syndrome means renal failure, and the longer such failure lasts the narrower becomes the margin for a return to full health.

A wide spectrum of specific conditions can injure the brain so as to result in coma or progressive defects of consciousness.

Unselected series have been published from the Cook County and the Boston City Hospitals.[243, 531] These series include many patients in whom the history or the findings made the cause of coma immediately obvious. Since one of the main purposes of this monograph is to discuss how to diagnose the cause of coma when the disease is not obvious, we tabulated cases for which the neurologist was consulted either because the patient's physician was unable to make a diagnosis or had serious doubts about it. Table 1 includes the final clinical, surgical or pathological diagnosis in these patients. Examples of these initially puzzling or obscure problems are discussed in subsequent sections, but before proceeding to that it may be helpful to define some terms.

Definitions

Consciousness. Consciousness means awareness of self and environment. Its precise limits are extremely hard to define satisfactorily for we can only infer the self-awareness of others by their appearances and acts. However, there are two aspects of consciousness, and different types and distributions of brain disease affect them differently. One is the *content* of consciousness, the sum of mental functions. The other is *arousal,* which, behaviorally at least, is closely linked to the appearance of wakefulness. Later sections discuss the evidence that assigns the content of consciousness largely to the functions of the cerebral hemispheres and the arousal parts of consciousness to brainstem structures (the diencephalon, midbrain, and pons). As will be seen, both content and arousal can vary independently through an almost infinite progression ranging from nil to a physiological maximum.

2

Table I. Final diagnosis in 386 patients admitted with "coma of unknown etiology"

I.	Supratentorial Mass Lesions		69
	Epidural hematoma	2	
	Subdural hematoma	21	
	Intracerebral hematoma	33	
	Cerebral infarct	5	
	Brain tumor	5	
	Brain abscess	3	
II.	Subtentorial Lesions		52
	Brainstem infarct	37	
	Brainstem tumor	2	
	Brainstem hemorrhage	7	
	Cerebellar hemorrhage	4	
	Cerebellar abscess	2	
III.	Metabolic and Diffuse Cerebral Disorders		261
	Anoxia or ischemia	51	
	Concussion and postictal states	9	
	Infection (Meningitis and encephalitis)	11	
	Subarachnoid hemorrhage	10	
	Exogenous toxins	99	
	Endogenous toxins and deficiencies	81	
IV.	Psychiatric Disorders		4

Since the consciousness of another individual can only be estimated from his behavior, its presence, degree, or absence can sometimes be difficult to judge medically, particularly during states of psychic withdrawal or when motor paralysis partially or completely blocks voluntary behavior. The diagnosis of these pseudo-unconscious states is treated elsewhere in these pages. Sleep is not fully conscious behavior, and, whatever significance dreams may have, they too closely resemble delirium to grant them any value in that adaptation to the external milieu that comprises full consciousness. Patients with sleeplike unresponsiveness are obviously unconscious by everyone's definition. However, semantic problems arise in dealing with certain chronically unresponsive patients who look awake but give little or no evidence of possessing any mental content. Some workers regard these states of wakeful unresponsiveness (called akinetic mutism or *coma vigile*) as a form of coma, while others consider them as examples of profound dementia and presumably restrict the term "coma" exclusively to sleeplike states in which the eyes remain closed.[169, 541] The importance of straightening out these terminological imprecisions is that clinicians, physiologists, pathologists, and psychologists can then reach a common discussion ground for adding their special expertise to unraveling the brain's unknowns.

States of altered consciousness. Restricted impairments of psychological function such as aphasia or memory loss reduce the content of consciousness but are localizable cerebral defects not generally regarded as altered states of consciousness. Acute, diffuse psychological losses, i.e., the confusional states and deliria, almost always combine a generalized reduction or alteration in the content of consciousness with at least some reduction in total arousal and comprise the states of altered or clouded consciousness. In stupor and sleeplike coma the defect in arousal predominates and it is impossible to estimate the potential mental content. With chronic states in which the content of consciousness is profoundly reduced but the capacity for arousal returns, it is best to avoid global, imprecise terms such as coma and to describe the mental content and the capacity for wakefulness separately. When the pathological processes strike the brain acutely or develop rapidly, the loss of cerebral function is proportionately large in relation to the size of the lesion so that sleeplike stupor and coma tend to reflect acute or subacute brain diseases while dementia more often characterizes insidiously developing or chronic processes, particularly those that spare the brainstem. However, even with acute lesions of the brain, the normal cerebral reserves are so extensive and pluripotential that altered or reduced consciousness can always be taken to reflect either diffuse and bilateral impairment of cerebral functions or failure of the brainstem ascending reticular activating system or both.

Clouding of consciousness. This is a state of reduced wakefulness or awareness that in its minimal form includes excitability and irritability alternating with drowsiness. The patient is startled by minor stimuli; he is distractible and he misjudges sensory perceptions, particularly visual ones. He cannot think quickly and clearly. More advanced clouding produces an acute or subacute *confusional state* in which stimuli are more consistently misinterpreted and the attention span is shortened. Confused patients are bewildered and often have difficulty following commands. They have at least a minor disorientation for time and sometimes for place or person. Memory is faulty, and confused subjects have difficulty in repeating numbers backward (the normal number is at least four or five) and in repeating the details or even the meaning of stories. Drowsiness often is prominent and daytime drowsiness may alternate with nighttime agitation.

Relatively few physiological or metabolic studies exist on the states of clouded consciousness, but those that do indicate the existence of generalized brain dysfunction. For example, in lethargic confused patients with liver disease, Posner and Plum[454] found that cerebral oxygen consumption had fallen 20 per cent below the normal level and Shimojyo, Scheinberg, and Reinmuth[513] noted a similar reduction in cerebral metabolism in confused subjects with Wernicke's disease.

Delirium is a more florid state characterized by disorientation, fear, irritability, misperception of sensory stimuli, and often visual hallucinations. Lucid periods can alternate with delirious episodes, and such patients are

4

commonly terrified of their own mental failure. Delirium commonly produces complex, systematized, and protracted delusions of a dreamlike nature during which patients are completely out of contact with the environment and unreachable by the examiner. They are commonly loud, talkative, offensive, suspicious, and agitated. Delirium is prominent with toxic and metabolic disorders of the nervous system such as acute poisoning with atropine or its congeners, the alcohol-barbiturate withdrawal syndrome, acute porphyria, uremia, acute hepatic failure, and encephalitis. Severe head injury often leads to delirium during recovery from unconsciousness. At one time delirium frequently accompanied acute systemic infections such as pneumonia, but it is much less common now that antibiotics have blunted the severity of those illnesses.

Delirium accompanies diffuse metabolic and multifocal cerebral illnesses and its presence implies a generalized impairment of brain functions or at least a bilateral involvement of limbic structures.[157] Cerebral metabolic studies on delirious patients are lacking, but Romano and Engel[473] reported that the EEG was always slowed in delirium and clinically the state is commonly a prelude or sequel to stupor or coma.

Stupor is unresponsiveness from which the subject can be aroused only by vigorous and repeated stimuli. Most stuporous patients have diffuse organic cerebral dysfunction, although deep physiological sleep can sometimes produce stupor and catatonic schizophrenia leads to a state of stupor sometimes requiring great skill to differentiate from organic causes (page 218).

Coma is unarousable unresponsiveness: ". . . the absence of any psychologically understandable response to external stimulus or inner need."[371] It is possible that coma has several gradations, but this generally defies quantitative appraisal once patients are completely unresponsive. Some authors equate the presence or absence of motor responses with the depth of coma, which confuses the issue since neural structures regulating consciousness and motor function are independent of each other (page 53).

It is not always easy to determine whether or not a patient is in coma. Under these circumstances, an accurate description of his behavior is preferable.

With *acute global aphasia* the failure of communication can sometimes make it extremely difficult on clinical grounds to determine whether the patient is mentally responsive or unresponsive.

Hypersomnia refers to excessive drowsiness. Particularly in the European literature, states of sleeplike coma are sometimes designated hypersomnia, but the physiological relationship to sleep has not been established and the usage is potentially confusing.

Akinetic mutism is a term coined by Cairns[74] to describe the silent, alert-looking immobility that characterizes certain subacute or chronic states of altered consciousness in which sleep-wake cycles have returned, but evidence for mental activity remains almost entirely absent.[303] The picturesque French term, *coma vigile,* refers to the same condition. The pathological basis for these disorders is given on page 23.

The *apallic state* is Kretschmer's term[318] to describe the diffuse bilateral cerebral cortical degeneration that sometimes follows anoxia, head injury, or encephalitis. Although an anatomical term, it has been applied to some patients whose condition resembles the akinetic mutism described above, while others are diffusely rigid or spastic, yet immobile.

Persistent or chronic vegetative state is the term proposed by Jennett and Plum[273a] to describe the condition of subjects who survive for prolonged periods (sometimes years) following a severe brain injury without recovering any manifestations of higher mental activity. All patients in coma begin to awaken within 2 to 4 weeks no matter how severe the brain damage, and once awake it is hardly possible to describe them as still in coma even though their behavior may never again demonstrate any evidence of a conscious intelligence. Since several different types of neuropathological abnormalities in the cortex or brainstem have turned out to underlie the condition, the behavioral description, vegetative, seems preferable to an anatomical term such as "neocortical death" or "apallic state," which implies a greater knowledge of the necessary morphological lesion than often turns out to be the case. Likewise, although many such patients are akinetic, not all are so, which is potentially confusing to the general physician. The term vegetative state focuses on the severe behavioral limitation, is immediately understood, and therefore is useful for communicating to physicians and laymen alike. Such a readily understood term may help medicine and society to focus on the increasing medical and social problem created by treatments that, by their effectiveness in saving life, increase the numbers of such unfortunate subjects.

The *locked-in syndrome* is a term we coined for the first edition of this monograph (see page 24) to describe a condition of paralysis of all four extremities and lower cranial nerves that may or may not be associated with impaired consciousness. Impairment of consciousness depends on the location and extent of the lesion. In this condition, bilateral supranuclear paralysis prohibits verbal or skeletal motor communication, leaving the patient only with vertical eye movements and blinking to communicate his consciousness. The terms "ventral pontine syndrome," indicating the size of the lesion, and "de-efferented state," indicating the absence of motor movement, have also been used but recent authors have preferred "locked-in syndrome."[159a, 412a]

Clinical Guides to Diagnosis

The diagnosis of the cause of coma or, at times, even whether an unresponsive patient suffers primarily from a physical or psychiatric illness can sometimes be dismayingly difficult. Unfortunately for those who seek simple solutions, no single laboratory test or screening procedure will sift out the critical initial diagnostic categories nearly so effectively as does a prompt and effective clinical appraisal. Faced with an acutely ill patient with severe neurological or behavioral symptoms suggesting impaired consciousness, the physician must accurately answer the following questions: Is the disturbance functional or organic? If organic, is it focal or diffuse? Is the patient getting better, holding his own or getting worse? How to differentiate between functional and organic causes of unresponsiveness is discussed in Chapter 5. Later sections of this chapter will make it clear that, although focal lesions of the cerebral hemispheres produce aphasia, apraxia, agnosia, or unilateral motor or sensory defects, they do not produce stupor or coma unless they secondarily impair remote intracranial structures so as to induce diffuse bilateral changes in the cerebral hemispheres. Small focal brain lesions must be in the brainstem to produce coma directly. Therefore, delirium, stupor, or coma complicating cerebral hemisphere disease implies brain dysfunction that is either diffuse or multifocal, and the course of signs and symptoms in patients with impaired consciousness is a crucial indication of the effectiveness of treatment and the potential outcome of the illness.

Clinical and experimental studies, reviewed later in this chapter, demonstrate that consciousness with an intact complement of its functions requires continuous and effective interaction between the relatively intact cerebral hemispheres and certain "nonspecific" physiological activating mechanisms in the upper brainstem. In keeping with these physiological concepts, two general types of pathological processes can impair consciousness. One consists of conditions that widely and directly depress the function of the cerebral hemispheres, and the other includes conditions that depress or destroy the brainstem activating mechanisms that lie in or near to the central core of gray matter of the diencephalon, midbrain, and rostral pons. These principles imply that diseases producing stupor or coma must either affect the brain widely or encroach directly upon its deep central structures or both. Such diseases fall into three categories: (1) supratentorial mass lesions, which secondarily encroach upon deep diencephalic structures so as to compress or damage physiological ascending reticular activating systems; (2) subtentorial mass or destructive lesions, which directly damage the brainstem central core; (3) metabolic disorders, which widely depress or interrupt brain function. Table 1 lists some of the specific causes of unconsciousness for these three categories and also includes psychogenic states that may at first resemble coma but are physiologically distinguishable from it. Subsequent chapters will explain and justify the classification.

Once having decided that a patient is in stupor or coma, the next question is anatomical, i.e., where do(es) the lesion(s) lie? A corollary question is: In what direction is the process evolving? The answers to these two place the disease in one of the above three categories and greatly reduce the number of inferences required to solve the final question: What is the specific pathological process and what can be done about it and its effects on the brain? However, before one attempts to answer these questions, the brain *must be protected immediately* against more serious or irreversible damage. Even preceding his detailed examination, the physician must guarantee the airway (the oxygen supply), the circulation (the oxygen-transport system), and the cerebral metabolic need (by giving glucose in any doubtful circumstance *after* first drawing blood for glucose determination).

The diagnosis of coma can be accomplished logically and accurately by moving from general causes to more-restricted categories, and finally to specific causes that can be verified objectively by laboratory methods. A full and accurate history often gives the answer so that telephone calls to a patient's family, associates, and local physicians commonly obviate the need for extensive and expensive diagnostic laboratory tests. Police and ambulance drivers often provide similarly valuable data.

In many cases of stupor or coma a reliable history cannot be obtained and the cause remains obscure, necessitating heavy reliance on the physical examination. A complete neurological examination must be made, but the pattern of changes in five physiological functions gives particularly valuable information about the *level* of the brain involved, the nature of the involvement, and the direction the disease process is taking. These functions are: (1) the state of consciousness, (2) the pattern of breathing, (3) the size and reactivity of the pupils, (4) the eye movements and the oculo-vestibular responses, (5) the skeletal muscle motor responses.

The following sections discuss these functions in detail and relate their pathological physiology to states of unconsciousness.

The Physiology and Pathology of Consciousness and Coma

Studies in Animals

The nature of consciousness and its alterations lies close to the most searching questions man asks about himself, no matter what his field of work. Several symposia and reviews that have thoughtfully discussed the subject are listed in the references.[1, 126, 147, 267, 272, 298, 552, 553, 602] Psychological and clinical-pathological studies in man have amply demonstrated that the content of consciousness depends on the cerebral hemispheres.[86] Physiological studies in animals have concentrated more on the arousal component of consciousness, seeking the anatomical substrate of crude consciousness and attempting to relate it to the naturally occurring states of wakefulness and sleep as well as to the pathological state of coma. These searches have focused mainly on structures resident in the brainstem.

More than a century ago Carpenter[80] stated in his *Principles of Human Physiology:*

The Sensory Ganglia (thalamus) constitute the seat of consciousness, not merely for impression on the Organ of Sense but also for changes in the cortical substance of the Cerebrum so that until the latter have reacted downwards upon the Sensorium we have no consciousness either of the formation of ideas or of any intellectual process of which these may be the subjects.

Direct evidence in recent years has justified these prescient speculations relating the brainstem to cortex.

Berger[37] discovered in 1928 that sleep is associated with a slower and more synchronous electroencephalographic (EEG) record than is wakefulness. The symmetrically increased synchrony could only be attributed to a sub-cortical "pacemaker" diffusely affecting the cortex but lying outside it. Further evidence of the importance of the brainstem to the hemispheres came from Bremer,[55] who in 1937 reported the effects of transection of the brainstem of cats at the pontine-midbrain and the medullary-spinal junctions, respectively. In both preparations, surgical damage to the rostral diencephalon and the hemispheres during the operation was minimal and the animals were physiologically well maintained. The animals with the midbrain transection looked asleep and had unarousable, synchronous, sleeplike waves in their EEG's. By contrast, the animals with the cervical-medullary transections looked awake and their EEG's contained desynchronized patterns, resembling normal arousal. Bremer emphasized that the cervical-medullary transected animals retained auditory and trigeminal sensory inputs, and concluded that wakefulness required constant stimulation of the cerebral hemispheres by incoming sensory impulses. Coma, by inference, would result when such stimulation was silenced or interrupted.

Bremer was correct in his observations, but nothing in his experiments implied that the diencephalon in any way transformed incoming stimuli when relaying them from the periphery to arouse an otherwise dormant cortex. However, Morison and Dempsey[389] in 1942 demonstrated a diffuse thalamocortical recruiting system that was nonspecific in that it was independent of a particular primary sensory relay. An even more important nonspecific activating mechanism, the ascending reticular activating system (ARAS), was discovered shortly after (1949) by Moruzzi and Magoun,[391] who along with their colleagues have made numerous important contributions to this field.[333, 352] Moruzzi and Magoun identified the ARAS within the rostral reticular formation, extending from the midbrain to the hypothalamus and thalamus, and demonstrated that it had diffuse projections to the cerebral cortex and profoundly influenced arousal and the EEG. When the ARAS of a sleeping animal was stimulated directly with an electrode placed in its substance, prompt EEG desynchronization and behavioral arousal resulted. When the ARAS was destroyed, a slow synchronized EEG and coma ensued, neither of which could be reversed by strong sensory stimulation even if the main sensory pathways from the periphery via thalamus to cortex were preserved. Coma was not a consequence of restricted cerebral hemispheric lesions as long as the ARAS and its connections to the cortex were preserved, even if the direct thalamocortical sensory relays were interrupted. Anesthetic drugs apparently selectively depressed the brainstem reticular core since they simultaneously blocked reticular activity, behavioral arousal, and EEG desynchronization (the amounts used were too small to interrupt direct impulses ascending to cortex via sensory lemnisci and thalamic sensory relay nuclei). There was much more seemingly concordant early evidence, and the view gradually became prevalent that consciousness was due to the specific arousal effects of the ARAS stimulating the hemispheres. It was initially assumed that sleep and coma were similar, both due to the passive failure of a physiologically or pathologically inactivated ARAS to arouse the cerebrum. As it turned out, this was too simple an explanation for these complex neural states, but before presenting current theories on sleep and coma, it may help briefly to outline the structure of the brainstem reticulum.

Anatomically, the reticular formation has vexingly indistinct boundaries and extends along the core of the central brainstem from the lower medulla to the thalamus, incorporating both small and large neurons. Short and long axons provide rich interconnections within the formation, endowing it with the property of both slow and rapid conduction. Individual cells extend their dendrites over large areas, providing a continuum of overlapping dendritic fields and a free intermingling of dendrites with passing myelinated and unmyelinated bundles. The entire architecture creates optimal anatomical opportunities for stimulation by collaterals coming both from many different specific fiber pathways and from adjacent brainstem nuclear masses.[461, 488]

In the thalamus, the reticular formation is interspersed among the main sensory nuclei. Morphologically, it includes most of the septal region, the hypothalamus, and the midbrain tegmentum. The reticular activating system receives collaterals from and is stimulated by every major somatic and special sensory pathway. Spinothalamic collaterals to the midbrain tegmental reticulum are especially numerous and may provide a morphological basis for the particularly arousing qualities of noxious stimuli. The cerebral cortex not only is stimulated by the ARAS but restimulates and modulates the reticulum in turn, and it has been postulated that this is the feedback mechanism by which the forebrain regulates incoming information.[352] Such a mechanism could also help to explain why incoming messages of equal intensity but different "meaning" have profoundly different capacities to arouse. There are close connections between the reticular formation and the rhinencephalon, that phylogenetically older and deeper part of the forebrain that is believed to mediate a large part of both emotional behavior and memory.

Because of its diffuse, polysynaptic anatomy, it is difficult to subdivide functional areas of the reticular formation on morphological grounds.[62] As a result, the ascending reticular activating system is more a physiological than an anatomical entity. Certain well-marked bundles such as the lateral reticulothalamic tract[480] conduct cephalically, but cells projecting cephalically occur at all levels of the brainstem reticular formation, and the final anatomical projection to the cerebral cortex is not fully understood. Some workers believe that all cortically directed reticular activity is first mediated through the thalamic reticular nucleus (a particular, identifiable thalamic structure), while others propose more widespread anatomical routes for cortical excitation. In either case, large portions of the brainstem neuronal reticulum are involved in the arousal mechanism. In animals, major damage to the structure anywhere rostral to the pons appears sufficient to interrupt or greatly reduce the cortical activation that maintains consciousness.[186, 418]

The caudal extent of the structures critical to cortical arousal is not exactly known, but it is probably not much lower than the trigeminal nerve entry. Thus, the reticular formation of the lower pons and medulla appears to have important influences on certain stages of sleep and on the EEG, but does not seem to be directly required for the maintenance of animal consciousness. Batini and associates[27] describe the appearance of alertness in cats with brainstem transections at midpons (midpontine pretrigeminal preparation) and Jouvet[283, 284] reports a similarly alert appearance in his "retropontine" preparations, which have their brainstems transected at the level of the trapezoid body, just rostral to the pontine-medullary junction.

The Relationship of Sleep to Coma

Sleep and coma share many apparent similarities. Conscious behavior is suspended in both, and they behaviorally resemble one another except in patients with prominent metabolic or motor changes. The EEG can be slow in both, and many lesions or illnesses that eventually cause coma in their late stages produce excessive drowsiness in their less severe or earlier periods. Our medical ancestors regarded sleep and coma as one, and until a few years ago there was a widespread tendency among physiologists to regard sleep and coma as both due to a damping or failure of the normally tonic flow of impulses from the reticular activating system to the cerebral hemispheres. But there were problems: This unitary view was hard to reconcile with the findings by Mangold and co-workers[357] that human cerebral oxygen uptake does not decline during sleep while it does fall below the normal resting level in every studied example of coma. It was also hard to reconcile with the fact that the EEG and behavioral manifestations that accompany each other during sleep often part company during pathological unconsciousness. In this regard some patients in coma from pontine lesions have normal rather than slow EEG patterns,[337] and drugs such as atropine can slow the EEG without dulling consciousness.[521] The premise that sleep and coma were one was gradually superseded when evidence emerged from several laboratories, especially those of Moruzzi[390] and

Jouvet,[283, 284] that sleep is an active physiological process with several distinct EEG and behavioral stages depending for its full expression on specific individual brainstem nuclear areas extending from the posterior diencephalon rostrally to the upper medulla caudally. At present no one equates physiological sleep with pathological clouding of consciousness and the unsolved problem lies more in determining where the two overlap and why they so often seem to blend into one another in patients with cerebral dysfunction.

The independence of sleep and coma is brought out in many clinical studies. It has already been emphasized that drowsiness is a prelude to stupor with both structural and metabolic disease of the brain. However, once patients become comatose from acutely or rapidly developing processes, they lie with the eyes unblinkingly shut and few display the behavioral changes of sleep-wake cycles during the first days or weeks of their unconsciousness, nor do those who fail to arouse appear to undergo the activated or REM stage of sleep. Later on, many patients with chronically severely impaired consciousness demonstrate periods of behavioral quietness or restlessness that imply the presence of sleep-wake cycles. Bricolo and associates[60] recorded the EEG in such chronically unresponsive patients after head injury and in a majority of them found changes indicating several stages of sleep. Interestingly enough, some patients with behavioral evidence of episodically greater wakefulness failed to undergo concurrent changes in the EEG frequency. If the results of acute animal studies apply to chronically brain-injured patients, intact sleep stages should imply a large measure of intact brainstem from hypothalamus to medulla and vice versa. Whether or not this will prove to be true in man remains to be seen. Bricolo and his group were unable to discern a fixed relationship between the presence and absence of organization of the EEG and the clinically appraised degree of coma. However, they lacked postmortem anatomical studies.

Evidence from undeveloped neonates may not necessarily be applicable to patients suffering injuries to fully developed nervous systems, but anencephalic monsters whose brains were intact only as far rostral as the midbrain level are reported to display behavioral sleep-wake cycles as well as primitive changes in emotional expression.[196] By implication, the absence of behavioral sleep-waking cycles would imply at least inhibition or depression of brainstem functions. Like many other aspects of the unconscious state, more extensive analyses of the relationship of behavioral and electroencephalographic sleep changes to the neuroanatomy of brain lesions promise rich rewards for the clinical investigator.

Studies in Man

The animal experiments referred to in previous sections have given to clinical medicine the immensely valuable concept of nonspecific reticular activating systems and have firmly established the indispensable role of the brainstem in maintaining the hemispheric tone required for the conscious state. They also have identified convincingly some of the definite properties that distinguish the normal physiology of sleep from the pathological physiology of coma. However, most of the experimental studies necessarily are limited to correlating anatomical and electrophysiological data with the behavioral appearances of the animal under study, and they thereby suffer unavoidable limitations. Different species do not always react similarly to similar lesions, and no species has a behavioral repertory comparable to man's. In animals most of the lesions have been produced abruptly, but the neurological effects differed significantly when similar destructive changes were induced more slowly in a manner more closely resembling what happens with human pathological processes.[2] Furthermore, acute lesions often produce behavioral and EEG effects that change significantly if the animal is nursed successfully to long survival. Demonstrating this, both Batsel,[28] in dogs, and Villablanca,[580] in cats, observed that permanent mesencephalic transections of the brainstem were followed at first by coma and EEG slowing but later by substantial neurological recovery with the isolated forebrain and diencephalon developing EEG patterns characteristic of alternating sleep and wakefulness. In this regard, electroencephalographic activation and behavioral arousal have sometimes been dissociated even in acute animal experiments. According to Feldman and Waller,[160] hypothalamic destruction sparing the midbrain reticular formation is followed by sustained somnolence even though stimulation of the midbrain or a peripheral afferent pathway can still evoke a low-voltage desynchronized EEG record. These inconsistencies and the difference between the neurological effects of anatomically comparable lesions in lower animals and man make well-documented clinical and pathological observations crucial to understanding the pathogenesis of impaired consciousness.

The cerebral hemispheres of man harbor the specific and well-localized faculties of language, vision, skilled motor function, and stereoperception. They also provide the neural machinery for the less easily localized qualities of thought, wit, memory and intellect, the meaningful content of consciousness. The integrity of these cerebral operations, as with language function, may depend more on one part of the brain than another (e.g., memory and orientation appear to depend particularly on rhinencephalic structures located in the medial temporal and orbital frontal regions[578, 595]), but the several cognitive functions are represented widely in both hemispheres and any substantial lesion in either hemisphere might be expected to diminish mental abilities roughly in proportion to its size. Chapman and Wolff,[86] for example, mustered considerable evidence to demonstrate that with cerebral damage man's "highest integrative functions," i.e., his mental capabilities, tend to be impaired roughly in proportion to the amount of tissue lost, no matter what part of the hemispheres sustains the attrition. Both these and other studies[83] show that with increasingly large lesions patients become duller until, finally, if the cortex is completely obliterated, all behavioral evidence for the content of consciousness also is lost, whether or not brainstem lesions coexist.[185, 449] However, total and selective obliteration of the cortex or its downstream connections is rare except occasionally in head injuries or anoxia (see below), and it will be seen that in humans as in animals structural lesions that cause coma do so most commonly by damaging the posterior basal diencephalon or the adjacent lower brainstem down to about the level of the midpons.

Historical Background

The record of well-studied patients having anatomical lesions that illuminate the basis for human consciousness and coma goes back a century. Gayet[200] in 1875 described a patient who was apathetic and limp when aroused and lapsed into a coma-like sleep when not actively stimulated. The illness lasted 5 months and at autopsy the brain contained inflammation, softening, and sclerosis of the reticular formation surrounding the third ventricle, aqueduct, and fourth ventricle. Mauthner[363] in 1890 reviewed Gayet's data, cited the association between somnolence and the presence of hemorrhagic necrosis in the same regions in patients with Wernicke's superior polioencephalitis, and correlated similarly distributed periaqueductal lesions with the somnolence of encephalitis. Mauthner concluded that midbrain lesions blocked wakefulness by blocking neural impulses between the periphery and the cerebral cortex: "'I . . . view the nature of sleep as an interruption of the centripetal and centrifugal conductor. . . . The location of sleep is in the central hollow gray." Explanations since then get more complicated but not necessarily more clear.

Mauthner's view was singular, and his contemporaries regarded sleep and coma as being due to cerebral anemia, or depression of conduction in the corona radiata of the cerebral hemispheres. Jackson[262] placed consciousness in the frontal lobes, and clinicians at least were disinclined to challenge him. In the 1920's, however, the finding of prominent midbrain damage in patients dying from encephalitis lethargica led von Economo[582] to refocus attention on the importance of brainstem lesions as a cause of coma. Similarly distributed abnormalities among patients in coma from brain tumors,[21, 193] brain infarcts,[52] and cerebral trauma[271] all demonstrated that relatively restricted lesions interrupt or markedly reduce consciousness if they involve the paramedian gray matter anywhere between the posterior hypothalamus and the tegmentum of the lower pons.[561]

Studies in recent years that have added new and useful details to these earlier findings are discussed in the following paragraphs. However, it should be noted that with the human as with the animal material the data are rarely sufficient to tell whether lesions that block consciousness acutely would necessarily forever prevent its emergence were the patient to survive.

Cerebral hemispheres. Focal purely unilateral lesions of the cerebral hemispheres do not diffusely blunt consciousness even when they destroy important selective psychological functions. Thus, Dandy's early search[121] for the source of consciousness in the territorial distribution of the anterior cerebral arteries proved fruitless and, as discussed in Chapter 2, most other reports attributing coma to focal lesions of the hemispheres are explained equally well or better by invoking a remote pathological effect of swelling or shift of deep brain structures. However, a seeming exception to this rule about the effects of unilateral cerebral lesions sometimes comes with large, acutely received lesions of the dominant hemisphere that greatly reduce or destroy language function and at the same time cause a hemiplegia and hemisensory defect. Such a loss, which is really more than 50 per cent of psychological function, can result from vascular occlusion of the internal carotid or middle cerebral arteries or from depression of the hemisphere by amobarbital sodium injected into the carotid artery. In both instances some patients become at least temporarily unresponsive to any but vigorous somatic sensory stimuli. Serafetinides, Hoare and Driver,[500] who first reported on the transient unresponsiveness caused by injecting amobarbital into the internal carotid artery of the dominant hemisphere, noted that only the homolateral side of the EEG usually slowed, yet they concluded that consciousness and not merely verbal responsiveness was lost. The inference was that consciousness, like speech, sometimes depended on the dominant hemisphere.

Rosadini and Rossi[475] subsequently examined the question of a cerebral dominance for consciousness and offered an explanation more in keeping with the traditionally held clinical and pathological interpretations of others. They studied 52 patients, most of whom had epilepsy. Loss of consciousness lasting more than 1 minute followed carotid amobarbital injection in 12 patients, in all of whom there were signs either that the opposite hemisphere was severely damaged from preexisting disease or that barbiturate had spread to depress the other hemisphere or the diencephalon. Another 10 patients underwent some very short-lasting signs suggesting impaired consciousness, but this occurred almost as often following right- as left-sided injections. No aspect of the studies suggested that hemispheric dominance is important to consciousness, although the results confirmed that the sudden loss of large amounts of cerebral function can impose a significant reduction in behavioral responses. It was of some interest that when the same investigators[9] injected barbiturate into the vertebral arteries, which presumably should have quickly delivered the depressant to the brainstem reticular formation, neither EEG slowing nor any depression of consciousness occurred. Paralysis of the eye muscles, pupillary responses, jaw and facial muscles occurred, indicating brainstem dysfunction, but neither respiration nor circulation was depressed, implying that much of the brainstem was intact and making the results equivocal.

15

When lesions strike the hemispheres bilaterally, the degree of impaired consciousness is determined partly by the size and rapidity of development and partly by how long the patient survives. The first experimental proofs of the importance of the brainstem reticular formation to consciousness were quickly followed by a widespread tendency to think that any unconscious patient must have a direct injury or depression of his brainstem, neglecting that one could hardly assess the reticulum behaviorally if there were no cerebral cortex to activate. However, it is now realized that even a morphologically intact brainstem cannot generate sentient activity in the presence of large, rapidly acquired bilateral cerebral lesions. A striking example is provided by patients with the condition of severe postanoxic demyelination of the cerebral hemispheres (Fig. 1A) since they first recover from anoxia and then deteriorate after a symptom-free interval as their hemispheres demyelinate. Morphologically, such patients lack any abnormality of the brainstem while having extensive bilateral destruction of the hemispheric white matter. Clinically, they are mainly in sleeplike coma, and the lucid interval between the time of anoxia and the demyelination eliminates any uncertainty that some unsuspected acute brainstem insult escaped the examiner's attention.

Case 1. A 59-year-old male was found unconscious in a room filled with illuminating gas. A companion was dead. On admission he was unresponsive. His blood pressure was 120/80 mm. Hg, pulse 120, and respirations 18 and regular. His rectal temperature was 102° F. His stretch reflexes were hypoactive, and plantar responses were absent. Coarse rhonchi were heard throughout both lung fields.

He was treated with nasal oxygen and began to awaken in 30 hours. On the second hospital day he was alert and oriented. On the fourth day he was afebrile, his chest was clear, and he was ambulated. The neurological examination was normal, and a psychological evaluation by a psychiatrist revealed a clear sensorium with "no evidence of organic brain damage." He was discharged to his relatives' care 9 days after the anoxia.

At home, he remained well for 2 days but then became quiet, speaking only when spoken to. The following day he merely shuffled about and responded only in monosyllables. The next day (13 days after the anoxia) he became incontinent and unable to walk, swallow, or chew. He neither spoke to nor recognized his family. He was admitted to a private sanatorium and diagnosed as having a depression. Deterioration continued, and 28 days after the initial anoxia he was readmitted to the hospital. His blood pressure was 170/100 mm. Hg, pulse 100, respirations 24, and temperature 101° F. There were coarse rales at both lung bases and bilateral decubitus ulcers. He perspired profusely and constantly. He did not respond to pain but would open his eyes momentarily to loud sounds. His extremities were flexed and rigid, his deep tendon reflexes were hyperactive, and his plantar responses were extensor. Laboratory studies, including examination of the spinal fluid, were normal. His pneumonia progressed and he died 3 days later.

At autopsy there was diffuse bronchopneumonia. The brain was grossly normal. There was no cerebral swelling. Coronal sections appeared normal with no evidence of pallidal necrosis. Histologically, neurons in the motor cortex, hippocampus, cerebellum, and occipital lobes were generally well preserved, although a few sections showed minimal cytodegenerative changes and reduction of neurons. There was occasional perivascular lymphocytic infiltration. Pathological changes were not present in blood vessels, nor was

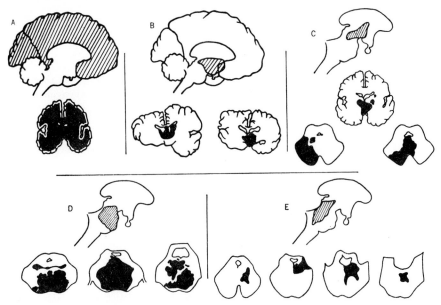

Figure 1. Brain lesions causing coma.

A, Diffuse demyelination of the hemispheral subcortex following anoxia. (See Case 1, page 16.)

B, Lymphoma of diencephalon. The findings are presented in full as Case 14 on page 117.

C, Diencephalic-midbrain infarct. A 66-year-old man was found unconscious in the street. For 6 months after his admission to the hospital he remained comatose, with eyes closed, and no spontaneous movement, but he grimaced and withdrew when stimulated noxiously. During the subsequent 2 months he opened his right eye in response to loud noises and once mumbled his first name. However, he never responded appropriately to command. He died 8 months after admission. There was severe arteriosclerosis of his cerebral arteries and a cystic infarct as diagramed involving the gray matter surrounding the posterior third ventricle and the aqueduct as well as the left cerebral peduncle.

D, High pontine infarct. A 56-year-old man with diabetes and hypertension was admitted to the hospital complaining of generalized weakness and vomiting. The day after admission he suddenly became unconscious and behaviorally unresponsive to noxious stimuli. He hyperventilated and developed skew deviation of his eyes. He died 26 days later without regaining consciousness. His basilar artery was thrombosed in its midportion. A large infarct involved the tegmentum of both the upper pons and lower midbrain.

E, Brainstem hemorrhage. A 49-year-old man with severe hypertension suddenly developed an occipital headache and right-sided weakness. Several hours later he lapsed into coma with decerebrate posturing in response to noxious stimuli. He remained in coma for 2 months and then gradually recovered consciousness but was left with severe dysarthria and dysphagia as well as bilateral weakness of the extremities. When he died 7 months after the original episode, residual damage from several small hemorrhages was scattered throughout the tegmentum of the lower midbrain, pons, and upper medulla.

there any interstitial edema. The striking alteration was diffuse demyelination involving all lobes of the cerebral hemispheres and sparing only arcuate fibers (the immediately subcortical portion of the cerebral white matter). Axis cylinders were also reduced in number but were better preserved than was the myelin. Oligodendroglia were preserved in demyelinated areas. Reactive astrocytes were considerably increased. The brainstem and cerebellum were not demyelinated. The pathological changes are illustrated in the original report of the case.[449]

Unresponsive behavior also has been described in children with Schilder's disease who have diffuse demyelination of the hemispheres but an intact brainstem. Brierley and co-workers[61] described two patients in coma following cardiac asystole who developed laminar degeneration of the hemispheres bilaterally plus anoxic degeneration of the basal ganglia, but who had relatively intact basal diencephalons and brainstems with sparing of the reticular formation. Both patients had isoelectric EEG's as well. Both patients remained entirely unresponsive for 5 months until death, and neither opened his eyes until the seventh week after the catastrophe.

Following head injury there is also evidence that damage confined or nearly so to the cerebral hemispheres can produce at least a transient sleep-like coma replaced only after several weeks or even months by a state of wakefulness devoid of the content of consciousness. Stritch[541] reported a series of patients in whom the cerebral hemispheres were extensively and bilaterally demyelinated yet the brainstem was spared from an extensive pathological change. Stritch describes her patients as severely demented although only after several weeks did any of them open their eyes. At least two never recovered more than the most rudimentary nonreflex responsiveness, and none recovered anything approaching the full faculties of consciousness. The difficulty in deciding when purely vegetative behavior, which can include waking and sleeping, passes over into true consciousness is partly semantic and is discussed in the section on akinetic mutism below. Crompton, Teare, and Bowen[112] and Jellinger and Seitelberger[273] all report that in their extensive studies on post-traumatic encephalopathy, coma was always associated with lesions at the base of the third ventricle and in the brainstem while those confined to the hemispheres resulted only in a profound or progressive dementia. Since they include no clinical details one cannot deduce whether by coma they refer to states in which sleeping and waking fail to return. However, even in their own reports, patients with entirely hemispheric lesions are described as spending days or weeks in coma, implying either that they had nonmorphological injury to brainstem arousal centers or that these were inhibited acutely following hemispheric injury. In either case, much evidence from many different kinds of neurological injury indicates that severe bilateral damage to the hemispheres alone produces at least temporary sleeplike coma and certainly is capable of wiping clean the content of man's consciousness.

Thalamus. Pure anatomical lesions of the thalamus that neither accompany a generalized disease nor involve adjacent structures are rare and probably almost never occur bilaterally. Unilateral thalamic destruction is not recorded as associated with behavioral unresponsiveness nor have we encountered such a patient. Bilateral lesions restricted to the thalamus are nearly always the consequence of vascular occlusion of arteries arising in the posterior perforated space, and infarcts found at postmortem examination in such a thalamic distribution imply that more widespread ischemia occurs acutely in the vascular distribution of the basilar artery apex. Castaigne and Escourolle[82] describe two patients with ischemic necrosis of the intralaminar nuclei of the thalamus. Both were initially in coma but in 10 days recovered to reach a permanent state of slow, apathetic dementia. The midbrain reticular formation, the hypothalamus, and the cerebral hemispheres were largely spared.

Hypothalamus. Paramedian bilateral destructive lesions of the posterior hypothalamus in man cause, with increasing size, progressively more severe clouding of consciousness, drowsiness, and eventually totally unresponsive coma. An example is diagramed in Figure 1B and described in detail on page 117 (Case 14). Since lesions in this area rarely spare the adjacent midbrain reticular formation, at least by compression, it is difficult to assign symptoms solely to injury of one or the other structure. However, the extensive literature on epidemic encephalitis[582] as well as that on neoplasms in this area[193] all suggest that posterior hypothalamic injury or destruction characteristically induces prolonged sleeplike coma.

Midbrain and pons. Abundant recent material corroborates the early conclusions about the relation of these structures to wakefulness cited in the pathological studies of Gayet,[200] Mauthner,[363] and von Economo.[582] Indeed, some of the lesions destroying the paramedian reticulum and producing well-documented coma in man are as precise and restricted as those created experimentally by Lindsley[333] that contributed to the establishment of the importance of the midbrain reticular formation in producing conscious arousal. The patient described by Brain[52] is such an example, as is the man whose pathological lesion is illustrated in Figure 1C.

The midbrain pontine area critical to consciousness in man is the paramedian tegmental gray matter immediately ventral to the ventricular system extending continuously from the posterior hypothalamic reticular formation rostrally to approximately the lower third of the pontine tegmentum caudally. Just how much of this critical gray matter is sufficient to activate the cerebral hemispheres can only be estimated, because only a very small number of well-studied patients have had small and restricted brain lesions and very few analyses differentiate between the immediate and long-term effects of such damage. To draw physiological conclusions one generally must rely on patients having had acute infarctions from vascular occlusions since the tissue alterations caused by hemorrhages or neoplasms generally change too much between the time of onset and autopsy to allow reliable inferences.

Small lesions involving the critical paramedian zone have been reported by only a few workers,[52, 259, 497] and the exact transverse or longitudinal size required to cause prolonged coma is conjectural. All recorded examples have at least involved both sides of the midline and most of the dorsal-ventral axis of the tegmentum. Chase, Moretti, and Prensky[88] described 20 patients, 8 of their own, with autopsy-confirmed tegmental lesions of the pons and lower midbrain. None of the 9 with bilateral lesions were alert and 8 were deeply obtunded. By contrast, only 3 of the 11 with unilateral tegmental destruction were obtunded and 2 of those were febrile or hypoxic. Lesions confined to the periaqueductal gray matter in man[231, 510] do not impair conscious behavior, an observation consistent with experimental findings.[522] According to von Glees and Bailey,[583] bilateral surgical severance of the medial lemnisci and spinothalamic tracts at midbrain level in man did not interrupt consciousness.

It is difficult to estimate the caudal extent of the tegmentum critical to consciousness because lesions that damage the lower pontine area also damage the lower cranial nerve pathways and both corticospinal tracts, cutting off the patient's ability to communicate (see page 24). The EEG is of no value in such instances since it usually resembles wakefulness in the presence of lesions of the pontine tegmentum. Patients with bilateral infarcts of the midpontine paramedian tegmentum are not arousable, at least acutely. We made a special effort to evoke appropriate responsiveness in two closely studied patients with such lesions, and no glimmer of appropriate reaction in ocular or any other movement could be elicited to any but noxious stimuli. Well-studied examples of chronically surviving patients with lesions confined to the lower pontine tegmentum have not been found.

Medulla oblongata. Paramedian medullary destruction does not interfere with conscious responses even when the lesion extends into the lower pons. Earlier workers, including Cairns[74] and Jefferson,[271] thought that medullary lesions did cause coma, but they observed patients with expanding lesions that commonly exert widespread effects. Reichardt's experience[468] has been cited to prove that medullary damage provokes coma. However, the example is equivocal. Reichardt described a woman who suffered an apparent medullary puncture during a cisternal tap. She cried out and become unresponsive, but promptly recovered after the needle was withdrawn. She complained bitterly of unilateral paresthesias of the body, and her pulse rate slowed to 55 per minute. The blood pressure was not taken, but it would seem that the attack could as easily have been vasovagal syncope as an interruption of specific physiological pathways subserving consciousness.

Our own material indicates that in man, as in the animal experiments cited on page 11, medullary structures exert little direct effect on neural functions regulating consciousness. The following patient preserved quick,

accurate responses to commands and the behavioral appearance of consciousness almost until death despite extensive destruction of the medulla extending rostrally to its junction with the pons. The findings at autopsy are
diagramed in Figure 2B and pictured in Figure 3.

Case 2. A 62-year-old woman was examined through the courtesy of Dr. Walter Camp
of Stamford, Conn. Twenty-five years earlier she had developed weakness and severely
impaired position and vibration sense of the right arm and leg. She improved little
but had no further symptoms until 2 years before we saw her, when she developed
paralysis of the right vocal cord and wasting of the right side of the tongue followed by
insidiously progressing disability with an unsteady gait and more weakness of the right
limbs. Four days before coming to the hospital, she became much weaker on the right
side and 2 days later she lost the ability to swallow.

When she entered the hospital, she was alert and in full possession of her faculties.
She had no difficulty in breathing and her blood pressure was 162/110 mm. Hg. She
had nystagmus confined to upward gaze with an upward fast component, and decreased
appreciation of pinprick on the left side of the face. The right side of the pharynx,
palate, and tongue was paralyzed. The right arm and leg were weak and atrophic,
consistent with disuse. Stretch reflexes below the neck were bilaterally brisk and the
right plantar response was extensor. Position and vibratory sensations were reduced on
the right side of the body and the appreciation of pinprick was reduced on the left.

The next day she was still alert and responsive, but she developed difficulty in cough-
ing and speaking and finally she ceased breathing. An endotracheal tube was placed
promptly (the patient and family at first refused tracheostomy) and connected to a
ventilator. Later, on that third hospital day she was still brightly alert, and quickly
and accurately answered questions by nodding or shaking her head The opening pressure
of CSF at lumbar puncture was 180 mm. of water and the xanthochromic fluid contained
8500 RBC and 14 WBC per cu. mm.

She lived for 23 more days. During that time she developed complete paralysis below
the face. There were several hypotensive crises that were treated promptly with infusions
of pressor agents, but no pressor drugs were needed during the last 2 weeks of life.
Intermittently during these final days, she had brief periods of unresponsiveness, but
then awakened and signaled quickly and appropriately to questions demanding a yes
or no answer and opened or closed her eyes and moved them laterally when commanded
to do so. There was no other voluntary movement. Four days before she died, she
developed ocular bobbing when commanded to look laterally, but although she clearly
responded to commands by moving her eyes, it was difficult to know whether or not her
responses were appropriate. During the ensuing 3 days, evidence of wakefulness became
less. She had a gastrointestinal hemorrhage and died suddenly 26 days after entering
the hospital.

The brain at autopsy contained a moderate amount of dark old blood overlying the
right lateral medulla adjacent to the fourth ventricle. A raspberry-appearing arteriovenous malformation, 1.4 cm. in greatest diameter, protruded from the right lateral
medulla, beginning with its lower border 2.5 cm. caudal to the obex. On section
the vascular malformation was seen to originate in the central medulla and to extend
rostrally to approximately 2 mm. above the obex. From this point a large hemorrhage
extended forward to destroy the central medulla all the way to the pontine junction
(Fig. 3). Microscopic study demonstrated that, at its most cranial end, the hemorrhage
destroyed the caudal part of the right vestibular nuclei and most of the adjacent lower
pontine tegmentum on the right. Caudal to this, the hemorrhage widened and destroyed
the entire dorsal center of the medulla from approximately the plane of the nucleus
of the glossopharyngeal nerve down to just below the plane of the nucleus ambiguus.

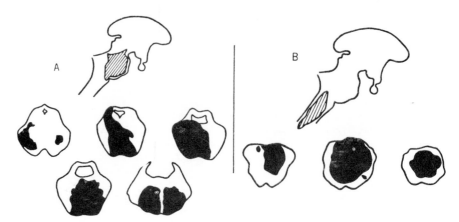

Figure 2. Brain lesions not causing sustained coma.

 A, Brainstem infarct. The clinical details are given as Case 16, page 126.

 B, Medullary hemorrhage, Case 2, page 21.

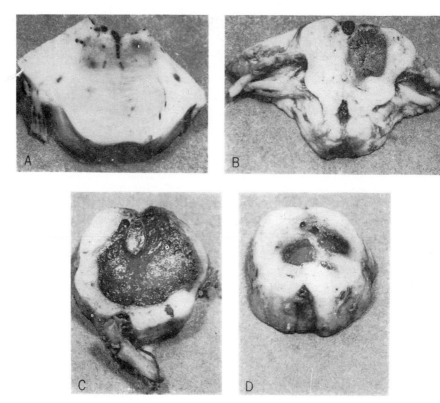

Figure 3. Section from lower pons **(A)** to upper cervical spinal cord **(D),** Case 2.

From this latter point caudally the hemorrhage was more restricted to the reticular formation of the medulla. The margins of this lesion contained an organizing clot with phagocytosis and reticulum formation indicating a process at least 2 weeks old. The center of the hemorrhage contained a degenerating clot estimated to be at least 72 hours old, and at several places along the lateral margin of the lesion were small fresh hemorrhages estimated to have occurred within a few hours of death. These latter comprised a minor part of the bulk of the lesion and in no area extended into adjacent brain. Thus it was considered unlikely that the lesion had changed substantially in size or extent of destruction in the few days before death.

Akinetic Mutism

The pathological basis of akinetic mutism. Many different structural pathological lesions will sooner or later after their onset produce variations on the state of akinetic mutism. The subject, although usually lying with eyes closed, retains cycles of self-sustained arousal, giving the appearance of vigilance but vocalizing little or not at all. He is totally incontinent and makes only the most rudimentary skeletal muscle movements even in response to noxious or disagreeable stimuli.[73] The crucial factors that attract the examiner's attention are (1) the seeming wakefulness without recognizable content and (2) the relative paucity of signs, implying severe damage to descending motor pathways despite the unmoving state. Cairns' original description[74] was of a girl with a craniopharyngiomatous cyst compressing the walls of the third ventricle, but more or less similar behavior has also been described in association with many different lesions, including: large bilateral frontal lobe lesions, particularly those that interfere with the anterior cerebral arteries so as to produce infarcts of the cingulate gyri and limbic system;[26] bilateral diffuse destruction of the cerebral cortical mantle, as following cardiac asystole or profound hypoglycemia; bilateral hemispheric demyelination, as sometimes follows carbon monoxide poisoning or head injury; hydrocephalus;[375] large bilateral lesions of the corpus striatum,[157] globus pallidus,[128] or of dorsomedial or ventrolateral thalamus;[317] paramedian lesions of the reticular formation of the midbrain and posterior diencephalon,[522] and cerebellar hemorrhage with brainstem compression.[134]

Inspection of the protocols of the above reports and others in the medical literature discloses two problems of interpretation. In many instances the inferred anatomical lesions were unverified by postmortem examination or were only part of more widespread pathological alterations, and among the several pathological states only some of them truly were accompanied by the distinctive appearance of motionless, mindless wakefulness that Cairns sagely recognized. Fewer still developed this as a presenting or early manifestation of illness. Thus, following severe head injury and other bilateral severe diffuse insults to the cerebrum, sleeplike coma tends to last for weeks or months and when the subject finally does reach a state of intermittent wakefulness devoid of mental content, the clinical state tends to be regarded as either a variation of coma or a profound dementia. Also, most patients

23

with large acute paramedian destructive lesions of the posterior diencephalon and midbrain have a clinical picture better termed hypersomnia than akinetic mutism, at least if one is to follow Cairns' lead in the matter. For example, Segarra[497] reports two patients with mesencephalic infarcts as having akinetic mutism and cites several other examples from the literature with ostensibly similar lesions and behavior. Segarra's two patients both had comparatively tiny areas of paramedian destruction of the midbrain and posterior diencephalon and by the limited clinical descriptions given apparently had frequent periods of spontaneous arousal during which they were apathetically immobile and verbally unresponsive. However, most of the patients with larger paramedian lesions culled from the literature and diagramed in Figure 1 were described by their original examiners as being either in coma or continuously asleep except when vigorously aroused. This is quite different from Cairns' original description but is in keeping with the well-documented association between hypersomnia and posterior hypothalamic destruction.[462]

The best presently available clinical and pathological evidence indicates that the classic appearance of akinetic mutism can arise early in the course of three types of lesions, all of which largely interfere with reticular-cortical integration but largely spare corticospinal pathways: subacute communicating hydrocephalus; large, bilateral, basal-medial, frontal lobe lesions involving the orbital cortex, septal area, and cingulate gyri; and tiny (and probably incomplete) lesions interrupting the reticular formation of the posterior diencephalon and adjacent midbrain. Even with the frontal lesions it is still an open question as to how much of the unresponsive akinesia can be attributed directly to frontal lobe damage and how much must be assigned to secondary compression or circulatory changes in the adjacent hypothalamus. It is noteworthy that neither large bilateral frontal lobotomy nor bilateral cingulectomy performed surgically to treat psychiatric disease blunts alertness, intellectual content, vocalization, or motor behavior.

The "Locked-In" Syndrome (The De-efferented State)

Certain neurological injuries can paralyze all expression by word or movement yet leave the patient in possession of full sentient consciousness. Although clinically somewhat resembling akinetic mutism and therefore sometimes confused with it, the pathogenesis and particularly the accompanying suffering are entirely different. When "locked-in," or de-efferented, the patient gives signs of being appropriately aware of himself and the environment whereas in akinetic mutism little or no awareness appears to exist. De-efferentation can occur to some degree with purely peripheral neurological lesions such as polyneuritis, poliomyelitis, or myasthenia gravis. However, such patients are recognized to be conscious and one can at least attempt to meet their emotional needs. A much more harrowing circumstance occurs when an acute destructive lesion such as an infarct or plaque of demyelination strikes the pontine base but spares the tegmentum[5, 293] or destroys the medulla. Such lesions produce an acute tetraplegia due to brainstem corticospinal tract involvement, plus aphonia due to lower corticobulbar interruption, and the combination can easily give the false impression of coma or mindless akinetic mutism. An example is described as Case 16 on page 126. Such patients reveal their awareness by moving their eyes appropriately, usually in the vertical plane only, or by blinking, since the supranuclear ocular motor pathways pass rostral to the main destructive lesion and remain unscathed. Patients chronically in this state have been taught Morse code with their eyes and have been able to communicate complex ideas.[159a]

RESPIRATION

Breathing serves both metabolic and behavioral functions and is an act integrated by nervous influences arising from nearly every level of the brain.[443] This influence of many different brain levels on the act of breathing means that diseases causing coma commonly induce respiratory abnormalities as well, making respiratory signs useful in diagnosis (Table 2). This section considers the neuroanatomical basis of respiratory abnormalities that accompany coma (Fig. 4), and Chapter 4 discusses respiratory responses to metabolic disturbances. A word of caution is in order. Metabolic and neurogenic influences on the respiratory act often overlap and

Table 2. Neuropathological correlates of breathing abnormalities

Forebrain Damage
    Epileptic respiratory inhibition[399, 438]
    Apraxia for deep breathing or breath-holding
    "Pseudobulbar" laughing or crying
    Posthyperventilation apnea
    Cheyne-Stokes respiration

Midbrain–Rostral Pons Tegmentum
    Central neurogenic hyperventilation

Pontine Base
    Pseudobulbar paralysis of voluntary control

Lower Pontine Tegmentum
    Apneustic breathing
    Cluster breathing
    Short-cycle anoxic-hypercapnic Cheyne-Stokes respiration
    Ataxic breathing

Medullary
    Ataxic breathing
    Slow regular breathing
    Loss of automatic breathing with preserved voluntary control

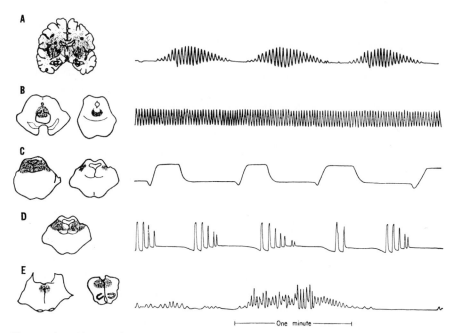

Figure 4. Abnormal respiratory patterns associated with pathological lesions (shaded areas) at various levels of the brain. Tracings by chest-abdomen pneumograph, inspiration reads up. **A,** Cheyne-Stokes respiration. **B,** Central neurogenic hyperventilation. **C,** Apneusis. **D,** Cluster breathing. **E,** Ataxic breathing. Except for Case E, the original discussion of the pathological material appears in references 66, 446, 452.

interact so that one must interpret respiratory changes cautiously. This particularly applies to patients with acute diencephalic dysfunction in whom pulmonary congestion and hypoxia are major causes of altered respiratory patterns.

Posthyperventilation Apnea (PHVA)

Normally, if the arterial carbon dioxide tension is lowered by a brief period of hyperventilation, most awake subjects resume the rhythm of regular breathing without delay, although tidal volume is reduced until normal carbon dioxide tension is restored. However, subjects with diffuse metabolic or structural forebrain disease commonly demonstrate posthyperventilation apnea, i.e., their respirations stop after deep breathing has lowered the arterial carbon dioxide content below its usual resting level. Rhythmic breathing begins again when endogenous CO_2 production raises the arterial value back to normal.

The demonstration of posthyperventilation apnea requires that the patient voluntarily take several deep breaths so that, strictly speaking, the test may be useful to evaluate obtunded or confused but not truly comatose patients. One instructs the patient to take five deep in-and-out breaths. No other instructions are given and no inferences should be given about breath-holding or even that the respiratory rhythm is being watched. If the lungs function well, the maneuver usually lowers the arterial carbon dioxide tension by 8 to 14 mm. Hg. At the end of the deep breathing, wakeful patients without brain damage experience little or no apnea (less than 10 seconds is the rule), but abnormal subjects have a period of apnea lasting 12 to 30 seconds or more. The neural stimulus that normally activates rhythmic breathing when CO_2 is reduced is believed to arise from the forebrain since it disappears with sleep, obtundation, or bilateral hemispheric dysfunction.[448]

Cheyne-Stokes Respiration (CSR)

This is a pattern of periodic breathing in which hyperpnea regularly alternates with apnea. The breathing waxes from breath to breath in a smooth crescendo and then, once a peak is reached, wanes in an equally smooth decrescendo. The hyperpneic phase usually lasts longer than the apneic phase.

CSR is a neurogenic alteration in respiratory control that most frequently results from intracranial causes, although anoxia and a prolonged circulation time enhance its appearance.[66] The most frequent anatomical abnormalities associated with CSR are bilaterally situated lesions deep in the cerebral hemispheres and basal ganglia that damage the internal capsules and are distributed much like the lesions causing pseudobulbar palsy. Metabolic brain dysfunction also causes CSR, presumably by impairing the function of similar cerebral regions.

The pathogenesis of CSR is the outcome of a combination of an abnormally increased ventilatory response to CO_2 stimulation causing hyperpnea and an abnormally decreased forebrain ventilatory stimulus subsequently permitting posthyperventilation apnea. Patients with bilateral hemispheric lesions overbreathe when stimulated by carbon dioxide, a phenomenon similar to other hyperactive responses to stimulation. As a result of the overbreathing, the blood's carbon dioxide content drops below the level where it stimulates the respiratory centers and breathing stops. During apnea, CO_2 reaccumulates until it exceeds the respiratory threshold, and the cycle then repeats itself and oscillates indefinitely, particularly if the circulation time is prolonged. Blood gases reflect mild overall hyperpnea with moderately lowered CO_2 values and with oxygen contents often slightly below normal.

The importance of CSR in patients with neurological disease is that the breathing pattern implies bilateral dysfunction of neurological structures, usually deep in the cerebral hemispheres or diencephalon, rarely as low as the upper pons. The abnormality is frequent in patients with bilateral

27

cerebral infarction, with hypertensive encephalopathy, and with metabolic diseases such as uremia. In addition, the emergence of CSR in patients with supratentorial mass lesions sometimes provides a valuable sign of incipient transtentorial herniation.

Occasionally, periodic breathing that may somewhat resemble CSR develops in association with expanding lesions of the posterior fossa, such as cerebellar hemorrhage. When this occurs, the respiratory thresholds are often elevated, the respiratory cycle is usually short, the patient appears to be underventilated, and the respiratory periodicity tends to be less regular than when CSR accompanies hemispheric lesions. The hypoventilatory periodic breathing of low brainstem injury often changes into cluster breathing (see below), which is more clearly a sign of pontomedullary dysfunction.

Central Neurogenic Hyperventilation (CNH)

Sustained, regular, rapid, and fairly deep hyperpnea occurs in certain patients with dysfunction in the brainstem tegmentum.[452] At autopsy, destructive lesions have been found in such patients between the low midbrain and the middle third of the pons, destroying the paramedian reticular formation just ventral to the aqueduct and fourth ventricle.

With CNH the respiratory threshold is low and arterial blood gases reveal a respiratory alkalosis with low CO_2 tensions ($<$ 30 mm. Hg) and elevated pH values ($>$ 7.48). In patients with pure CNH the arterial blood oxygen tension also will be normal or above normal ($>$ 80 mm. Hg) when the patient is breathing room air. If the blood oxygen tension is low ($<$ 70 mm. Hg) in a hyperpneic comatose patient with respiratory alkalosis, several factors may be operating singly or together. Heart failure, pneumonitis, neurogenic pulmonary edema,[139-141] and hepatic coma[454] all produce hypoxic, hypocapnic hyperpnea. One cannot conclude that the hyperpnea originates centrally in the brain unless the arterial blood oxygen tension has been above 70 to 80 mm. Hg for at least the previous 24 hours since values below that level stimulate the peripheral chemoreceptors and could themselves account for the increased ventilation. Giving oxygen to inhale for even a few hours to a hyperpneic patient will not rule out a peripheral chemoreceptor drive since at least several hours are required for the central respiratory chemoreceptor to "acclimatize" to the lessened peripheral stimulus.[501]

Although not always a pure physiological effect because of the high incidence of pulmonary edema accompanying lesions in this area, central hyperventilation does occur with midbrain-pontine infarcts and with anoxia or hypoglycemia affecting the same area. The breathing pattern is often observed in patients with midbrain compression secondary to transtentorial herniation, particularly when cerebral hemorrhage is the cause. In the latter instance, the noxious effects of intraventricular blood may enhance the respiratory response. Lange and Laszlo[321] observed central hyperventilation as the main feature of a neoplasm invading the midbrain region. Similarly, we have studied closely a child in whom sustained regular tachypneic hyperpnea with a rate of 40 to 60 per minute, including during sleep, was an early feature of an intrapontine neoplasm. The associated blood gases were Pao_2 105 mm. Hg, $Paco_2$ 16 mm. Hg, ruling out hypoxemia as the stimulus.

Apneustic Breathing and Its Variants

Apneusis is a prolonged inspiratory cramp—a pause at full inspiration. Fully developed apneustic breathing is rare in man but does occur. A more common abnormality consists of brief end-inspiratory pauses lasting 2 to 3 seconds, often alternating with expiratory pauses as well as with other irregularities of the respiratory rhythm[446] (Fig. 4). Apneustic breathing is a localizing sign of great value that reflects damage to the respiratory control mechanisms located at the mid- or caudal-pontine level, approximately at and below the segment where the trigeminal root emerges. The brainstem lesions reported usually have been extensive, consisting of a nearly complete dorsal transection, with a predilection for the dorsolateral tegmental areas. More prolonged apneusis has developed when these dorsolateral lesions extended caudally to involve the dorsolateral pontine nuclei.

Clinically, apneustic breathing usually denotes pontine infarction due to basilar artery occlusion. Occasionally, apneustic breathing accompanies hypoglycemia, anoxia, or severe meningitis. Apneusis has not been observed in patients with progressive brainstem dysfunction secondary to transtentorial herniation, possibly because the major injury to the brainstem in these cases is medial rather than lateral.

Ataxic Breathing

The respiratory centers that ultimately regulate the to-and-fro of breathing are located in the reticular formation of the dorsomedial part of the medulla and extend down to or just below the obex. Lesions in this area in man cause respiratory ataxia.[451] Ataxic breathing has a completely irregular pattern in which both deep and shallow breaths occur randomly. Irregular pauses appear haphazardly, and there is no predicting the future respiratory rhythm from the pattern of past breaths. The respiratory rate tends to be slow and may progressively decelerate to apnea. Ataxia is the respiratory abnormality that Biot described in severe meningitis. Its irregularity differentiates it from the regular waxing and waning of Cheyne-Stokes respiration.

Physiologically, ataxic breathing represents primary disruption of the reciprocal interrelationships between the medullary inspiratory and expiratory neuron populations. The irregular pattern usually is accompanied by hyposensitivity of the respiratory center to endogenous chemical stimuli, as well as an undue susceptibility to depressant drugs. As a result, mild

29

sedation or natural sleep sometimes induces apnea. Conversely, the respiratory apparatus often remains responsive to voluntary efforts so that patients who hypoventilate when left alone can still breathe adequately when commanded to do so.

Many different pathological processes in the posterior fossa can impair the respiratory rhythm. It is typical of medullary compression that respiration fails long before circulation. Rapidly expanding lesions such as cerebellar hemorrhage or pontine hemorrhage are prone to produce acute respiratory arrest, and direct medullary destruction from trauma or hemorrhage will do the same (Fig. 3). Lesions that expand more slowly affect respiration less often unless they directly compress or destroy the central part of the caudal medulla. With ischemia from cerebral vascular disease, medullary respiratory involvement is rare since an unusual abnormality such as bilateral involvement of the vertebral arteries is required to produce infarction of the central medulla. Chronic demyelinating illnesses seldom cause ataxic breathing, but acute parainfectious demyelination is prone to involve the medulla and leads directly to respiratory failure. Similar involvement is frequent in poliomyelitis. Complete respiratory assistance should be readied for patients who show ataxic breathing.

Other Abnormal Forms of Breathing with Medullary Lesions

When the lesion is high in the medulla, or low in the pons, *clusters* of breaths may follow each other in disorderly sequence with irregular pauses between. These merge with various patterns of *gasping* respiration in which deep "all-or-none" breaths occur, usually at a slow rate. One of our patients with an intramedullary glioma breathed with a slow *ratchet-like*, jerky inspiration followed by expiration, then pauses lasting 6 to 10 seconds. Finally, drugs can depress the medulla so gradually that breathing fails almost imperceptibly with tidal volume insidiously decreasing and rate slowing until the system stops altogether.

Yawning, Vomiting, and Hiccup

All three of these stereotyped complex acts involve the respiratory musculature, yet only the first has a primary respiratory function. Their importance to neurological diagnosis is that each is integrated by neural mechanisms in the lower brainstem, a site where disease or dysfunction can produce the reflex by direct stimulation, bypassing the normal afferent pathway.

Yawning is physiologically the least well studied of the three. Closely related to generalized body stretching, yawning must certainly help maintain chest, lung, and respiratory muscle compliance, but whether this is its primary function is unknown. The sparse available literature on yawning practically confines itself to descriptions of its associations and often somewhat whimsical speculations about its possible biological advantages.[23, 237]

Whether the medulla oblongata contains an integrating area for yawning similar to that for hiccup and vomiting is likely but unknown. Gamper[197] states that his well-studied anencephalic human neonate, who possessed no brain higher than the midbrain, yawned and stretched in normal fashion. Yawning commonly accompanies posterior fossa expanding lesions, but these also raise the intracranial pressure and the associated yawning could possibly be simply part of the resulting drowsiness. Both Penfield and Jasper[438] and Wilson[599] describe forced and repeated yawning in association with structural lesions located around the medial temporal lobe and the third ventricle, but the material is hard to interpret because of uncertain remote effects and scanty details.

Vomiting is primarily a gastrointestinal reflex with a strong efferent component involving the respiratory muscles. The act is integrated by an area in the lateral reticular formation of the medulla oblongata in the region of the tractus solitarius.[51] Nausea and gastrointestinal atony characteristically accompany vomiting evoked by visceral stimulation. By contrast, direct involvement of the central vomiting mechanism by neurological lesions usually short-circuits the afferent arc to produce vomiting without preceding nausea: Having no warning, vomitus escapes as a "projectile" with the full force of the suddenly contracted thoracoabdominal muscles behind it.

In relation to the total incidence of vomiting, central neurological lesions must only seldom take the blame, but for this reason when they do occur they are often overlooked while other body systems are fruitlessly explored. Central neurological lesions that produce vomiting are, respectively, those that involve the vestibular nuclei or their immediate projections, particularly when they cause diplopia as well; those that directly impinge on the floor of the fourth ventricle, such as the medulloblastoma or ependymoma; and, less often, those that produce brainstem compression secondary to increased intracranial pressure. Since many of this last group also consist of posterior fossa neoplasms, general and local medullary compression is often hard to differentiate.

Hiccup, like vomiting, appears to be mainly a gastrointestinal reflex involving the respiratory musculature.[408] Sustained hiccuping is peculiarly an abnormality of males, so that in the Mayo Clinic series of 220 cases, for example, there were only 39 women, 36 of whom had "psychogenic" hiccup.[532]

Most hiccup is stimulated by thoracoabdominal disease or by the ingestion of drugs. Neurological causes include parenchymal abnormalities of the medulla oblongata such as infections, syringomyelia, neoplasm, or infarction, and lesions surrounding or compressing the medulla such as neoplasms or hematomas.

Although central mechanisms in hiccup are less worked out experimentally than those in vomiting, the peripheral physiology has been well studied. According to Newsom Davis[408] the reflex is accentuated by a low arterial carbon dioxide tension and inhibited by hypercarbia or breath-holding. The act consists of spasmodic bursts of inspiratory muscle activity followed within 35 milliseconds or so by abrupt glottic closure so that the ventilatory effect is negligible. However, if a tracheotomy bypasses the glottis, the vigorous inspiratory spasm produces a large tidal volume that is enough to hyperventilate the patient and to self-accentuate the phenomenon. One such patient at The New York Hospital with a low brainstem infarct maintained his total ventilation for several days by hiccup alone. Another, after surgical manipulation of the floor of the fourth ventricle, developed recurrent, abrupt, inspiratory spasms without glottic closure. We lacked the necessary physiological data to say whether this latter was a fragment of hiccup or a respiratory abnormality, but the phenomenon carried the same implication of parenchymal low brainstem dysfunction.

CIRCULATION

The cardiovascular system is influenced by a series of central nervous system centers that operate from as many levels of the brain as those that modulate and regulate the act of breathing. However, in contrast to breathing, which is expressed through skeletal muscle and cannot function without central regulation, the cardiovascular system readily maintains its rhythm after complete separation from all nervous influences. Also, purely peripheral reflexes can influence the blood vessels almost as much as central ones. Because of this peripheral semiautonomy, and for other reasons as well, the monitoring of changes in the EKG, blood pressure, and pulse has proved disappointingly unhelpful in the diagnosis of many instances of stupor or coma. The development of the classic Cushing changes[116-118] of a slow pulse and elevated blood pressure in association with increased intracranial pressure are practically limited to children if one seeks to employ them as consistently useful general guides to worsening neurological conditions. Otherwise the changes occur either inconstantly, not at all, or only in association with lesions that directly compromise the posterior fossa. Johnston, Johnston, and Jennett[280] demonstrated vividly the unreliability of monitoring systemic arterial pressure as a guide to intracranial pressures. When they simultaneously recorded the pressures of the arterial blood and cerebral ventricular fluids in 32 patients after head injury, the relation was variable and unpredictable. Little or no blood pressure changes sometimes accompanied waves of increasing intracranial pressure that closely approximated the mean arterial pressure. We have been equally disappointed in our efforts to identify patterns of altered circulatory reflexes that would usefully differentiate the cause or clinical course of patients in coma and thus have given little attention to the significance of circulatory changes in this book.

PUPILS

The pupillary reactions, constriction and dilation, are controlled by the sympathetic and parasympathetic nervous systems (Fig. 5). The sympathetic pathways begin in the hypothalamus and traverse the entire ipsilateral brainstem. The parasympathetic pathways can be traced with certainty from the pretectal area into the midbrain. Because the brainstem areas controlling consciousness are anatomically adjacent to those controlling pupils, pupillary changes are a valuable guide to the presence and location of brainstem diseases causing coma. In addition, because pupillary pathways are relatively resistant to metabolic insult, the presence or absence of the light reflex is the single most important physical sign distinguishing structural from metabolic coma.

Functional Anatomy

Sympathetic stimulation contracts the pupillodilator muscle and the pupil widens (mydriasis). Parasympathetic stimulation contracts the pupilloconstrictor fibers and the pupil narrows (miosis). Both innervations are normally active, and the resting pupil represents a balance with a moderate

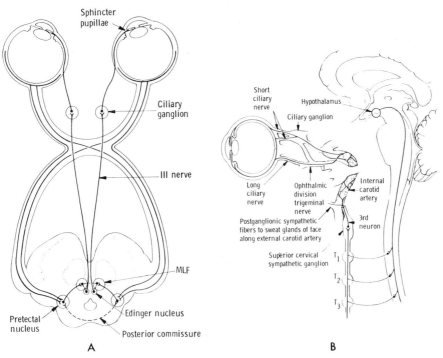

Figure 5. **A,** The parasympathetic pupilloconstrictor pathway. **B,** The sympathetic pupillodilator pathway.

preponderance of one innervation over the other, depending on incident light and other factors. The tonic resting pupillary stimulation is considerable, since when either the sympathetic or parasympathetic supply is blocked, the remaining, unopposed, system evokes a near-maximal pupillary response of miosis (1.5 to 2 mm.) with sympathetic, or mydriasis (8 to 9 mm.) with parasympathetic, paralysis.

Both Walsh and Hoyt[586] and Cogan[96] review the central pathway for sympathetic regulation of the human pupil. Evidence suggests that pupillary regulation begins in the cerebral cortex since removal of a cerebral hemisphere results in pupillary constriction, and stimulation of several hemispheric points produces pupillary dilatation.[67, 266]

Stimulating the ventrolateral hypothalamus in animals produces homolateral pupillary dilatation. Destruction or functional depression of this area results in pupilloconstriction. The pathway by which the sympathetic fibers descend through the caudal diencephalon, midbrain, and pons is unknown in man, but lesions in the upper brainstem immediately rostral and dorsal to the red nucleus[77] and at the subthalamic nucleus[198] produce ipsilateral pupilloconstriction. In animals, descending pupillodilator fibers in the midbrain lie ventral to the posterior commissure. Caudal to this level they branch into a lateral pathway and a centrally lying pathway that accompanies the medial longitudinal fasciculus. In man, the descending medullary pathway is apparently dorsolateral since lesions in this area produce a homolateral Horner's syndrome. It is presumed that in man one pathway also lies laterally in the pons. It is not known whether an additional, central, pathway lies near the medial longitudinal fasciculus.

In the cervical spinal cord the descending sympathetic pupillodilator fibers descend superficially in the ventrolateral region[297] to synapse with neurons in the intermediate lateral gray column of the upper thoracic segments. Preganglionic fibers leave the cord, usually with the upper three thoracic roots,[464] pass through the inferior and middle cervical ganglia, and synapse in the superior cervical ganglion. This ganglion lies near the ganglion of the glossopharyngeal and vagus nerves, between the internal carotid artery and the internal jugular vein just below the base of the skull. The postganglionic sympathetic fibers then travel with the internal carotid artery into the skull. They leave the artery to accompany the tympanic branch of the glossopharyngeal nerve into the middle ear, an association that explains the occasional occurrence of Horner's syndrome with otitis media.[504] The nerve then rejoins the carotid artery, lying within its sheath as far as the cavernous sinus, reaching the eye via filaments accompanying the ophthalmic artery and the nasociliary division of the trigeminal nerve.

The parasympathetic innervation of the pupil has a more direct route, but whether or not it has cerebral representation is unknown. Stimulation of both the occipital and frontal lobes in animals evokes pupillary con-

34

striction, as does stimulation of the pretectal region (that part of the hypothalamic gray matter lying immediately rostral to the midbrain tegmentum). Comparable observations are unavailable in man. The major sources of parasympathetic preganglionic supply to the pupil are the Edinger-Westphal nuclei, lying in the midbrain between the oculomotor nuclei and sending fibers that accompany the oculomotor nerve. Outside the brainstem the parasympathetic fibers lie mainly in the superior periphery of this nerve and split away from the inferior oblique branch of the oculomotor nerve in the orbit to reach the ciliary ganglia.

The Pupillary Light Reflex

Figure 5 diagrams the neural pathway for the pupillary light reflex. The afferent stimulus is relayed from retinal ganglion cells via fibers that travel in the optic nerves and accompany homotopic fibers from retinal visual receptors through crossed and uncrossed chiasmatic pathways into the optic tracts. From the optic tract, the pathway bypasses the lateral geniculate body, turning medially to synapse in the prectectal nucleus of the posterior diencephalon. From the pretectal nucleus, fibers connect bilaterally to the Edinger-Westphal nuclei, crossing both ventral and dorsal to the aqueduct, the latter pathway being via the posterior commissure.

The Ciliospinal Reflex

The ciliospinal reflex consists of bilateral 1 to 2 mm. pupillary dilatation evoked by noxious cutaneous stimulation. It is most easily elicited by a pinch to the face, neck, or upper trunk. The reflex is more prominent during sleep or coma than during wakefulness and clinically tests the integrity of sympathetic pathways in lightly comatose patients. However, because the synapse between afferent pain pathways and efferent pupillodilator pathways is in the spinal cord, the reflex is not particularly useful in evaluating brainstem function.[467]

The Localizing Value of Pupillary Abnormalities in Coma

The incidence of pupillary abnormalities in comatose patients is high and justifies giving careful attention to pupillary size and shape. The light reflex should be examined with a bright light, and if the pupils are small a magnifying glass may demonstrate a reflex constriction not apparent to the naked eye. Some important pupillary abnormalities in comatose patients are illustrated in Figure 6.

Cerebral effects on the pupil are not helpful in diagnosis.

Hypothalamic damage, especially to its posterior and ventrolateral portions, produces ipsilateral pupillary constriction usually associated with ptosis and anhidrosis (Horner's syndrome). The associated anhidrosis involves the entire ipsilateral half of the body and not just the face, neck, and arm as in cervical sympathetic lesions. The importance of recognizing hypo-

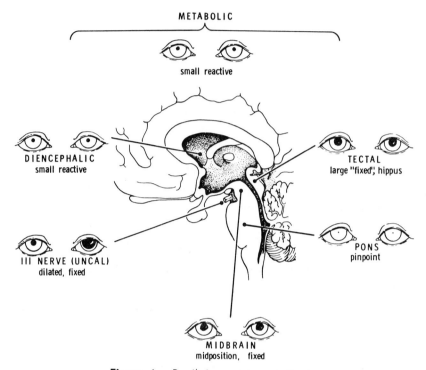

Figure 6. Pupils in comatose patients.

thalamic dysfunction in coma is that downward displacement of the hypothalamus with a unilateral Horner's syndrome is often the first clear sign
of incipient transtentorial herniation (Chapter 2). Crill[109] reported five
cases of supratentorial hemorrhage associated with ipsilateral Horner's
syndrome. In none was there carotid occlusion (see below). Of the four
patients who died and underwent autopsy, two had cerebral hemorrhages
directly involving the thalamus and hypothalamus, and one had a subdural
hematoma with transtentorial herniation and a secondary hemorrhage
involving the upper midbrain and diencephalon. The fourth had hemorrhage into a cortical metastatic tumor with no direct hypothalamic
destruction.

Horner's syndrome sometimes accompanies occlusion of the internal
carotid artery and often has been attributed to involvement of the perivascular sheath in such instances. However, asymptomatic carotid artery
occlusion almost never causes Horner's syndrome, so we suspect that hypothalamic damage rather than a peripheral sympathetic lesion is probably
the explanation for most examples of the Horner's syndrome reported in
association with carotid artery occlusion.[276] In keeping with this suggestion
is the fact that several of the patients with Horner's syndrome attributed to

carotid artery disease in clinical reports did not have an actual occlusion of the artery but only stenosis or, rarely, even a normal vessel.[416] However, all had ipsilateral cerebral symptoms. One of our patients with a carotid occlusion and ipsilateral Horner's syndrome was anhidrotic on the entire ipsilateral side, a finding that points to a central lesion.

The pupils shrink in sleep and also become symmetrically small when the diencephalon is bilaterally involved during rostral-caudal deterioration secondary to supratentorial mass lesions. In both instances, the reaction to light is preserved.

Midbrain damage produces clear-cut pupillary signs. Dorsal tectal or pretectal lesions interrupt the pupillary light reflex (Fig. 6) but may spare the response to accommodation. The result is midposition or slightly widened (5 to 6 mm. in diameter), round, regular pupils that are light fixed but spontaneously fluctuate in size and may show hippus and retain their ciliospinal reflex. Recognition of these tectal effects on the pupil is important since small lesions in the midbrain tegmental area often involve the periaqueductal gray matter and interrupt consciousness. In such instances, the accompanying pupillary changes localize the anatomical lesion.

Nuclear midbrain lesions nearly always interrupt both the sympathetic and parasympathetic pathways to the eye (Fig. 6). The resulting pupils are midposition (4 to 5 mm. in diameter), fixed to light, usually slightly irregular, and often unequal. They occur most commonly with midbrain damage from transtentorial herniation but also when neoplasms, granulomas, or infarcts involve the midbrain. Lesions involving the third nerves between their nuclei and point of emergence from the brainstem produce external oculomotor paralysis accompanied by wide pupillary dilatation. Such parenchymal third nerve paralyses are frequently bilateral, in contrast to peripheral third nerve palsies, which are usually unilateral.

Pontine lesions of the tegmentum interrupt descending sympathetic pathways and produce bilaterally small pupils. If no drugs have been taken or instilled in the eye, pinpoint pupils generally mean pontine hemorrhage and are believed by Walsh and Hoyt[586] to result from parasympathetic irritation in combination with sympathetic interruption. The pupillary light reflex with pontine hemorrhage is usually present if examined with a magnifying glass,[168] although the degree of constriction is sometimes so intense that the casually observed light reflex is absent for several hours.

Lateral medullary and *ventrolateral cervical spinal cord lesions* cause homolateral mild Horner's syndrome with slight ptosis and pupillary constriction, never obliterating the light reflex.

Peripheral lesions involving either the third nerves or the sympathetic pathways affect the pupils of comatose patients. The pupillary fibers in the third nerve are particularly susceptible when uncal herniation compresses the nerve against the posterior cerebral artery or tentorium. In these instances, pupillary dilatation often precedes extraocular motor abnormalities. More distally along the nerve, the oculomotor and pupillomotor fibers are equally susceptible to damage, although occasionally the pupil is spared. More rarely, lesions compressing the third nerve near its origin can produce oculomotor palsy without pupillary dilatation. The reason for this selective involvement is unknown.

Pupillary Reflexes in Comatose Patients

A bilateral absence of the pupillary light reflex accompanies pretectal lesions and has been mentioned earlier. Lesions of any portion of the neural pathway, illustrated in Figure 5A, produce abnormalities of the light reflex. In lesions of the retina or the optic nerve anterior to the optic chiasm, the pupils are usually equal even if one eye is completely blind.[562] With such unilateral lesions, the direct pupillary light reflex is diminished or absent, but the consensual reflex is intact. Incomplete lesions may be detected by rapidly swinging a bright light from one eye to the other (the "swinging flashlight test").[536] There is dilatation of the involved eye when the light is moved to it from the uninvolved side. With lesions of the optic tract, the pupils are equal but may constrict only weakly when the light is restricted to the hemianopic retina (Wernicke's pupillary phenomenon). Small, light-fixed, irregular pupils without oculomotor paralysis are characteristic of central nervous system syphilis (Argyll Robertson pupil) and are occasionally seen in patients with diabetes. These diagnoses must always be considered when differentiating the causes of acute focal brainstem disease. With midbrain lesions at the level of the pretectal nucleus, the pupils are midposition or large. They do not respond to light but constrict on accommodation. *Lesions of the midbrain at the level of the Edinger-Westphal nucleus produce midposition, often irregular, 4 to 5 mm. fixed pupils,* probably because both sympathetic and parasympathetic descending pathways are involved. Lesions of the third nerve produce ipsilateral pupillary dilatation with absence of direct and consensual light responses.

Pharmacological and Metabolic Effects on the Pupil

The following drugs have effects that are likely to confuse the interpretation of pupillary changes in coma:

Atropine and *scopolamine,* when ingested in large amounts, produce fully dilated and fixed pupils, often accompanied by delirium or stupor.

Glutethimide (Doriden) characteristically produces midposition or moderately dilated (4 to 8 mm.) pupils that are unequal and frequently are fixed to light for several hours following ingestion of enough of the drug to produce profound coma. Fixed pupils in glutethimide poisoning do not necessarily signify a poor prognosis as they do under most other circumstances.

Opiates, particularly heroin and morphine, produce pinpoint pupils resembling those seen with pontine hemorrhage. The light reflex may be difficult to elicit but can be demonstrated with a bright light.

Anoxia or *ischemia,* if severe, may lead to bilaterally wide and fixed pupils. The clinical paradigm is that observed after cardiac arrest, in which if resuscitative measures are successful the pupils rapidly become small and reactive. Pupillary dilatation is not an invariable accompaniment of anoxia, however, and the pupils can sometimes remain small or midposition throughout an episode of profound hypoxia leading to death.[282] Experimentally, acute anoxia produces pupillary constriction until asystole occurs or the cardiac output is reduced more than 70 per cent,[46] at which point the pupils dilate only to return to the midposition 3 to 20 minutes after death. Pupillary dilatation follows circulatory arrest even in pupils with sympathetic or parasympathetic denervation. If the pupil has lost both sympathetic and parasympathetic supply, maximum dilatation follows restoration of circulation,[287] suggesting that circulating humors as well as neural impulses play a role in anoxic pupillary dilatation. Clinically, anoxic pupillary dilatation lasting more than a few minutes implies very severe and usually irreversible brain damage, although efforts at resuscitation should not be abandoned on that account alone since occasional recoveries, especially in younger patients, have been reported after the pupils have been fixed and dilated for hours.[93]

Hypothermia[564] and, rarely, *extremely severe barbiturate intoxication*[48] can fix the pupils. The patients with barbiturate intoxication whose pupils are fixed are usually apneic and hypotensive as well.

Pant, Benton, and Dodge[427] report transient anisocoria in 12 patients during or following *seizures.* The larger pupil usually reacted sluggishly to light.

Small pupils accompany many metabolic encephalopathies. The difference between pharmacogenic and destructive lesions causing sympathetic hypofunction cannot be made by examining the eyes alone. *The most important point is that, with the exceptions noted above, the pupillary light reflex is preserved until the terminal stages of metabolic brain disease producing coma. Since destructive lesions of the midbrain abolish the light reflex, it follows that patients showing other signs of severe midbrain depression, yet retaining the pupillary light reflex, have a metabolic disturbance.*

OCULAR MOVEMENTS

Pathways for vestibulo-ocular reflexes lie adjacent to brainstem areas necessary for consciousness, making it clinically useful to search for both gross and subtle oculomotor abnormalities when evaluating patients in stupor and coma. Asymmetrical oculomotor dysfunction more often accompanies structural than metabolic causes of unconsciousness.

39

Anatomy

Figure 7 schematically represents currently accepted concepts of the major neural pathways for ocular motility. Although there is dispute about the exact localization of these pathways, the general outlines are sufficiently reproducible to help in localizing clinical lesions, even if some anatomical details remain controversial or unknown.[33, 96]

Supranuclear Fibers (Fig. 7A and B)

The "frontal gaze center" (Brodmann's area 8) subserves rapid, voluntary, or saccadic eye movements. Loss of frontal lobe function impairs voluntary eye movement as well as the fast phases of optokinetic and vestibular nystagmus. Stimulation of the frontal center moves the eyes conjugately to the opposite side, and a combined stimulation of both frontal lobes together produces vertical eye movements. Fibers from the frontal cortex probably reach the brainstem by descending through the genu of the internal capsule. The "occipital gaze center" (Brodmann's areas 18 and 19) subserves slow, tracking, or pursuit eye movements. Loss of occipital function impairs smooth following or tracking responses. Stimulation of the occipital cortex also moves the eyes conjugately to the opposite side, and bilateral stimulation produces vertical movements, but if one frontal and the contralateral occipital lobe are stimulated simultaneously, the frontal stimulus dominates[245] and the eyes move away from the stimulated frontal lobe. Fibers from the occipital area descend to the internal sagittal stratum and the pulvinar to reach the midbrain.[586]

The supranuclear fibers subserving conjugate lateral eye movement descend to the midbrain in two bundles: The first bundle, the "aberrant pyramidal system of Déjerine," descends in the medial third of the cerebral peduncle and leaves the pyramidal system somewhere caudal to the oculomotor nucleus, where it crosses the substantia nigra and gathers in a bundle that passes to the medial tegmentum of the opposite side. Once crossed, these fibers descend to end chiefly in the paramedian zone of the pontine reticular formation. Goebel and co-workers[208] were able to produce paralysis of ipsilateral conjugate horizontal gaze by lesions in the medial portion of the nucleus reticularis magnocellularis and believe this area, which they have designated the paramedian pontine reticular formation, is the major area of confluence of pathways producing horizontal eye movements. Brucher[67] has described a second, noncrossed, cortical diencephalic-mesencephalic pathway that he believes to be important in subserving lateral conjugate as well as vertical eye movements. The fibers of Brucher's pathway course largely in the homolateral mesencephalic reticular formation and decussate just caudal to the oculomotor nucleus. They synapse in the contralateral pons near the abducens nucleus.

Fibers controlling conjugate vertical gaze (Fig. 7B) pass through the cerebral hemispheres with those subserving lateral gaze. Those from the

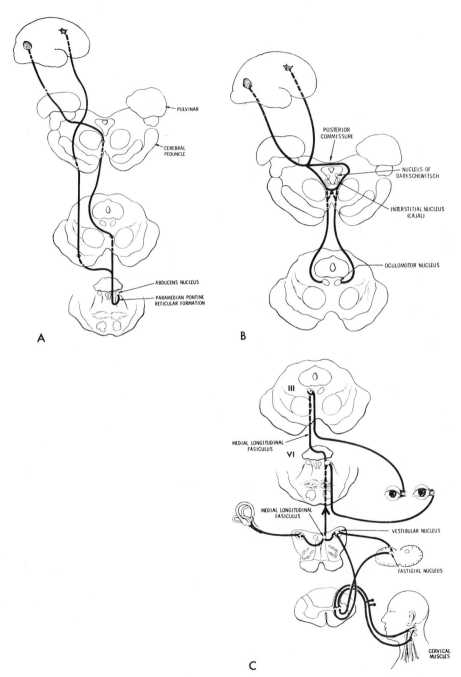

Figure 7. A, Schematic drawing of supranuclear pathways subserving lateral conjugate gaze. **B,** Schematic drawing of supranuclear pathways subserving vertical conjugate gaze. **C,** Schematic drawing illustrating internuclear oculomotor pathways and vestibular cerebellar and cervical proprioceptive eye movements.

frontal eye fields probably reach the oculomotor and trochlear nuclei by the noncrossed cortical diencephalic-mesencephalic pathway of Brucher.[67] Those from the occipital eye fields probably reach the oculomotor nuclei bilaterally, traveling through the regions of the pretectal and posterior commissural nuclei.

The pathways for vertical eye movement are only partially understood. In experimental animals, both voluntary and reflex upward gaze can be abolished by selective lesions of the posterior commissure,[431] and this is the pathway that probably is damaged by structural lesions involving the region of the superior colliculus. The earlier view that fibers subserving vertical gaze traveled through the superior colliculi is probably incorrect since removal of this structure does not affect ocular motility. There is some physiological evidence for a system of supranuclear vertical gaze fibers descending to the pons before reaching the oculomotor nuclei. Bender and Shanzer[34] produced loss of vertical gaze in both upward and downward directions by placing bilateral lesions in the pontine reticular formation. The clinical significance of this observation is somewhat doubtful since patients with pontine reticular lesions sufficient to produce total absence of conjugate lateral gaze characteristically retain vertical gaze movements (see Case 16, page 126). Hoyt and Daroff[249a] report transient loss of vertical gaze with normal eyelid and pupillary function after surgery of posterior fossa lesions. They assume that midbrain structures were not damaged and that the vertical gaze palsy resulted from bilateral edema of the pontine tegmentum. Some workers believe that the supranuclear fibers controlling upward gaze have different pathways from those controlling downward gaze since brainstem lesions can impair one of these functions and not the other.[144, 431]

Internuclear, Vestibular, and Proprioceptive Fibers (Fig. 7C)

The medial longitudinal fasciculus (MLF) connects the oculomotor, trochlear, and abducens nuclei. This pathway lies immediately ventral to the periaqueductal gray matter and decussates in the pons just rostral to the abducens nerve.[97] Interruption of one MLF prevents abduction of the ipsilateral medial rectus when conjugate lateral gaze is attempted voluntarily or when one tries to evoke it by optokinetic,[527] vestibular, or oculocephalic stimulation. Fibers from the semicircular canals and the fastigial nucleus of the cerebellum[63, 555] synapse in the vestibular nuclei and traverse the medial longitudinal fasciculus to supply the ocular nuclei, thereby linking the semicircular canals and the cerebellum with the eye muscles. The cerebellum probably serves the saccadic eye movement system since lesions restricted to the cerebellum result in disorders of saccadic eye movements (i.e., ocular dysmetria, ocular flutter, or opsoclonus[95]). Fibers subserving proprioception from vertebral joints, ligaments, and possibly neck muscles[43] enter the spinal cord through the dorsal roots of C2, C3, and C4. They ascend both by direct pathways and through spinocerebellar and spinal reticular tracts to reach the vestibular nuclei.[183] From there they project to the medial longitudinal fasciculus. Fibers of the medial longitudinal fasciculus subserve the slow phase of vestibular nystagmus. Fibers subserving the fast phase probably ascend in the pontine tegmentum via a polysynaptic pathway.[554]

Examination of Ocular Motility

One examines extraocular movement in awake, cooperative patients by comparing both voluntary and reflex eye movements. In patients in stupor or coma, reflex eye and eyelid movements must suffice. The paragraphs that follow give our methods for examining ocular motility, including the oculocephalic and oculovestibular responses. The physiological explanation for these responses is given in the next section.

The position of the eyes and eyelids at rest is noted and the patient observed for spontaneous eye movements. A small flashlight or bright ophthalmoscope, when shined in the eyes, reflects from the same point on each pupil if the eyes are conjugate.

Eyelid and Corneal Reflexes

Observe the position of the eyelids. In most stuporous or comatose patients, as in sleep, the eyes are closed by tonic contraction of the orbicularis oculi muscles. (The situation changes in chronic coma when sleep-wake cycles return.) Lift the lids and release them, noting their tonus. In unconscious patients the eyelids close gradually after they are released, a movement that cannot be duplicated voluntarily by a hysterical patient.[169] Absence of tone or failure to close either lid suggests facial nerve dysfunction on that side. Strong resistance to eye opening or rapid closure upon release, or both, can be voluntary, as in psychogenic unresponsiveness, or a result of reflex blephorospasm, which occurs in both structural and metabolic brain disease.[169] *Observe if blinking is present* either at rest or in response to a bright light, a threat, or a loud sound. The presence of spontaneous blinking implies that the pontine reticular formation is intact, and if blinks can be provoked by light or sound, those special sensory afferent pathways must also be intact. Blinking in response to a bright light may be present when there is no response to threat and probably does not imply an intact visual cortex since the reflex can be elicited in decorticate animals.[431a] Absence of blinking on one side is usually a sign of facial nerve dysfunction. Bilateral absence of blinking suggests either structural or metabolic dysfunction of the pontine reticular formation. *Test the corneal response.* In unconscious patients, a stronger stimulus must often be used to elicit this reflex than in alert patients. Observe both the eyelid and the eye. A positive bilateral response of eyelid closure and upward deviation of the eye (Bell's phenomenon) indicates normal function of the brainstem

43

tegmental pathways from the midbrain (third nerve nucleus) to the low pons (seventh nerve nucleus). With structural brainstem lesions above the midpons (trigeminal nucleus), Bell's phenomenon disappears, but the jaw may deviate to the opposite side (corneal pterygoid reflex). When Bell's phenomenon is present but eyelid closure absent, the facial nerves or nuclei are damaged.

The Oculocephalic Reflex (Proprioceptive Head-Turning Reflex, Doll's-Head Eye Phenomenon)

The eyelids are held open and the head is briskly rotated from side to side. A positive response is contraversive conjugate eye deviation (e.g., if the head is rotated to the right the eyes deviate to the left). Next, the neck is briskly flexed and extended. A positive response is deviation of the eyes upward when the neck is flexed and downward when the neck is extended. The eyelids may open reflexly when the neck is flexed (doll's-eyelid phenomenon[169]), allowing one to test levator palpebrae function as well. The eyes rapidly return to the resting position after the head is moved even if the head position is maintained.

Caloric Stimulation (Oculovestibular Reflex)

After the auditory canal is examined to be certain that the tympanic membrane is intact, and any impacted cerumen is removed, the head is elevated 30 degrees above the horizontal so that the lateral semicircular canal is vertical and stimulation can evoke a maximal response. A small catheter is placed in the external canal near the tympanic membrane and, with a large syringe, ice water is slowly introduced into the canal of unresponsive patients until either nystagmus or ocular deviation occurs, or until 200 cc. have been introduced. Cool water (30° C.) or small amounts of ice water (< 1 cc.)[400] are effective and less noxious for awake patients. In a normal awake patient the response to ice water caloric testing is nystagmus with the slow component toward the irrigated ear and the fast component away from the irrigated ear. The nystagmus is regular, rhythmic, and lasts 2 to 3 minutes. There is little excursion of the eye from the midline. As consciousness is lost acutely from metabolic or supratentorial brain disease, the fast component progressively disappears and the slow component carries the eyes tonically toward the irrigated ear. In obtunded or lightly comatose patients there may be a slow drift toward the irrigated ear with quick return to the midline. Even in unresponsive patients, occasional irregular beats of nystagmus are encountered, but the eyes are usually fully and conjugately deviated toward the irrigated ear for 2 to 3 minutes before returning to their original position. One should allow 5 minutes for the oculovestibular system to stabilize before performing the caloric test in the opposite ear. When brainstem lesions produce coma and involve the oculovestibular system as well, perversion of the caloric response may be observed, e.g., caloric irrigation may produce downward deviation of the ipsilateral eye with a few rotatory nystagmoid jerks (see Case 3).

With chronic brain injuries producing coma, the oculovestibular responses are less predictable than those just outlined. Mentally unresponsive patients surviving for several weeks after severe supratentorial injuries, for example, may demonstrate unsustained conjugate ocular movements down and away from the caloric irrigation as well as a number of other less-well-characterized responses. The pathological physiology of these responses is not well worked out.

The above caloric stimuli test lateral eye movements. To test vertical eye movements, one can irrigate both auditory canals simultaneously with ice water. In a comatose patient with intact brainstem function, the eyes deviate downward. To produce upward gaze, either irrigate both canals simultaneously with warm water (44° C.) or position the head 60 degrees below the horizontal and use ice water.

The Physiology of Oculocephalic and Oculovestibular Reflexes

Despite its empirical value in diagnosis, the physiological basis of the oculocephalic reflex is debated. Neither visual fixation nor occipital connections are involved in the reflex since it persists after blindness,[246] in coma or darkness,[397] and after occipital lobectomy.[430] Awake patients whose eyes are open do not have doll's-head eye responses unless they either voluntarily fix vision or suffer from interrupted frontopontine pathways bilaterally.[10] With the latter lesion, full doll's-eye responses are present but are said by Bielschowsky[42] to reflect a different reflex, requiring visual fixation. The stimulus for the oculocephalic reflex involves either the vestibular system or the proprioceptive afferents from the neck, or possibly both. Ford and Walsh[178] favor a vestibular basis for the reflex and state that the afferent pathways originate in the otolith. They point out that in healthy subjects neck reflexes elicit only 2 to 3 degrees of ocular movements and that the doll's-eye response can be elicited with the neck fixed if the patient is moved through space or tilted on a table. However, evidence for a contribution from proprioceptor impulses originating in neck muscles is compelling since the oculocephalic reflexes can be elicited in patients with vestibular systems unresponsive to caloric stimulation.[246] Case 3 illustrates this phenomenon.

Case 3. A 51-year-old man was admitted in deep coma. Eight years earlier he had had a subarachnoid hemorrhage treated by ligation of the left internal carotid artery, and followed by right hemiplegia and aphasia.

His body temperature was 32.6° C. (92° F.); his blood pressure was 110/70 mm. Hg, and his pulse was 64 per minute and regular. His respiratory pattern was apneustic. His pupils were 2 mm. in diameter and constricted briskly to a bright light stimulus. His right eye was in the straight-ahead position at rest. His left eye showed intermittent, spontaneous, rotatory jerking movements from the straight-ahead position to an infero-medial position. Cold caloric testing intensified the movements of the left eye, but neither eye deviated appropriately. *Vigorous head turning elicited a full range of lateral and vertical eye movements.* Noxious stimuli to the right side of the body elicited flexion of the legs and decerebrate posturing of the right arm. The EEG showed 3 to 4 cps background with lower voltage over the left hemisphere. He died several days later.

Autopsy disclosed a recent occlusion of the basilar artery from its midpoint to a level 2 to 3 cm. rostrally. There was an old left internal carotid thrombosis with an old cavitary left hemispheral infarct. There was a large recent infarct almost transecting the pons at the level of the trigeminal motor nucleus (see ref. 446; Figs. 5 and 6). Below and above this level, the infarction was primarily in the lateral tegmentum, and medial tegmental structures were relatively spared.

The fundamental physiology of the caloric response has been extensively studied by Szentágothai,[554, 555] Cohen and associates,[98, 99] and others.[174] It is generally accepted that in caloric tests, convection currents in the endolymph activate receptors in the semicircular canals. Cold stimuli produce downward currents away from the ampulla of the horizontal canal when the head is 30 degrees above horizontal, and warm stimuli produce upward currents[165] toward the ampulla. The vestibular nerve is tonically active at rest; stimulation with electrical impulses increases activity, as does warm water. Cold water gives the opposite response, decreasing the frequency of discharge below the resting level.[203a] When individual semicircular canals are selectively activated by pressure or electricity,[174, 555] stimulation of the horizontal canal excites, concurrently, the contralateral lateral rectus and the ipsilateral medial rectus muscles (an opposite effect is produced by ice water caloric tests). Stimulation of the posterior canal excites the ipsilateral superior oblique and the contralateral inferior rectus muscle. Stimulation of the superior canal excites the ipsilateral superior rectus muscle and the contralateral inferior oblique muscle. The excitatory stimuli to the extraocular muscles travel over three neuron arcs via the medial longitudinal fasciculus. Neural influences inhibiting reciprocal muscles during caloric stimulation appear to travel not in the medial longitudinal fasciculus but perhaps through the reticular formation.[555]

Abnormal Clinical Findings in Coma

Resting Eye Position and Spontaneous Eye Movements

ROVING EYE MOVEMENTS. The eyes of comatose patients with intact brainstem oculomotor function often rove spontaneously with slow, random deviations much like the "slow eye movements" of light sleep in normal persons. The movements may vary from conjugate to dysconjugate in the same patient, the dysconjugate aspect having no known additional pathological significance. The movements are usually horizontal, but vertical eye movements also occur. Roving eye movement cannot be mimicked voluntarily[169] and their presence rules out psychogenic unresponsiveness. Most patients with roving eye movements also have active oculocephalic reflexes (see below). Roving eye movements disappear if brainstem function becomes depressed much as slow eye movements disappear in deep sleep. Roving eye movements are slower than the always conjugate rapid eye movements (REM) of the dreaming phase of sleep.[127]

NYSTAGMUS. Spontaneous nystagmus is uncommon in coma since the quick or compensatory phase depends upon interaction between the oculovestibular system and the cerebral cortex and disappears as cortical influences are reduced. One does encounter, however, the following patterns of spontaneous eye movements resembling nystagmus, which may be of localizing value in comatose states:

Retractory nystagmus was first described by Koerber.[309] The movements consist of irregular jerks of the eyes backward into the orbit, sometimes occurring spontaneously but usually precipitated by attempted upward gaze. The phenomenon usually accompanies mesencephalic tegmental lesions.[153] Daroff and Hoyt[249a] reviewed the electromyographic findings in this disorder, which showed simultaneous co-contraction of all six ocular muscles. They suggested that the mesencephalic lesion produces dysfunction of cortical mesencephalic inhibitory fibers, and thus all six muscles contract when any one is stimulated.

Convergence nystagmus consists of spontaneous, slow, drifting, ocular divergence followed by a quick convergent jerk. The abnormality also reflects a mesencephalic lesion and may be interspersed with retractory nystagmus.

Ocular bobbing is Fisher's term[167] for attacks of intermittent, usually conjugate, brisk, downward eye movement followed by return to the primary position "in a kind of bobbing action." The movement occurs with severe destructive caudal pontine lesions (see Case 2) and is not altered by caloric tests. Nelson and Johnston[401] suggest that the sign is so specific for primary pontine hemorrhage or infarction as to eliminate the need to search for a cerebellar, subdural, or epidural mass lesion. However, there is a report of the phenomenon produced by brainstem compression from cerebellar hematoma[228] and a report of dysconjugate bobbing in a conscious patient with a pontine lesion.[407]

Nystagmoid jerking of a single eye in a lateral, vertical, or rotational direction also accompanies severe midpontine to lower pontine damage. Case 3 illustrates this phenomenon. Like other patients with this disorder, this man had severe abnormalities of his resting ocular position. Occasionally, slow, irregular, rotatory movements of the eyes occur in patients with pontine lesions; these are bilateral and sometimes reciprocal so that one eye moves down and extorts as the other moves up and intorts.

Not to be confused with these reciprocal eye movements is "seesaw" nystagmus,[342] a rapid, pendular, disjunctive movement of the eyes in which as one eye rises and intorts the other falls and extorts. The nystagmus is most marked on visual fixation, decreases with relaxation of visual attention, and is not present in comatose patients. Patients with seesaw nystagmus usually have lesions of the anterior third ventricular region and not of the brainstem. The nystagmus is invariably associated with severe visual field defects and loss of visual acuity and may be ocular in origin.

EYE POSITION AT REST. Patients with intact extraocular muscle pathways have eyes directed straight ahead[96] or slightly divergent during both consciousness and unconsciousness. Deviation of either eye more than a few degrees of arc from the physiological position of rest signifies abnormal extraocular function, although the abnormality may represent the emergence of latent strabismus rather than a new oculomotor lesion.

ABNORMALITIES OF LATERAL GAZE. Most conjugate gaze disorders occurring in unconscious patients result from destructive lesions since neither compression nor metabolic disorders usually affect the supranuclear oculomotor pathways asymmetrically. Conditions causing coma are likely to produce one of three types of abnormal conjugate lateral gaze, two originating in the hemisphere and the third in the brainstem. The first is a temporary loss of contraversion when a hemispheral lesion disrupts supranuclear cerebral pathways. Contralateral gaze being suddenly deprived of descending neural influences, the eyes deviate fully and conjugately to the still innervated side (the side of the lesion). The cerebral lesion usually also causes associated contralateral hemiparesis so that the eyes "look" at the normal arm and leg. There is usually no nystagmus.

The second hemispheral abnormality is an irritative or epileptic phenomenon that conjugately deviates the eyes *away* from a cerebral lesion. This contraversion of the eyes often accompanies cerebral hemorrhage and lasts only a matter of minutes or hours, to be replaced by the more common supranuclear paralysis of conjugate gaze. Less frequently, contraversion of the eyes provides a clue that coma is due to status epilepticus. Under these circumstances, the ocular contraversion has a jerking, nystagmoid, clonic quality similar to that of focal motor seizures in the extremities.

The third conjugate gaze abnormality comes from the brainstem. Lesions in the pons involving supranuclear oculomotor fibers below their decussation produce conjugate ocular deviation in which the eyes usually cannot be brought past the midline toward the lesion and spontaneously deviate away from the lesion. The deviation usually is less than with hemispheral lesions. If the responsible lesion affects the corticospinal pathway as well, the hemiparesis is contralateral to the lesion so that the eyes "look" at the paralyzed side.

Fisher[168] reports three patients with supratentorial hemorrhage whose eyes deviated to the "wrong" side. In each instance the hemorrhage was located in the medial thalamus with rupture into the third ventricle. All three patients had signs of upper brainstem disease as well (i.e., unreactive pupils in all three, downward deviation of the eyes in one, absence of full oculocephalic responses in two), suggesting that the eye deviation was produced by midbrain involvement just below the decussation of the corticobulbar fibers. We have made similar clinical observations, but our material lacks pathological confirmation. Daroff and Hoyt[249a] describe ipsilateral conjugate paresis with preserved reflex eye movements in patients with acute deep medial cerebellar hemispheral lesions. We have not observed such a patient.

To epitomize: Sustained, involuntary, conjugate ocular deviation toward a normal arm and leg suggests a hemispheral lesion, and toward a paralyzed arm and leg, a pontine brainstem lesion. Localization of conjugate gaze disorders is aided by caloric and oculocephalic testing as discussed below.

Resting dysconjugate lateral position of the eyes results when nuclear or infranuclear oculomotor pathways are damaged. Lesions involving the oculomotor nucleus or nerve cause the involved eye to deviate outward. If the oculomotor lesion is in the brainstem, the pupil is dilated to at least some degree, and light fixed. If the oculomotor lesion is in the peripheral fibers, the pupil is usually, but not always, dilated (see page 37). With unilateral abducens paralysis the involved eye deviates inward; with bilateral paralysis the eyes converge.

Latent strabismus can be accentuated or made manifest by acute neurological illness, even when oculomotor function is not directly involved. Brainstem lesions causing strabismus produce defects in a neurological distribution as described above, whereas congenital strabismus involves single muscles. Conversely, in *deeply* comatose patients preexisting dysconjugate gaze disappears since, when innervation is removed from all ocular muscles, the eyes assume the physiological position of rest.

ABNORMALITIES OF VERTICAL GAZE. Many otherwise healthy elderly patients have a limited capacity for upward gaze, but, with that exception, abnormalities of upward gaze imply a brainstem lesion. The most common abnormality is *paralysis* of upward gaze, which usually results from a lesion compressing or destroying the pretectal and posterior commissural areas at the midbrain-diencephalic junction. Bilateral lesions of the medial longitudinal fasciculus also may produce defects in upward gaze, particularly if the lesion extends ventrally into the adjacent reticular formation. In patients in light coma, upward gaze can be tested by holding the lid open and stimulating the cornea. This normally results in lid closure and upward ocular deviation (Bell's phenomenon). In patients in deeper coma, oculocephalic or caloric stimulation is usually required. Resting deviation of the eyes below the horizontal meridian always denotes brainstem dysfunction, which most often results from compression upon the midbrain tectum. However, extensive brainstem destruction or metabolic depression, as in hepatic coma, can also cause conjugate downward deviation.

Resting vertical dysconjugate gaze implies a lesion of internuclear or, rarely, supranuclear pathways. Bielschowsky[41, 42] reports this phenomenon following interruption of supranuclear fibers with a midbrain lesion involving the tectum but sparing the oculomotor nuclei. Presumably, the

49

supranuclear fibers are involved unilaterally after they separate to innervate their respective oculomotor nuclei.

In skew deviation the eyes diverge, one "looking" down, the other, up. Patients able to cooperate and who possess this ocular abnormality may show mild vertical nystagmus in either eye and occasionally have slow seesaw movements of both eyes. The specific fibers involved in skew deviation have not been identified, but the causative lesions are characteristically localized in or around the brachium pontis on the side of the inferiorly rotated eye[528] or in the medial longitudinal fasciculus on the side of the elevated eye.[526] Since skew deviation is diagnostic of brainstem lesions, it is imperative to be certain that one is not misinterpreting preexisting vertical strabismus.[528]

Abnormalities of Oculocephalic (Doll's-Head) and Oculovestibular (Caloric) Reflexes

With certain important exceptions, discussed below, the oculomotor responses to caloric stimulation and passive head turning relate to each other as if the two stimuli differed only in degree, the first being stronger than the second. Both reflexes, therefore, are discussed together.

In normal awake subjects or those with psychogenic unresponsiveness, oculocephalic responses are inconsistent and caloric stimulation produces nystagmus. Awake patients with bifrontal[10] or diffuse hemispheral and basal ganglia disease[538] have active doll's-head oculomotor responses, possibly, as Bielschowsky pointed out, because damaged frontal eye field pathways no longer inhibit visual fixation; caloric stimulation may produce tonic deviation rather than nystagmus.

In light coma, cortical influences are lost. The oculocephalic reflexes can be demonstrated consistently, and caloric stimuli produce tonic lateral deviation rather than nystagmus. Several vigorous turns of the head may be necessary to elicit the oculocephalic response, particularly if the subject has roving eye movements. With greater cortical depression, but still leaving the brainstem intact, both doll's-head and caloric responses become very brisk and the oculocephalic response can be elicited by a single turn of the head.

Oculocephalic and particularly oculovestibular reflexes are usually powerful enough to overcome the conjugate lateral eye deviation that results from unilateral lesions of the frontal or occipital eye fields. However, in the first few hours after a massive hemispheral lesion, it may require both vigorous passive head turning and caloric stimulation in combination to overcome the ocular deviation toward the damaged hemisphere.

Patients with metabolic cerebral depression generally retain reflex eye movements even when certain other signs of brainstem depression such as decerebrate rigidity and central hyperventilation have already appeared.

With more severe depression of brainstem function, as with deep sedative poisoning, the reflexes become sluggish and finally disappear, caloric responses outlasting oculocephalic reflexes.

Lesions that destroy or compress the brainstem produce oculocephalic and caloric reflex abnormalities that depend on the location of the lesion. Pretectal or midbrain tegmental compression destroys reflex upward gaze. Compression or destruction of the oculomotor nerves or nuclei obliterates all homolateral oculocephalic and caloric responses except as mediated by the external rectus muscle.

Midbrain or pontine lesions involving the medial longitudinal fasciculus (MLF) produce internuclear ophthalmoplegia. In comatose patients, the effects of MLF lesions can be detected by passive head turning or caloric irrigation. The eye ipsilateral to the lesion fails to adduct when the other eye abducts. Strictly speaking, the presence of intact convergence (this function not requiring MLF pathways) is required to distinguish between internuclear ophthalmoplegia and isolated medial rectus palsy. However, isolated medial rectus weakness is so rare that reflex failure of one or both eyes to adduct is almost diagnostic of internuclear ophthalmoplegia. The clinical usefulness of this identification is that unilateral or bilateral internuclear ophthalmoplegia occurs frequently in patients with structural brainstem lesions. Internuclear ophthalmoplegia is less common with metabolic brain disease. Nathanson[396] failed to demonstrate internuclear ophthalmoplegia by caloric tests in any of 250 subjects after giving amobarbital intravenously. Blegvad,[50] however, reports that internuclear ophthalmoplegia and other dysconjugate eye movements are common in patients with barbiturate intoxication and therefore are of no diagnostic value. Our experience has been that internuclear ophthalmoplegia may often be encountered at some stage during barbiturate intoxication, although it is usually transient. We have also noted the phenomenon in other forms of metabolic coma (e.g., hepatic encephalopathy), especially when small quantities of ice water were used. In these instances, the stronger stimulus of larger irrigation may produce adduction of the contralateral medial rectus, a finding not encountered with structural disease of the MLF.

Acute or subacute lateral pontine lesions in the area of the abducens nuclei produce conjugate gaze paralysis, which cannot be modified by either passive head turning or caloric stimulation. It is believed that vestibular and proprioceptive impulses enter the neural pathways controlling extraocular movements at this locus and are involved in the lesion.

In bilateral lateral brainstem lesions involving the vestibular nuclei caloric responses are absent, but oculocephalic reflexes are retained because the pathways remain for proprioceptive afferent impulses from the neck (Case 3). This or circumstances in which both labyrinths are destroyed (e.g., streptomycin toxicity) are the only conditions in which absence of caloric responses accompanies preserved oculocephalic responses.

51

Summary of Oculomotor Signs

In awake alert patients the eyes are directed straight ahead at rest and there are no involuntary movements. Oculocephalic responses cannot normally be elicited, and caloric stimulation yields nystagmus rather than sustained deviation.

Unconscious patients suffering from diffuse or bilateral hemispheral dysfunction without direct destruction or compression of the neural pathways influencing ocular movements have eyes directed straight ahead or slightly divergent with no involuntary movements except slow roving eye movements. Oculocephalic responses are brisk, and caloric stimulation causes sustained eye deviation.

Unconscious patients with acute damage to a frontal eye field have eyes deviated to the side of the lesion, occasionally with some nystagmus to that side. Oculocephalic and caloric responses are usually present although they may be difficult to demonstrate in the early hours after injury.

In metabolic coma, responses to oculocephalic and caloric stimulation at first are brisk, then become more difficult to demonstrate as coma deepens. In very deep metabolic coma, the eyes are immobile.

The eyes of comatose patients with midbrain lesions are immobile and directed straight ahead. The eyes of patients with small lesions involving the medial longitudinal fasciculus look straight ahead, but the globe on the side of the lesion fails to adduct to oculocephalic or caloric stimulation. More laterally placed unilateral pontine lesions cause the eyes to deviate conjugately away from the lesion with absence of oculocephalic and caloric responses in the paralyzed field. Skew deviation results from dorsolaterally placed pontine lesions or from lesions of the medial longitudinal fasciculus.

Eyes that are directed straight ahead have no localizing value in the unconscious patient. Eyes that are conjugately deviated in the horizontal meridian mean either an ipsilateral hemispheral lesion (usually frontal) or a contralateral pontine lesion. If the eyes are fully deviated but can be brought beyond the midline toward the other side by either passive head turning or caloric stimulation, the lesion is almost certainly hemispheral. If the eyes are partially deviated and repeated efforts fail to bring them beyond the midline toward the other side, the lesion is almost certainly pontine. If the eyes are conjugately deviated downward, a lesion is either compressing or metabolically depressing the mesencephalon; downward deviation rarely occurs with direct destruction of the mesencephalon. If the eyes can be raised above the horizontal meridian by oculocephalic or caloric response, the lesion is probably metabolic; if not, it is probably compressive.

Except for mild ocular divergence, dysconjugate ocular deviation in coma means a structural brainstem lesion if pre-existing strabismus can be ruled out. Dysconjugate eye movements may be evoked by caloric or oculocephalic responses. If one or both eyes selectively fail to adduct, the lesion is in the medial longitudinal fasciculus (if pupillary responses indicate that there is no oculomotor palsy). Failure of abduction with intact contralateral adduction indicates a lesion of the abducens nerve below its nucleus. Oculocephalic and caloric stimulation only rarely produce dysconjugate vertical movements, but if they do the lesion is intrinsic to the brainstem.

MOTOR FUNCTION

Clinical accounts often equate motor responses with depth of coma. This is unjustified and often misleading since the nuclear masses and pathways that regulate movement stand almost entirely apart from those that mediate either mental activity or arousal. As a result, neurological disease often affects motor function and consciousness at independent levels of integration.[226] Examples of this dissociation are given above in the section on de-efferentation, which cites examples of patients having motor decerebration with the full retention of consciousness. Neurologists commonly encounter similar examples in patients with multiple sclerosis. Also, as Chapter 4 will emphasize, dissociation between the functional level of impaired motor function and the degree of impairment of other functions, including consciousness, respiration, pupils, and eye movements, is characteristic of metabolic coma. Thus, the importance of the motor examination of the patient in coma is that it gives information about the geographical distribution of neurological dysfunction because injury at almost every level of the nervous system affects motor behavior differently so as to produce a distinctive and recognizable response. If one can deduce where the motor abnormality arises, this yields a clue as to the site, cause, and possible progression of the lesion or lesions causing stupor or coma.

Most motor abnormalities in patients in coma are associated with typical and well-known patterns of monoplegia, hemiplegia, and other abnormal reflexes or postures that have a limited localizing value. However, certain less frequently emphasized motor changes are also useful in evaluating states of impaired consciousness as they either indicate the development of more subtle changes or provide a more precise anatomical localization. These are discussed in the following paragraphs.

Impaired cerebral hemispheric function reflects itself in the emergence of several motor behavioral patterns and responses that are similar to functions exhibited by a normal infant in the early months of life, a time when the child is functioning essentially at the thalamic level.[432] Included are posthyperventilation apnea and respiratory apraxia, oculomotor avoidance reactions, reflex blepharospasm, exaggerated prehensile sucking and snouting reactions, flexion tetraparesis with lordosis (paraplegia in flexion of cerebral origin),[606] skeletal muscle paratonia or gegenhalten, motor perseveration, and reflex tonic grasping of the hand or the foot. In most instances the responses are bilateral, although some, such as tonic grasping, can at times be detected entirely unilaterally in the hand or foot opposite to large frontal lobe lesions.[6, 503] However, even when only unilateral clinical signs are found, such abnormal reflexes almost always accompany bilateral cerebral dysfunction. Grasping, for example, is seldom elicited in patients with small frontal lobe neoplasms or entirely focal vascular disease, and its presence is usually a reliable clinical sign not only of contralateral frontal lobe dysfunction but of increased intracranial pressure, abnormal intracranial shifts, or diffuse vascular or metabolic changes in addition.

The precise pathological physiology of these motor signs of impaired cerebral function is in many instances unknown. Publications on the subject that include full details of pathological structural changes almost always depict widespread abnormalities in the frontal lobes, the basal ganglia, and even the brainstem reticulum. It helps little to relate the signs to a loss of putative cortical inhibition, since cortical inhibition of behavioral responses is itself physiologically unexplained. However, in many instances, as with the grasp reflex and forced grasping, it is likely that the responses have two components, one mediated as a short latency, primitive, cutaneous spinal reflex analogous to the normal flexor plantar response[437] and the second (a sign of more severe frontal lobe damage) combining the abnormally manifest spinal reflex with motor perseveration.[505] Thus, a very brisk, brief palmar flexor reflex without sustained grasping is readily elicited by finger or palmar extension in patients with decerebrate rigidity. The biological advantage of the grasp reflex presumably has its full expression in our simian ancestors where the neonate tonically grasps the mother's underbelly, leaving the maternal arms and legs free to swing and run. Similar ontogenic advantages may favor other motor patterns in the infant.

Paratonia or gegenhalten (motor negativism)[305] is a plastic-like increase in muscle resistance to passive movements of the extremities, head, or trunk. The resistance is constant or nearly so throughout the movement arc and of similar intensity regardless of the initial position of the body part. The phenomenon is differentiated from parkinsonian rigidity in that it almost disappears if the part is moved very slowly and is made much worse by rapid passive movement. It is generally greatly enhanced by brusque urgings to the patient to "relax," often giving to the resistance a quality suggesting that the patient actively opposes every effort to move his parts. The degree of resistance varies widely from a just perceptible molasses-like "stickiness" to an intense rigidity that can involve the entire body. The associated stretch reflexes are unaltered, but a weak palmar grasp reflex and a tonic flexor plantar or extensor plantar response are commonly elicited on the same side as the resistance. The physiological basis of paratonic rigidity is unknown, although it blends into the more familiar extrapyramidal rigidity of certain forms of parkinsonism. Both it and the grasp reflex are present in normal infants between the second and eighth week of life.

In adults, paratonic rigidity usually accompanies diffuse forebrain dysfunction such as occurs with metabolic encephalopathy, diffuse cerebral atrophy, or hypertensive vascular disease. When the abnormality is predominantly unilateral it occurs most consistently in association with disease of the frontal lobes, particularly when the process is accompanied by increased intracranial pressure or metabolic abnormalities. In such instances, it can be an early sign of a hemispheric mass lesion, whether or not the patient is in coma.

Motor and sensory function in patients with clouded or reduced consciousness can be estimated by applying noxious stimuli to various parts of the body and observing the responses. The motor responses are of three types: appropriate, inappropriate, and absent. *Appropriate* responses in a patient with acute brain dysfunction imply that sensory pathways are functioning and that the corticospinal pathways from the cerebral cortex to effector are at least partially functioning. Provided stimuli are applied to both sides of the body so as to rule out sensory impairment, unilateral *absence of* responses is consistent with interruption of the corticospinal tract anywhere along its length. Bilateral absence of responses means one of three things: In the brainstem, both corticospinal tracts are interrupted, there is depression or destruction of the pontomedullary reticular formation and associated extrapyramidal pathways, or the motor unresponsiveness is psychogenic. *Inappropriate* motor responses are stereotypes whose pattern depends on the level of injury. Three principal responses are seen with brain injury: decorticate rigidity, classical decerebrate rigidity, and decerebrate changes in the arms combined with flexor responses in the legs (Fig. 8).

Decorticate rigidity consists of flexion of the arm, wrist, and fingers, with adduction in the upper extremity and extension, internal rotation, and plantar flexion in the lower extremity. In man this motor pattern characterizes chronic spastic hemiplegia and typically emerges in the wake of lesions of the internal capsule or cerebral hemisphere which interrupt the corticospinal pathways (Fig. 8, top). Experimentally, decorticate rigidity follows frontal lobe removal or thalamic decerebration,[40] and postmortem findings in humans[369] correlate well with the experimental results. Thus, decorticate responses are characteristic of patients with moderate- to large-sized destructive lesions of the internal capsule and rostral cerebral peduncle. Sometimes the adjacent basal ganglia and thalamus are involved. To bring out decorticate responses during the early hours after acute cerebral injuries it may be necessary to apply noxious stimulation by supraorbital pressure, tracheal suction, or vigorous cutaneous stimulation. Spontaneous spasms of rigidity often complicate the course of patients with acute hemispheric hemorrhages.

Decerebrate rigidity, when fully developed in man, consists of opisthotonos with the teeth clenched, the arms stiffly extended, adducted, and hyperpronated, and the legs stiffly extended with the feet plantar flexed

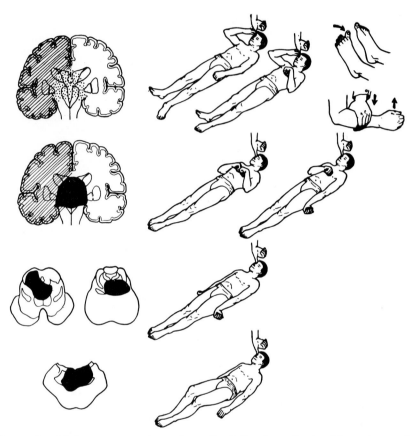

Figure 8. Motor responses to noxious stimulation in patients with acute cerebral dysfunction.

(Fig. 8, third line). The full response usually emerges only on application of a noxious stimulus. With acute lesions of the brain, waves of shivering and hyperpnea accompany decerebrate spasms, particularly when subarachnoid bleeding or massive cerebral and intraventricular hemorrhages provide endogenous noxious stimulation. In less severely ill patients with the appropriate neural lesions, external noxious stimulation sometimes elicits fragments of the decerebrate response consisting of brief hyperextension of the body or an arm, pronation of the hand, and clenching of the jaws with head retraction. It should be emphasized that clinical disease sometimes blurs the dividing line between decorticate and decerebrate rigidity, particularly with deep hemispheric lesions that are beginning to exert pressure effects on the upper brainstem. In such instances, the motor responses can shift back and forth from one combination to the other, presumably reflecting physiological changes in the tissue's circulation. It is not unusual under

56

such circumstances for decerebrate responses to be present on one side of the body (usually contralateral to the hemispheric lesion) while the other side undergoes either an appropriate response or yields the decorticate posture (Fig. 8, second line).

Decerebrate rigidity is induced in experimental animals by midbrain transections that spare the vestibular nuclei and the adjacent pontine reticular formation.[511, 589] Lesions found at autopsy in patients seldom provide anatomical correlation as precise as the sherringtonian section in animals, but decerebrate rigidity occurs in patients with infarcts destroying all brainstem rostral to the midpons as well as in patients suffering large cerebral hemorrhages that destroy or compress the lower thalamus and midbrain (Chapter 2). These observations as well as the experimental studies alluded to imply that decerebrate rigidity in man requires at least partial and bilateral separation of midbrain-pontine structures from more rostral neural influences.

The clinician usually encounters decerebrate rigidity under one of three circumstances: (1) during rostral-caudal deterioration as diencephalic dysfunction progresses into midbrain damage (Chapter 2); (2) with destructive or expanding posterior fossa lesions that damage the midbrain and rostral pons; and (3) with severe metabolic disorders such as hepatic coma, hypoglycemia, anoxia, or drug intoxication that depress the function of the upper brainstem.

Decerebrate rigidity also is observed with certain subacute and severe bilateral, diffuse hemispheric abnormalities such as postanoxic cerebral demyelination and Schilder's disease. The pathological physiology of the motor response is not readily explained in such cases unless one postulates either that the rapid and extensive damage to rostral structures has a shock effect that particularly interrupts cerebral inhibition of more caudal structures or that functional abnormalities exceed the anatomical change and extend to nuclear masses below the hemispheres.

Decerebrate posturing in the upper extremities combined with either flaccidity or weak flexor responses in the lower is a primitive stereotyped motor response to noxious stimulation found in patients with extensive brainstem damage extending down to or across the pons at the trigeminal level (Fig. 8, bottom).

ELECTROENCEPHALOGRAM

The electroencephalogram may differentiate coma from psychogenic unresponsiveness (e.g., hysteria and catatonia) (see Chapter 5) and helps to distinguish among the various causes of coma. The following paragraphs outline the common normal and abnormal EEG patterns. More detailed descriptions can be found elsewhere.[238, 300]

The Normal EEG

Physiology

The electroencephalogram records the electrical activity of those layers of the cerebral cortex that are adjacent to the skull. It is generally believed that EEG activity represents the graded potential changes in the massed dendrites of cortical neurons.[54] Despite its superficial cortical origin, however, the form of the normal EEG depends on stimuli reaching the cortex from deeper brain structures. Several facts support this statement. (1) Normal EEG rhythms are absent from undercut and isolated cortex.[56] (2) Many EEG waves appear synchronously in both hemispheres, suggesting that a midline diencephalic or brainstem pacemaker controls the synchronous waves. (3) The entire EEG is modified by stimulating certain deep midline brain structures with the resulting EEG modification often outlasting the stimulus.

Waking Patterns

The outstanding feature of the EEG in the normal awake adult is the 8 to 13 cycles per second alpha rhythm, which is most prominent in the posterior parts of the head. Alpha activity has an amplitude of 1 to 100 microvolts (μV.) (average 25 to 50 μV.), and although this amplitude may differ substantially between the hemispheres, alpha frequency is normally identical in both hemispheres (a persistent difference of greater than 1 per second is abnormal). Alpha activity responds to environmental alterations and usually "blocks" (i.e., is replaced by low voltage fast activity) when the eyes are opened, during mental effort,[207] or after a sudden sound or touch. The frequency of the alpha rhythm is generally quite constant[588] for a given subject. Alpha frequency, however, is slowed by metabolic changes such as are induced by anoxia and hypoglycemia. Emotional tension and anxiety lead to a decrease in the total amount of alpha activity, but not to a decrease in the alpha frequency.

Beta activity (faster than 13 cycles per second) appears in all normal adult records, most prominently in the frontal and central areas. It is normally of low amplitude, averaging less than 20 μV. Beta rhythm predominates in some normal individuals (producing so-called low voltage fast records) and frequently replaces the alpha activity in tense and anxious patients.

Theta (4 to 7 cycles per second) waves are normally less than 20 μV. in amplitude. They are most prominent in the frontotemporal areas and occupy as much as 5 per cent of some normal EEG's.

Delta waves are slower than 4 cycles per second and do not occur in the normal adult EEG.

Sleeping Patterns

There are several different EEG patterns, correlating with the different stages of normal sleep.[127, 340] Dement and Kleitman recognize four:

Stage 1 (drowsiness and light sleep) begins with slowing of the alpha frequency by a fraction of a cycle per second and rapidly progresses to replacement of alpha by low amplitude fast waves. Short runs of alpha activity reappear from time to time.

Stage 2 (light sleep). Superimposed on a low amplitude background are 1-second bursts of 12 to 14 cps high amplitude waves called sleep spindles. High potential, bilaterally synchronous waves, maximal at the central vertex and often followed by spindle activity, are called K complexes and appear at this stage.

Stage 3 (moderate sleep). Some spindle activity remains, and high amplitude 1-to-2-per-second waves appear.

Stage 4 (deep sleep). No sleep spindles are seen. The record is dominated by 1-to-2-per-second waves of 100 μV. or more in amplitude.

A normal sleeper proceeds sequentially through these stages several times during the night. Episodes of stage 1 EEG that occur after the initial one are associated with sudden jerky conjugate eye movements in any direction called rapid eye movements (REM). Rapid eye movements are related to dreaming. Sleep associated with the initial stage 1 EEG episodes is very light, but later stage 1 episodes are associated with deeper sleep.[127] The rhombencephalic stage (a stage of sleep in animals inferred to emanate from controlling influences in the caudal pons[283]) resembles this "emergent stage 1" EEG phase of sleep in man. Both are associated with EEG patterns suggesting wakefulness when the subjects are asleep, and both are associated with rapid eye movements. The emergent stage 1 phase of sleep in man, however, may not be as deep as the rhombencephalic stage in animals.

The Abnormal EEG

Physiology

Since normal EEG activity depends on the integrity of both cortex and deep structures, it follows that an EEG may be altered by dysfunction of cortical neurons, by dysfunction of diencephalic or brainstem structures influencing the EEG, or by interruption of connections between the cortex and deeper brain structures.

Neural centers that influence consciousness tend to have an important effect on the EEG, and most conditions that alter consciousness in the behavioral sense also alter the EEG. In animals, stimulation of "nonspecific" thalamic nuclei (including mainly the midline nuclei, the interlaminar nuclei, and the reticular and anterior ventral nuclei) leads to widespread, bilateral EEG changes either in the form of sleep spindles or high potential slow waves. The type of evoked EEG activity depends on the location and type of stimulation, and under various experimental conditions the EEG changes can be accompanied by cessation of normal motor activity,[253] by drowsiness, or even by sleep.[7] At the level of the mesencephalic reticulum, stimulation in a sleeping intact animal causes both behavioral and EEG arousal; destructive lesions cause coma and a synchronous pattern of EEG activity reminiscent of sleep. More caudally, stimulation of the nucleus reticularis pontis caudalis is followed by the EEG and behavioral correlates of so-called rhombencephalic sleep.[283]

EEG abnormalities in man do not always correlate this closely with anatomical lesions, as the following paragraphs indicate.

Supratentorial Lesions

Supratentorial lesions generally cause focal EEG abnormalities because they either directly involve the cortex or interrupt thalamocortical projections. The first change, the appearance of unilateral or focal slow activity, occurs in the vast majority of hemorrhages, infarcts, tumors, and abscesses. Slow activity is more prominent with acute or rapidly progressive lesions and may be minimal or absent with slow-growing lesions. As the lesions spread to invade or compress diencephalic structures, bilateral slow activity occurs, probably because the diffuse projection system of the thalamus is damaged. At this stage, EEG activity is usually slower on the side of the lesion, but often the bilateral slowing obscures the original focus. Frequently sleep spindles and K complexes are decreased on the side of the structural lesion, a change which has been attributed to interruption of thalamocortical pathways.[518] Theoretically, coma should not occur until diencephalic structures are sufficiently involved that the EEG is bilaterally slow. This usual pattern, however, is not invariable, and there are reports of patients in moderate or deep coma having only unilateral EEG slowing.[336]

Subtentorial Lesions

When infratentorial lesions involve the mesencephalic reticular formation, bilateral synchronous EEG slowing is usually noted.[336] Sleep spindles, vertex sharp waves, and K complexes are often present, suggesting that the lesion is below the still intact thalamocortical system.[268] In patients with caudally placed subtentorial lesions, there is poor correlation between the EEG and the state of consciousness. Chase, Moretti, and Prensky[88] compared EEG and clinical observations with pathological findings in 20 cases of lower midbrain and pontine infarction. Of the eight alert patients, four had normal tracings; bilaterally synchronous high voltage delta activity was present in one alert patient. Of the eight unresponsive patients, only one had a normal record, but one was borderline; three records contained marked but intermittent theta activity and three showed high voltage delta activity. Some alpha activity was present in most of the unresponsive patients but, unlike alpha activity in alert patients, it was not affected by light, noise, or noxious stimuli.

Metabolic Disorders

Metabolic brain disease produces diffuse and symmetrical slowing of the EEG with the severity of the encephalopathy and degree of slowing generally paralleling one another.[473] Even the mildest delirium is usually accompanied by reduction in alpha frequency, but this may be difficult to ascertain unless previous normal records are available for the subject. With more severe cerebral depression to the point of lethargy, slower 5- to 8-per-second waves replace the background alpha activity.

When the patient becomes lethargic, paroxysmal bursts of high voltage, bifrontally synchronous, 2- to 4-per-second waves appear and spread laterally and posteriorly as cerebral depression deepens. These paroxysmal waves may take several forms, which have been called by various authors "blunt spike and wave,"[175] "triphasic waves,"[39] and "pseudoparoxysmal waves."[517] Because the activity is bilaterally synchronous, Foley, Watson, and Adams[175] postulated that it results from a metabolic disturbance of thalamocortical systems. It occurs most commonly in hepatic encephalopathy and was originally thought to be characteristic of this disorder. However, similar patterns are encountered in metabolic brain disease of other causes (e.g., uremia[263]) and occasionally accompany deep midline brain tumors. With deep coma the entire electroencephalogram consists of continuous 1- to 3-per-second diffuse slow activity of high voltage. A normal EEG in an unresponsive patient rules out metabolic brain disease as the cause. However, although the EEG is always slow in metabolic coma, EEG recovery may lag behind clinical recovery and very slow coma-like records may persist for days or weeks after patients reawaken.

Chapter 2

Supratentorial Lesions Causing Coma

Three types of supratentorial processes have been reported to cause loss of consciousness. (1) Lesions producing diffuse bilateral impairment of either the cortical mantle or its underlying white matter without abnormalities in the brainstem. Some of these can follow traumatic head injuries, as discussed in this chapter, but more often such diffuse lesions have a metabolic origin and are discussed in Chapter 4. (2) Bilateral subcortical destructive lesions ostensibly selectively involving rhinencephalic structures. As discussed below, these lesions probably extend to involve structures beyond the rhinencephalon as well, making it doubtful that abnormalities confined to the rhinencephalon cause coma. (3) Localized hemispheric mass and destructive lesions. These cause coma when they either encroach directly upon deep medial diencephalic structures or secondarily compress them.

RHINENCEPHALIC AND SUBCORTICAL DESTRUCTIVE LESIONS

Several workers have described patients in whom coma was associated with lesions of the corpora striata,[121] the cingulate gyri,[409] or the territorial distribution of the anterior cerebral arteries.[120] However, other patients with similar lesions have not been unconscious[380] and a review of the protocols of the unconscious patients suggests that in some of them metabolic or circulatory complications caused the coma, and in others that the pathological changes were distributed more widely than was at first suspected or emphasized. An example of the latter is a patient in whom coma was attributed to bilateral infarction of the cingulate gyrus.[409] She had a cerebral hemorrhage above the cingulum and, while there certainly was cingulate gyrus damage, an accompanying illustration of a sagittal brain section shows downward displacement of the diencephalon consistent with tentorial coning. Another example is a patient in whom coma was ascribed to occlusion of the anterior cerebral artery proximal to the origin of Heubner's recurrent artery,[110] but the autopsy description indicated pathological changes considerably beyond the usual territorial distribution of this vessel. Thus, it appears unlikely that restricted rhinencephalic or subcortical hemispheral destructive lesions cause coma although acute, large, bilateral frontal-medial destruction does appear capable of producing akinetic mutism (page 23).

SUPRATENTORIAL MASS LESIONS

Clinical-pathological correlations repeatedly have demonstrated that large, one-sided cortical and subcortical lesions dampen total behavior and produce dull apathy, particularly when they involve the thalamoparietal sensory radiations. However, disease processes causing unilateral destruction confined to a single cerebral hemisphere, basal ganglia, or lateral thalamus do not appear to cause coma unless their effects extend beyond these anatomical boundaries. The way that supratentorial mass lesions do produce coma is by enlarging sufficiently so that they displace tissues either across the midline to compress the other hemisphere (which is a comparatively uncommon cause) or caudally to compress and damage the deep diencephalic and midbrain structures that normally activate or arouse the cerebrum. Occasionally a supratentorial mass directly invades these deep structures; more often the mass evokes local and remote intracranial tissue reactions that secondarily displace the brain down toward the tentorial incisura, compressing the diencephalon and interfering with its blood supply.

Anatomy of the Intracranial Compartments

The dural and meningeal supporting structures have a negligible volume. In the dog the remaining intracranial contents are divided approximately as follows: brain (of which 65 per cent is water) 88.8 per cent, blood 2.3 per cent, and cerebrospinal fluid 8.9 per cent.[478] The values are probably similar in man. Since the intracranial volume is essentially constant, any new mass must develop and enlarge at the expense of an existing component.

Several factors limit the brain's ability to adjust to a space-occupying mass. The skull is inelastic and allows for only minimal expansion through the foramen magnum and the smaller foramina that transmit blood vessels and nerves. Furthermore, supporting septa divide the intracranial cavity into fossae that normally protect the brain against excessive movement but limit the amount of compensatory shift and displacement that can develop in response to abnormal conditions.

The tentorium cerebelli divides the cranial vault into anterior and posterior fossae (Fig. 9). This inflexible fibrous dural lamina extends posteriorly from the petrous ridges and anterior clinoid processes, sloping downward and outward from its medial edge to attach laterally to the occipital bone along the line of the lateral sinus. Posteriorly, the tentorium slopes down to attach to the internal occipital protuberance. Extending posteriorly into the center of the tentorium from the posterior clinoid processes is a large semioval opening, the incisura or tentorial notch, whose diameters are usually between 50 and 70 mm. in the fronto-occipital axis and 25 and 40 mm. on the interparietal axis.[163, 270, 543]

The temporal lobes rest on the tentorial incisura, and their medial surfaces slightly overhang it so that ordinarily 3 to 4 mm. of the medial-anterior part of the temporal uncus bulges into the notch. A small crescent of the hippocampal gyrus also overhangs the edge and becomes more narrow posteriorly. At postmortem examinations, the uncus normally contains a visible, shallow, 1 to 2 mm. groove marking its tentorial edge. In pathological herniations this groove deepens and extends back over the hippocampal gyrus as well (Fig. 10).

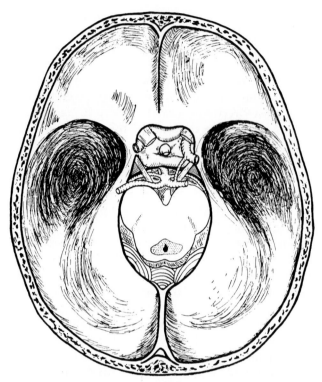

Figure 9. The floor of the anterior and middle fossae, illustrating the tentorial notch and how the third nerve passes between the posterior cerebral and superior cerebellar arteries and over the petroclinoid ligaments.

Changes in the relationships between the tentorial incisura and its surrounding structures explain most of the complications and many of the symptoms of supratentorial mass lesions producing coma. The midbrain occupies the anterior portion of the notch (Fig. 9). The important anatomical relationships of the midbrain are those of the arteries, the third nerves, and the cisterns, whose size varies considerably among different individuals. The cerebellum is closely apposed to the dorsum of the midbrain and fills the posterior part of the notch. Ventral to the brainstem lies the basilar artery, which splits into the two diverging posterior cerebral arteries just below the tentorial incisura. Each posterior cerebral artery crosses the oculomotor nerve that emerges caudal to it. The artery then circles around the homolateral cerebral peduncle and the adjacent lateral midbrain and reaches the ventral surface of the hippocampal gyrus of the temporal lobe, where it crosses the tentorial edge and proceeds toward the occipital lobe. Another important vascular structure in this region is the anterior choroidal artery, which branches directly from the internal carotid artery and runs in a narrow space between the dentate gyrus of the temporal lobe and the free lateral margin of the tentorium, over which it is sometimes displaced by masses pressing the temporal lobe downward.

The oculomotor nerves emerge from the medial-basal surface of each cerebral peduncle just caudal to the tentorium. They proceed across the basal cistern (or tentorial gap, as Sunderland[543] calls it), first passing between the superior cerebellar (below the nerve) and posterior cerebral (above the nerve) arteries. These nerves then lie adjacent to each temporal lobe uncus at the point where this structure overhangs the lateral incisural edge. Each nerve passes over the homolateral petroclinoid ligament just lateral to the posterior clinoid process, and enters the cavernous sinus.

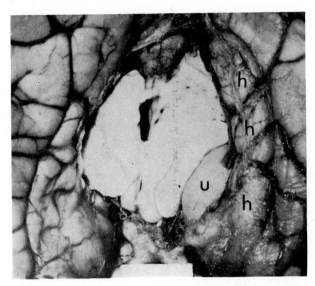

Figure 10. Right-sided uncal (u) and hippocampal (h) herniation compressing the midbrain, seen from below. Note the swelling of the right side of the midbrain.

The trochlear nerve is clinically unimportant, being protected on the under surface of the tentorium. The abducens nerve is infratentorial and becomes impaired by supratentorial lesions only when slowly progressing processes displace the entire brainstem downward, stretching the nerve.

The foramen magnum is another potential site for intracranial herniation. Here the medulla, the cerebellum, and the vertebral arteries are juxtaposed, and their normal relationships to one another often vary. Usually a small portion of the cerebellar tonsils protrudes into the aperture, and the inferior surface of the cerebellum is grooved against the foramen's posterior lip. Variations in the normal degree of grooving make it difficult to interpret cerebellar impaction or tonsillar herniation at the autopsy table unless changes are extensive.

67

Pathology and Pathological Physiology

Recognition of the Importance of Tentorial Herniation

Many investigators have attempted to explain the mechanisms whereby supratentorial lesions produce stupor, coma, and other signs of widespread neurological dysfunction. In the nineteenth century, Macewen,[349] Gower,[216] Oppenheim,[420] and Déjerine[125] all cited coma with supratentorial lesions as a manifestation of widespread or rapid involvement of the cortical mantle. This view was largely supplanted during the first part of this century by Cushing's belief that the major remote or indirect symptoms of cerebral compression were due to capillary anemia of the medulla oblongata.[116] However, Cushing based many of his conclusions upon acute animal experiments in which he produced rapidly accumulating supratentorial masses,[117] which tend to bypass intermediate brain segments and produce medullary abnormalities early in their course.[274, 563] As models they resemble problems such as certain examples of intracerebral hemorrhage, but they are much less useful in explaining the symptoms of patients harboring more gradually enlarging supratentorial masses. Most clinically occurring masses enlarge more slowly than do masses experimentally produced in animals, and such patients almost always develop symptoms reflecting more rostral brainstem dysfunction before showing evidence of medullary failure.[369]

Understanding how supratentorial mass lesions cause coma and other signs of serious brainstem dysfunction in man has come as much from studies of postmortem pathology as from experimental physiology. Adolph Meyer,[376] in 1920, first called attention to temporal lobe herniation into the tentorial gap in cases of brain tumor. His accompanying text was sparse and perhaps for that reason his contemporaries paid little attention to the tentorial notch. During the next decade, several observers reemphasized the earlier point made by Hutchinson[255] and Macewen[348] that the pupil may dilate on the same side as a cerebral mass because of pressure of the temporal lobe on the third nerve.

In 1929, Kernohan and Woltman[296] demonstrated grooving and histological change in the cerebral peduncle as it was compressed against the edge of the tentorium opposite to a supratentorial mass, thus explaining why some patients with brain tumor show homolateral paresis (see Fig. 11). Thenceforth, attention turned increasingly to how changes at the tentorial region explained the remote and catastrophic effects of certain supratentorial masses. Spatz and Stroescu[533] in 1934 published detailed illustrations of the intracranial cisterns and how they were altered by various hernias, and 2 years later Vincent, David, and Thiebaut[581] related the development of anxiety, stiff neck, vasomotor troubles, and cardiac arrhythmias to transtentorial herniation in patients with brain tumor. Van Gehuchten[571] drew attention to the hemorrhages in the midbrain and the pons that sometimes accompany tentorial pressure cones. Both he and Vincent stressed that death might follow lumbar puncture in patients with tentorial herniation. This was the period during which much of the physiology of the hypothalamus in respiratory, circulatory, and thermal regulation was delineated. As a result, when Jefferson[270] in 1938 reviewed the problems of tentorial pressure cone, he cited four general signs that indicated its presence: (1) "vegetative storm"; (2) stiff neck; (3) bilateral motor signs (often decerebrate rigidity), and (4) a dilated pupil. Jefferson attributed death in these patients to subthalamic vegetative damage and pointed out that signs of medullary failure are uncommon and, if present, are late manifestations of decompensating supratentorial masses.

Since Jefferson's paper it has generally been accepted that the dividing line between survival and death with supratentorial masses is whether or not irreversible tentorial herniation can be prevented. For this reason, a clear understanding of the mechanisms leading to this process and their accompanying symptoms becomes a major step in planning effective treatment.

Mechanical Factors Enhancing the Effects of Intracranial Masses

The pathological tissue reactions surrounding all intracranial masses are qualitatively similar, whether the masses are neoplasms, infections, infarcts, hemorrhages, or foreign bodies. They include glial proliferation, dilatation and multiplication of blood vessels, invasion by histiocytic and inflammatory cells, and at least some edema of the adjacent brain. The histological type of the lesion itself and the rate of its development modify these reactions: acute lesions such as bacterial abscesses, parenchymal hemorrhages, or metastatic tumors for reasons unknown evoke more edema and a brisker vascular and inflammatory response than do slow-growing lesions such as intracranial neoplasms that lie outside the brain. Sooner or later, however, nearly all masses enlarge so much, either through their own growth or by the edema added to their periphery, that the surrounding brain can no longer accommodate them. The expanding cerebral structures shift across the midline or downward toward the base of the brain; the sheer bulk of the shifting tissues compresses new regions, and these, in turn, begin to swell and shift. Eventually, the brain, thus progressively increased in volume, has no choice but to squeeze into the only available supratentorial exit, the tentorial notch.

Vascular Factors Enhancing the Effects of Supratentorial Lesions

Alteration or abolition of the normal physiological responses of the cerebral vascular bed contributes importantly to the remote and progressive pathological effects of supratentorial injuries and masses, and the same principles undoubtedly apply to the subtentorial vasculature as well. Normally, the resistance and size of the cerebral arterial and arteriolar bed are

69

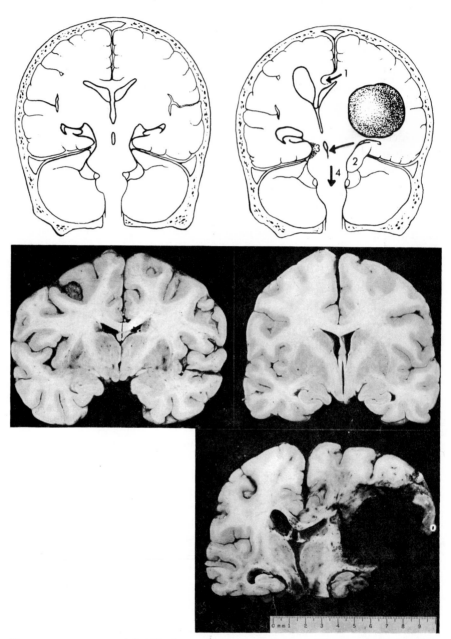

Figure 11. Intracranial shifts from supratentorial lesions. The drawing on the left shows the relationships of the various supratentorial and infratentorial compartments as seen in a coronal section. Immediately below it is a photograph of a normal brain section. The drawing on the right illustrates: herniation of the

(Legend continued on opposite page)

subject to two governing influences. The bed is *autoregulated,* i.e., it intrinsically constricts or dilates when the systemic arterial pressure is raised or lowered so as to assure a constant blood supply as long as the tissue itself is metabolically constant, and *chemically regulated,* i.e., its smooth muscle contracts or relaxes in response to appropriate changes in carbon dioxide and oxygen tensions in the blood and local tissue. Except possibly with the prodromata of migraine, the intracranial vessels do not spontaneously go into *spasm.* Intracranial disease can disrupt all three of these physiological properties of blood vessels, with autoregulation being perhaps the most sensitive to injury and, when lost, the most important vascular factor enhancing the pathological effects of still-reversible mass lesions. The additional loss of chemical regulation produces a dilated, entirely passive arterial bed in the zone where regulation is lost and is a much more severe physiological injury, probably confined to areas of profound ischemia or necrosis. Vasospasm mainly follows more or less direct vascular injuries from hypertension, direct trauma, blood extravasation or perivascular inflammation and is usually a diffuse response described more fully in Chapter 4.

The normal cerebral autoregulation is at least briefly but diffusely suspended after a concussive injury, after generalized seizures,[447] and following brief generalized ischemia or anoxia.[322] Local trauma,[493] infarcts,[162, 434] and neoplasms[425] are commonly surrounded by pressure-passive hyperemic zones that retain their endogenous ability to constrict if one lowers the arterial blood CO_2 tension, but passively increase or decrease their resistance (and therefore their blood volume and flow) if the systemic arterial pressure rises or falls. Even with well-localized infarcts or neoplasms, the loss of autoregulation can be widespread, sometimes including the entirety of the same or even both hemispheres. Such margins of vasodilatation can con-

---

cingulate gyrus under the falx (1), herniation of the temporal lobe into the tentorial notch (2), compression of the opposite cerebral peduncle against the unyielding tentorium, producing Kernohan's notch (3), and downward displacement of the brainstem through the tentorial notch (4). The photograph immediately below that is taken from a patient with carcinoma of the lung and multiple cerebral metastases (none are apparent in this section) who died after developing signs and symptoms of the central syndrome of rostral-caudal deterioration (see text). The brain is swollen; the diencephalon is compressed and elongated, and the mammillary bodies lie far caudal to those in the normal brain. Neither the cingulate gyrus nor the uncus is herniated. The lowest photograph is taken from a patient who developed a massive hemorrhagic infarct and who died after developing the syndrome of uncal herniation (see text). The cingulate gyrus is herniated under the falx; there is hemorrhagic infarction of the opposite cerebral peduncle, and marked swelling and grooving of the uncus on the side of the lesion. Central downward displacement is also present but is less marked than in the figure above. The drawings are modified from a drawing by Miles and Dott.

siderably extend the pathological boundaries of the primary lesion since the increased bulk of blood creates an additional mass and the arteriolar vasodilatation leads to edema by increasing the local capillary hydrostatic pressure.[361] Neither the mechanisms that normally govern cerebral auto-regulation nor those that destroy it are precisely known, but an abnormal, passive cerebral vascular response to pressure is clearly a significant factor contributing to "decompensation" in progressive supratentorial mass lesions.

Related closely to the functional loss of intracranial vasomotor regulation that accompanies the above-mentioned diseased states is the development of intraventricular pressure waves first described extensively in the clinical setting by Lundberg.[345] Lundberg described several different types of fluc-tuating intracranial pressure patterns in patients with expanding brain lesions. Particularly important were large fluctuations in pressure that occurred at intervals as often as 15 to 30 minutes apart, sometimes main-taining long plateaus for considerable periods with pressures approaching the mean blood pressure. Although some of the pressure fluctuations pre-cipitated no apparent neurological worsening, others were associated with alarming (although often temporary) neurological deterioration. Lang-fitt[322] postulates that these pressure waves reflect intracranial vasomotor paralysis and that similar fluctuations are responsible for some of the changing symptoms in patients with chronic subdural hematoma or decompensating neoplasms.

Increased Intracranial Pressure as a Cause of Symptoms

There is sometimes a tendency to regard increased intracranial pressure as dangerous in its own right. This is commonly a misinterpretation of cause and effect. Elevations in the intracranial pressure of less than 500 to 600 mm. of CSF and not caused by masses or obstruction to cerebrospinal fluid outflow are probably dangerous only to the optic nerves because of optic ischemia secondary to papilledema and usually do not cause obtunda-tion, stupor, or coma. The relatively benign effects of moderately high in-tracranial pressure are seen in many circumstances. No serious cerebral symptoms accompany increased intracranial pressure due to obstruction of venous outflow such as occurs with blockage of the superior vena cava, of the jugular veins in the neck, or even of the posterior part of the sagittal sinus.[463] Similarly, when Browder and Meyers[65] and Schumacher and Wolff[492] raised the intracranial pressure by injecting saline into the lumbar subarachnoid space, the subjects developed no adverse symptoms, not even headache, until the pressure approached the diastolic blood pressure (800 to 1000 mm. CSF).

The above examples demonstrate the benign nature of intracranial hypertension caused either by obstructing the veins or by directly increasing the spinal fluid pressure, but what of raising the pressure by increasing the size of the intracranial substance, the brain itself? Here again, the

72

evidence is that if the expanding brain substance does not shift or obstruct the flow of arterial blood or spinal fluid, the ensuing increase in intracranial pressure has a relatively benign effect on the central nervous system. In the condition known as *pseudotumor cerebri,* brain bulk is increased and the intracranial pressure is raised, but the intracranial structures maintain their normal anatomical relationships to one another and nothing obstructs the flow of CSF within either the ventricles or the subarachnoid space. The remarkable thing is that despite intracranial pressures that often are as high as 400 to 600 mm. CSF and sometimes closely approach the mean systemic arterial pressure,[383] the majority of these patients look and feel well and remain free of confusion, obtundation, or coma.

These examples suggest that increased intracranial pressure is associated with neurological symptoms only when it reflects the presence of an expanding or obstructing mass for which the intracranial structures cannot fully compensate. Increased pressure from this cause implies a lesion enlarging in one intracranial compartment that threatens sooner or later to expand into or encroach upon the others.

Intracranial Shift in the Pathogenesis of Coma

There are three major patterns of supratentorial brain shift, and they can be identified by their end stages: cingulate herniation, central transtentorial herniation, and uncal herniation (Fig. 11).

CINGULATE HERNIATION. This occurs when the expanding hemisphere shifts laterally across the intracranial cavity, forcing the cingulate gyrus under the falx cerebri and compressing and displacing the internal cerebral vein. The main danger of cingulate herniation is that it compresses blood vessels and tissues, causing cerebral ischemia and edema which, in turn, enhance the expanding process.

CENTRAL OR TRANSTENTORIAL HERNIATION. Central or transtentorial herniation of the diencephalon is the end result of downward displacement of the hemispheres and the basal nuclei, compressing and eventually displacing the diencephalon and the adjoining midbrain rostrocaudally through the tentorial notch.[490] Shift of this kind occurs mainly in response to parenchymal lesions of the frontal, parietal, and occipital lobes and to extracerebral lesions lying more toward the vertex or the frontal-occipital poles. With unilateral expanding lesions, shift across the midline and herniation of the cingulate gyrus under the falx commonly precede downward shift and central transtentorial herniation.

The changes at the tentorium in central transtentorial herniation consist of an actual caudal displacement of the diencephalon, sometimes to such a distance that it partially avulses the pituitary stalk[278] and buckles the diencephalon against the midbrain.[249] Cross-section examinations of such cases show the diencephalon to be edematous and enlarged, often containing hemorrhages in the pretectal region and sometimes also in the thalamus

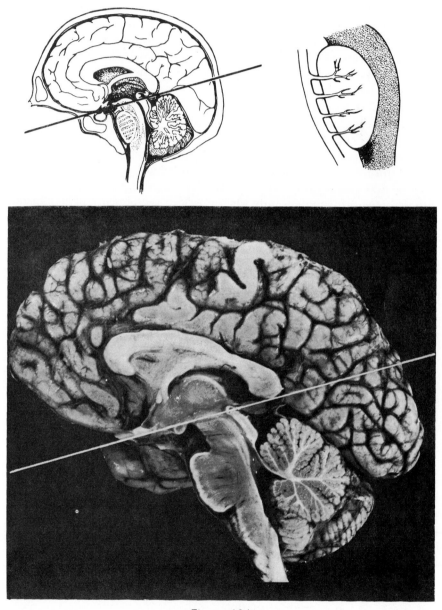

Figure 12A

Figure 12. Downward displacement of the brainstem with transtentorial herniation. The drawings in the upper part of each figure illustrate the relationship of the brainstem to the supratentorial compartment (left) and to the penetrating branches of the basilar artery (right). In drawing 12**B** there is downward displacement of the diencephalon and stretching of the penetrating branches of

(Legend continued on opposite page)

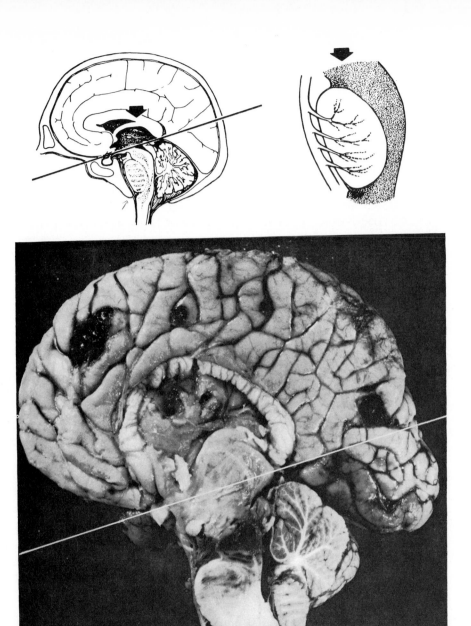

Figure 12B

the basilar artery. The photograph in 12A is that of a sagittal section of a normal brain. The line drawn between the inferior margin of the splenium of the corpus callosum and the optic chiasm passes just above the quadrigeminal plate and either through or just above the mammillary body. The photograph in 12B is from a patient with multiple metastatic brain tumors (melanoma) who died following a clinical course suggesting central transtentorial herniation (see text). The multiple tumors are apparent in the supratentorial compartment. The line drawn from landmarks similar to those in 12A now passes well above both the quadrigeminal plate, which is foreshortened as well as displaced posteriorly, and the mammillary bodies. A midbrain hemorrhage is apparent in this section as well.

adjacent to the thalamostriate veins, which normally drain into the internal cerebral vein. These severe paramedian changes need not necessarily be accompanied by prominent morphological evidence of uncal or hippocampal herniation into the incisura. Severe secondary brainstem changes develop caudal to the incisura and are discussed in the next section.

UNCAL HERNIATION. When the abscess is seated in the temporosphenoidal or frontal lobe, the pupil on the same side as the abscess may become . . . mydriatic, accompanied by a degree of stability. . . . Sections of the frozen head show well the relationships of the third nerve to the temporal lobe and how destruction of this lobe may exercise pressure on the third nerve. These words of Macewen,[349] written almost 80 years ago, emphasize that the earliest warnings of uncal herniation signal dysfunction in structures outside the brain parenchyma in contrast to central herniation where the first signs are of diencephalic dysfunction. Uncal herniation characteristically occurs when expanding lesions in the lateral middle fossa or temporal lobe shift the inner, basal edge of the uncus and hippocampal gyrus toward the midline and over the lateral edge of the tentorium. The resultant crowding at the notch flattens the adjacent midbrain, pushing it against the opposite incisural edge (Figs. 10 and 11). At the same time, the third nerve and the posterior cerebral artery on the side of the expanding temporal lobe are often caught between the overhanging swollen uncus and the free edge of the tentorium or some other resistant structure such as the petroclinoid ligament.

The particular danger of supratentorial displacements and herniations is that they initiate vascular and obstructive complications that aggravate the original expanding lesion and convert a potentially reversible into an irreversible pathological process. Herniation under the falx compresses the anterior cerebral artery and accentuates already existing ischemia and edema of the herniating hemisphere. Displacement across the midline posteriorly compresses the great cerebral vein and raises the hydrostatic pressure of the entire deep cerebral territory it drains. Either central or uncal herniation into the tentorial notch compresses the posterior cerebral artery to produce occipital infarction and swelling. Equally important to any of these processes is that both uncal and transtentorial herniation can compress the aqueduct so as to block spinal fluid circulation.[494] The blockage has two consequences. One is that spinal fluid can no longer escape from the ventricular system to accommodate an enlargement in the brain, and the pressure in the supratentorial cavity rises above that in the posterior fossa.[593] The other, proposed by Bering,[38] is that when the ventricular system is obstructed, arterial pulsations in the choroid plexus act like a water hammer, steadily pounding the surrounding brain. However, anyone who has observed the brain itself pulsate when the skull is open would suspect that the brain is actually pounded between the pulsating arterial bed and the unyielding cerebral extracellular and ventricular fluid. This pounding may be a factor impacting the posterior diencephalon into and through the tentorial incisura, which is the terminal common denominator of both the central and the uncal patterns of herniation.

Herniation into or across the tentorium also produces brainstem ischemia and hemorrhages that characteristically involve the central core of the structure from the diencephalon to the lower pons, and are particularly prominent when the supratentorial lesion enlarges rapidly. The exact pathogenesis of these secondary brainstem vascular lesions is debated, and both a venous and arterial origin were originally suggested.[75, 132, 278] However, their arterial origin now seems well established.[188] Transtentorial herniation displaces the midbrain and pons downward, stretching the medial perforating branches of the basilar artery, because the artery itself is tethered to the circle of Willis and cannot shift downward. Pathologically, the first brainstem change is that of paramedian ischemia,[601] and when Johnson and Yates[278] injected the intracranial arteries in such cases post mortem, contrast media leaked out of the now necrosed arteries along the brainstem, just as blood would have done had their perfusion continued during life. Indeed, Klintworth[306, 307] produced midbrain hemorrhages experimentally by following a procedure of first markedly increasing the supratentorial pressure, then releasing the pressure and producing hypertension sufficient to reperfuse the ischemic arteries. Friede and Roessmann[188] serially sectioned the brainstem in patients with midbrain hemorrhages and found 101 of arterial to 1 of venous origin.

Clinical evidence as outlined in the next section suggests that the ischemic process rather deliberately advances down the brainstem once transtentorial herniation occurs. Pathological confirmation of this kind of steady advancement is almost always impossible to reconstruct from postmortem material, which usually discloses only the terminal stage of severe central brainstem destruction down to lower pontine levels.

To epitomize: Pathological changes in most brains with supratentorial mass lesions consist of vasomotor nonreactivity and edema that spreads from the lesion, at first radially and then downward in a progressively contiguous manner. Even when tentorial herniation and downward displacement finally damage the brainstem, the pathological changes tend to move in an orderly rostral-caudal plane almost as if an inexorably advancing wave were producing serial functional transections.

Two infrequent exceptions break the rule that untreated supratentorial mass lesions paralyze the brain in a progressively contiguous rostral-caudal direction. One occurs in patients with acute cerebral hemorrhage, the other follows ill-timed lumbar punctures in patients with incipient transtentorial herniation. In both instances, clinical signs can jump from reflecting hemispheral or diencephalic dysfunction to indicating sudden medullary failure. Special pathological circumstances explain both of these exceptions to the usual rostral-caudal progression. Most cerebral hemorrhages produce rapid medullary failure only after bleeding extends into the ventricular system. Presumably the sudden outpouring of blood produces a fluid wave that compresses the region around the fourth ventricle almost as much as the parenchyma of the immediately surrounding brain. Experimentally, this effect can be reproduced in animals: An intraventricular injection of saline produces medullary failure much more rapidly than comparable amounts of saline injected into the cerebral parenchyma.[379, 563] Similar considerations explain the lumbar puncture effect, except that here the stopper has been removed from below rather than the compression applied from above. Anatomical lesions in patients with supratentorial lesions dying from sudden medullary failure following lumbar puncture usually are not distinctive except that all such patients show either incipient or fully developed tentorial herniation and most have compression of the aqueduct as well. Apparently, withdrawal of spinal fluid from the reservoir of the posterior fossa must suddenly reduce its supporting pressure so that the intracranial contents are abruptly pushed downward, compressing the medulla into the foramen magnum. As already mentioned, this sudden sequence of events is difficult to reconstruct at autopsy.

The Diagnosis of Coma from Supratentorial Mass Lesions

The previous section described how intracranial pathological changes radiate progressively downward and away from supratentorial mass lesions. Clinical signs develop the same way, so that patients with progressing, unreversed supratentorial lesions develop a sequence of respiratory, ocular, and motor signs that indicate the gradual, orderly failure of first dien-cephalic, and then midbrain, pontine, and medullary functions, in that order. Indeed, this orderly progression is almost invariable unless a hemorrhage or abscess ruptures into the ventricles or an ill-advised lumbar puncture rapidly changes the intracranial dynamics to produce medullary compression. The classical Kocher-Cushing signs[118, 308] of a rising blood pressure and slow pulse rate do not occur with most supratentorial masses.[65] These "classical" signs of increased intracranial pressure are more common with posterior fossa lesions, and on the rare occasions when they do accompany supratentorial lesions, they usually imply that an epidural hemorrhage or a massive cerebral hemorrhage has *suddenly* increased the supratentorial and intraventricular pressure and transmitted its effects directly to the posterior fossa.

Decompensating focal cerebral lesions produce either of two distinct clinical pictures. One, the *uncal syndrome,* is the classical picture of uncal herniation and includes the early signs of compression of the third nerve and lateral midbrain. The uncal syndrome is particularly likely to develop in neurosurgical emergencies, especially rapidly expanding traumatic hematomas and overwhelmingly severe head injuries associated with generalized

78

intracranial vasomotor paralysis. In these instances, the pathological sequence resembles that produced by inflating balloons in the heads of experimental animals. The other, the *central syndrome,* is less commonly recognized but occurs more frequently among subacute or chronically ill patients, where diagnosis is a greater problem, and reflects bilateral progressive parenchymal impairment of the diencephalon.[369] The syndromes conform to the differences in pathology between uncal and central tentorial herniation. Clinically, they are recognizably distinct early in their course, but both merge into a similar picture once pathological changes extend to involve the midbrain level or below.

Table 3. The nature and location of supratentorial lesions producing rostral-caudal deterioration in 67 verified cases*

	No. of Cases	Type of Syndrome		
		Central	Uncal	Combined
Infarction				
Massive middle cerebral a. distribution	8	8		
Parieto-occipital	I	I		
Parietotemporal	3	3		
Hemorrhage				
Basal ganglia	6	4	I	I
Frontotemporal	3	2	I	
Frontoparietal	2	2		
Frontal	3	3		
Parietal	I	I		
Temporal	5	I	3	I
Neoplasm				
Frontal	3	3		
Parietal	5	4		I
Thalamic	3	3		
Abscess				
Temporal	2		2	
Thalamoparietal	I	I		
Trauma (acute epidural 3, acute subdural 4, chronic subdural hematoma 14)				
Hemisphere	12	7	3	2
Frontal	4	3	I	
Biparietal	2	2		
Temporal	3		2	I

* These patients do not in all instances correspond with those in Category I of Table I because coma was not a problem in diagnosis in many of these patients and, conversely, several patients in Table I were not observed fully for evidence of rostral-caudal deterioration.

Whether patients with intracranial disease develop a central syndrome or an uncal syndrome depends partly on the site of the lesion and partly on unknown influences. Table 3 includes 67 well-documented cases of supratentorial lesions producing transtentorial herniation. All the patients were studied for the evolution of signs and symptoms leading to coma. The diagnoses were confirmed by autopsy in 42 cases, by surgery in 15, and by radiological procedures or a combination of these in the remainder. Radiographic evidence alone was accepted only in patients having entirely consistent clinical findings and a neurological disability fully reversed by treatment; this minimized the possibility that undiagnosed primary brain-stem lesions caused the symptoms. As can be seen from the table, medially placed supratentorial lesions of relatively slow development more often produced signs of the central syndrome, while temporal lobe and lateral extracerebral masses most often caused the uncal syndrome. In only a small proportion of cases, however, were these anatomical correlations sufficiently consistent to predict confidently the site of the lesion or its histology from the pattern of herniation alone.

The Central Syndrome of Rostral-Caudal Deterioration

DIENCEPHALIC STAGE—CLINICAL SIGNS. Figures 13 and 14 illustrate the clinical signs that accompany the early and late diencephalic stages of the central syndrome. The first evidence that a supratentorial mass is beginning to impair the diencephalon is usually a change in alertness or behavior. Initially, subjects with such lesions find it difficult to concentrate, and tend to lose the orderly details of recent events. Some patients become agitated; others sink slowly into torpid drowsiness. Admittedly, it some-times is difficult to distinguish between the apathy accompanying purely unilateral hemispheric abnormalities such as aphasia or severe hemisensory defects and a more global reduction in consciousness caused by direct encroachment on subhemispheric neural structures. Under such circum-stances the respiratory, ocular, and motor signs described below can provide evidence for or against the presence of bilateral dysfunction in these other neurologically controlled systems. If the supratentorial lesion continues to enlarge and displace tissues toward the deep midline of the cerebrum, stupor and then coma occur. Once this stage is reached, the state of con-sciousness per se is less useful as a localizing sign and has little value as an immediate index to whether patients are improving or worsening. When consciousness is lost, the careful attention to respiratory, ocular, and motor signs not only helps in diagnosing supratentorial causes of coma but also helps in determining whether the direction of the disease process is for the better or worse.

Respiration in the early diencephalic stage of the central syndrome is commonly interrupted by deep sighs, yawns, and occasional pauses. Many

CENTRAL SYNDROME – EARLY DIENCEPHALIC

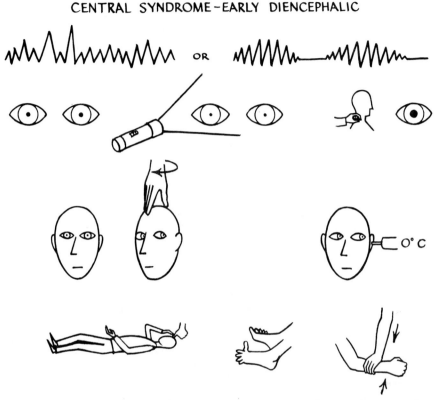

Figure 13. Figures 13–18 are from McNealy, D. E., and Plum, F.: Brainstem Dysfunction with Supratentorial Mass Lesions. Arch. Neurol. 7:10-32, 1962. In these figures the top line is a pneumographic record of the respiratory pattern; the second gives the pupillary size and reaction to light; the third demonstrates the characteristic oculocephalic and oculovestibular responses; and the bottom line illustrates motor responses at rest and to stimulation.

patients have periodic breathing of the Cheyne-Stokes type, particularly as they sink into deeper somnolence. The pupils are small (1 to 3 mm.) and, if examined superficially, may appear to have lost their reaction to light. Close scrutiny with a bright light brings out reactions that are brisk, but with a small range of contraction. Whether these small pupils reflect the effects of functional decortication or hypothalamic sympathetic dysfunction is unknown; either mechanism could explain them.

Examination of eye movements reveals one of two abnormalities in the early diencephalic stage of the central syndrome. Some patients show conjugate or slightly divergent roving eye movements that are only weakly interrupted by the doll's-head maneuver. These always mean that the brainstem is intact and probably indicate a relatively slight degree of

81

CENTRAL SYNDROME – LATE DIENCEPHALIC

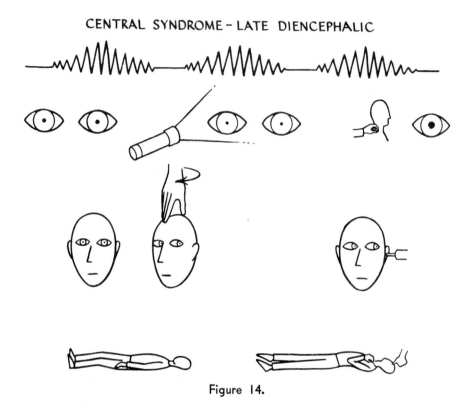

Figure 14.

diencephalic impairment. More frequently, the eyes are conjugate and quiet at rest but respond briskly to passive side-to-side head rotation. Caloric tests with cold water evoke a full and conjugate slow tonic movement to the side irrigated with impairment or absence of the fast component of the response. (Temporarily, patients with acute primary lesions of a cerebral frontal eye field may not demonstrate reflex lateral eye movement to the contralateral side with the doll's-head maneuver—see page 50.) Tests of vertical reflex eye movements also furnish valuable information in this early stage. Lesions producing downward pressure through the posterior part of the tentorial incisura compress the region of the superior colliculi and the adjacent diencephalic pretectum and impair upward conjugate deviation of the eyes. This can be demonstrated in stuporous patients by briskly flexing the head and observing that the eyes fail to roll upward.

In the motor system, early diencephalic involvement is signaled by the development of bilateral signs of corticospinal and extrapyramidal dysfunction. Commonly with hemispheral lesions, there is a preexisting hemiparesis or hemiplegia contralateral to the original focal brain lesion. As the diencephalic stage of the central syndrome evolves, the contralateral hemiplegia may worsen, but in addition the extremities *homolateral* to the brain lesion commonly develop paratonic resistance, or gegenhalten, but continue to respond appropriately to noxious stimuli. The generalized muscular hypertonus often extends to the neck, which initially resists both flexion and lateral motion. (A truly stiff neck or head retraction without lateral limitation of movement results from stretching pain-sensitive meninges at the base of the brain and is more consistent with meningitis or cerebellar tonsillar herniation than with tentorial herniation.) Along with the development of paratonic rigidity homolateral to the hemispheral lesion, both plantar responses commonly become extensor. Later, as diencephalic impairment progresses, paratonic resistance to passive stretch increases and grasp reflexes commonly emerge, particularly when the initiating lesion is contralateral in the prefrontal area. Finally, decorticate responses appear— nearly always at first contralateral to the primary expanding lesion and in response to a noxious stimulus such as supraorbital pressure or firm compression of the pectoralis muscle. In some patients with a hemispheral lesion whose deterioration indicates rostral-caudal progression, the initially hemiplegic side responds to noxious stimulation with decerebrate posturing while the opposite extremity, homolateral to the primary lesion, responds with the decorticate posture. The physiological explanation for this difference is unknown.

PATHOGENESIS AND SIGNIFICANCE OF THE DIENCEPHALIC STAGE. Many of the above mentioned signs could result from either diffuse bilateral hemispheral dysfunction or impaired function of the upper brainstem. Obtundation and progressively increasing stupor are more compatible with brainstem than unilateral hemispheric dysfunction, but a hard and fast distinction is not always possible because hemispheral shift across the midline is a possible cause of bilateral functional changes. The few patients coming to autopsy at this early stage usually have had at least some edema in both hemispheres. Almost all patients at this stage also have functional abnormalities of their cerebral circulation (page 69), but how much this contributes to their symptoms is unknown. Some investigators, as reviewed by Heiskanen,[234] have suggested that increased intracranial pressure in these patients compresses the intracranial blood vessels, which, in turn, decreases the cerebral blood flow. Since intracranial pressures exceeding arteriolar-capillary pressure would be required, it seems unlikely that this happens very often, although sudden rises of increased pressure sufficient to impede the circulation have also been suggested by Ethelberg and Jensen[156] to cause visual obscurations and other transient worsenings in patients with brain tumor. The mechanism merits direct investigation as a potential cause of symptoms. Often, however, slowed cerebral circulation as measured by angiography or other techniques is observed in these patients only after intracranial bleeding or meningitis, and in these instances, at least, a direct effect of the disease on the blood vessels can be held responsible for much of the arterial narrowing.

It is our view that the clinical course of patients having signs of the early central syndrome is most compatible with early diencephalic dysfunction. Most commonly the intracranial pressure is not high enough to compress the vascular bed, and x-ray studies of many patients with central signs show downward displacement of the anterior choroidal artery or other structures, indicating diencephalic displacement. If patients with diencephalic signs of the central syndrome continue to worsen, they tend rapidly to develop manifestations of midbrain damage, suggesting that the pathological process has simply extended to the next more caudal level.

The clinical importance of the diencephalic stage of stupor or coma due to supratentorial mass lesions is that it warns that a potentially reversible lesion is about to become irreversible by progressively destroying the brain at the level of the tentorium or below. If the enlarging supratentorial process can be alleviated or removed before the aforementioned signs of diencephalic dysfunction give way to signs of midbrain damage, chances are good for complete neurological recovery. Once signs of lower diencephalic and, particularly, midbrain dysfunction appear, it becomes increasingly likely that they will reflect infarction rather than reversible ischemia and compression, and although a few patients may still be treatable the outlook for neurological recovery is poor.

MIDBRAIN – UPPER PONS

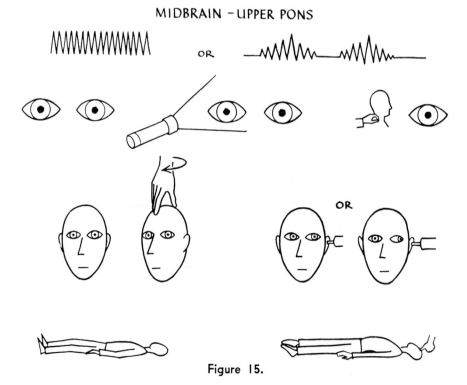

Figure 15.

MIDBRAIN–UPPER PONS STAGE—CLINICAL SIGNS. If treatment is delayed or ineffective and patients progress beyond the diencephalic stage of the central syndrome, the clinical signs give way to those of midbrain failure (Fig. 15). A few patients develop diabetes insipidus, reflecting severe downward traction on the pituitary stalk and the hypothalamic median eminence.[278] Wide fluctuations of body temperature are common and hyperthermia often surrenders to hypothermia. Cheyne-Stokes respiration gradually changes to sustained central hyperventilation. The initially small pupils dilate moderately to fix irregularly at midposition (3 to 5 mm.), but do not dilate widely except terminally, when generalized anoxia may cause a systemic release of epinephrine. Ciliospinal reflexes may disappear and the oculovestibular responses become progressively more difficult to elicit, requiring either repeated side-to-side head movement or a combination of lateral head movement and cold caloric irrigation. When elicited, the eye movements often are dysconjugate with the medially moving eye failing to move as far as the laterally moving eye. Meanwhile, motor dysfunction progresses from decorticate to bilateral decerebrate rigidity in response to noxious stimulation. Decerebrate rigidity sometimes occurs spontaneously and sporadically, particularly in the presence of irritative intracranial processes such as hemorrhages or infections; more commonly, patients rest quietly until stimuli are applied.

Midbrain damage after tentorial herniation is due to secondary ischemia, which rapidly produces necrosis, particularly in paramedian structures. In our adult patients, no subject with a supratentorial lesion has recovered full neurological function once midbrain signs were fully developed, and most have either died or remained in coma for months until transferred for custodial care. Brendler and Selverstone[57] report a somewhat less gloomy experience, but even their series implies a high incidence of neurological residua. The prognosis is often considerably better in children, however.

LOWER PONTINE–UPPER MEDULLARY STAGE. Gradually, ischemia moves down the brainstem (Fig. 16). Hyperventilation quiets down and a more or less regular breathing pattern resembling eupnea supervenes, but often with a more rapid rate (20 to 40 per minute) and shallow depth. Unless the patient has been severely anoxic or has been given drugs that affect the autonomic nervous system, the pupils maintain midposition and do not respond to light. Oculovestibular responses are unobtainable, and the subject becomes flaccid, retaining bilateral extensor plantar responses and, occasionally, flexor responses in the lower extremities to noxious stimulation.

MEDULLARY STAGE. The medullary stage is terminal. Respiration slows, often becomes irregular in rate and depth, and frequently is interrupted by deep sighs or gasps. Occasionally, brief episodes of hyperpnea alternate with relatively long periods of apnea. The pulse is variably slow or fast and the blood pressure drops. Finally, breathing stops and during the

LOWER PONS – UPPER MEDULLA

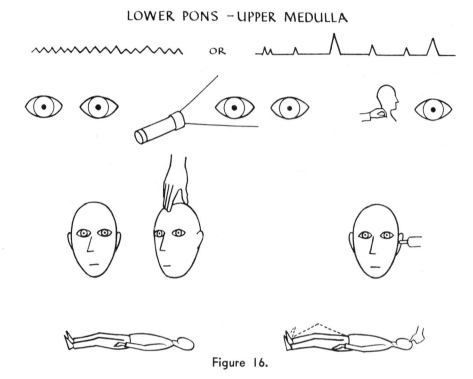

Figure 16.

ensuing hypoxia the pupils often dilate widely. With artificial respiration the blood pressure can be maintained for several hours, but death is inevitable.

The following case illustrates the full development of the central syndrome due to an acute cerebral hemorrhage:

Case 4. A 74-year-old retired lawyer had mild hypertension for several years but was otherwise in excellent health. On the day of admission he suddenly developed pain behind the right ear along with weakness of the left side of his body and dysarthria. He was brought immediately to the hospital where he was observed to be afebrile, to have a pulse rate of 88 per minute, regular breathing at a rate of 16 per minute, and blood pressure of 200/112 mm. Hg. He was awake, oriented, and followed commands. He was dysarthric and complained of a steady, moderately severe pain above and behind the right ear. His head and eyes deviated moderately to the right, and there was a left homonymous hemianopsia.

He was able voluntarily to deviate his eyes just past the midline to the left. With the doll's-head maneuver, however, the eyes conjugately deviated all the way to the left. The pupils were unequal, the right being 2 mm. and the left 3 mm.; both reacted to light. The inequality was interpreted as a right partial Horner's syndrome due to incipient diencephalic compression. Sensation was reduced in the left side of the face and cornea. There was a moderately severe, flaccid left hemiparesis interrupted intermittently by clonic movements of the left leg and tonic flexor movements of the left arm. Stretch reflexes on the left side were reduced, but the plantar response was extensor. Laboratory work was unremarkable. At lumbar puncture, the opening pressure of the

CSF was 200 mm. with brisk arterial pulsations and crystal clear fluid. Microscopic examination of the fluid disclosed 1143 red cells per cu. mm. in the first tube and 288 red cells in the third tube. After centrifugation the supernatant fluid was not xanthochromic. The protein content was 57 mg. per 100 cc. Despite the equivocal spinal fluid findings, the clinical diagnosis of cerebral hemorrhage was made.

By an hour after admission, the patient was having periodic decorticate postural spasms on the left side. The right plantar response had become extensor. He gradually lost consciousness and by 4 hours after admission was unresponsive except to noxious stimuli, which produced at first decerebrate responses on the left but decorticate responses on the right, and finally bilateral decerebrate posturings slightly more pronounced on the left than on the right. By this time the right pupil had dilated and fixed in an oval shape, being vertically 7 mm. and horizontally 3 mm. Minimal oculomotor responses could be elicited to cold caloric stimulation, and the patient was hyperventilating. The blood pressure had risen to 235/150 mm. Hg.

Treatment with intravenous urea was started and during the next hour the patient's condition stabilized except that the right pupil became round and regained a minimal reaction to light. The blood pressure dropped to 160/60 mm. Hg. However, the patient began to vomit, and his temperature rose to 39.6° C. He began to sweat profusely. By 6 hours after admission, decerebrate responses became less intense; the pupils were fixed, slightly irregular at 3 to 4 mm. diameter, and unequal; oculocephalic responses were absent; respiration was quiet and shallow. By 8 hours after admission, respiration was ataxic; the pupils remained slightly unequal with absence of oculovestibular responses; the patient was diffusely flaccid but had bilateral extensor plantar responses and mild flexor responses in the legs to noxious stimulation of the soles of the feet. He died half an hour later.

At postmortem examination there was hypertrophy of the heart and a massive right-sided cerebral hemorrhage arising in the region of the posterior aspect of the basal ganglia and creating both uncal and transtentorial herniations. The posterior diencephalon was displaced an estimated 8 mm. down through the tentorial incisura. Acute hemorrhages and hemorrhagic infarction extended down the brainstem to the lower third of the pons.

The Syndrome of Uncal Herniation and Lateral Brainstem Compression

EARLY THIRD NERVE STAGE. As discussed on page 76, expanding lesions in the lateral middle fossa or temporal lobe commonly push the medial edge of the uncus and hippocampal gyrus toward the midline and over the free lateral edge of the tentorium. Because the diencephalon may not be the first structure encroached upon, impaired consciousness is not consistently an early sign of impending uncal herniation, and the state of alertness in different subjects may vary from near-wakefulness through stupor to coma. The earliest consistent sign is the unilaterally dilating pupil (Fig. 17).

Moderate anisocoria with a sluggish light reaction of the dilated pupil can sometimes last for hours before other signs appear. During early uncal herniation, this may be the only abnormality, respiration remaining eupneic, extraocular movements and oculovestibular responses being unimpaired, and motor abnormalities, if any, reflecting no more than could be expected in someone with a supratentorial lesion. But the alarming feature of uncal herniation is that once any signs of herniation or brainstem com-

UNCAL SYNDROME – EARLY III NERVE

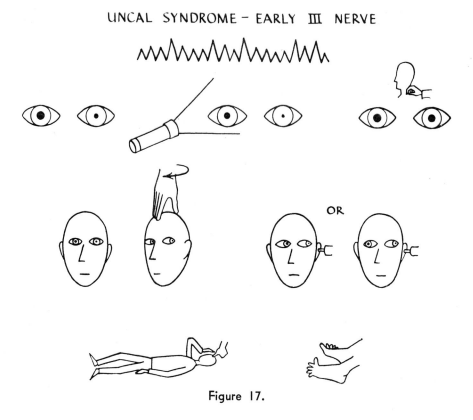

Figure 17.

pression appear, deterioration may proceed rapidly with patients slipping from full consciousness to deep coma in a few hours.

LATE THIRD NERVE STAGE. A striking feature of the clinical syndrome of uncal herniation is that, once the patient progresses beyond the stage where his signs are entirely explained by a restricted cerebral lesion, there is a tendency for midbrain dysfunction to occur almost immediately (Fig. 18). This quick progression with a tendency to bypass the rostral diencephalon is associated with rapid encroachment upon the brainstem by the herniating hippocampal gyrus and implies great clinical danger since delays in effective treatment invite irreversible damage. Once the pupil fully dilates, external oculomotor ophthalmoplegia soon follows. Concomitantly, patients usually become deeply stuporous, then comatose. The oculovestibular responses at first reveal oculomotor impairment, then rapidly become sluggish and disappear as ischemia spreads to the midbrain. As the opposite cerebral peduncle becomes compressed against the contralateral tentorial edge (producing Kernohan's notch),[296] hemiplegia commonly develops *ipsilateral* to the expanding supratentorial lesion. Soon afterward, bilateral

88

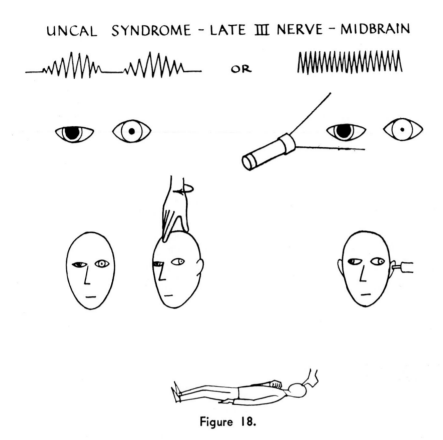

Figure 18.

motor signs evolve and noxious stimuli elicit bilateral extensor plantar responses succeeded by decerebrate posturing. Decorticate posturing is unusual. Treatment must remove the initiating lesion or alleviate the brain swelling at this point or the patient will not recover. The example described in Case 11 on page 110 illustrates the rapid development of uncal herniation in a young woman with a cerebral hemorrhage and its equally rapid reversal by treatment.

MIDBRAIN—UPPER PONS STAGE. If treatment is delayed or is unsuccessful in reversing uncal herniation, signs of midbrain damage appear and progress caudally. The pupil opposite the one originally dilated may show either of two reactions: It may dilate widely and fix or it may enlarge to fix in midposition. Sooner or later both pupils assume the midposition (5 to 6 mm.) and remain fixed. Most patients at this stage show sustained hyperventilation, impairment or absence of oculovestibular responses, and bilateral decerebrate rigidity. From this point, progression of the uncal syndrome is clinically indistinguishable from that of the central syndrome.

89

PATHOGENESIS OF THE UNCAL SYNDROME. Macewen's description quoted on page 76 can hardly be improved upon. As the temporal lobe slides medially over the edge of the tentorium, the uncus herniates over the free edge, pushes the posterior cerebral artery down, and in turn compresses the third nerve. The midbrain is squeezed directly, and the cerebral peduncle presses against the opposite tentorial edge. The temporal lobe tissue herniating into the notch traps the posterior cerebral artery against the free edge of the tentorium: Ischemia of the occipital lobe, obstruction of the aqueduct, and expansion of the original lesion all combine to increase the supratentorial contents. Transtentorial impaction and secondary brainstem ischemia follow. Once this occurs, few survive.

The following case illustrates the development of the uncal syndrome in a young man with cerebral hemorrhage.

Case 5. A 16-year-old boy suddenly complained of frontal headache and collapsed. He was admitted almost immediately to the hospital. His previous health had been good.

His blood pressure was 158/64 mm. Hg, his pulse 44 per minute, and his breathing eupneic at 18 per minute. The general examination was normal. He was obtunded but with encouragement could be aroused to complain of headache. He retched frequently. The pupils were equal (4 mm.) and reacted to light and cervical pinch. The eyes roved spontaneously with a full lateral range. The corneal reflexes were present. There was a flaccid left hemiplegia and hemihypalgesia with complete areflexia, including no plantar response. His neck was slightly stiff. The right retina contained small flame-shaped hemorrhages.

The CSF pressure was 280 mm., and the fluid was bloody with a hematocrit of 14 per cent. Shortly after lumbar puncture, the right pupil dilated to 6 mm. but remained sluggishly reactive; the left pupil was 4 mm. and reactive. The right eye failed to move completely medially on doll's-head maneuvers (internuclear ophthalmoplegia). He became more difficult to arouse. Five hours after admission, the right pupil dilated widely (8 mm.) and became fixed. Right medial rectus function was absent. He developed sustained regular hyperventilation at a rate of 26 per minute. He was unresponsive, and the left arm and leg showed fragmentary decerebrate responses following deep supraorbital pressure. Urea was given intravenously. During the next 15 to 30 minutes he became agitated and pulled out his oral airway and intravenous infusion. The pupils became equal at 4 mm. and were equally reactive. Respiration lessened in depth and rate but continued to be slightly labored. The eye movements were again roving and complete. The blood pressure was 120/60 mm. Hg (intramuscular reserpine had been given), and the pulse rate was 60 per minute. Ten hours after admission he was restless, had intense nuchal rigidity, and his pupils were 2 to 3 mm. and reactive. One hour later he suddenly became deeply comatose with widely dilated and fixed pupils and flaccid areflexia. The blood pressure had increased to 210 mm. Hg systolic, and the pulse had risen to 140 per minute. Respiration ceased for 5 minutes, then resumed with occasional irregular gasps. The blood pressure disappeared 1 hour later.

At autopsy, the lungs weighed 870 gm. and were congested. The heart weighed 310 gm. and was normal. The formalin-fixed brain revealed a 1 × 3 mm. aneurysm at the right internal carotid artery bifurcation. Coronal section of the hemispheres showed a large hematoma in the right frontal lobe, which had ruptured into the lateral ventricle and filled the entire ventricular system with blood. There was a right uncal hernia, and the right third nerve was compressed by the posterior cerebral artery. The right calcarine cortex was infarcted. There were no gross brainstem hemorrhages.

Combined Central and Uncal Herniation

The differences between the pathological anatomy of diencephalic compression with central herniation and lateral temporal lobe shift with uncal herniation are usually sufficiently different that patients show either the central or the uncal syndromes in relatively pure form. But occasionally the same patient will combine features of both clinical pictures with an equally serious progression of neurological dysfunction. Such patients show moderate pupillary dilatation or even early signs of peripheral third nerve weakness combined with early stupor and periodic breathing. The whole picture evolves more in the slow, deliberate rostral-caudal fashion of the central syndrome than in the rapid jump from early third nerve signs to midbrain damage and coma, as so commonly happens in the uncal syndrome.

Combined Supratentorial and Subtentorial Damage

Head injury, diffuse intracranial bleeding (as with blood dyscrasias), encephalitis, and meningitis often damage both brainstem and supratentorial functions simultaneously. Initially, the appearance of signs different from the expected rostral-caudal pattern helps to estimate the extent and locus of the immediate brainstem injury. Later, if the supratentorial lesion swells and induces secondary brainstem compression, signs of rostral-caudal deterioration may be limited to changes in only one or more functions (respiratory, oculomotor, skeletal muscle) because others are already impaired. Nevertheless, a change in only a single function can help to indicate increasing secondary brainstem compression requiring active therapy. The following patient illustrates this principle: A change in respiratory abnormalities led to the diagnosis of an expanding supratentorial lesion needing surgical relief.

Case 6. A 15-year-old boy was struck by an automobile and brought to the hospital within 30 minutes in deep coma. His blood pressure was 168/60 mm. Hg. He had a pulse rate of 60 per minute, Cheyne-Stokes breathing, widely dilated and fixed pupils, absence of oculocephalic reflexes, and decerebrate posturing. A lumbar puncture yielded moderately bloody spinal fluid with a pressure of 330 mm. A sagittal fracture line across the coronal suture was seen in the skull x-ray film. During the next 2 hours, sustained hyperventilation replaced periodic breathing and the patient became flaccid. Both of these signs suggested deterioration in the rostral-caudal direction: Burr holes were placed in the skull and subdural and epidural hematomas containing an estimated 90 cc. were encountered over the left hemisphere and drained. Postoperatively, the pupils shrank to approximately 3 mm., left greater than right, and the oculovestibular responses returned. Breathing quieted and he moved his left arm spontaneously. The patient gradually regained consciousness, but with the passage of time was left with mild residual aphasia and a right hemiparesis.

False Localizing Signs with Supratentorial Lesions

When obstructive hydrocephalus or supratentorial masses develop slowly, they sometimes distort and displace the intracranial tissues a great deal before they dampen the function of the brainstem core enough to produce stupor or coma. The results can be to produce dysfunction in cranial nerve and brainstem structures that lie remote from the primary lesion, and the resulting abnormal clinical signs can trap an unwary observer into incorrect localizing diagnoses. The most frequent deception, as Collier[101] long ago pointed out, is for a supratentorial tumor or obstruction to induce signs suggesting primary trouble in the posterior fossa. A striking example of this from our own service was a girl of 16 years with an unsuspected chronic aqueductal stenosis. She was at first thought to have disseminated sclerosis and treated inappropriately for 2 years for trigeminal neuralgia, nystagmus, and intermittent deafness before her hydrocephalus was discovered and all her posterior fossa symptoms were cured by a lateral ventricular shunt.

Although most signs of remote dysfunction involve the cranial nerves, a few have a parenchymal origin. A cerebellar-like ataxia can emerge if a frontal lobe tumor interrupts or compresses cerebello-frontal projection pathways, and the same mimicry can confuse the clinical picture if a parietal lobe lesion blunts or destroys proprioception. Nystagmus sometimes accompanies supratentorial mass lesions, presumably as the result of severe downward displacement of the vestibular region of the brainstem. Evidence of just how misleading such changes can be comes from the neurosurgical writings of 50 years ago: Accurate diagnostic radiology was lacking, and despite the clinical skills of the day inappropriate posterior fossa exploration was by no means rare in patients with entirely supratentorial tumors.

Dysfunction of each and every cranial nerve sometimes results as the indirect effect of increased intracranial pressure or downward displacement of the brainstem. The details of these impairments and their individual pathogenesis are beyond our scope here, but the changes can include anosmia, papilledema, congruent and incongruent visual field defects, unilateral (tentorial herniation) or bilateral pupillary change, unilateral or bilateral ophthalmoplegias involving the sixth, fourth, and third nerves, trigeminal sensory loss (rarely accompanied by tic douloureux), facial monoplegia or diplegia, bilateral deafness, and even bilateral weakness in swallowing, speaking, or use of the tongue.[398] Except for papilledema, unilateral or bilateral abducens paralysis is both the most frequent and the earliest of these remote changes to appear.

The pathogenesis of remote intracranial abnormalities includes, in varying degree, compression of the involved nerves against their cranial outflow foramina (much as toothpaste is squeezed from a tube), stasis-ischemia and edema of the nerves, and traction of the involved nerves downward with compression against various angular protuberances of the dura and skull as the brainstem is pushed further caudally by the supratentorial mass.[249] In some instances the lower cranial nerve defects involving facial, speaking, and swallowing movements are undoubtedly part of a pseudobulbar palsy induced by hydrocephalic impairment of supratentorial corticobulbar motor

92

pathways; other examples of these lower cranial nerve weaknesses appear to be part of a generalized akinesia that accompanies extensive frontal lobe dysfunction. But whether due to direct traction, to compression of cortico-bulbar pathways, or to supranuclear akinesia, the weakness usually quickly resolves if the surgeon can relieve the abnormal supratentorial pressure and the resulting brainstem displacement.

The false localizing signs of intracranial lesions are potentially puzzling diagnostically and clinically important because they reflect hydrocephalus, brainstem distortion, or (as with oculomotor paralysis) transtentorial herniation. However, they should seldom confuse or interfere with the orderly diagnosis of coma. For one thing, the abnormalities are most frequent in the still-conscious patient whose central brainstem function has accommodated to mechanical displacement, and with the exception of oculomotor paralysis (page 88) or abducens nerve paralysis, their development rarely parallels any acute decline in consciousness. For another, when diencephalic and central brainstem dysfunction finally does reach a stage to cause stupor or coma, more prominent and characteristic changes in respiration, pupillary, oculovestibular, and motor function still evolve in their characteristic progression, only partly obscured by these independent cranial nerve weaknesses.

Lumbar Puncture in Patients with Mass Lesions

The question is often asked, "Under what circumstances is a lumbar puncture indicated in patients suspected of suffering from an intracranial mass lesion?"[119, 184, 362] Lumbar puncture is often useful in the differential diagnosis of such lesions: Bloody spinal fluid is present in all but a few patients with supratentorial hemorrhages; xanthochromia without red cells is a frequent finding of patients with subdural hematoma; malignant cells are occasionally identified in the spinal fluid of patients with primary or metastatic supratentorial tumors. At times acute bacterial meningitis may mimic supratentorial mass lesions and a lumbar puncture becomes essential in establishing both the diagnosis and the etiological agent. However, lumbar puncture also can be dangerous in patients with supratentorial mass lesions. There are often large pressure gradients between the supratentorial compartment and the lumbar compartment,[290] and lowering the lumbar pressure by removing CSF may increase the gradient, promoting both transtentorial and foramen magnum herniation. How frequently a lumbar puncture produces or hastens the clinical signs of transtentorial herniation is unclear because it is difficult to be certain in an individual patient whether the patient would have spontaneously developed transtentorial herniation had the diagnostic procedure not been undertaken. The literature presents conflicting opinions. Lubic and Marotta[344] analyzed 401 lumbar punctures in patients with brain tumors, of whom 127 had increased intracranial pressure. Only 1 patient became worse following the procedure. Of their 127 patients with increased intracranial pressure, only 33 had papilledema, and in another 40 the funduscopic findings were equivocal. Korein, Cravioto, and Leicach[310] reported the findings in 129 patients with either papilledema or increased intracranial pressure on lumbar puncture. Fifteen patients (or 11.9 per cent) developed possible complications of the lumbar puncture (any change for the worse in 48 hours). The authors, however, estimate the actual complication rate at 1.2 per cent. Another series[499] reports 38 patients with papilledema secondary to brain tumors, of which 10 were subtentorial and the remainder supratentorial masses. The authors noted no complications but noted that 7 of their patients had normal lumbar pressure despite the obvious evidence of increased intracranial pressure. A much more disturbing series was reported by Duffy[142] involving 30 patients referred to a neurosurgical service in 1 year because of complications of lumbar puncture. Twenty-nine of the patients had had headache and 22 had had focal neurological signs before the puncture. Thirteen patients lost consciousness immediately following the lumbar puncture, and another 15 showed decreases in their state of consciousness within 12 hours following lumbar puncture. Three patients stopped breathing, and 7 developed unequal pupils during or immediately after the procedure; 12 died within 10 days of the lumbar puncture. Of their 30 patients, only 10 had papilledema, and in half of the patients the lumbar puncture pressure was normal.

Our own experience has been that lumbar punctures, even when meticulously performed, can be dangerous in patients with increased intracranial pressure, as the case below illustrates:

Case 7. A 43-year-old woman was admitted complaining of "terrible headache with nausea and vomiting for 3 days." She had been employed at the hospital for 5 years and during that time had visited the outpatient department over 30 times for evaluation and treatment of headache. The headaches, which had troubled her for 25 years, were usually right-sided and throbbing, occasionally preceded by blurred vision. They had been treated with ergotamine tartrate, aspirin, and other analgesic drugs (including narcotics) and tranquilizing and antidepressant drugs. She was depressed and had often visited the psychiatrist. Two months before her admission she complained that she had fallen and bumped her right parietal area and had developed daily headaches. Her physical and neurological examinations at that time were normal, as were skull x-ray studies; the pineal gland was not calcified. Ten days before her hospital admission she returned to the outpatient department complaining of 5 days of bilateral frontal and occipital headache unlike her usual headache and unrelieved by aspirin. The headache did not respond to ergotamine tartrate or to an interview with the psychiatrist, and she was admitted to the hospital.

On examination she was depressed, crying and appeared exhausted, complaining of severe head pain. Her physical and neurological examinations were reportedly normal, as were routine blood and urine examinations. At 9:30 the evening of admission a lumbar puncture was performed with an opening pressure of 125 mm. of CSF. The fluid was crystal clear; there was one mononuclear cell and no red cells were seen; the protein concentration was 10 mg. per 100 ml. and the glucose concentration 60 mg. per 100 ml. During the night she was given 100 mg. pentobarbital, 10 mg. prochlorperazine, 30 mg. pentazocine, and 50 mg. Demerol. At 6:00 A.M. the nurse found her unarousable. Neurological examination at that time revealed her to be unresponsive to all verbal stimuli, but she withdrew appropriately from noxious stimuli. There was equivocal blurring of the right optic disc; the right pupil was 3 mm. and the left pupil was 1.5 mm.; both reacted sluggishly. Doll's-eye reactions were sluggish, but the ice water caloric test produced tonic movement toward the appropriate side. Her neck was supple; deep tendon reflexes were symmetrical, and plantar responses were extensor bilaterally. Despite the anisocoria, it was the impression of her physicians that she was suffering from depressant drug poisoning; however, 4 hours later she was unresponsive to noxious stimuli and the oculocephalic and oculovestibular responses had disappeared; her pupils were 6 mm. and unreactive, and stretch reflexes were absent. Respirations ceased and an endotracheal tube was placed and she was put on artificial respiration. Lumbar puncture was repeated and again the opening pressure of the clear fluid was 125 mm. of CSF. Bilateral trephination yielded 150 to 200 cc. of subdural blood that was removed from over the right cerebral hemisphere. No subdural blood was found on the left side. She did not recover spontaneous respirations and died 4 days later. At autopsy there was evidence of the evacuated subdural hematoma as well as cerebral swelling with uncal and transtentorial herniation.

Experiences such as this indicate that lumbar puncture can induce intracranial herniation even in patients who are relatively stable. A meticulous neurological examination should be performed before lumbar puncture is undertaken in any patient. When there is evidence of a mass lesion increasing intracranial pressure, we believe that lumbar punctures should be performed as the *primary* diagnostic procedure only if there is a suspicion of infection. In other instances, other diagnostic tests (usually arteriography) should be performed before lumbar puncture is undertaken. Since most complications of the procedure occur within 12 hours, lumbar puncture should, when possible, be performed during the daytime, permitting observation of the patient during his waking hours.

SPECIFIC SUPRATENTORIAL LESIONS AS CAUSES OF COMA

The preceding pages have described how the normal relationships among intracranial structures "decompensate" in response to supratentorial space-occupying lesions and have delineated the general clinical syndromes that result. Because of the physiological implications of coma, it follows that when any supratentorial process impairs consciousness, the physician must either find a way promptly to halt the progression or risk seeing his patient suffer irreversible brain damage or death. Beyond this generality, different supratentorial lesions have individual characteristics that govern their rate of development, modify their treatment, and sometimes hint at their specific diagnosis. The following sections of this chapter group these lesions according to their geographical distribution within the supratentorial space and discuss their symptoms. It has not been possible to discuss in detail every space-occupying lesion, and the examples selected have been those that most frequently present problems in the diagnosis and management of coma.

Extracerebral Lesions

General characteristics: Neoplasms, infections, and hematomas are included in this category. Except with acute head injuries, these extracerebral lesions seldom produce a problem in the diagnosis of stupor or coma except when they and their surrounding tissue reaction change the intracranial dynamics so as to impair consciousness without producing prominent focal neurological signs. Under such circumstances, the signs and symptoms of diffuse brain dysfunction often can be more prominent than those of focal brain disease. In the early stages, such a course of events is sometimes misdiagnosed as having a psychogenic or metabolic origin.

NEOPLASMS. The major intracranial extracerebral neoplasms rarely produce problems in the diagnosis of coma. Most meningiomas, neuromas, pituitary adenomas, and lymphomas tend to evoke prominent focal local-izing signs in the form of seizures, motor and sensory abnormalities, cranial nerve defects, or endocrine changes *before* they impair alertness or aware-ness. Lymphomas and metastatic carcinomas can sometimes grow in the sub-dural space over the cerebral convexity to produce a clinical syndrome similar to chronic subdural hematoma discussed below. However, only in the rare instance of hemorrhage into a tumor (e.g., pituitary apoplexy) is coma a presenting complaint with most extracerebral neoplasms. Rarely, large meningiomas underlying the frontal lobes grow so insidiously and displace the brain so gradually that quiet apathy bordering on akinetic mutism overcomes the patient before he presents for medical care. But even in such patients, brain tumors are seldom unsuspected and conventional objective tests confirm the diagnosis.

CLOSED HEAD TRAUMA. When acute head injury causes unconsciousness, the fact of the trauma seldom escapes attention so that diagnostic problems related to impaired consciousness usually center on secondary questions, particularly on whether the patient might have an intracranial extracerebral hemorrhage requiring neurosurgical treatment. Although Jennett and asso-ciates will discuss the full spectrum of head injuries and their treatment in a forthcoming monograph of this series, sufficient diagnostic problems sur-round the patient with impaired consciousness after head injury to justify brief discussion here. Blunt cranial trauma produces both extracerebral and intracerebral lesions and damage to the brainstem as well. However, almost all the directly treatable acute and subacute conditions are extra-cerebral so that it is convenient to present the whole problem in this section insofar as it relates to supratentorial structures.

The mechanism of unconsciousness following closed head injury. Sur-prisingly enough, this is unknown although both the forces required to produce it and some of its physiological accompaniments have been well delineated.[222] Thus, at this time it is impossible to say whether the changes that cause concussion and those responsible for prolonged post-traumatic coma differ from one another in kind or only in degree. Nor is it possible to conclude from the evidence at hand whether acute traumatic uncon-sciousness represents mainly a suspension of function in the cerebral hemispheres, in the brainstem, or both. Foltz and Schmidt[176] found that activity in the brainstem reticular formation was at least temporarily suspended in experimental animals receiving a concussive injury, but this important observation has not been extended into comparable analyses of this or other cerebral functions over longer periods.

Brief unconsciousness from which the subject recovers in minutes to hours with no detectable residua other than transient post-traumatic amnesia and, perhaps, some more slowly subsiding nonspecific symptoms of giddiness and headache is universally termed *concussion*. Symonds[551] would make this only quantitatively different from more long-lasting unresponsive states, while others, including ourselves, suspect that the pathological vascular-necrotic[273] and nerve fiber damage[541] that one finds in the brains of patients dying after protracted coma have no anatomical counterpart in commonplace, brief concussion. One problem is that most reports of large series of patients with head injury are singularly free of the detailed clinical observations on breathing, oculomotor function, and motor responsiveness that one requires to evaluate whether the brainstem was functioning normally or abnormally. Similarly, no satisfactory long-term followup studies analyze whether patients following head injury tolerate subsequent stresses such as aging as well as the rest of the population. Without such data, it is impossible to guess whether brief concussion invariably leaves its neuropathological mark.

Concussion. Patients with brief concussion whom we have examined have almost always been arousable to semiappropriate responses by vigorous stimuli or have possessed conjugate or dysconjugate roving eye movements, responsive pupils that spontaneously fluctuated considerably in size, and a motor abnormality that at worst was confined to extensor plantar responses. When neurological abnormalities exceeded these, the coma usually lasted a minimum of several hours and often much longer, and the patients suffered substantial post-traumatic amnesia and confusion coupled with a recovery period that stretched out over several days and often much longer. However, our experience is limited, and the physiological changes of these early clinical cases need much more careful attention to establish prognostic guides.

The adequate stimulus to produce concussion is either a rapid acceleration-deceleration injury[129] or a sudden blow that deforms the skull sharply, raising the intracranial pressure.[222] According to Gurdjian and associates,[222] the common denominator to both injuries is a sudden pressure rise in the region of neurons critical to consciousness. Cerebral ischemia, cerebral edema, depolarization of neurons from sudden acetylcholine release, and destruction of neurons and nerve fibers from shearing effects have all been invoked to explain how sudden deceleration or pressure changes interfere with neuronal function.[551] Although no gross neuropathological changes consistently follow experimental concussion, considerable individual neuronal disruption can usually be found on microscopic examination, especially in the brainstem reticular formation.

Clinically, the coma of concussion is usually brief, with consciousness returning within minutes or at most a few hours after the blow. Respiration is usually eupneic and pupillary and ocular reflexes are retained, caloric tests often producing quick-phase nystagmus.[381] Decorticate or decerebrate rigidity may be present transiently, but usually patients are flaccid, although they do have bilateral extensor plantar responses. After consciousness is regained, confusion persists for variable periods but seldom more than 24 hours. At least some amnesia is always present and includes the brief period of confusion after re-awakening (post-traumatic amnesia) as well as a shorter period before the concussion (retrograde amnesia).

The coma and post-traumatic confusion of concussion is nonspecific and resembles a number of other causes of coma, including the postictal state and some metabolic abnormalities. Unless there is direct physical evidence of head injury, the diagnosis can only be inferred from the situation in which the patient is found so that an especially careful examination of the head should be made to uncover contusions or lacerations of the scalp. Diffuse or localized scalp edema without lacerations suggests multiple underlying fractures produced by a blunt instrument (e.g., "sandbagging"). An ecchymosis over the mastoid area (Battle's sign) results from a fracture through the temporal bone, and bilateral medial orbital ecchymoses ("raccoon eyes") suggest an anterior basal skull fracture. Both the nose and ears should be examined for blood or cerebrospinal fluid leakage. A clear, glucose-containing fluid in these cavities is CSF, which can only have seeped out via a basal skull fracture. Fracture lines over the vault also may be evident on skull x-ray films. Lumbar puncture is normal with uncomplicated concussion. Blood in the CSF suggests more severe brain damage (e.g., contusion or laceration) but in the absence of focal neurological signs does not necessarily carry a worse prognosis.

Other than concussion, three conditions may impair or block consciousness after head injury so as to present diagnostic problems. These are extradural hemorrhage, acute post-traumatic stupor, and chronic subdural hematoma. In all three, the evolution of new neurological signs coming after an interval from the initial trauma and implying rostral-caudal deterioration or incipient central or uncal herniation provides the danger signal that prompt and direct treatment may be necessary.

Extradural hemorrhage can arise frontally, laterally, or occipitally, with the lateral two presentations running the more rapid and usually more dangerous course. The bleeding can originate from veins, arteries, or both.

Frontal extradural hematomas most often arise in children and in the elderly, are relatively self-limited and often run a slow course more like that of subdural hematoma. Occipital hematomas tend to compress posterior fossa structures and are discussed in Chapter 3. The most common extradural hemorrhages arise in the lateral temporal fossa from laceration of the middle meningeal artery or vein by skull fracture. Such hemorrhages tend to enlarge rapidly until they self-seal the bleeding vessel, are surgically repaired or cause the death of the subject. Although an occasional hematoma arrests its own progress after 30 to 50 cc. of blood has accumulated and thereafter acts as a unilateral focal mass lesion, the more frequent rule is for extradural hematomas to produce a rapidly progressing uncal syndrome within a few hours or days after injury.

Extradural hematomas push the brain laterally away from the skull and in so doing stretch and tear pain-sensitive meninges and blood vessels at the base of the middle fossa. They then compress the ipsilateral temporal lobe and adjacent hemispheric tissue, finally inducing uncal herniation and pressure on the third nerve, resulting in dilatation of the homolateral pupil *early* as brain swelling, shift, and herniation evolve.

As one might expect with such a sequence, the first symptom in conscious patients with extradural hematoma is headache, followed by clouding of consciousness or agitation and then by signs and symptoms of the uncal syndrome. Once clouding of consciousness develops, pupillary signs, hemiparesis, and deeper coma evolve within a few hours because, as the shifting uncus reaches far enough to compress the third nerve, it also encroaches upon the midbrain. Sunderland and Bradley[544] emphasized the sensitivity of pupillary signs as indicators in this condition and described their evolution and frequency: Only 2 of their 25 patients with epidural hemorrhage lacked pupillary abnormalities, and both of these had evidence for subacute or chronic lesions rather than acute ones. In the remaining patients the homolateral pupil first constricted, then gradually dilated to become widely fixed, and oculomotor palsy ensued. Each of these three distinct signs of dysfunction, i.e., pupillary dilatation, pupillary fixation, and oculomotor paralysis, passed from the homolateral to the contralateral eye before the next more severe ophthalmologic change occurred. Maximum pupillary dilatation and fixation were ominous, requiring urgent action since patients failed to survive if fixed bilateral mydriasis persisted longer than 30 minutes.

Motor signs occur only late in the course of extradural hematoma and usually are those of an acute uncal syndrome. In addition, the rapid development of the lesion and the irritative effect of the blood frequently produce focal or general convulsions.

The diagnosis of extradural hemorrhage can be puzzling, for many of them follow trivial blows to the head such as can arise in minor home accidents or sports. Another, smaller, group must be detected by signs of clinical worsening in patients who remain unconscious from the time of the initial head injury. Among Jamieson and Yelland's 167 patients with extradural hemorrhage[265] almost half had no initial loss of consciousness, and in Gallagher and Browder's equally large series,[195] two thirds had an initial injury too mild to command hospital attention. Only about 15 to 20 per cent of patients undergo the "classical" sequence of an initial traumatic unconsciousness followed by a lucid interval and then a relapse into coma.

Headache is the most common symptom among conscious patients, but a subtle change in behavior, consisting of irritability, a lessening of mental alertness, or somnolence, is usually the first clear warning of impending trouble. Once stupor, pupillary or motor signs, or convulsions evolve, the chance of death increases rapidly, and less than half of patients operated on in coma survive. Plain skull x-ray films will identify a fracture line in 80 per cent but miss approximately 10 per cent of fractures that turn up later at autopsy or operation. If the fracture line overlies the middle meningeal groove, it is essentially diagnostic.

Carotid arteriography is the most informative indirect diagnostic procedure and usually outlines the lesion, showing separation of the cerebral vasculature from the inner table of the skull. However, with rapid clinical progression, particularly when altered consciousness or pupillary dilatation has already developed and there is a history of recent head trauma or a known temporal skull fracture, delay can be fatal. In such instances, diagnosis and treatment can be made simultaneously by proceeding immediately to trephination, which should be done quadrantically in the frontoparietal and temporoparietal regions of the skull.

POST-TRAUMATIC STUPOR IN CHILDREN. This syndrome involves a lesion of neither the epidural nor the subdural space, but since its symptoms are often confused with these more serious conditions it is included here.

Head injuries in children often initiate a clinical picture of post-traumatic stupor, which is briefly alarming but ultimately benign. The children are typically under 14 years of age and suffer a moderate or severe direct closed head injury such as occurs after falling from a tree, being hit on the head by a ball, or being struck in an accident. Usually there is brief unconsciousness after which children go through either of two early courses. Most recover immediately and are clinically well so that physicians rarely see them. A smaller number recover for 30 to 60 minutes but then relapse and undergo several hours of lethargy accompanied by fluctuating but consensual changes in the pupil size, muscular hypertonus shifting from one side of the body to the other, and unilateral or bilateral extensor plantar responses. Focal seizures[441] and cortical blindness[205, 220] have been observed during such periods. The children often are nauseated and vomit, but as a rule awaken from their lethargic state within 2 to 6 hours after the injury and are alert with no apparent residua. Sometimes, however, that night the child declines into a stuporous sleep and is abnormally difficult to arouse, a state that superficially may suggest the presence of a cerebral contusion or even an epidural hematoma. The arousability, the lack of focal signs, and the lack of progression belie these more serious diagnoses, and the children usually recover with no residua the following day.

The cause of childhood post-traumatic stupor is unknown (see the next section). The patients have normal x-ray findings and EEG records. Lumbar puncture usually is unremarkable except for occasional high pressures of 160 to 200 mm., a finding difficult to interpret in children. The illness is short-lived, and the benign features that distinguish it from serious head injury are that, after brief worsening, the children improve spontaneously and progressively, do not show evolving focal cerebral signs, and, despite sleeping deeply, can be awakened at least briefly if vigorously stimulated.

DELAYED BRAIN LESIONS FOLLOWING MILD OR TRIVIAL HEAD TRAUMA. This disorder may differ only in degree and permanence from the delayed encephalopathy in children described above. Delayed post-traumatic cortical blindness, for example, occurs in younger adults as well as children[205] although it is more common in the latter. Fortunately, delayed encephalopathy in adults is rare, for the course of the clearly documented cases observed in our own hospital and by others has been devastating. The reported patients have been young people below the age of 25 years, mainly adolescents. Following a relatively mild head injury sufficient to stun but not cause sustained unconsciousness, the patients lapse into coma or develop a severe focal neurological deficit (cortical blindness, hemiplegia, aphasia) after an awake, relatively symptom-free, immediate post-traumatic period lasting from 15 minutes to 2 or more hours. In no instance has the clinical examination at the time of delayed unconsciousness been sufficiently detailed to estimate how much brainstem function was lost. A 24-year-old woman examined by us several years ago at The New York Hospital had signs of a progressive left hemispheric dysfunction without brainstem dysfunction that began after a closed head injury and a 30-minute clear period following the trauma. The duration and evolution of her signs over a period of less than 2 hours resembled the course of ischemic cerebral infarction. Trephination and ventriculography were unremarkable and failed to reveal the expected epidural hematoma. Arteriography was not performed. She was left with a significant residual motor and language defect.

Autopsy findings have been reported on four such patients.[217, 524, 542] The brains of all four contained multifocal ischemic or necrotic lesions; in two the abnormalities were confined to cortical diencephalic and brainstem gray matter, but the other two lacked such a clear geographical distribution. The ultimate pathogenesis of this lesion is unknown. Neither the appearance of any of the patients nor the pathological changes at autopsy suggested that they suffered from an unsuspected period of hypotension or an asystole. The obviously ischemic lesions found at postmortem examination suggest a link to the functional cerebral vascular abnormalities that follow trauma described on page 69, but no direct evidence supports this speculation.

SUBDURAL HEMATOMA. Acute and subacute hematomas are complications of acute, severe head injuries, and their effects usually are ancillary to the primary cause of coma, which is contusion of the brainstem and hemispheres. These acute traumatic lesions seldom present problems of differential diagnosis and are not discussed in this book.

Chronic subdural hematoma is a more difficult diagnostic problem that is a fairly frequent cause of stupor or coma and often deceptive in its manifestations. Although the hematomas occur in all age groups, they are more frequent among the elderly, in chronic alcoholics, and in patients receiving anticoagulant drugs.

Chronic subdural hematomas are collections of weeks-to-months-old partially decomposed blood, blood pigments, and proteins in the subdural space. The lining of the hematoma is supplied with luxuriously proliferating small vessels, and fresh blood that leaks from the delicate channels undoubtedly is one factor that explains why a chronic hematoma can suddenly cause symptoms after many months of clinical silence. Small clots containing 40 to 60 cc. probably cause no symptoms. Larger clots vary greatly in their size by the time they cause symptoms, because of differences in how fast they accumulate as well as in the degree of brain displacement and compression that individual hematomas produce. Since subdural hematomas do not directly invade the brain, it is not uncommon for them to produce signs of generalized supratentorial dysfunction in advance of or instead of paralysis, seizures, or other focal changes.

During recent years 73 patients with subdural hematomas have been treated at The New York Hospital (Table 4); 27 were in stupor or coma. Most of them were initially admitted to general medical or surgical services where it was notable that a supratentorial mass lesion was correctly diagnosed in less than half and not even considered in more than one third. The most serious and frequent error was to diagnose a subdural hematoma as cerebral infarction, although infection of the central nervous system was an incorrect diagnosis made almost as frequently.

Table 4. Clinical features of 73 patients with subdural hematoma

Unilateral hematoma	62	
Bilateral hematomas	11	
Mortality	14 (3 unoperated)	
Number of patients in stupor or coma	27	
Principal Clinical Diagnosis before Hematoma Discovered:		
Intracranial mass lesion or subdural hematoma		24
Cerebral vascular disease, but subdural hematoma possible		17
Cerebral infarction or arteriosclerosis		12
Cerebral atrophy		5
Encephalitis		8
Meningitis		3
Metabolic encephalopathy secondary to systemic illness		3
Psychosis		1

Subdural hematomas cause coma because they compress the brain and displace it downward or laterally to produce central or uncal herniation. About 80 per cent of all patients with subdural hematoma have headache and even if stuporous will recoil if the skull is percussed over the hematoma. Beyond this, the diagnosis is suggested by either of two clinical pictures. (A history of trauma cannot be relied upon.) One is that of a straightforward expanding hemispheral mass lesion, and the physician needs only the history of headache combined with signs of progressive clouding of consciousness and hemispheric dysfunction to suspect the diagnosis and proceed with specific diagnostic studies. The other is more frequent and consists of headache, diffuse mental changes, obtundation, and signs signifying bilateral cerebral dysfunction (the presence of posthyperventilation apnea, sucking and snouting reflexes, diffuse gegenhalten, minor stretch reflex differences), blending into the early symptoms of the central herniation syndrome. In their early stages, these imprecise symptoms may remotely suggest a subacute delirious reaction or even a primary dementia, but headache, drowsiness, asymmetry of signs, and a neurological picture that characteristically changes or fluctuates under observation will usually provide the diagnostic impression. Neither psychiatric nor metabolic brain disease produces the typical rostral-caudal deterioration that sooner or later characterizes a progressive subdural hematoma.

The symptoms of subdural hematoma have a remarkable tendency to fluctuate from day to day and even from hour to hour, and the nature of these fluctuations is both alarming and suggestive of their possible cause. Many types of expanding supratentorial mass lesions produce fluctuations in their symptomatology once they reach the stage where the intracranial structures can barely compensate for the mass and the associated downward shift it produces. When these masses are brain tumors, the fluctuations are usually associated with worsening or improvement of motor, sensory, or other focal signs. What is different (and deceptive) with subdural hematoma is that the downward shift and generalized supratentorial dysfunction often occur without substantial accompanying focal signs of a hemispheral mass lesion. Under these circumstances, as Case 8 illustrates, the fluctuations are associated with changes in pupillary, ocular, and motor function that indicate the patient is moving in and out of the diencephalic stage of the central syndrome.

In making the diagnosis of chronic subdural hematoma, one cannot depend on distinctive pupillary abnormalities being present. Most patients in our own series had small, reactive pupils consistent with the early stages of the central syndrome. In the large series of 216 patients with chronic subdural hematomas reported by Pevehouse, Bloom, and McKissock[440] only 11 per cent had pupillary inequality, and when a larger pupil was present, it was homolateral to the hematoma in 91 per cent. One fifth of their patients with chronic hematomas had papilledema, and 10 per cent had homolateral abducens palsy.

General laboratory aids help only moderately when subdural hematoma is suspected (Table 5). In The New York Hospital series, examination of the spinal fluid was undependable as the fluid was xanthochromic or under increased pressure in less than half of the patients. The EEG was frequently abnormal but often not focal. Skull x-ray pictures contained evidence of a pineal shift in only 12 of 73 cases, although, when present, this was an obviously valuable sign of a mass lesion. Brain scanning after radionuclide injection detects an abnormal uptake in the region of the hematoma in about 80 per cent of such cases, and in an even higher percentage when the lesion is over 2 weeks old and membranes have formed.[106]

A suspected diagnosis of subdural hematoma requires cerebral angiography or well-placed parieto-occipital burr holes to confirm it. The latter technique is almost without complication, and in cases strongly suspected of hematomas may be preferred as it also treats the lesions. Carotid

Table 5. Diagnostic features of 73 patients with subdural hematoma

Skull X-Ray Examination		Spinal Fluid (51 patients)	
Negative	53	Protein under 50	24
Fracture	8	Protein over 50	25
Pineal shift	12	Less than 5 RBC	21
		More than 5 RBC	28
Electroencephalogram		More than 2 WBC	11
Focal abnormality	19	Xanthochromia	23
General abnormality	18	CSF pressure < 150	24
Normal	8	CFS pressure > 150	25
Unsatisfactory	1		

arteriograms are almost equally accurate in diagnosis and in doubtful cases have the advantage of outlining other intracranial structures as well as unusually placed hematomas tucked between or underneath the hemispheres, where trephination would miss them.[92] When clinical signs strongly suggest subdural hematoma, the exact diagnosis and treatment should not be delayed. As implied above, symptoms in these patients often reflect a delicate balance between compensation and decompensation of the neural and vascular structures grouped around the tentorial notch, and patients can rapidly develop serious and irreversible cerebral damage if not properly and promptly treated.

Case 8. A 35-year-old woman had been well until the last trimester of her uncomplicated pregnancy in September, when she became lethargic. After the uncomplicated delivery of a premature child, she continued to be drowsy, and, despite the demands of the newborn, she slept for long periods during both the day and night. In early November, she had a brief tonic seizure. Her lethargy increased, and by mid-November she developed headaches, which were at first biocciptal and subsequently changed position

104

to become dull and constant behind the left eye. Concurrently she developed intermittent nausea and vomiting. A neurological examination was reportedly negative at that time. At the beginning of December she was found early one morning by her husband speaking incoherently. She was admitted to The New York Hospital later the same day, irrational, bewildered, and agitated. The somatic neurological examination was unremarkable at that time. Her serum potassium was 2.5 mEq. per L. (the patient had been receiving chlorothiazide) and her serum bicarbonate was 30 mEq. per L. The lumbar puncture yielded faintly xanthochromic, clear fluid, with a pressure of 205 mm., no cells, and 56 mg. of protein per 100 cc. An electroencephalogram showed bursts of high amplitude 2 cps waves in the frontal areas bilaterally, but predominating on the left side. Skull x-ray findings were negative.

The electrolyte abnormalities were corrected parenterally, and later the same day the patient had recovered remarkably. She was alert, oriented, and cooperative and had no memory of her recent confusion. She continued to have left-sided headaches, however. Six hours later she became obtunded—indeed, almost stuporous—and she was disoriented when aroused. Her pupils were 2 mm. and reactive, and she had bilateral paratonic resistance to passive stretch in the extremities as well as mild right-sided weakness and an abnormal plantar response on the right. The fluctuation of signs in and out of stupor along with bilateral motor signs suggested incipient transtentorial herniation, and biparietal burr holes were placed by a neurosurgeon. These yielded a large chronic subdural hematoma on the left containing both fresh and decomposed blood. Within minutes after evacuation of the hematoma she was alert, oriented, and rational. A detailed neurological examination 3 days later encountered no abnormalities. Subsequently it was learned that the patient probably suffered from recurrent alcoholism and falls, but this information was pointedly withheld by the family when she was first examined.

Comment: This is a typical history for subdural hematoma and illustrates how difficult it is to determine retrospectively when these lesions begin or first produce clinical symptoms. Whether her bouts of exacerbation represented additional head trauma with fresh bleeding cannot be known. When she came under our care, her fluctuating symptoms clearly reflected diffuse, intermittent, bilateral cerebral dysfunction, and these fluctuations plus the other clinical and EEG signs of diencephalic dysfunction suggested early transtentorial herniation. Her rapid recovery when the hematoma was evacuated was evidence that her clinical picture was due to shift and displacement of the brain rather than to structural compression of vessels and neurons, for the latter would hardly have responded so rapidly.

The following patient with subdural hematoma illustrates well the fluctuating nature of rostral-caudal signs of upper brainstem dysfunction in this disorder as well as the close relation between delirium and coma in cerebral disorders.

Case 9. A 34-year-old male clerk of exemplary habits had had bitemporal headaches for a month, and for 5 days had had an increase in headache accompanied by confusion, agitation, and somnolence. He had had some weakness of his right side the day before admission, and his wife, a nurse, had noted that his left eye lagged behind the right when he looked to the right.

When he was admitted to The New York Hospital, his blood pressure, pulse, respiration, and body temperature were unremarkable. He was obtunded, restless when aroused, and oriented only to person. The pupils were dilated to 7 mm. bilaterally but reacted to light. Examination of extraocular movements showed loss of upward conjugate gaze. There was a mild right hemiparesis; the stretch reflexes were bilaterally hyperactive, and both plantar responses were extensor.

During the 2 hours after admission the patient became more agitated and developed more spasticity and intermittent decorticate spasms on the right. His pupils shrank symmetrically to 5 mm. but retained their light reaction. At lumbar puncture the CSF pressure was 240 mm., and the fluid was otherwise unremarkable. Following the puncture, the right facial weakness was briefly more pronounced, but within 2 hours he was alert, talking coherently, and the right-sided signs had almost disappeared. Diffuse headache persisted, however.

The improvement misled his examining physicians into believing that he might have a metabolic cerebral lesion, and it was decided to observe him and obtain more laboratory work. During the next 5 hours he again developed obtundation accompanied by increased spasticity on the right side and bilateral extensor plantar responses. The cycle reversed again, and by the next morning, 6 hours later, he was alert and responsive and a neurological consultant found a loss of upward conjugate gaze as the only certain abnormality. The patient was scheduled for arteriography, but as preparation for the procedure was made he became progressively more somnolent. The right pupil shrank to 3 mm. and lost its light reaction. The left pupil remained at 5 mm. but with a minimal light and ciliospinal reaction. The right eye turned outward (third nerve palsy) and did not move during the doll's-eye maneuver. Decorticate posturing developed first on the right, then on the left side of the body. The arteriogram demonstrated a large nonvascular area in the left parietotemporal subdural space. On the way to the operating room, the man became first extremely agitated, then quiet and unresponsive. The left pupil became fixed, and the left eye deviated laterally. Shortly thereafter, the patient's eyes deviated in a skewed manner: the right up and the left down. Respiration rose to 30 per minute, then quieted and became small in amplitude and slow (8 per minute) in frequency.

Burr holes were placed promptly, and 150 cc. of dark red blood were removed from the subdural space on the left. The underlying brain was slack and re-expanded only after lumbar subarachnoid saline injection. During operation, the respiratory rate gradually rose to 60 per minute. One hour later the pupils were 3 mm. and reacted to light, and the eyes were conjugately midposition with intact horizontal oculovestibular responses to head turning. Four hours after the surgical procedure the patient responded verbally to vigorous stimulation and moved all four extremities. Thereafter, he made an uneventful recovery and left the hospital on the twelfth day with no neurological residuals other than a slight weakness on the lower right side of the face. No history of relevant head trauma could be recalled.

SUBDURAL EMPYEMA.   Subdural empyema is a rare but important cause of coma, which can be cured if treated promptly but damages the brain irreversibly if neglected. The condition is usually a complication of otorhinological disease, particularly of acute sinusitis. Less commonly, the empyema follows the rupture of an intracerebral abscess or complicates a penetrating wound of the skull. Males are affected more than females, and a significant proportion of the patients give a history of either ear, nose, and throat surgery or head trauma shortly before they develop symptoms of the empyema. The infection gets to the subdural space either by extending directly through the skull (otitic infection) or along the penetrating veins, the latter route being most common with sinus infection. Pus sometimes accumulates between the hemispheres or at the base of the brain, but the most frequent distribution is a collection extending posteriorly from the frontal pole over the dorsolateral part of the hemisphere.[240] Streptococci are the most common causative organisms, the anaerobes being frequent.

Subdural empyema produces stupor or coma by two mechanisms. The principal mechanism results from an expanding supratentorial mass, which, together with the adjacent brain swelling, produces rostral-caudal displacement and compression of the brain at its base. The other is that of an intracranial infection, which either spreads to involve the adjacent brain or whose toxic effects impair brain metabolism. At least in the early stages, the latter effect is usually less prominent because the arachnoid membrane is relatively impermeable to both toxins and infection. As the illness evolves, however, meningitis, underlying bacterial encephalitis, and cortical thrombophlebitis become more prominent and are accompanied by increasing focal signs of seizures, hemiplegia, or aphasia.[319]

The clinical picture of subdural empyema resembles in many ways the symptoms of subdural hematoma except that there is a greater tendency to produce stupor or coma in advance of focal hemispheral signs, the time course is greatly truncated, and the patient with empyema has fever and toxic signs. A small proportion of patients have cutaneous swelling over the infected sinus (Pott's puffy tumor). The diagnosis should be suspected in a patient with clouded consciousness who has the history or x-ray findings of rhino-otitic infection, headache, skull tenderness, fever, and the early signs of transtentorial herniation (which are the principal differentiating features from acute, uncomplicated meningitis). Typically, patients with subdural empyema have mild bilateral motor signs at this early stage. Meningismus is sometimes present, and the spinal fluid is under increased pressure. The spinal fluid contents are rarely normal, although their cell count is often low (we view more than 2 lymphocytes suspiciously and even a single neutrophil as abnormal) and the CSF protein may be only modestly elevated. Organisms can almost never be cultured from the CSF in the early stage of the illness. Skull x-ray films are helpful only if they disclose evidence of sinusitis or sinus or mastoid osteomyelitis.

When subdural empyema is suspected as a cause of coma, cerebral angiography is probably the most valuable indirect technique to establish the diagnosis and also frequently reveals sites of clinically unsuspected pus.[240] When patients are severely and acutely ill, however, it is desirable to proceed immediately to trephination, which not only provides a definitive diagnosis but permits drainage as well. Antibiotics in large doses are indicated as soon as one suspects an intracranial infection.

The following young man had subdural empyema. It was of interest that burr holes were delayed several hours because asterixis, fever, and vomiting originally suggested metabolic disease. The importance of only a few cells in the CSF was not initially recognized.

Case 10. A 28-year-old man had been healthy except for chronic sinusitis. Two weeks before his admission to the hospital, he developed a dull, right frontal headache that persisted and gradually became more severe. His physician gave him penicillin intramuscularly and for 12 hours after this he developed fever (39.6° C.), nausea, and vomiting. He then improved for 3 days, after which increasing headache and a return of fever led to another penicillin injection, which again was followed by transient nausea and vomiting and then improvement. Five days before we saw him, his headaches became "excruciating" and because of this, as well as the fever and vomiting, he was admitted to another hospital. A diagnosis of acute and chronic sinusitis was made and the patient was placed on a regimen of penicillin, 1,200,000 units every 4 hours. The neurological examination initially was reported to be within normal limits, but during the ensuing 3 days he gradually became first obtunded and finally almost unresponsive. A lumbar puncture revealed an initial pressure of 240 mm. of CSF, no white cells, 92 mg. of sugar and 30 mg. of protein per 100 cc.

When he was admitted to The New York Hospital, his rectal temperature was 37.5° C.; his pulse was 70 per minute; his respirations were 40 per minute and regular, and his blood pressure was 120/75 mm. Hg. He was stuporous and responded only to vigorous and repetitive stimuli. Once aroused, he was disoriented to time, but followed commands slowly and appropriately. He complained of right hemicranial headache, and the right side of the skull was tender. The neck was not stiff. He had had an old injury of the left iris that reduced its light reaction, but both pupils were 2 mm. in diameter and reacted to light, the right briskly so. The retinal veins were full. Testing of extraocular movements showed limitation of both voluntary and reflex upward gaze. There was bilateral paratonic resistance to passive stretch in the extremities and very mild right-sided hemiparesis. Bilateral extensor plantar responses were elicited, more briskly on the left than on the right. A striking finding was the presence of asterixis involving particularly the left upper and lower extremity with occasional myoclonic twitches involving the same area.

A lumbar puncture released crystal-clear spinal fluid with a pressure of 120 mm. There were 32 red blood cells and 3 lymphocytes per cu. mm. The protein was 47 mg. per 100 cc. The white blood count was 13,000 with 80 per cent neutrophilic forms. Skull x-ray films showed evidence of bilateral frontal and maxillary sinusitis.

The asterixis was puzzling, and the sinusitis and fever not at first given sufficient weight. However, the progressive obtundation, small pupils, loss of upward gaze, and bilateral mild motor signs all suggested a supratentorial poorly localized mass, probably subdural hematoma, producing the diencephalic stage of the central syndrome. With the history of sinus infection and fever, abscess formation was considered possible. Bilateral parietal-occipital burr holes were placed, and copious amounts of pus were evacuated from the right subdural space. The next day a frontal sinus antrotomy was performed to drain that cavity as well. Postoperatively, the patient developed left-sided motor seizures and weakness. Transient left homonymous hemianopsia was noted at the same time, but he had not previously been sufficiently alert to enable vision to be tested. Cultures of the empyema yielded a microaerophilic streptococcus. Penicillin was continued for 2 weeks parenterally. Recovery was uneventful, and the patient has subsequently remained well and returned to work.

Comment: This patient developed the typical signs of the central syndrome of transtentorial herniation with rostral-caudal deterioration. The persistent headache and lack of clear localizing signs suggested a lesion in the subdural space, and the fever, rapid course, and history of sinusitis should have made us suspect empyema even more promptly. The asterixis was a finding of great interest, particularly as it developed maximally in the extremities opposite to the abscess. We tentatively ascribed this to "toxic" effects of the infection, but the important thing was to learn that it did not rule out a mass lesion.

Intracerebral Lesions

Neoplasms, hemorrhages, infarctions, and abscesses are included in this category. Most of these lesions are easier to localize and identify than the extracerebral lesions because they impinge upon or directly destroy the cerebral structures dealing with movement, sensation, speech, or the special senses. By the time they produce coma, therefore, most intracerebral masses have also produced specific localizing neurological signs that warn of their presence and sometimes imply their histological construction. There are two exceptions to the rule that intracerebral masses produce focal signs before generalized ones: Frontal lobe and intraventricular masses are both in neurologically "silent" areas and even when they produce widespread anatomical effects they may result in few recognizable focal symptoms in advance of confusion, stupor, or coma.

CEREBRAL VASCULAR LESIONS CAUSING COMA. *Cerebral hemorrhage.* About half of all cerebral hemorrhages produce unconsciousness, making them the most common cause of coma among supratentorial vascular lesions. Cerebral hemorrhage is due to: (1) most commonly, rupture of an intracerebral blood vessel deep in the parenchyma, usually an artery, occasionally a vein; (2) leakage from or rupture of arterial aneurysms at the base of the brain; (3) leakage from or rupture of arteriovenous malformations[350] or microangiomas[359] (the least common cause). In the case of aneurysms or of large arteriovenous malformations, the source of bleeding can usually be identified, but with hypertensive hemorrhages deep in the parencyhma, it is almost the rule for the pathologist not to find the actual bleeding vessel.

Hemorrhages producing coma are deep in the hemisphere, extensive, and usually involve structures in and around the internal capsule and adjacent basal ganglia. This anatomical distribution means that hemorrhages severe enough to cause coma usually produce hemiplegia or hemisensory defects as well. Although cerebral hemorrhage is almost the only supratentorial vascular lesion that produces coma within minutes of its onset, unconsciousness is rarely the very first sign of even these catastrophes. Thus, almost all patients with cerebral hemorrhage have at least a brief headache before losing consciousness, and many suffer a gradual or stair-step progression of symptoms for several hours. Some of these worsenings are because brain swelling and inflammation progressively surround the fresh area of bleeding, but many instances also reflect repeated severe hemorrhages.

Our studies include 34 patients who died from hemispheral cerebral hemorrhage and subsequently were examined post mortem. An additional 15 patients were initally severely obtunded or barely arousable but survived. No patient in our series has survived deep coma produced by cerebral hemorrhage.

All of our patients bled during wakefulness, several while exercising. Only five were not hypertensive: Three of these bled into the cerebral parenchyma from ruptured aneurysms, and the other two were receiving anticoagulants. Almost every patient who was observed by witnesses at the onset of the hemorrhage complained of sudden headache. This was followed occasionally by sudden collapse and coma (a sequence that we believe means intraventricular bleeding), but more often progressive neurological signs radiated from the initial hemispheric focus and evolved gradually into the typical picture of either the central or uncal syndromes of rostral-caudal deterioration. Examples of cerebral hemorrhages producing the central and uncal syndromes, respectively, have been given on pages 86 and 90 as Cases 4 and 5. The following report illustrates how patients with cerebral hemorrhage sometimes rapidly develop signs of diencephalic dysfunction and how effective treatment can equally rapidly reverse these signs.

Case 11. A 34-year-old woman developed a sudden right-sided headache that rapidly spread over the right hemicranium. She could not see clearly to the left, and her family noted that she was confused. Two days later she was brought to the hospital. At that time she had a blood pressure of 160/100 mm. Hg. She was lethargic, oriented, and coherent but had left homonymous hemianopsia and a left hemisensory defect for stereoperception. She denied her neurological abnormalities in a manner typical of patients with parietal lobe damage.

Laboratory work was unremarkable, lumbar puncture being omitted because cerebral hemorrhage was suspected. A right internal carotid arteriogram showed evidence of a moderately large right posterior temporal lobe mass with the internal cerebral vein shifted 10 mm. to the left.

The day after admission her blood pressure slowly rose from 140/110 to 190/100 mm. Hg and her pulse rate fell from 72 to 54 per minute. After 60 to 90 minutes, she became suddenly unresponsive with periodic breathing, bilaterally dilated (8 mm.) and fixed pupils, flaccid extremities, and extensor plantar responses. She was given the hyperosmotic agent, sodium mannitol, 50 gm. in 250 cc. of 5 per cent dextrose in water over the next hour. Prednisone was given intravenously, a tracheostomy was performed, and she was placed on artificial respiration. (Hyperosmotic agents shrink the brain, and lowering the arterial carbon dioxide content by artificial ventilation reduces the intracranial blood volume, also shrinking the intracranial contents.) After 60 minutes of treatment, the pupils constricted to 5 mm. and regained their light reflex. She began to move her right side.

Over the next 3 days she gradually improved and awakened, although she remained obtunded when not stimulated. She was oriented but showed almost complete denial of her rather severe left homonymous hemianopsia, her left-sided hemisory defect, and her mild left hemiparesis. The breathing pattern was normal, and the pupils were 4 mm., reacted to light and were equal. She could gaze conjugately to both lateral extremes but could not follow an object with her eyes to the left of the midline. There was paralysis of voluntary and reflex upward gaze.

She continued to improve, but suddenly one evening she became apneic and flaccid with dilated fixed pupils and divergent eyes. She died after receiving artificial respiration and pressor agents for 2 days.

At postmortem examination, the brain was soft, reflecting the 2-day-period of artificial survival. The inferior and posterior portions of the right temporal lobe were destroyed by a large, partly clotted and partly fresh hemorrhage, which had lacerated the base of the temporal lobe, pushing the homolateral uncus into the tentorial incisura and displacing the opposite third nerve downward and compressing it against the petroclinoid ligament. The entire upper brainstem was displaced caudally, but the brainstem was free of gross hemorrhage. The exact source of the hemorrhage could not be found.

Intraventricular hemorrhage. Intraventricular hemorrhage occurred in 24 of the 34 patients in our own series who died from cerebral hemorrhage, and a retrospective analysis suggested that in many this catastrophe produced a characteristic group of symptoms. Ten patients presented with sudden profound coma after either very brief or no recognized initial symptoms. They died within minutes to hours and often demonstrated signs of pontine or medullary failure when first examined a few minutes following onset. The 14 remaining patients had a double-phased illness: Their early symptoms clinically resembled those of any kind of progressive supratentorial mass lesion producing incipient rostral-caudal deterioration. Suddenly this orderly progression of signs was interrupted by deeper coma, convulsions, and the abrupt appearance of signs indicating low brainstem damage. We believe that these signs reflect sudden pressure transmitted through the ventricular system to the floor of the fourth ventricle at the moment of intraventricular rupture. Experimental data are consistent with this interpretation. Blood, per se, in the ventricular system has little or no ill effects on the brain.[79] However, Meyers[379] found that saline injected into a lateral cerebral ventricle adversely affected blood pressure, pulse rate, and respiration more than equal amounts injected over the hemispheral surface. More recently, Thompson and Malina[563] demonstrated that a sudden injection of saline into a lateral ventricle created acute pressure gradients between the anterior and posterior fossae with rapid medullary failure.

The following patient's course was typical of intraventricular hemorrhage. The effects of sudden bleeding into the ventricular system were difficult to distinguish from primary pontine hemorrhage (page 131).

Case 12. A 70-year-old woman was known to be well the evening before admission. On the morning of admission, she was found semicomatose and incontinent of urine and feces. She spoke briefly to a friend, asking for water, but then vomited and lost consciousness altogether. She had a rectal temperature of 38.5° C. and a regular pulse of 88, regular respirations at 30, and a blood pressure of 150/80 mm. Hg. She was in moderately deep coma. The pupils were 2 mm. and reacted to light stimulation. Oculocephalic responses could not be elicited. She was diffusely flaccid with bilateral Babinski signs but flexed the lower extremities in response to noxious stimulation.

Laboratory work included a white blood count of 27,800 per cu. mm.; the lumbar spinal fluid was grossly bloody, had a hematocrit of 10 per cent and a pressure of 460 mm. By 6 hours after admission she had bilaterally midposition and fixed pupils, and no responses to noxious stimulation; she was mildly hyperpneic, and the extensor plantar responses remained. There was little change between then and her death 18 hours later.

At the autopsy there was a large ruptured aneurysm on the right anterior cerebral artery with a huge blood clot filling the lateral ventricle on that side as well as the third ventricle, the aqueduct, and the fourth ventricle. There was little subarachnoid blood, but microscopic sections showed blood dissecting through the ependymal floor of the fourth ventricle into the pons and medulla. The brain was grossly and diffusely swollen, and there was both uncal and transtentorial herniation. Hemorrhages were present throughout the parenchyma of the brainstem as well as in the right hemisphere.

Comment: This patient suddenly completely lost consciousness and presented with pupillary, oculomotor, and motor system signs suggestive of a primary low brainstem lesion (see Chapter 3). The tamponade effect of the downwardly dissecting blood must have simultaneously produced abnormalities in both supratentorial and subtentorial neural systems, a supposition supported at postmortem examination by the finding of subependymal fourth ventricle blood.

Cerebral ischemic infarction. Unconsciousness is seldom the initial sign of uncomplicated cerebral hemispheric infarction. Among 106 patients with hemispheric infarcts whom we studied,[445] the only instances of coma at the onset of illness were in patients with either myocardial infarction or cardiac arrhythmias, both of which reduce the cardiac output and the cerebral blood flow.[150] Several patients with large infarcts were dull, drowsy, and apathetic. This, combined with severe aphasia, sometimes led the family or the referring medical examiners to call them unconscious, but a detailed appraisal almost always indicated a less global reduction of faculties. Others, notably Merritt and Aring,[374] report that as many as 30 per cent of their patients with acute cerebral infarction were unconscious at the onset. This high figure may be partly explained by their including many patients with basilar artery thrombosis. Also, the analyses were made entirely on patients who died from their illness, and several may have had myocardial infarcts or other lesions.

Although coma is rare with the onset of a hemispheric infarct, several conditions favor its development during the ensuing few days. Many patients with acute strokes develop pneumonitis, heart failure, or electrolyte disorders, and these complications can impair brain metabolism and lead to stupor. In addition, a cerebral infarct becomes an expanding mass as vascular congestion, inflammation, and edema increase its bulk. This can be a life-threatening complication.

Shaw, Alvord, and Berry[509] pointed out that patients dying within a week after acute cerebral hemispheric infarction have considerable brain swelling with hemispheral shift across the midline and usually transtentorial herniation. In their pathological material, swelling reached a maximum within 2 to 4 days and then gradually became less as the interval from the onset of the stroke lengthened.

Clinical criteria suggest that cerebral edema causes worsening of signs in about one out of every five cases of acute cerebral infarction. We studied 106 cases in which there were clinical signs of large cerebral hemispheric infarctions specifically for this complication.[445] Fourteen patients developed a gradual worsening into stupor and then deep coma with signs of progressive rostral-caudal deterioration typical of an expanding supratentorial mass. Eight of the fourteen died and were examined post mortem. The brain of each showed gross cerebral edema and secondary transtentorial herniation. An additional eight patients developed part of this progression, but the signs of dysfunction halted at the diencephalic level and were followed by slow recovery. Most of the patients who developed coma secondary to cerebral infarction had clinical signs of the central syndrome of rostral-caudal deterioration. Pupillary dilatation was recorded only twice.

Cerebral embolism. Acute cerebral embolism is frequently regarded as a potential cause of coma, even when the region of ischemic infarction is limited to the cerebral hemispheres. Wells,[594] for example, states that 20 of 63 episodes of acute cerebral embolism were associated with coma, and his statistics indicate that at least some of these patients had hemispheric lesions.

Our experience, cited below, is that coma rarely accompanies the onset of embolism to the cerebral hemispheres. Fisher[166] implies the same conclusion since his diagnostic criteria for suspecting cerebral embolism include the preservation of consciousness in the presence of a severe neurological deficit. Carter[81] also regards unconsciousness as uncommon, although it is difficult to assess exact incidence from his figures.

We have examined 17 patients who, by autopsy or a combination of clinical history and examination plus an arteriogram, were diagnosed as having an embolus restricted to the internal carotid or proximal middle cerebral artery with large hemispheric infarcts. Two had convulsions with transient unconsciousness immediately, and four more progressed into coma within 8 to 24 hours after the onset of the acute lesion. All four of these died, and the three in whom autopsy was done were found to have extensive edema of the infarcted hemisphere with a tentorial pressure cone. Among the remaining 13 patients, 1 with a dominant hemisphere lesion (see page 15) was apparently in coma from the onset of his illness, and 9 others had signs of bilateral hemispheric dysfunction (usually consisting of paratonia and an extensor plantar response opposite to the major hemiplegia plus varying degrees of obtundation) but not coma when they were first examined. Most of these patients became somewhat more torpid during the next 48 to 72 hours, but the mechanism of the immediate bilateral functional impairment with an ostensibly unilateral vascular lesion is, physiologically, still something of a mystery. (The time course is too rapid for cerebral swelling.)

At least three explanations have been offered for the immediate development of bilateral signs of coma with acute embolism. One is that sudden hemispheral loss alone can cause coma. This is unlikely, as discussed on page 16. A second is that emboli may have gone to both sides of the brain in these acutely comatose patients, a postulate that is hard to evaluate. In experimental cerebral embolism, emboli are usually found in all parts of the cerebral circulation, even when great care is taken to inject them only into a single carotid artery.[372] In man, however, it is rare to find bilateral emboli at postmortem examination except when a source exists for multiple and repeated embolism such as mitral valvular disease or bacterial endocarditis. The third is that the effect on the contralateral hemisphere is physiological, i.e., it is a sudden inhibition of remote neural or vascular tissue function due to the injury, a process called by von Monakow "diaschisis."

Although there is little doubt that remote neurological effects can follow cerebral injury, the nature of diaschisis is unknown. Some have postulated that diffuse vascular shock or vasospam occurs when embolism strikes one part of a previously healthy cerebral circulation. No evidence supports this contention, and most workers liken the contralateral hemispheric depression to the sudden depression of the remaining intact, spinal cord that follows a rostral transection (spinal shock). Kempinsky's[294] experiments are in keeping with this interpretation and demonstrate that acute embolism to one hemisphere in animals induces in the other immediate EEG abnormalities not accompanied by any vascular changes. This chapter earlier discussed (page 112) evidence that purely focal ischemic lesions can be associated with widespread functional abnormalities of the cerebral vascular bed, but whether these vascular changes also affect brain function is unknown.

The likelihood is that stupor and coma after a hemispheral cerebral embolism probably mean that the embolus has lodged opposite to a previously damaged hemisphere or that dissemination of embolic material has either caused bilateral hemispheric abnormalities or has directly struck the diencephalon or brainstem. With large emboli occluding the internal carotid or middle cerebral arteries and causing extensive unilateral injury, there is probably an acute physiological inhibition of neural and vascular function, and for this there is presently no known treatment. Later, within the first hours or days after the embolus strikes, cerebral edema forms in and around the fresh infarct and produces a supratentorial mass lesion that induces or accentuates coma by producing rostral-caudal deterioration.

Cerebral venous and sinus thrombosis. These most often arise in the adult as a complication of a predisposing condition; Krayenbühl's experience[316] with 20 per cent arising in the setting of good health stands as an exception. The principal stage setters include pregnancy and the postpartum period, the ingestion of contraceptive pills, abscesses of the skull, sinuses, mastoids or brain, migratory thrombophlebitis, ulcerative colitis, systemic infection, senile marasmus and, particularly, invasion of the venous sinuses by neoplasms.[17, 286] All engender either a hypercoagulable state or a mechanical nidus to which intravascular clotting elements can attach.

Local venous thrombosis or occlusion of the cavernous or lateral sinuses complicating facial or aural infections produces signs and symptoms that depend on the site of occlusion, and the clinical picture is likely to be dominated by signs of the local infection plus focal cerebral defects (see also Subdural Empyema, page 106). However, thrombosis of the superior longitudinal sinus precipitates a more insidious illness, often with impaired consciousness as an early or even the initiating symptom. When they precipitate serious neurological illnesses, most such occlusions lie in the anterior two thirds of the sinus, from which collateral drainage is less easily established (posterior sinus occlusions are often silent or cause headache, papilledema, and, occasionally, drowsiness or mild neurological abnormalities, but rarely stupor or coma). Bifrontal or generalized headache usually develops early, often with nausea and vomiting. Irritability, drowsiness or delirium follows, proceeding to stupor or coma. Papilledema arises in about half the cases. Kalbag and Woolf[286] found lower extremity sensory loss more often than motor impairment, but lower extremity monoparesis, paraparesis, hemiparesis, or language defects all may develop, depending upon the exact site of the thrombosis and whether it occludes the venous drainage of the central fissure or more lateral hemispheric areas. A history of jacksonian, multifocal, or generalized convulsions corresponds at autopsy with those patients in whom the thrombosis has extended into cortical veins, a stage too late for anticoagulants to have their maximal value.

Diagnosis depends upon the above clinical features, particularly when they evolve without other obvious cause during the puerperium or in women receiving hormonal contraceptives. There is usually accompanying fever, the erythrocyte sedimentation rate is always elevated, and the white blood count usually so. Two thirds of the patients have elevated CSF pressure, the fluid containing up to 5000 RBC and, uncommonly, as many as 150 to 200 WBC. Cerebral arteriograms usually suggest the diagnosis, revealing, at a maximum, large bilateral avascular areas without a midline shift and, at a minimum, a lack of filling of the anterior portion of the longitudinal sinus and its immediate venous tributaries.

Alternative diagnostic possibilities are few once one considers this complication of an appropriate predisposing condition. Among several of our patients, an acute hemorrhagic or necrotizing encephalitis (page 207) seemed the main clinical alternative until arteriograms settled the matter. The following patient's natural history is characteristic and illustrates superior longitudinal sinus occlusion associated with a malignant neoplasm.

Case 13. A 42-year-old woman developed acute myelomonocytic leukemia with anemia, abnormal leukocytosis, a decrease in blood platelets (30,000 per cu. mm.), and characteristic bone marrow changes. She was treated with platelet transfusions, leukophoresis, thioguanine, and arabinosylcytosine. Later, prednisone and vincristine were added.

One month later the patient had a generalized convulsion without prodromal symptoms. When examined immediately afterward, she was stuporous but awakened quickly. Her pupils were normal; her eyes deviated conjugately to the right, and both plantar responses were extensor. The lumbar puncture pressure was 210 mm., and the pink fluid contained 4 lymphocytes and 715 RBC per cu. mm. The protein was 28 and the sugar 90 mg. per 100 cc. Two similar seizures occurred during the next 2 hours, after which she was disoriented for exact dates but otherwise had an unremarkable general medical and detailed neurological examination except for bilateral extensor plantar responses. However, as the day passed the patient gradually became lethargic and confused and developed a left hemiparesis with the eyes tending to deviate toward the right. Subsequently she developed repetitive focal left facial seizures and a low grade fever. Left carotid arteriography failed to fill a large zone in the superior frontal region, and no contrast material appeared in the superior longitudinal sinus. Despite the large frontal avascular area, there was no shift of midline structures, strongly suggesting the presence of bilateral lesions.

The patient was treated with dehydrating agents, corticosteroid hormones, and platelet transfusions with the mistaken belief that she had suffered a cerebral hemorrhage although the arteriographic results should have led us to the correct diagnosis. She failed to improve, developed a more severe hemiplegia followed by progressive signs of rostral-caudal deterioration and died 4 days later.

At autopsy, the positive findings included a single adherent embolus in each of two small pulmonary arteries. There was no area of infarction grossly. Microscopically, fresh thromboemboli were present in small arteries, and there were microscopic areas of infarction in both lower lobes. The femoral veins and other major vessels were patent.. There was a hypercellular marrow with large clumps of granulocytes, and a decrease in erythrocyte precursors and megakaryocytes.

The brain weighed 1450 gm. and was grossly edematous. At about the midportion of the superior sagittal sinus there was an adherent thrombus occluding the sinus. Coronal sections of the brain revealed hemorrhagic infarction of both frontal lobes, larger on the right. There was also evidence of both uncal and transtentorial herniation. On microscopic examination, the superior sagittal sinus was occluded by a fresh and nonorganizing thrombus. Cortical veins entering the area of the superior sagittal sinus were also thrombosed, and there was hemorrhagic infarction of both frontal lobes.

INTRACEREBRAL TUMORS. The early symptoms of brain tumor have become generally recognized in recent years, and during the same time the diagnostic accuracy of electroencephalography and neuroradiology has very greatly improved. As a result, supratentorial brain tumors are now usually diagnosed before they impair consciousness, and are a relatively uncommon cause of coma of unknown origin. Nevertheless, these masses sometimes present vexingly difficult diagnostic problems, particularly when the patient's past history is unknown and the tumor's effects have impaired consciousness so much that a clear story cannot be obtained.

If supratentorial neoplasms produce coma, they do so by one or more of the following mechanisms: (1) They cause convulsions followed by a postictal state in all ways similar to that which follows other convulsive disorders (page 214). (2) Bleeding occurs into the neoplasm superimposing the effects of a cerebral hemorrhage onto the natural history of the tumor. This is comparatively unusual. (3) A neoplasm enlarges progressively and evokes swelling and displacement of the brain to produce the central or uncal syndromes of tentorial herniation. The type of tumor usually influences only the rate at which the symptoms develop. (4) A tumor, located in the lateral or third ventricle, suddenly obstructs ventricular flow, which produces acute, ventricular hypertension and sudden downward compres-

116

sion or displacement of the brainstem. This is the presumed mechanism of the recurrent attacks of unconsciousness that mark the natural history of third ventricle cysts.[292] (5) A neoplasm directly infiltrates or destroys the cerebral activating structures located in the thalamus and hypothalamus and thereby produces an encephalitis-like picture of progressively deepening obtundation.

Among the above causes of coma with supratentorial brain tumors, the first four involve mechanisms that have already been discussed. The final mechanism, that of a neoplasm directly invading the diencephalon, merits more comment. The early stages of these lesions are often marked primarily by changes in mentation, behavior, and consciousness, and they may produce very few accompanying long tract signs of abnormal motor or sensory function. At such times, physicians must give particular heed to evidence of excessive drowsiness, memory loss, impaired concentration, or changes in personal habits, as these early signs of dementia signify that a structural lesion rather than a purely emotional illness is causing the obtundation. An additional source of potential difficulty in diagnosis is that many diencephalic neoplasms lie adjacent to the meninges and may produce an encephalitic-like or meningitic picture, complete with pleocytosis and, sometimes, a lowered sugar content as well. Similar EEG abnormalities accompany either infections or neoplasms involving this region and, in such instances, radiological contrast procedures are required to decide the cause of the progressive signs of diencephalic failure. The following report illustrates such a course.

Case 14. A 44-year-old petroleum engineer noted gradual difficulty in concentration, accompanied by lethargy, approximately 3 months before he was first examined by a physician. These symptoms insidiously progressed so that he was sleeping for longer and longer periods at night and napping during the day as well. His wife found him increasingly inattentive, but he had no headache, no evidence of motor or sensory abnormalities, and no apparent symptoms of autonomic dysfunction. Finally, his drowsiness became so severe that he fell asleep driving his automobile and his wife insisted that he see a physician.

At another hospital he was noted to be lethargic but had few other neurological abnormalities. A diagnosis of encephalitis was suspected and seemed to be supported by the spinal fluid findings of 138 lymphocytes per cu. mm. and 120 mg. of protein and 70 mg. of sugar per 100 cc. Cultures of the CSF were sterile. Agglutination tests for viruses and rickettsia were inconclusive, and when the patient failed to improve he was referred to The New York Hospital 4 weeks later.

Upon admission he was only intermittently responsive and appeared to sleep most of the time. When he did answer, he was disoriented for time and he perseverated. He was unable to perform even simple calculations and could not follow commands. Language function per se appeared preserved. Respiration was marked by intermittent deep sighs. The pupils were bilaterally tiny, 1 to 2 mm., but equal, and they retained their light reaction. Extraocular movements were intact, and it was possible during his intermittent periods of unresponsiveness to elicit full lateral and vertical oculovestibular responses. The motor examination showed an occasional myoclonic jerk, occurring in either arm and sometimes the trunk. One observer thought that the right lower face

117

drooped, but there were no other focal neurological signs. Laboratory work added nothing to what was already known except that an EEG was diffusely moderately slow, particularly in the right posterior temporal-occipital lead, and showed bursts of bilateral frontal 2 cps slow activity, typical of deep midline supratentorial lesions.

The coma, pinpoint pupils, intact oculovestibular responses, and typical EEG all indicated a hypothalamic lesion. Radiographic contrast procedures failed to fill the posterior part of the third ventricle and aqueduct of Sylvius, and an arteriogram indicated a mass in the right thalamus.

He gradually declined into uninterrupted coma. Periodic breathing and intermittent spasms of decerebrate rigidity followed. He finally developed brainstem failure and died 3 weeks after admission. The general autopsy was unremarkable. The brain showed moderately dilated lateral ventricles. There was a yellow-gray tumor involving both thalamic regions, more on the left than on the right (Fig. 1B). The neoplasm invaded the floor of the third ventricle and the paraventricular region of the diencephalon from the posterior commissure dorsally to the mammillary bodies ventrally. The third ventricle was compressed and shifted to the right, and the rostral portion of the aqueduct appeared to be closed by adjacent tumor. There was no tumor in or caudal to the midbrain, but central hemorrhages down the brainstem had occurred terminally. Histologically, the tumor was a malignant lymphoma of the microglial type.

Chapter 3

Subtentorial Lesions
Causing Coma

PATHOLOGY AND PATHOLOGICAL PHYSIOLOGY

Two kinds of posterior fossa lesions cause coma: those located within the brainstem that *destroy* the paramedian midbrain-pontine reticular formation and those located outside the brainstem that *compress* its reticulum. Since the reticular formation and the lateral brainstem structures, respectively, have different blood supplies, a detailed knowledge of the vascular anatomy of the subtentorial compartment is essential for discrete diagnosis.

Figures 19 and 20 diagram the brainstem, illustrating the blood supply, the regions critical to consciousness, and the functional anatomy of the adjacent parts. The paramedian branches of the basilar artery supply the reticular formation, the oculomotor nuclei, the medial longitudinal fasciculus, and the pyramidal tracts. The lateral circumferential arteries, namely, the superior and anterior inferior cerebellar arteries, supply the important lateral structures mediating especially cerebellar and sensory functions, but they do not participate in the irrigation of structures dealing with consciousness.

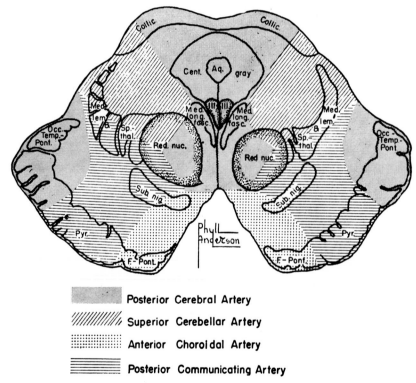

Posterior Cerebral Artery

Superior Cerebellar Artery

Anterior Choroidal Artery

Posterior Communicating Artery

Figure 19. Vascular distribution to the midbrain. From CEREBROVASCULAR DISEASE, by J. P. Murphy. Copyright © 1954, Year Book Medical Publishers, Inc. Used by permission of Year Book Medical Publishers.

120

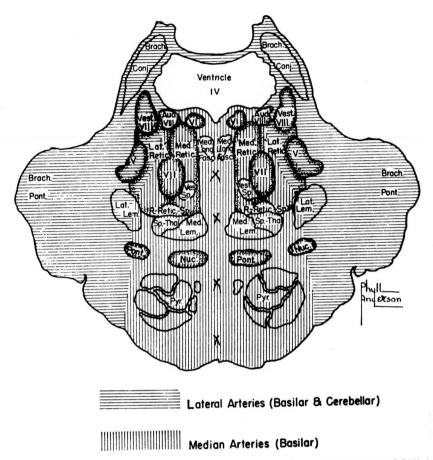

▬▬▬▬▬ **Lateral Arteries (Basilar & Cerebellar)**

||||||||||||||||||||| **Median Arteries (Basilar)**

Figure 20. Vascular distribution to the pons. From CEREBROVASCULAR DISEASE, by J. P. Murphy. Copyright © 1954, Year Book Medical Publishers, Inc. Used by permission of Year Book Medical Publishers.

Brainstem Destruction

Lesions within the brainstem can cause coma either by directly invading and destroying the brainstem central core or by impairing its blood supply to produce ischemia, necrosis, or hemorrhage. The most common pathological process that causes such primary destruction of the brainstem is cerebral vascular disease, but nutritional deficiencies (page 139), neoplasms, granulomas, and abscesses produce similar effects, which are individually discussed in the second half of this chapter. Head trauma also can damage the subtentorial reticulum,[332] but this usually presents no problem in diagnosis.

121

Brainstem Compression

Posterior fossa lesions lying outside the brainstem can cause coma in three possible ways: (1) by direct pressure upon the tegmentum, usually at the pontine level, (2) by upward herniation of the cerebellum and midbrain through the tentorial notch, compressing the mesencephalic tegmentum, (3) by downward herniation of the cerebellar tonsils through the foramen magnum, compressing the medulla.

DIRECT COMPRESSION.   The anatomical and physiological principles that underlie swelling, displacement, and compression of the brain were discussed in Chapter 2. With posterior fossa lesions, just as with supratentorial lesions, the rate at which these changes develop has an important bearing on the severity of symptoms.   Large or rapidly developing masses, such as cerebellar hemorrhage, are frequently associated with coma, presumably because there is insufficient time for other posterior fossa structures, such as the brain itself, the CSF, and the blood vessels, to readjust their size and compensate for the lesion.   By contrast, more slowly developing lesions sometimes reach an equal or greater size and produce extraordinary brainstem deformities without impairing consciousness.   Sooner or later, however, compression of the brainstem directly damages neural tissue and distorts the blood vessels to produce ischemia.   Whichever the initial step, necrosis of both neural and vascular elements is the ultimate effect, and the resulting coma is an ominous development.

UPWARD TRANSTENTORIAL HERNIATION.   When tissues in the posterior fossa selectively expand, the cerebellum and mesencephalon may herniate upward through the tentorial notch.   This compresses the dorsal aspect of the mesencephalon as well as adjacent blood vessels and induces changes in the midbrain and surrounding structures drained by the central cerebral veins.[20] Figure 21 illustrates Ecker's reconstruction of upward herniation of the midbrain through the tentorium.[148] The posterior third ventricle is distorted, and the potential vascular obstructions can be appreciated.   The spinal fluid flow can be blocked either by obstruction of the aqueduct, which prevents caudal exit of CSF from the lateral ventricles, or by obliteration of the pontine and ambient cisterns, which dams back the rostral flow of CSF over the surface of the brain from the posterior to the anterior fossa. Upward herniation also compresses and distorts the veins of Galen and Rosenthal, raising the supratentorial venous pressure, a process which partly counteracts and compensates for the upward herniation from below. Finally, the superior cerebellar arteries can be compressed against the tentorium from upward herniation, resulting in infarcts of the superior cerebellum.

Upward tentorial herniation occurs frequently with expanding lesions in the posterior fossa.   Vastine and Kinney[575] reported that the pineal body

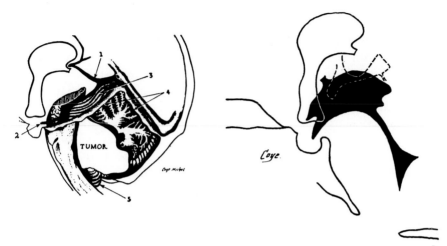

Figure 21. Upward herniation of the cerebellum **(3)** and midbrain through the tentorium **(4),** as diagramed by Ecker from necropsy, venograms, and ventriculograms. Figure on the left illustrates distortion and compression of the veins of Galen **(1)** and Rosenthal **(2)** with displacement of the posterior third ventricle rostrally. The cerebellar tonsils **(5)** are herniated into the foramen magnum. The solid black area in the figure on the right illustrates the normal position of the third and fourth ventricles. From Ecker, A.: Upward transtentorial herniation of the brainstem and cerebellum due to tumor of the posterior fossa. With special note on tumors of the acoustic nerve. J. Neurosurg. 5:51-61, 1948. Reprinted with permission of the Harvey Cushing Society, publisher of the Journal of Neurosurgery.

was displaced upward in one third of their 15 patients with subtentorial gliomas and in 22 per cent of their 28 patients with acoustic neurinomas. More "normally placed" pineal bodies in their patients with subtentorial tumors were nearer the upper than the lower margin of the normal range.

DOWNWARD HERNIATION INTO THE FORAMEN MAGNUM. The cerebellar tonsils may normally project as much as 2 cm. into the cervical canal,[248] and five out of six normal brains show grooving of the under surface of the cerebellum against the foramen magnum. In patients with foraminal impaction, the groove extends more deeply and ventrally to involve cerebellar tissue on either side of the medulla. If such patients survive long enough, the tonsils as well as the medulla and upper cervical spinal cord may become infarcted. This is an extreme situation, however, and the usual problem for the pathologist is that foraminal herniation with medullary compression so quickly produces fatal respiratory and circulatory arrest that morphological changes are equivocal. Physiologically the mechanism of coma in foraminal impaction is anoxia secondary to the respiratory and circulatory changes and not medullary compression per se.

123

CLINICAL SIGNS OF SUBTENTORIAL LESIONS

Destructive Lesions

Patients with destructive subtentorial lesions often lose consciousness immediately, and the ensuing coma is accompanied by distinctive patterns of respiratory, pupillary, oculovestibular, and motor signs that clearly indicate whether it is the tegmentum of the midbrain, the rostral pons, or the caudal pons that is most severely damaged. Since the brainstem reticulum lies so close to nuclei and pathways influencing the pupils, the eye movements and other major functions, it is characteristic of primary brainstem destructive lesions that they produce restricted and asymmetrical signs of focal neurological disease that often can be precisely localized anatomically by the clinical findings, with all the signs pointing to a single lesion that produces less than a full physiological brainstem transection. This restricted, discrete localization is unlike metabolic lesions causing coma, where the signs commonly indicate incomplete dysfunction at several different levels, and also is unlike the secondary brainstem dysfunction that follows supratentorial herniation, in which *all* function at any given brainstem level tends to be lost as the process descends from rostral to caudal along the neuraxis.

Certain combinations of signs stand out prominently in patients with subtentorial destructive lesions causing coma. At the *midbrain* level, centrally placed brainstem lesions interrupt the pathway for the pupillary light reflex and often damage the oculomotor nuclei as well. The resulting deep coma commonly is accompanied by pupils that are fixed at midposition or slightly wider, by a nuclear or infranuclear type of ophthalmoplegia, and by abnormal, long tract motor signs. These last mentioned result from involvement of the cerebral peduncles and commonly are bilateral, although asymmetrical. Destructive lesions of the *rostral pons* commonly spare the oculomotor nuclei but interrupt the medial longitudinal fasciculus and the adjacent ocular sympathetic pathways. One observes tiny pupils, internuclear ophthalmoplegia, and, in many instances, cranial nerve signs of trigeminal or facial weakness betraying pontine destruction.

Sometimes severe *lower pontine destruction* causes a functional transection with physiological effects that may be difficult to differentiate from metabolic coma. The pupils of such patients are miotic but may react minimally to light since midbrain parasympathetic oculomotor fibers are spared. Reflex lateral eye movements are absent since the pontine structures for lateral conjugate eye movements are destroyed. However, upward and downward ocular deviation occasionally is retained either spontaneously or in response to the oculocephalic maneuvers, and, if present, this dissociation between lateral and vertical movement clearly identifies pontine destruction. Ocular bobbing sometimes accompanies such acute destructive lesions and also indicates the diagnosis when present. The motor signs of

124

severe pontine destruction are not the same in every patient and include flac-cid quadriplegia, less often decerebrate rigidity or, occasionally, decerebrate responses in the arms with flexor responses in the legs. Respiration may show any of the patterns characteristic of low brainstem dysfunction de-scribed in Chapter 1, but cluster breathing, apneusis, gasping, and ataxic breathing are most common.

Compressive Lesions

With posterior fossa lesions the effects of direct brainstem compression can be difficult to separate clinically from the effects produced by upward or downward herniation of the brain out of the posterior fossa since all three processes accompany almost every sizable lesion. Abnormal lateral conjugate gaze, ocular bobbing, and other oculomotor signs frequently occur because pontine ocular pathways are compressed. Vomiting and cranial nerve abnormalities accompany many of these compressive lesions.

It is not certain whether or not posterior fossa lesions causing *upward transtentorial herniation* produce a consistent syndrome. As herniation occurs, it compresses the pretectal area, an effect that results in either conjugate downward deviation of the eyes or at least failure to elicit voluntary or reflex upward deviation of the eyes. Severe upward herniation also obstructs the vein of Galen, and this may be the mechanism of those rare instances of proptosis with acute posterior fossa hemorrhage.

The following patient illustrates the clinical picture of a combination of direct brainstem compression and upward transtentorial herniation due to an expanding cerebellar abscess.

Case 15. A 52-year-old alcoholic male became progressively obtunded in jail. By the time he reached the hospital, he was unable to give a history. His body temperature was 39.2° C., and he was diffusely rigid and hyperventilating at a rate of 34 per minute. At lumbar puncture the opening pressure of CSF was 230 mm. The CSF contained 4 mononuclear cells, and the protein content was later reported to be 242 mg. per 100 cc. Despite the ominous story, he was initially suspected of having delirium tremens and little was done. The next morning he was in coma and had decerebrate motor responses on the left side of his body and decorticate posturing on the right. He was mildly hyperp-neic with a rate of 28 per minute. His pupils measured 1.5 mm. and were *unreactive* to a bright light. Vertical doll's-eye movements were absent but the lateral responses were hyperactive. His extremities and neck were diffusely rigid and his plantar responses were extensor. Skull x-ray findings were unremarkable, and a right carotid arteriogram showed a sweeping anterior cerebral artery consistent with dilation of the lateral ventricles, as well as elevation of the basal vein consistent with upward transtentorial herniation. Air could not be introduced into the aqueduct or fourth ventricle by ventriculography, and air injected into the lumbar subarachnoid space stopped at the cervical region, a finding compatible with cerebellar tonsillar herniation. The posterior fossa was explored, and 10 cc. of pus was removed from the greatly swollen right cerebellar hemisphere. The patient recovered.

Comment: The combination of coma, hyperventilation, miotic fixed pupils (pontine compression), loss of upward gaze (pretectal compression), and brisk lateral oculocephalic responses was, in retrospect, diagnostic of a posterior fossa lesion with upward herniation. Before obtaining the ventriculogram, observers failed to heed these signs and believed that the patient had a metabolic or diencephalic lesion despite the hyperventilation, the nearly pinpoint, fixed pupils, and the dissociated oculovestibular responses, all of which spelled direct brainstem dysfunction.

Brainstem Lesions Not Causing Coma

Brainstem lesions lying outside the pontine-midbrain reticular formation sometimes destroy a remarkable amount of brain without causing coma. Patient 2, described in Chapter 1, who was awake despite widespread destruction of the medulla, illustrates this principle, as does the following patient who retained consciousness and responded appropriately despite almost total destruction of the basis pontis with sparing of the pontine reticular formation.

Case 16. A 44-year-old white man was healthy until approximately the middle of February when he had a 15-minute episode of vertigo and nausea. A physical examination the following day was normal. Seven days later, the patient again experienced vertigo, nausea, and vomiting, followed by weakness of all extremities and inability to talk. On admission to a hospital, the diagnosis of basilar artery thrombosis was made. He was transferred to our observation 1 month later. His blood pressure was 140/80 mm. Hg; his pulse rate was 100 per minute; his respirations were 20 per minute, deep and regular. He was well developed and well nourished. He was awake but unable to move his limbs or talk. When instructed to respond to questions by moving his eyes up and down to indicate yes or no, he could do so appropriately. He apparently recognized large images although detailed testing of visual acuity was not possible. There was no lateral motion of the eyes either on command or on passive head turning. Cold caloric irrigation on the left evoked no response; on the right it evoked tonic deviation of the eyes to the right, which lasted approximately 4 minutes. Nystagmus was not present in either direction. The corneal reflexes and facial sensation appeared to be present bilaterally. There was bilateral facial weakness. The brow had a normal contour but no voluntary motion. Hearing was intact bilaterally. There was no voluntary movement in structures innervated by cranial nerves IX to XII or in the extremities, which lay motionless and flaccid. Perception of noxious stimuli appeared to be preserved. The stretch reflexes were equally hyperactive bilaterally throughout the arms and legs, with bilateral extensor plantar responses.

Laboratory findings were unremarkable, including the EEG which contained symmetrical, well-formed parietal-occipital 8 per second alpha activity and was interpreted as being within normal limits. The course in hospital was unremarkable except for the development of some voluntary motion in the left ankle. The patient died 1 month later from pneumonia, having retained responsiveness to questions almost until death.

Autopsy revealed severe arteriosclerosis of the basilar artery with complete occlusion 1 cm. above its origin. The cerebral hemispheres were normal. There was a cystic infarct in the brainstem that destroyed most of the upper two thirds of the basis pontis and a small portion of the cerebal peduncles (Fig. 2A). The mesencephalic tegmentum was intact, and a small portion of the periventricular pontine tegmentum was also spared. At no point did the reticular formation appear to be completely interrupted in its course. The lower pons and medulla were not involved by the lesion.

Comment: Like M. Noirtier de Villefort in Dumas' *The Count of Monte Cristo,* this patient was awake but had lost all power to communicate except with his eyes—"a corpse with living eyes." Although both akinetic and mute, he did not suffer from the syndrome of akinetic mutism in which patients are unconscious and make no appropriate responses.[73, 108] Great care must be exercised in distinguishing "a mind . . . encumbered by a body over which it has lost the power of compelling obedience" from typical akinetic mutism, since the former usually results from a low or midpontine lesion, as with this patient, and the latter from much more extensive impairment of the arousal systems or the hemispheres (see page 23). The implications for humane patient care are profound. This constellation of alert wakefulness accompanied by mute tetraplegia of brainstem origin has been variously termed the "locked-in" syndrome, the ventral-pontine syndrome and the de-efferented state to distinguish it from akinetic mutism, which is properly a form of coma.

SPECIFIC SUBTENTORIAL LESIONS CAUSING COMA

Basilar Artery Occlusion with Midbrain-Pontine Infarction

Occlusion of the basilar artery either by thrombosis or embolism is a relatively common cause of coma, and several patients with this disorder are admitted every year to large clinical services. The occlusions are usually the result of atherosclerotic or hypertensive disease, rarer vascular diseases such as periarteritis and other collagen diseases tending to spare the basilar artery. Emboli to the basilar artery are unusual with valvular heart disease but do occur with arteriosclerosis. Kubik and Adams[320] reported that 7 of their 18 patients with basilar occlusion had an embolism, but did not identify the origin.

The usual age of patients in coma from brainstem infarction is over 50 years, but this is not an exclusive limit. One of our patients was only 34 years old. Characteristic transient symptoms and signs due to brief ischemia of the brainstem often precede coma by days or weeks. These transient attacks typically change from episode to episode but always reflect subtentorial central nervous system dysfunction and include headaches (mainly occipital), diplopia, vertigo, dysarthria, dysphagia, and bilateral or alternating motor or sensory symptoms. The attacks usually last for as short a period as 10 seconds or as long as several minutes. Seldom are they more prolonged, although recurrent transient attacks of otherwise unexplained akinetic coma lasting 20 to 30 minutes occurred in one of our patients who later died from pontine infarction due to total occlusion of the middle portion of the basilar artery. Except in patients who additionally have recurrent asystole or other severe cardiac arrhythmias, transient ischemic attacks due to vertebrobasilar artery insufficiency nearly always occur in the erect or sitting position.

Segmental thrombi can occlude the midportion of the basilar artery, producing only limited and temporary symptoms of brainstem dysfunction. However, such limited occlusions are rare, and most patients with basilar artery occlusion are much more seriously ill—about half are in coma from the onset of their disease, and most of the rest are either confused, obtunded, or delirious. The degree of impairment of consciousness presumably depends on how extensively the reticular formation is damaged. The coma usually begins abruptly or within a few hours of other clinical signs and is accompanied by other signs reflecting infarction of the midbrain or pons. Most patients have respiratory abnormalities that include periodic breathing, central hyperventilation, or various types of ataxic respiration. The pupils are almost always abnormal and may be small (pontine), midposition (midbrain), or dilated (third nerve outflow in midbrain). Most patients have divergent or skewed optical axes reflecting direct nuclear and internuclear damage. Other cranial nerve functions are often impaired. Signs of motor long-tract abnormalities are characteristically bilateral and include defects in swallowing as well as hemiplegia or quadriplegia and extensor plantar responses.

The differential diagnosis of acute brainstem infarction can usually be made from clinical clues alone. With brainstem infarction, the fact that signs of midbrain or pontine damage accompany the *onset* of coma immediately places the site of the lesion as subtentorial. The illness is maximal at onset or evolves rapidly and in a series of steps, as would be expected with ischemic vascular disease. Supratentorial ischemic vascular lesions, by contrast, are not likely to cause coma with such an abrupt onset and never begin with pupillary abnormalities or other signs of direct brainstem injury. Pontine and cerebellar hemorrhages, since they also destroy or depress the brainstem, sometimes resemble brainstem infarction in their manifestations. However, hemorrhages nearly always arise in hypertensive patients, nearly always cause occipital headache (which is unusual with infarction), and are accompanied by a bloody spinal fluid under increased pressure. Metabolic depression of the brainstem only rarely is mimicked by brainstem infarction; in the few cases in which this distinction is a problem it is usually because the history of onset is unavailable and the infarct has involved the low pons. Such infarcts can produce defects in the sympathetic control of the pupil as well as interruption of oculovestibular reflexes. The differentiation between pontine infarction and a metabolic lesion is made easier by recalling that among metabolic causes for coma only glutethimide produces deep coma with fixed pupils and that metabolic lesions rarely produce a sustained dissociation between the lateral and vertical oculovestibular responses.

Case 16 illustrated the symptoms of one type of basilar artery occlusion with sparing of much of the tegmentum. The following example illustrates the syndrome of acute infarction of the lower midbrain tegmentum due to basilar artery occlusion.

Case 17. A 79-year-old white woman was admitted in coma. She had been in good health, except for known hypertension, until 4 hours earlier when she suddenly vomited and became unconscious. Her blood pressure was 180/100 mm. Hg. She had sighing respirations, which shortly changed to a Cheyne-Stokes pattern. The pupils were 4 mm. in diameter and unreactive to light. The oculocephalic responses were absent, but cold caloric irrigation induced a bilateral, dysconjugate response with abduction of the eye only on the side being irrigated. She responded to noxious stimuli with decerebrate posturing and occasionally was wracked by spontaneous waves of decerebrate rigidity. On the way to the ward from the emergency room, she vomited bloody material. Her blood pressure subsequently was 120/80 mm. Hg, her pulse 80 per minute, and her respirations periodic at 11 per minute. The pineal gland was seen in the midline on a skull x-ray film. The CSF pressure on lumbar puncture was 140 mm.; the fluid was clear, without cells, contained 35 mg. per 100 cc. of protein. Two days later, the patient continued in coma with decerebrate responses to noxious stimulation; the pupils remained fixed in midposition, and there was no ocular response to cold caloric irrigation. Respirations were eupneic. The next day she died. The brain was examined post mortem. The basilar artery was occluded in its midportion by a recent thrombus 1 cm. in length. There was extensive infarction of the upper portion of the basis pontis and of medial pontine and midbrain tegmentum. The lower portion of the pons and the medulla were intact.

Comment: This woman suffered an acute brainstem infarction with unusually symmetrical neurological signs. It was at first thought that she might have had a cerebral hemorrhage with sudden acute transtentorial herniation producing a picture of acute midbrain transection. However, such rapid progression to a midbrain level (within 4 hours) almost never occurs in cerebral hemorrhage, probably because overwhelmingly severe hemorrhages are fatal within minutes. Patients with large cerebral hemorrhages rarely vomit initially, and their spinal fluid is almost never completely free of red cells. Finally, the neurological signs of midbrain damage in this patient remained nearly constant from onset, whereas transtentorial herniation would rapidly have produced further rostral-caudal deterioration.

Nonvascular Brainstem Destructive Lesions

Abscesses, granulomas, and both primary and secondary neoplasms may arise in the pontine and midbrain tegmentum and destroy or compress the reticular formation. Generally speaking, coma is a late or nonexistent development with these lesions, presumably because the primitive brainstem reticulum undergoes a considerable physiological adjustment to partial destruction and distortion if given time. For example, slowly proliferating neoplasms such as pontine gliomas in children may enlarge the brainstem to twice the usual size, disrupt motor pathways almost completely, and paralyze extraocular function without altering consciousness until their terminal stages. Even when the content of consciousness is impaired with slowly expanding brainstem lesions, the result is more frequently dementia, memory loss, and abnormal behavior than coma.[404, 424]

The differential diagnosis of posterior fossa infiltrative or destructive lesions depends heavily on indirect evidence. Abscesses produce acute or subacute meningitis plus focal brainstem signs, which continue despite the

129

adequate use of antibiotics. The diagnosis of brainstem abscess has rarely been suspected during life, but can be considered when fever, occipital-nuchal headache, cranial nerve signs, low-grade persistent meningitis, and stupor or coma develop in a patient with an extrameningeal source of infection.[590] In about one fourth of the cases reported in the literature the infection extended from the middle ear; the others stemmed from a more remote source.

The presence of brainstem granulomas or metastatic tumors is suggested by signs of a posterior fossa infiltrating lesion in patients with identifiable primary lesions elsewhere in the body. Usually the exact diagnosis must be made by x-ray contrast studies or posterior fossa surgical exploration.

Subtentorial Hemorrhage

POSTERIOR FOSSA SUBDURAL AND EXTRADURAL HEMATOMAS. In the posterior fossa, space-occupying lesions in the subdural and extradural space produce similar clinical disorders[90, 94, 311] whose recognition is important because proper treatment leads to a high incidence of full recovery. Underlying cerebellar hematomas accompany many of these lesions[90] but with no distinguishable differences in symptoms. A history of trauma precedes about three fourths of the cases.

These hematomas usually originate from veins rather than arteries, which may explain why most of the patients have a subacute or chronic illness. Direct occipital injury with skull fracture frequently precedes bleeding into either space, but extradural hematomas generally originate from tears in the sinuses or torcular, while subdural collections have more often been described in association with cerebellar lacerations. With severe head injury, both supratentorial and subtentorial extracerebral bleeding can combine.[469]

The history and findings are characteristic. In acute cases, occipital injury produces acute unconsciousness or a dazed state followed in most instances by a lucid interval during which occipital headache becomes progressively more severe. This is followed within a few hours by vomiting, vertigo, ataxia, stiff neck, drowsiness, restlessness and, finally, coma with bilateral corticospinal tract dysfunction plus signs of diffuse posterior fossa dysfunction and, eventually, respiratory failure. Skull x-ray examinations disclose an occipital fracture line in about three quarters of the patients, and vertebral arteriograms or ventriculograms are usually diagnostic. (Direct trephination is preferable to such contrast studies in acute cases with a strong clinical story since these illnesses when untreated can run their full course to severe brain damage or death in less than 12 to 15 hours.)

Subacute or chronic hematomas tell a similar tale but more slowly. Post-traumatic lucid intervals lasting as long as 4 months have been reported, followed by occipital headache, stiff neck, papilledema, ataxia, and dysarthria, plus other signs of cerebellar dysfunction, and finally, impaired consciousness. Occipital fracture lines are usually present. The CSF is noncharacteristic and lumbar puncture risky so that most hematomas are ultimately diagnosed by contrast studies, surgical exploration or postmortem examination. Surgical drainage, if initiated early, results in a cure.

PRIMARY PONTINE HEMORRHAGE. Hemorrhage into the pons arises from the paramedian arterioles, begins at the base of the tegmentum, and dissects in all directions in a relatively symmetrical fashion.[134] Rupture into the fourth ventricle occurs in most patients, but dissection into the medulla is rare. Although pontine hemorrhages nearly always produce coma, they are a comparatively uncommon cause, accounting for only 7 cases in our own series of 386 patients. Almost all primary pontine hemorrhages occur in hypertensive persons, few of whom, according to Dinsdale,[134] have prior symptoms of cerebral vascular disease. Among our own 7 patients, however, 3 had histories of previous hemiplegic strokes.

Coma due to pontine hemorrhage begins abruptly, usually during the hours when patients are awake and active and usually without prodromata.[134, 537] Only one of our patients had symptoms of sudden occipital headache, vomiting, speechlessness, and collapse before losing consciousness. Almost every patient has respiratory abnormalities of the brainstem type. Cheyne-Stokes breathing, apneustic or gasping breathing, and progressive slowing of respiration to apnea occur. Steegman[537] reported that 30 per cent of his patients developed progressive respiratory failure.

The pupils are nearly always abnormal and usually pinpoint. The light reaction is often lost immediately after the hemorrhage but ordinarily returns if the patient survives 24 hours or more. The ciliospinal response disappears. Large hemorrhages, extending to the midbrain, may cause asymmetrical or dilated pupils. About one third of the patients suffer from oculomotor abnormalities such as skewed or lateral ocular deviations or ocular bobbing,[167] and the oculocephalic responses disappear. Motor signs vary according to the extent of the hemorrhage. Some subjects become diffusely rigid and trembling and suffer repeated waves of decerebrate rigidity. More frequently, however, the patients are quadriplegic and flaccid with flexor responses at hip, knee, and great toe to plantar stimulation, a reflex combination characteristic of acute low brainstem damage when it accompanies acute coma. Nearly all patients with pontine hemorrhage who survive more than a few hours develop hyperthermia with body temperatures of 38.5 to 41° C.

The diagnosis of pontine hemorrhage is usually straightforward. Almost no other lesion, except occasionally cerebellar hemorrhage with secondary dissection into the brainstem, produces sudden coma with periodic or ataxic breathing, pinpoint pupils, absence of oculovestibular responses, quadriplegia, and bloody spinal fluid. Before lumbar puncture, a severe metabolic disease might be suspected, but in metabolic coma the pupils are rarely so small and, even if pinpoint, are not light fixed. Finally, the flexor spasms that accompany the flaccid quadriplegia of low brainstem injury do not occur in patients who have motor flaccidity from metabolic disease. The patient reported below had a clinical picture typical of pontine hemorrhage.

Case 18. A 75-year-old man had a "stroke" with a left hemiparesis from which he subsequently recovered. Seven months later he collapsed in coma. The blood pressure was 170/90 mm. Hg; the pulse was 84 per minute, respirations were Cheyne-Stokes in character and 16 per minute. The pupils were pinpoint but reacted equally to light. Oculovestibular responses were absent. The patient was flaccid with symmetrical stretch reflexes of normal amplitude and bilateral flexor responses in the lower extremities to plantar stimulation. The spinal fluid was bloody with an opening pressure of 200 mm. and a protein content greater than 100 mg. per 100 cc. There was no shift of the well-calcified pineal gland in the x-ray films. The next morning he was still in deep coma, but now was diffusely flaccid except for flexor responses to noxious stimuli in the legs. He had slow, shallow, eupneic respiration, small, equally reactive pupils, and eyes in neutral position. Shortly thereafter, breathing became irregular and he died. A 3-cm. primary hemorrhage destroying the central pons and its tegmentum was found at autopsy.

CEREBELLAR HEMORRHAGE. Cerebellar hemorrhages account for about 10 per cent of parenchymal intracranial hemorrhages and frequently cause coma by compressing or infiltrating the brainstem. McKissock, Richardson, and Walsh[368] as well as Logue and Monckton[339] indicate that if the diagnosis can be made promptly, many such patients can be treated successfully by evacuating the clot or removing an associated angioma. Approximately three quarters of patients with cerebellar hemorrhage have hypertension; most of the remaining have angiomas of the posterior fossa. Among our own 23 patients, 5 had posterior fossa arteriovenous vascular malformations, 1 had thrombocytopenic purpura, and the remainder, who ranged between 39 and 83 years of age, had hypertensive vascular disease. Hemorrhages in hypertensive patients arise in the neighborhood of the dentate nuclei; those coming from angiomas tend to lie more superficially. Both types usually rupture into the subarachnoid space or fourth ventricle and appear to produce coma chiefly by compressing the brainstem.

There are three relatively distinct syndromes of cerebellar apoplexy, and consciousness tends to be impaired or lost sooner or later in all. About one fifth of the patients suddenly lose consciousness and develop respiratory irregularity, pinpoint pupils, and absence of the oculovestibular responses— a picture indistinguishable from primary pontine hemorrhage. A larger percentage develop occipital headache, vomiting, and progressive neurological impairment, including confusion, nausea, vertigo, tonic deviation of the eyes, and weakness or paralysis of the legs. Consciousness is more gradually lost and coma may develop only after many hours or days of progression. Dinsdale[134] describes wakeful mutism in several such patients. This second group also tends to have respiratory slowing or irregularity and most of the patients have pupillary constriction. A third group of patients with cerebellar hemorrhage have occipital headache and drowsiness plus the slow or episodic development of signs of cerebellar or oculomotor dysfunction. In them, as well as the above patients, severe impairment of consciousness is sometimes delayed for several days. Presumably some of these individuals recover spontaneously, but evidence of this is hard to find in the literature, and we have no examples of proved cerebellar hemorrhage with spontaneous recovery.

The diagnosis of cerebellar hemorrhage is suggested by one of the above syndromes plus a bloody spinal fluid. Clinical signs and symptoms alone are usually insufficient to distinguish immediately a slowly expanding cerebellar hemorrhage from other causes of posterior fossa vascular disease or even an angiomatous neoplasm, so that cerebral angiograms and, sometimes, ventriculograms must be obtained in patients strongly suspected of having such lesions. In patients already in coma, these measures are not urgent since treatment offers very little hope once patients have lost consciousness.

At The New York Hospital we have treated 12 men and women in whom an acute or subacute cerebellar hemorrhage was found at operation or autopsy. The ages ranged from 32 to 75 years. Seven patients were known previously to be hypertensive, and two were receiving anticoagulant therapy. Severe headache, nausea, and vomiting were initial symptoms common to all patients. Vertigo and unsteadiness of gait were frequent. Of ten patients with an acute form of cerebellar hemorrhage, only two showed pronounced alterations of consciousness when first examined. All of the remaining eight rapidly or gradually progressed to stupor or coma within the ensuing 18 hours. The frequency of clinical signs on initial examination appears in Table 6. None of the three unoperated patients survived beyond 48 hours from the onset of their symptoms. Of nine patients undergoing surgery, six survived and three, including the two patients with a subacute form of cerebellar hemorrhage, are now without significant disability. Of the remainder, one patient has mild and two moderate residual cerebellar ataxia, but all are mentally unimpaired and largely self-sufficient.

The following histories compare the clinical courses of two patients, one with a methodically evolving (Case 19) and the other with a much more explosive (Case 20) cerebellar hemorrhage.

Case 19. A 64-year-old woman had a 15-year history of hypertension medically well controlled with blood pressure in the region of 160/95 mm. Hg. At 7:30 in the evening, while cooking dinner, she experienced a sudden onset of vertigo associated with nausea and vomiting. She sat down and did not have occasion to walk thereafter. She also developed a severe occipital headache, but this was far overshadowed by the vertigo in terms of subjective distress. A physician examined her at 9:00 P.M. and noted that her head and eyes were deviated to the right. When she arrived at The New York Hospital 1½ hours later she was lethargic, anxious to sleep, experiencing vertigo, and vomiting in a nonprojectile fashion. Her blood pressure was 230/130 mm. Hg. Her pupils were 4 mm.

133

Table 6. Neurological signs in 12 patients with cerebellar hemorrhage

1. Hypertension		10/12
2. Disturbance in Respiration		
	Cheyne-Stokes	5/12
	Ataxic	3/12
3. Pupils		
	Small (< 5 mm.), equal, reactive	10/12
	Smaller on ipsilateral side, reactive	2/12
4. Nystagmus		
	Horizontal, to ipsilateral side	6/12
	Vertical	2/12
5. Ocular Bobbing		1/12
6. Conjugate Gaze Deficit		
	Ipsilateral	6/12
	Vertical	2/12
7. Skew Deviation		3/12
8. Contralateral Conjugate Ocular Deviation		6/12
9. Oculovestibular Response		
	Abnormal	2/5
	Absent	3/5
10. Cranial Nerve Signs		
	VI	
	bilateral	2/12
	unilateral	1/12
	VII, unilateral	3/12
	X, unilateral	1/12
	XI, unilateral	1/12
	XII, unilateral	2/12
11. Dysarthria		8/12
12. Dysmetria, Upper Extremity		
	Ipsilateral	6/12
	Bilateral	2/12
13. Unilateral Extremity Weakness, Mild		
	Contralateral	3/12
	Ipsilateral	2/12
14. Extensor Plantar Response		
	Bilateral	7/12
	Unilateral	1/12

in diameter and reactive, but her head and eyes deviated to the right and she did not follow commands to move them from that position. She had decreased, rapid, alternating movements in the left upper and lower extremities along with mild dysmetria and striking hypotonia in the left arm. A left extensor plantar response was noted. Ice water (50 cc.) irrigated against the left tympanum failed to bring the eyes beyond the midline. Forty-five minutes later the patient had become more lethargic and had developed bilateral extensor plantar responses. A lumbar puncture opening pressure was 345 mm. with the patient in the lateral recumbent position, and the fluid contained 3800 red cells in the third tube. The protein was 150 mg. per 100 cc. At midnight the patient had a posterior fossa exploration, and a 3- to 4-cm. fresh hematoma was evacuated from the left cerebellar hemisphere. The next day she was greatly improved, with normal extraocular movements and near-complete resolution of cerebellar and corticospinal tract dysfunction. She recovered gradually and by 2 months later had barely detectable cerebellar abnormalities on the left side. Postoperatively the blood pressure returned to the pre-illness level and was easily controlled medically.

Comment: The sudden onset of vertigo and occipital headache associated with conjugate ocular deviation away from the side of cerebellar signs strongly suggested a posterior fossa lesion. Had the hemorrhage, which was proved by lumbar puncture, been in the brainstem, consciousness would surely have been lost since the neurological signs indicated a pontine defect and not a medullary one. The steady and comparatively rapid progression led her physicians to act promptly and directly, without wasting valuable time on superfluous x-ray contrast studies. In restrospect, even the lumbar puncture probably needlessly delayed things.

Case 20. A 22-year-old woman had a spontaneous subarachnoid hemorrhage at the age of 9 years with loss of consciousness, difficult breathing, and proptosis of the left eye. Carotid arteriograms were unremarkable; posterior fossa arteriograms were not obtained. In the interim she had been well and had married. At 7 A.M. on the day of admission, she had a sudden occipital headache. She went to her mother's house approximately 20 minutes later and soon began to vomit. The headache became generalized and more severe, and she lost consciousness. She was admitted to hospital at 8:15 A.M. in deep coma. The blood pressure was 180/110 mm. Hg; the pulse was 60 per minute. Respiration was ataxic. The pupils were 1.5 mm. in diameter and fixed

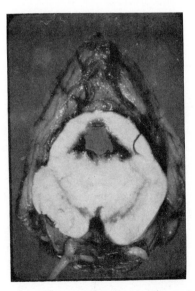

Figure 22. Distention of midbrain aqueduct with periaqueductal necrosis in a patient in coma from cerebellar hemorrhage with rupture into the fourth ventricle (Case 20).

to light stimulation. The oculocephalic reflexes were absent. The arms and legs were flaccid, and stretch reflexes were just perceptible and symmetrical. Plantar responses were flexor. She occasionally had a withdrawal movement of the left side of her body but not of the right. Twenty minutes later, her blood pressure dropped to 110/70 mm. Hg, and respirations became more ataxic. After 2 hours, hyperactive stretch reflexes were elicited, more on the right than on the left. On lumbar puncture, the CSF had a pressure of 300 mm. with pink fluid having a hematocrit of 2.5 per cent. Intermittent positive pressure breathing with oxygen therapy was initiated. Ten hours later, she developed intermittent decerebrate spasms. She died that next morning without further change.

Autopsy disclosed a tangled mass of tortuous arteries and veins almost replacing the inferior and medial portion of the left cerebellar hemisphere. The malformation was supplied mainly by the posterior inferior cerebellar artery, and several large venous branches drained directly into the left transverse sinus. The entire structure was densely adherent to the adjacent dura, which prevented extensive subarachnoid bleeding, but a 3-cm. hemorrhage had infiltrated the cerebellum, ruptured into the fourth ventricle, and distended the aqueduct. The cerebellum was herniated upward through the tentorium, and the periaqueductal gray matter of the midbrain was raggedly necrotic, presumably from pressure from the hemorrhage (Fig. 22). The lower pons and medulla were compressed, but contained no gross abnormalities, and the interpretation of microscopic changes was made equivocal by the antemortem use of the ventilator.

Comment: The occipital headache and pinpoint pupils, flaccidity, external ophthalmoplegia, and respiratory failure are what one would expect with posterior fossa bleeding and medullary compression. Coma was undoubtedly related to this and the periaqueductal ischemic necrosis. The late development of decerebrate rigidity may have been the clinical result of upward herniation compressing the more rostral brainstem, but with such severe other changes this is a tenuous conclusion. Of interest was the history of proptosis with the first subarachnoid hemorrhage, suggesting that even at that time partial obstruction of the left transverse and petrosal sinuses by hemorrhage may have dammed back blood in the ipsilateral cavernous sinus.

Acute hemorrhagic cerebellar infarction. This is a recently recognized clinical entity[327, 603] that closely resembles cerebellar hemorrhage in its evolution and outcome but that possesses a few distinctive features. Most, but not all, of the patients have had hypertension, and the great majority have been men ranging between 34 and 69 years of age. Their ages have reached considerably less than most patients with vertebro-basilar ischemic infarction, which may mean that they have small underlying angiomas or other predisposing lesions not yet discovered at operation or autopsy.

The onset is with progressive occipital headache lasting as long as 2 months, eventually coupled with "dizziness," cerebellar dysfunction, pupillary changes, lethargy, somnolence and eventually bilateral corticospinal tract signs. X-ray examinations disclose obstructive hydrocephalus and sometimes an avascular lateral cerebellar mass. The CSF pressure is elevated, and the fluid often microscopically bloody. Operation or postmortem examination uncovers severe cerebellar swelling due to hemorrhagic infarction with ventricular obstruction and brainstem compression. Survival follows promptly timed surgery, but many patients have had fairly severe residual neurological deficits. The following story is typical:

Case 21. A 32-year-old athletically inclined woman was in good health except for labile hypertension until 5 days prior to a New York Hospital admission when she noted the onset of vertex headache. She attributed this to a fall the day before, which occurred while she was attempting a headstand. Her headache was dull, aching, not lateralized, nonthrobbing, and made worse by any movement of the head. She was otherwise well and continued to work but sought medical help because of persistent headache. Her neurological examination was entirely normal, and a lumbar puncture was cell free and the fluid under normal pressure. Over the next 3 days she remained at home complaining of increasingly more severe headache and some dizziness. She was admitted for further evaluation.

The general physical and neurological examinations were normal except for pain on palpation over the midcervical vertebrae and slight restriction of neck flexion. On lumbar punctures performed during the first 2 days of hospitalization, there were 300 to 800 red blood cells, with protein concentrations of 42 and 111 mg. per 100 ml. Her headache continued without specific lateralizing features and required narcotic analgesics for relief. On the morning of the third hospital day the patient developed horizontal nystagmus to the left on left lateral gaze and a slight conjugate gaze palsy to the left. The left pupil was 1 mm. smaller than the right and there was mild left ptosis. Rapid movements in the left upper extremity were dysmetric. There was mild flattening of the left lower face without weakness and some depression of gag reflex on the left. A left vertebral and a right brachial arteriogram revealed narrowing of the extracranial portions of the left vertebral artery together with signs of a cerebellar mass within the left hemisphere. The posterior inferior cerebellar arteries were angulated forward and depressed, and the superior cerebellar arteries were stretched upward. The right lateral ventricle was minimally enlarged. Twelve hours later she developed a left lateral rectus muscle palsy and the posterior fossa was explored. At operation, the lateral inferior portion of the left cerebellar hemisphere was soft and mushy and the left tonsil of the cerebellum was widened, discolored, and extended well below the margin of the foramen magnum. The abnormal tissue was resected and had the gross and microscopic consistency of a hemorrhagic infarction. She made a gradual recovery.

BRAINSTEM ANGIOMAS. Arteriovenous malformations and hemangiomas can occur at any level of the brainstem.[557] These lesions, when small, are sometimes asymptomatic until they bleed; the larger ones may induce progressive cranial nerve changes and motor loss, but in both instances coma occurs only with rupture, producing the characteristic picture of brainstem hemorrhage.[339] Those that directly communicate with a lateral sinus sometimes produce homolateral proptosis at the time of rupture: Case 20 is an example.

VERTEBRO-BASILAR ARTERY ANEURYSM. Increased attention is being focused on ruptured aneurysms of the vertebral and basilar arteries as causes of coma since recent experience indicates that some of them can be treated surgically without paying too high a price in associated neurological damage.[133, 264, 338] Unruptured aneurysms of the basilar and vertebral arteries sometimes grow to a size of several centimeters and act like posterior fossa extramedullary tumors.[145, 227, 433] They do not cause coma, however, unless they rupture.

When a vertebro-basilar aneurysm ruptures, the event is characteristically sudden and frequently is marked by the complaint of suddenly weak legs, collapse, or coma. Most patients also have sudden occipital headache, but in contrast with anterior fossa aneurysms in which the story of coma, if present, is usually clear cut, it sometimes is difficult to be certain whether a patient with a ruptured posterior fossa aneurysm had briefly lost consciousness or merely collapsed because of paralysis of the lower extremities. Ruptured vertebro-basilar aneurysms are often reported as presenting few clinical signs that clearly localize the source of the subarachnoid bleeding to the posterior fossa. In Logue's 12 patients,[338] 4 had unilateral sixth nerve weakness (which can occur with any subarachnoid hemorrhage), 1 had bilateral sixth nerve weakness, and only 2 had other cranial abnormalities to signify a posterior fossa localization. Duvoisin and Yahr[145] say that only about half of their patients with ruptured posterior fossa aneurysms had signs that suggested the origin of their bleeding. Jamieson[264] reported 19 cases with even fewer localizing signs: 5 patients suffered third nerve weakness, and 2 had sixth nerve palsies.

Table 7. Localizing signs in 6 cases of ruptured vertebro-basilar aneurysms

Occipital headache	5
Skew deviation of the eyes	3
Third nerve paralysis	2
Cerebellar signs	3
Acute paraplegia before loss of consciousness	2

Our own experience differs somewhat from the above. We have had 8 patients with ruptured vertebro-basilar aneurysms found at arteriography or autopsy, and 6 had respiratory, pupillary, or oculomotor signs indicating a primary fossa lesion (Table 7). Despite these clinical hints, however, posterior fossa angiography ultimately must be resorted to in order to diagnose vertebro-basilar aneurysms and should be employed without hesitation whenever acute subarachnoid hemorrhage is accompanied by signs of primary brainstem dysfunction or is unexplained by the findings of carotid angiography.

Nonvascular Lesions Compressing the Brainstem

These are rare causes of coma. Cerebellar abscesses may cause coma if they suddenly rupture into the fourth ventricle and compress the brainstem, but most abscesses are clinically evident long before this. Cerebellar neoplasms may produce drowsiness and dementia if they cause obstructive hydrocephalus, but they rarely cause coma except as a terminal event when foraminal impaction produces respiratory arrest, neurogenic hypotension, and asphyxia. Extramedullary neoplasms in the posterior fossa rarely cause coma as an early sign, even if they distort, compress, and displace the brainstem.

Demyelinating Lesions

The plaques of *multiple sclerosis* frequently involve the brainstem, and in this region, where areas of gray and bundles of white matter are closely juxtaposed, the acute lesions frequently produce drowsiness or even stupor. The diagnosis presents no difficulty when a new exacerbation of a chronic problem produces acute signs of cranial nerve, internuclear, or vestibular dysfunction coupled with reduced alertness. However, when the first attack of demyelination involves the brainstem, multiple sclerosis cannot with any certainty be differentiated from other causes of focal encephalitis or demyelination of this region[291] except at autopsy or by finding serological evidence of one of the specific viral diseases.

Central pontine myelinolysis is an uncommon disorder in which the myelin sheaths in the central basis pontis are destroyed in a single confluent and symmetrical lesion.[5] The lesions vary from a few millimeters in size to ones large enough to spare only a rim of peripheral myelin, and these latter involve the ventral part of the tegmentum as well. Children as well as adults are affected.[72] The cause is unknown, but presumably relates closely to nutritional insufficiency as the great majority of patients have chronic alcoholism or some other severely debilitating illness. Small demyelinations cause no symptoms. The larger lesions characteristically produce ocular and pupillary paralyses, dysarthria or mutism, quadriparesis, and incontinence. About a quarter of the patients have become drowsy, stuporous or unresponsive as their illness progressed.[364] The diagnosis would be suspected in a chronic alcoholic or patient with severe nutritional deficit who develops cranial nerve weaknesses, quadriplegia, and reduced consciousness despite receiving thiamine and other vitamins. Confirmation can come only at autopsy.

Chapter 4

Metabolic Brain Diseases
Causing Coma

This final category of comatose states is caused by diffuse failure of neuronal metabolism (Table 8).

Table 8. Metabolic causes of stupor and coma

I. Stupor or Coma Arising from Intrinsic Diseases of the Neurons or Neuroglial Cells (Primary Metabolic Encephalopathy)

    A. Gray Matter Diseases:

        Jakob-Creutzfeldt disease
        Pick's disease[405]
        Alzheimer's disease and senile dementia[406, 546]
        Huntington's chorea[49]
        Progressive myoclonic epilepsy[436]
        Lipid storage diseases[413, 483]

    B. White Matter Diseases:

        Schilder's disease
        Marchiafava-Bignami disease
        The leukodystrophies[114, 235]

II. Stupor or Coma Arising from Diseases Extrinsic to Neurons and Glia (Secondary Metabolic Encephalopathy)

    A. Deprivation of Oxygen, Substrate, or Metabolic Cofactors

        1. Hypoxia (interference with oxygen supply to the entire brain—cerebral blood flow (CBF) normal)

            a. Decreased oxygen tension and content of blood
                Pulmonary disease
                Alveolar hypoventilation
                Decreased atmospheric oxygen tension

            b. Decreased oxygen content of blood—normal tension
                Anemia
                Carbon monoxide poisoning
                Methemoglobinemia

        2. Ischemia (diffuse or widespread multifocal interference with blood supply to brain)

            a. Decreased CBF resulting from decreased cardiac output
                Stokes-Adams; cardiac arrest; cardiac arrhythmias
                Myocardial infarction
                Congestive heart failure
                Aortic stenosis
                Pulmonary infarction

            b. Decreased CBF resulting from decreased peripheral resistance in systemic circulation
                Syncope; orthostatic, vasovagal
                Carotid sinus hypersensitivity
                Low blood volume

            c. Decreased CBF due to generalized or multifocal increased vascular resistance
                Hypertensive encephalopathy
                Hyperventilation syndrome
                Hyperviscosity (polycythemia, cryoglobulinemia or macroglobulinemia, sickle cell anemia)

            d. Decreased CBF due to widespread small vessel occlusions
                Disseminated intravascular coagulation
                Systemic lupus erythematosus
                Subacute bacterial endocarditis
                Fat embolism
                Cerebral malaria
                Cardiopulmonary bypass

Table 8 (continued)

3. Hypoglycemia
   Resulting from exogenous insulin
   Spontaneous (endogenous insulin, liver disease, etc.)

4. Cofactor deficiency
   Thiamine (Wernicke's encephalopathy)
   Niacin
   Pyridoxine
   Cyanocobalamin

B. Diseases of Organs Other Than Brain
   1. Diseases of nonendocrine organs
      Liver (hepatic coma)
      Kidney (uremic coma)
      Lung (CO_2 narcosis)

   2. Hyperfunction and/or hypofunction of endocrine organs
      Pituitary[395]
      Thyroid (myxedema-thyrotoxicosis)
      Parathyroid (hypoparathyroidism and hyperparathyroidism)
      Adrenal (Addison's disease, Cushing's disease, pheochromocytoma)
      Pancreas (diabetes, hypoglycemia)

   3. Other systemic diseases:
      Cancer (remote effects)
      Porphyria[151, 567]

C. Exogenous Poisons
   1. Sedative drugs
      Barbiturates
      Nonbarbiturate hypnotics
      Tranquilizers
      Bromides
      Ethanol
      Anticholinergics
      Opiates

   2. Acid poisons or poisons with acidic breakdown products
      Paraldehyde
      Methyl alcohol
      Ethylene glycol
      Ammonium chloride

   3. Enzyme inhibitors
      Heavy metals[16, 115]
      Organic phosphates
      Cyanide[104]
      Salicylates

D. Abnormalities of Ionic or Acid-Base Environment of CNS
   1. Water and sodium (hypernatremia and hyponatremia)
   2. Acidosis (metabolic and respiratory)
   3. Alkalosis (metabolic and respiratory)
   4. Potassium (hyperkalemia and hypokalemia)
   5. Magnesium (hypermagnesemia and hypomagnesemia)[171]
   6. Calcium (hypercalcemia and hypocalcemia)

E. Diseases Producing Toxins or Enzyme Inhibition in CNS
   Meningitis
   Encephalitis
   Subarachnoid hemorrhage

F. Disordered Temperature Regulation
   Hypothermia
   Heat stroke

143

Primary metabolic encephalopathy results from intrinsic disorders of neuronal or glial cell metabolism. The group encompasses the degenerative cerebral diseases that culminate in coma and, in their early stages, often produce the symptoms of dementia, organic psychosis, or "chronic brain syndrome." These disorders usually develop insidiously and are mostly irreversible. A typical example is Alzheimer's disease.

Secondary metabolic encephalopathy results when extracerebral diseases interfere with brain metabolism, either by causing nutritional deficiencies or by producing electrolyte imbalances or intoxication. Secondary metabolic encephalopathy is the chief cause of metabolic coma, and this chapter is devoted largely to a description of it. Examples range from drug poisoning to uremia, and the early symptoms include what have been called delirium, toxic psychosis, and acute confusional states. These illnesses usually develop acutely or subacutely and, unlike the primary metabolic encephalopathies, are often reversible if the systemic disorder is treated.

ASPECTS OF CEREBRAL METABOLISM PERTINENT TO COMA

Cerebral oxidative metabolism supplies the energy for three major brain functions: (1) The maintenance across neuronal membranes of electrical potentials that frequently discharge and ultimately must be recharged by transporting sodium out of and potassium into cells. (2) The synthesis of important, active compounds such as acetylcholine and other transmitter substances. (3) The replacement of catabolized enzymes and structural cellular elements. To meet these needs, the brain rapidly and constantly synthesizes high energy phosphate compounds such as ATP. If the extrinsic supply of substrate for oxidative metabolism fails, normal neuronal function fails also. Then, deprived of extrinsic energy sources, the brain proceeds to catabolize itself to maintain activity, and in so doing it becomes irreparably damaged. As Haldane put it, anoxia not only causes "the mere stoppage of a machine, it is also the total ruin of the supposed machinery." [225]

Most of the elements that the brain requires either exist abundantly within it or can be synthesized there from glucose. Others such as vitamins must be brought from outside in small and inconstant quantities. Glucose and oxygen, however, must be supplied constantly and in large amounts.

Glucose Metabolism

Glucose is the brain's only substrate under physiological conditions. During starvation and absence of glucose ingestion, however, gluconeogenesis by the liver is insufficient to meet cerebral glucose demands.[421] Under these circumstances the brain utilizes β-hydroxybutyrate and other ketones as substrates. The mechanism depends on the induction of the affected enzymes in brain tissue by fasting.[525] The usual exclusive dependence of the brain on glucose is not because neural tissue cannot metabolize other substances, since slices of cerebral cortex utilize a variety of substrates,[152] but rather is because the blood-brain barrier generally prevents other circulating substrates from entering the brain in sufficient quantity to maintain normal metabolic rates.

Glucose crosses the blood-brain barrier by a non-energy-requiring transport system called facilitated transport.[170] Insulin does not appear to affect either cerebral glucose uptake or metabolism in any important way,[152] although Rafaelsen[460] reports that large amounts of insulin increase the in vitro glucose metabolism of cortex slices and spinal cord fragments. However, others have interpreted these results as possibly due to contamination of neural tissue by insulin-sensitive meninges.[152]

Each 100 gm. of brain in a normal human takes up about 5.5 mg. of glucose per minute, and the brain's consumption of glucose in the basal state is almost as much as the total that the liver produces.[191] All but about 15 per cent of this uptake is accounted for by combustion with O_2

$$\text{Glucose} + 6 \text{ Oxygen} \longrightarrow 6 \text{ Carbon dioxide} + 6 \text{ Water} + 690{,}000 \text{ calories}$$
$$\downarrow$$
$$32 \text{ ATP}$$

$$\text{Glucose} \xrightarrow{\text{No oxygen}} 2 \text{ Pyruvic acid} \longrightarrow 2 \text{ Lactic acid} + 54{,}000 \text{ calories}$$
$$\downarrow$$
$$2 \text{ ATP}$$

Figure 23.

to form CO_2, H_2O, and energy as in the formula in Figure 23. Whether the remaining glucose is partially oxidized to lactic acid as in formula 2 is disputed: some studies reveal a consistent but small lactate output by brain[482] and others none.[489] In any event, the fact that glucose fully accounts for the oxidative metabolism of brain should not be taken to imply that other metabolic pathways are not operative as well. Only about 35 per cent of the glucose entering the brain is rapidly metabolized to CO_2,[202] the rest is incorporated into cerebral amino acids, proteins, and lipids. It appears that while there is no net use of substrate other than glucose in vivo, other substrates are nevertheless being constantly catabolized from brain stores and these must be replenished by synthesis from glucose.

The brain contains about 2 gm. of glucose in reserve, both as such and as glycogen.[565] Subjects in deep insulin coma use these reserves and consequently survive about 90 minutes before developing irreversible cerebral damage by autodigesting structural proteins or lipids. Long before 90 minutes have elapsed, however, severely hypoglycemic patients become deeply unconscious, although they usually retain primitive vegetative neural functions such as those that regulate the blood pressure and breathing. The implication is that some neural structures are more sensitive to hypoglycemia than others. This differential susceptibility is borne out by anatomical studies, and the brains of patients dying of hypoglycemia contain more

145

marked abnormalities in neurons of the hippocampus and cerebral cortex than elsewhere.[472]

Alteration in consciousness is an early sign of hypoglycemia as well as of most other acute or subacute metabolic encephalopathies. Since the clinical manifestations and pathological physiology of hypoglycemic coma have been particularly well studied, they serve as an illustrative model for metabolic coma.

When alterations in consciousness occur in hypoglycemia, which neural structures are involved? The discussion presented in Chapter 1 provides two choices: either the cortex must be diffusely impaired or the brainstem-activating structures must be functionally affected (or both). Experimental work supports both choices. Himwich[239] took the first view and conceived of hypoglycemia and anoxia as damaging the brain in progressively descending levels; at first dysfunction of cortical neurons occurred, then subcorticodiencephalic, mesencephalic, premyelencephalic, and myelencephalic areas became involved later, in that order. Both morphological and physiological evidence can be mustered to support this view. Studies of the pathology of man[472] and animals[241] dying from hypoglycemia demonstrate the earliest and most severe damage in neurons of the cerebral cortex; the neurons of the brainstem and basal ganglia are less vulnerable. In physiological studies, Hoagland and his colleagues[241] found grossly abnormal cortical EEG's in hypoglycemic animals at a time when direct recordings from anterior and posterior hypothalamic areas were normal.

Arduini and Arduini[15] took the second view and postulated a subcortical cause for metabolic coma since their experiments indicated selective reticular depression by hypoglycemia. Using auditory stimuli, the Arduinis recorded responses both from the cerebral cortex and the brainstem reticular formation. When hypoglycemia was induced, the response to sound was diminished or absent in the reticular formation but remained unchanged in the auditory cortex. Anoxia yielded similar results with responses in the auditory cortex persisting long after the reticular response disappeared. These authors and others made similar observations of the predilective susceptibility of the reticular formation to cyanide,[15] anesthestic drugs,[15, 187] and concussion.[176]

In contrast to the orderly conclusions derived from experimental data, clinical evidence suggests that several different levels of the neuraxis can undergo the first dysfunction in hypoglycemia, with the locus sometimes varying capriciously from attack to attack. Some patients first suffer loss of consciousness and have bilaterally synchronous slow waves in their EEG, suggesting an initial reticular involvement. Others first exhibit restricted signs of cerebral motor or sensory dysfunction unaccompanied by either EEG abnormalities or impaired consciousness. Sometimes each subsequent attack irreversibly damages more cortical neurons, so that there is a high incidence of permanent dementia in patients who survive repeated hypoglycemia. These inconsistencies among different patients illustrate how in the clinical situation regional cerebral factors such as blood flow and energy requirements vary from moment to moment to predispose first one part of the brain and then another to metabolic insult.

Oxygen Metabolism

A constant supply of oxygen is vital for cerebral energy metabolism. Formulas 1 and 2 (Fig. 23) demonstrate that without oxygen it is still possible to metabolize glucose to lactic acid and supply some energy as ATP. But this is only a fraction of the energy that glucose supplies when it is fully metabolized oxidatively, and even the most rapid acceleration of anaerobic glycolysis cannot sustain the adult brain for more than a few seconds. (The energy requirements of the neonatal brain are different, as is demonstrated by newborn rats who can survive 50 minutes of total anoxia by using anaerobic glycolysis for energy.[158] Adult rats, like man, succumb in minutes.) Unlike glucose, no reserves of oxygen are maintained in the brain (one estimate is a 10-second supply) so that metabolic failure in anoxia occurs almost immediately. The normal brain consumes about 3.3 cc. of oxygen per 100 gm. of brain per minute. This figure, called the cerebral metabolic rate for oxygen ($CMRO_2$), is remarkably constant in normal man, both awake[299] and asleep,[357] and represents 15 to 20 per cent of the total body resting O_2 consumption even though the brain equals only about 2 per cent of body weight. The $CMRO_2$ is not increased by mental activity or fever although it sometimes rises slightly following administration of epinephrine[302] and increases greatly during seizures.[102] With impaired brain function, the $CMRO_2$ declines, paralleling the degree of cerebral depression.[454] Significant mental changes usually accompany $CMRO_2$ values below 2.5 cc. per 100 gm. per minute, and when the $CMRO_2$ falls below 2.0 cc., most patients are in coma.

Cerebral Blood Flow

The common denominator to glucose and oxygen requirement is the cerebral blood flow. Under resting conditions, the cerebral blood flow (CBF) is normally about 55 cc. per 100 gm. per minute, or about 15 to 20 per cent of the total cardiac output. The cerebral blood flow is considerably less constant than the $CMRO_2$ and it increases or decreases in response to a variety of physiological stimuli (e.g., CO_2 inhalation increases CBF and hypocapnia decreases it). When the cerebral blood flow is decreased the brain at first merely extracts more oxygen per unit volume. If the arterial oxygen supply is normal, the brain's metabolic rate continues to be normal with decreasing blood flow until so much oxygen is extracted that the jugular venous oxygen tension falls to about 20 mm. Hg, a value which usually requires that the CBF drops to about 50 per cent of normal. At this point, the oxygen tension in brain tissue remote from capillaries falls to levels that will no longer maintain metabolism.[559] The $CMRO_2$ falls rapidly,[491] and subjects lose consciousness.[329] When the cerebral blood flow fails, the primary insult to neurons is anoxia, but stasis also occurs and results in an accumulation of potentially toxic waste products and local lactic acidosis as well.

To deprive the brain of glucose or oxygen is not the only way to interfere with its energy metabolism and cause metabolic coma. The brain requires cofactors such as thiamine and pyridoxine to oxidize glucose; these are not intrinsically synthesized and must be included in the diet.

Other disorders theoretically could cause metabolic coma without interfering with the pathway of glucose oxidation. These include processes that interfere with the synthesis or breakdown of transmitter substances,[367] abnormalities of or inhibition of enzymes involved in lipid metabolism,[19] and abnormalities of non-energy-producing carbohydrate metabolism.[483] Clinically, none of these processes has yet been confirmed as a cause of coma, and in all instances of metabolic coma so far studied, the cerebral oxygen uptake has been reduced. However, this reduction could reflect a lesser metabolic need and not necessarily be the cause of coma. Ingvar and associates[257] presented a case that illustrates this principle: The subject was in coma following a brainstem infarct, presumably interrupting the midbrain reticular activating system. Despite normal glucose metabolism and a histologically intact cerebral cortex found at biopsy, the $CMRO_2$ was very low, indicating the metabolic indolence of the nonactivated cerebrum. McIlwain[365] has demonstrated how important activation is in maintaining cerebral metabolism: The oxygen consumption of resting cortical slices in vitro is much lower than brain in vivo, but electrical stimulation of the slices increases their oxygen consumption to approach the in vivo rate.

CLASSIFICATION OF METABOLIC ENCEPHALOPATHY

The physician examining a patient in coma is confronted with two questions: Is metabolic brain disease the cause, and if so, which of the large number of metabolic abnormalities is responsible? Table 8 lists many of the metabolic causes of coma. Included in addition to such illnesses as hypoglycemia, uremia, and hepatic coma, which are universally accepted as metabolic, are others not ordinarily classed as metabolic cerebral disorders. These latter include postictal coma, coma due to meningitis, and coma due to subarachnoid hemorrhage. We have included these conditions for two reasons. One is that they appear to cause unconsciousness by widespread and often reversible interference with brain metabolism. The other is that they clinically resemble other forms of metabolic coma rather than the coma states caused by supratentorial masses or by infratentorial mass and destructive lesions.

Table 8 attempts to classify metabolic coma in such a way that the table can be used as a check list of the major causes to be considered when the physician is presented with an unconscious patient suspected of having metabolic brain disease. Category I includes the primary metabolic encephalopathies, and category II, the secondary metabolic encephalopathies. Heading A under category II presents conditions in which there is a deficiency of essential metabolic factors. Headings B, C, and E include conditions that result from intoxications that probably interfere with normal enzyme function. Heading D lists abnormalities that can occur in a variety of illnesses (i.e., hypercalcemia can result from hyperparathyroidism, cancer, or sarcoid) and that probably exert their deleterious effect on the nervous system by interfering with a normal membrane or action potential. Reference citations are included to certain diseases such as heavy metal poisonings, which are such rare causes of coma in the adult that we have omitted discussing them.

CLINICAL SIGNS OF METABOLIC ENCEPHALOPATHY

Each patient with metabolic coma has a distinctive clinical flavor, depending on the particular causative illness, the depth of coma, and the complications provided by other illnesses or by treatment. Despite these individualities, however, specific illnesses often produce certain clinical patterns that occur again and again, and once these are recognized, they betray the diagnosis. A careful evaluation of consciousness, respiration, pupillary reactions, extraocular movements, motor function, and the EEG may differentiate metabolic encephalopathy from psychiatric dysfunction on the one hand, and from supratentorial or infratentorial structural disease on the other. Since these general characteristics of metabolic coma are so important, they are discussed before the specific disease entities.

Consciousness

Clinical Aspects

Changes in mentation and awareness are the earliest and most reliable warnings of the more slowly developing varieties of metabolic encephalopathy and almost invariably precede coma. The importance of these warnings is so great that we have stepped outside the literal bounds of coma to review briefly some of the mental symptoms that often precede metabolic coma and, by their presence, help to make the diagnosis. The mental changes are best looked for in terms of: alertness, orientation and grasp, cognition and attention, memory, affect, and perception.

ALERTNESS. With metabolic encephalopathy, the level of alertness and awareness of the environment varies from mild drowsiness to unresponsiveness. Altered awareness is the first and most subtle index of brain dysfunction, especially in patients with acute or subacute metabolic disorders. Initially the patient appears preoccupied or just uninterested. He

149

foregoes reading to lie quietly or sleep when left alone. Often he concedes that thinking or reading requires undue effort. As the disease progresses, drowsiness becomes more apparent, and the patient must be prodded or shaken to give answers, many of which emerge with insouciant incorrectness. This pattern of drowsiness preceding other changes is more characteristic of secondary metabolic encephalopathy than of primary; demented patients tend to lose orientation and cognition long before lethargy occurs. However, both primary and secondary metabolic encephalopathy eventually lead to stupor and finally coma, and when this point is reached, mental testing no longer helps to distinguish metabolic from other causes of brain dysfunction.

ORIENTATION AND GRASP. Although awareness and cognition are the first of man's faculties to be impaired with either primary or secondary metabolic encephalopathies, they are difficult to test and interpret unless the physician knows his patient's pre-illness personality and intellect. As a result, defects in orientation and immediate grasp of test situations often become the earliest unequivocal symptoms of brain dysfunction. When examining patients suspected of metabolic or cerebral disorders, one must ask specifically the date, the time, the place, and how long it takes to reach home or some other well-defined place. Even patients with limited intellects should know the month and year, and most should know the day and date, particularly if there has been a recent holiday. Patients with early metabolic encephalopathy lose orientation for time and as frequently miss the year as the month or the day. Orientation for distance is usually impaired next, and finally, persons and places are confused. Disorientation for person and place but not time is unusual in structural disease but sometimes is a symptom of hysteria.

COGNITION AND ATTENTION. The content and progression of thought are always disturbed in delirium and dementia, sometimes as the incipient symptoms. To detect these changes requires asking specific questions employing abstract definitions and problems. Since attention and concentration are nearly always impaired, patients with metabolic brain disease usually make errors in serial subtractions, and rarely can they repeat more than three or four numbers in reverse.

MEMORY. Loss of recent memory is a hallmark of dementia and a frequent accompaniment of delirium. Most patients with metabolic brain disease have a memory loss that is proportional to other losses of highest integrative functions. When the maximal pathological changes involve the limbic system, however, recent memory loss outstrips other intellectual impairments (page 152). Thus, memory loss and an inability to form new associations can be a sign of either diffuse or bilateral focal brain disease.

AFFECT. Patients with metabolic brain disease tend to be apathetic and withdrawn, and since they volunteer little, the examiner must directly test their highest integrative functions. (The apathy of these patients sometimes has pathetically ludicrous consequences. One elderly patient suffering from brain damage due to a hypotensive episode, during the week following a herniorrhaphy, each day responded to his doctor's question of, "How are you?" by saying, "Fine!" Only when an effort was made to send him home was it discovered that this was nearly his total vocabulary and that he had no idea of where he was, much less of the date or the purpose of his hospitalization.) A smaller proportion of patients, especially those suffering from anoxia, from sepsis, from acute withdrawal of drugs or alcohol, from acute intermittent porphyria, or from liver necrosis, are anxious, fearful, agitated, and tremulous. The two affective responses, the one quiet and the other agitated, sometimes alternate in the same patient. More frequently, the two occur in different subjects, with quiet delirium chiefly characterizing slowly developing, recurrent, or chronic processes and agitated delirium characterizing rapidly developing changes of an acute process in a previously healthy or at least metabolically stable subject.

PERCEPTION. Patients with metabolic brain disease frequently make perceptual errors, mistaking the members of the hospital staff for old friends and relatives, and granting vitality to inanimate objects. Illusions are common and invariably involve stimuli from the immediate environment. Quiet and apathetic patients suffer illusory experiences but these must be asked about since they are rarely volunteered. Anxious and fearful patients, on the other hand, frequently express concern about their illusions and misperceptions to the accompaniment of loud and violent behavior. Visual hallucinations are common; auditory ones, unusual.

Pathogenesis of the Mental Changes

There are two views about the mechanism of mental symptoms in metabolic brain disease. One is that the severity of symptoms is directly related to the mass of impaired brain, with the clinical changes depending on an interaction between the patient's premorbid personality and the gross amount of impaired cerebral tissue, regardless of its location (specific motor, speech, or visual areas being exceptions). The other is that the symptoms and signs distinctively reflect dysfunction in specific selected areas of the brain.

The first, or quantitative, view of brain function has a distinguished history in neurology beginning with Lashley. Its most recent support comes from the study of Chapman and Wolff,[86] who concluded that in diseases of the forebrain, man's highest integrative functions were reduced in proportion to the total quantity of brain destroyed by injury, operation, or degeneration. Except when speech and motor areas were involved, the behavioral impairment was directly related to the total mass of inadequately functioning neurons, regardless of whether the neuronal loss was aggregated in one area or diffusely distributed throughout the cortex.

The other, or focal, view of brain function is supported more by the studies of Penfield and Milner,[439] Scoville and Milner,[496] Victor and associates,[578] Whitty and Lewin,[596] and Spiegel and colleagues.[534] Each of these workers correlated specific defects in memory and orientation with specific anatomically verified brain lesions. Victor and his group, as well as others,[439, 496] described lesions involving the temporal lobes and hippocampus bilaterally. The patients afflicted with this rhinencephalic defect could neither retain new information nor remember information presented at variable times before the illness (retrograde amnesia). Whitty and Lewin, after placing lesions bilaterally in the cingulate gyrus, noted a postoperative period of confusion, disorientation, and memory loss, which in at least one patient remained permanently. Spiegel and co-workers reported that disorientation for time persisted for days to weeks after placing specific lesions in the anterior thalamic area. These results make it appear that fairly discrete but usually bilateral lesions in the limbic system reduce alertness and memory with the memory changes being the most striking.

The two views described above are not incompatible, and a combination of both pathological processes is probably the basis for the clinical picture of most metabolic brain disease. The general loss of highest integrative functions in metabolic diseases is compatible with a diffuse dysfunction of neurons and, as judged by measurements of cerebral metabolism, the severity of the clinical signs is directly related to the mass of neurons affected. However, certain distinctive clinical signs in different patients and in different diseases probably reflect damage to more discrete areas having to do with memory and other selective aspects of integrative behavior. An example is the encephalopathy resulting from thiamine deficiency (Wernicke-Korsakoff syndrome).[579] In this illness patients show acutely the clinical signs of delirium. All neuronal areas lose thiamine at about the same rate,[137] but certain nuclear collections such as the mammillary bodies, the periaqueductal gray matter, and the oculomotor nuclei are morphologically more sensitive to the deficiency and show the major anatomical pathology. A diffuse disease thus has a focal maximum. Clinically, recent memory is impaired more severely than are other mental functions and, indeed, memory loss may persist to produce the Korsakoff syndrome after other mental functions and overall cerebral metabolism have improved to a near-normal level.

Respiration

Sooner or later metabolic brain disease nearly always results in an abnormality of either the depth or rhythm of respiration. Most of the time this is a nonspecific alteration and simply a part of more widespread brainstem depression. Sometimes, however, the respiratory changes stand out separately from the rest of the neurological defects and are more or less specific to the disease in question. Some of these specific respiratory responses are homeostatic adjustments to the metabolic process causing encephalopathy. The others occur in illnesses that particularly affect the respiratory mechanisms. Either way, proper evaluation and interpretation of the specific respiratory changes facilitate diagnosis and often suggest an urgent need for treatment.

As a first step in appraising the breathing of patients with metabolically caused coma, increased or decreased respiratory efforts must be confirmed as truly reflecting hyperventilation or hypoventilation. Increased chest efforts do not spell hyperventilation if they merely overcome obstruction or pneumonitis, and conversely, seemingly shallow breathing can fulfill the reduced metabolic needs of subjects in deep coma. Although careful clinical evaluation usually avoids those potential deceptions, the bedside observations are most helpful when anchored by direct determinations of the arterial blood pH, Pco_2, Po_2, and bicarbonate concentration.

"Nonspecific" Respiratory Effects of Metabolic Disease

Lethargic or lightly obtunded patients have posthyperventilation apnea, and those in stupor or light coma commonly exhibit Cheyne-Stokes respiration. With more profound brainstem depression, transient neurogenic hyperventilation can ensue from suppression of brainstem inhibitory regions. As an illustration, poisoning with short- or intermediate-acting barbiturate preparations often induces brief episodes of hyperventilation and motor hypertonus, both during the stage of deepening coma and as patients reawaken. Hypoglycemia and anoxic damage are even more frequent causes of transient hyperpnea. In these instances, the increased breathing sometimes outlasts the immediate metabolic trauma, and if the subject also has decerebrate rigidity, the clinical picture may superficially resemble structural disease or severe metabolic acidosis. However, attention to other neurological details usually leads to the proper diagnosis, as the following case illustrates:

Case 22. A 28-year-old man was brought unconscious to the emergency room. Fifteen minutes earlier, with slurred speech, he had instructed a taxi driver to take him to the hospital, then "passed out." His pulse was 100 per minute, and his blood pressure was 130/90 mm. Hg. His respirations were 40 per minute and deep. His pupils were small (2 mm.), but the light and ciliospinal reflexes were preserved. Oculocephalic reflexes were present. His deep tendon reflexes were hyperactive; there were bilateral extensor plantar responses, and he periodically had bilateral decerebrate spasms. After 25 gm. of glucose were given intravenously, respirations quieted, the decerebrate spasms ceased, and he withdrew appropriately from noxious stimuli. After 75 gm. of glucose, he awoke and disclosed that he was diabetic, taking insulin, and had neglected to eat that day. The preglucose blood sugar level was 20 mg. per 100 cc.

Comment: This man's hyperpnea and decerebrate rigidity initially suggested structural brainstem disease to the emergency room physicians. Normal oculovestibular and oculocephalic responses, normal pupillary reactions, and the absence of focal signs made metabolic coma more likely, and the diagnosis was confirmed by the subsequent findings.

153

The effectiveness of respiration must be evaluated repeatedly when metabolic disease depresses the brain because the brainstem reticular formation is especially vulnerable to chemical depression. Anoxia, hypoglycemia, and drugs all are capable of suppressing breathing to the point of apnea and yet at the same time may fail to depress other brainstem functions such as pupillary responses and blood pressure control. Barbiturates exemplify this: Experimentally, only one fourth as much drug is required to depress respiration as to depress cardiovascular responses,[325] and clinically, many more patients with barbiturate intoxication require artificial respiration than require support of the blood pressure.[450]

"Specific" Respiratory Effects of Metabolic Disease

Respiration is the first and most rapid defense against systemic acid-base imbalance, and chemoreceptors located in the carotid body and aortic arterial wall as well as in the low brainstem[384, 428] quickly respond to alterations in the blood of either hydrogen ion concentration or Pco_2.

HYPERVENTILATION. In a stuporous or comatose patient, hyperventilation is a danger sign meaning one of two things: either compensation for metabolic acidosis or a response to primary respiratory stimulation (respiratory alkalosis). Metabolic acidosis and respiratory alkalosis are differentiated by blood biochemical analyses. In the first instance, the arterial blood pH is low (less than 7.30 if hyperpnea is to be attributed to acidosis), and the serum bicarbonate is also low (usually below 10 mEq. per L.). In the second case, the arterial pH is high (over 7.45), and the serum bicarbonate is normal or slightly reduced. In both respiratory alkalosis and metabolic acidosis, the arterial carbon dioxide tension ($Paco_2$) is reduced, usually below 30 mm. Hg. Table 9 lists some of the causes of hyperventilation in patients with metabolic encephalopathy.

Metabolic acidosis sufficient to produce coma and hyperpnea has only four important causes: uremia, diabetes, lactic acidosis (anoxic or spontaneous), and the ingestion of poisons that are acidic or have acidic breakdown products. In any given patient, a quick and accurate selection can and must be made from among these. Diabetes and uremia are diagnosed by appropriate laboratory tests, and diabetic acidosis is confirmed by identifying serum ketonemia. An important observation[419, 566] is that diabetics, especially those who have been treated with oral hypoglycemic agents, are subject to lactic acidosis as well as to diabetic ketoacidosis, but in the former condition ketonemia is lacking. If diabetes and uremia are eliminated in a patient as causes of acidosis it can be inferred either that he has spontaneous lactic acidosis or has been poisoned with an exogenous toxin such as ethylene glycol, methyl alcohol, or decomposed paraldehyde. Anoxic lactic acidosis would be suspected only if anoxia or shock were present, and severe anoxic acidosis is relatively uncommon even then.

Table 9. A differential analysis of abnormal ventilation in unresponsive patients

CLINICAL AND LABORATORY FINDINGS	PROBABLE DIAGNOSIS
I. Hyperventilation:	
A. Serum pH $<$ 7.30, Pa_{CO_2} $<$ 35 mm. Hg, serum HCO_3^- $<$ 10 mEq./L. (if pH $<$ 7.30, Pa_{CO_2} $>$ 40 mm. Hg, HCO_3^- $>$ 20 mEq./L., see respiratory acidosis)	Metabolic acidosis
1. BUN $>$ 60 mg./100 cc.	Uremic encephalopathy
2. Hyperglycemia (blood sugar $>$ 250 mg /100 cc.)	Diabetic coma
a. 4+ serum acetone	Diabetic ketoacidosis
b. no acetonemia	Diabetic lactic acidosis
3. Cyanosis (P_{O_2} $<$ 50 mm. Hg), shock	Anoxic lactic acidosis[250]
4. BUN, sugar, oxygen, blood pressure—normal	Exogenous poisoning
a. paraldehyde odor on breath	Acidosis secondary to paraldehyde ingestion[232]
b. hyperemic optic discs, dilated sluggish pupils	Methyl alcohol poisoning[35]
c. oxalate crystals in urine	Ethylene glycol poisoning[189]
5. None of the abnormal findings above	Spontaneous lactic acidosis[251, 419]
B. Serum pH $>$ 7.45, Pa_{CO_2} $<$ 30 mm. Hg, serum HCO_3^- $>$ but $<$ 25 mEq./L. (if pH $>$ 7.45 and HCO_3^- $>$ 30 mEq./L. see metabolic alkalosis)	Respiratory alkalosis
1. Serum HCO_3^- $<$ 15 mEq./L., hyperthermia, positive urine $FeCl_3$ test	Salicylate poisoning
2. Serum HCO_3^- $<$ 15 mEq./L., fever, tachycardia, hypotension	Gram-negative sepsis
3. Serum HCO_3^- $>$ 15 mEq./L., Pa_{O_2} $>$ 50 mm. Hg, hepatomegaly, serum NH_3 elevated	Hepatic encephalopathy
4. Serum HCO_3^- $>$ 15 mEq./L., cyanosis (P_{O_2} $<$ 50 mm. Hg)	Cardiopulmonary disease
a. rales, elevated venous pressure, cardiomegaly	Pulmonary edema
b. no heart disease	Pneumonia, alveolar-capillary block, pulmonary emboli
5. Serum HCO_3^- $>$ 15 mEq./L., absence of pupillary and oculovestibular responses, decerebrate rigidity	Central neurogenic hyperventilation
6. Serum HCO_3^- $>$ 15 mEq./L., nystagmus on caloric testing, normal examination	Psychogenic hyperventilation
II. Hypoventilation	
A. Serum pH $<$ 7.35, Pa_{CO_2} $>$ 45 mm. Hg, serum HCO_3^- $>$ 20 mEq./L.	Respiratory acidosis

Table 9 (continued)

CLINICAL AND LABORATORY FINDINGS	PROBABLE DIAGNOSIS
1. Serum $HCO_3^- >$ 20 mEq./L. but $<$ 30 mEq./L.	
a. normal lungs	Depressant drug poisoning
b. rales, emphysema, $P_{O_2} <$ 40 mm. Hg	Chronic pulmonary disease with acute CO_2 retention
2. Serum $HCO_3^- >$ 30 mEq./L.	
a. normal lungs	
(1) obesity	Pickwick's syndrome[71]
(2) not obese	"Primary alveolar hypoventilation"[181]
b. rales, emphysema, $P_{O_2} <$ 40 mm. Hg	Chronic pulmonary disease with slowly developing CO_2 retention
B. Serum pH $>$ 7.45, $Pa_{CO_2} <$ 55 mm. Hg, serum $HCO_3^- >$ 30 mEq./L.	Metabolic alkalosis
a. vomiting, hypotension, hypovolemia	Gastric HCl depletion
b. edema, heart disease	Diuretic therapy
c. hypokalemia, moon face, truncal obesity	Cushing's syndrome secondary to: adrenal hyperfunction steroid therapy hormone-secreting lung neoplasms
d. hypertension, hypokalemia	Primary hyperaldosteronism
e. renal disease	Hypokalemic alkalosis
f. peptic ulcer	$NaHCO_3$ ingestion alkalosis

Unfortunately, tests for most ingested agents causing acidosis cannot be made quickly. However, once diabetes, uremia, and acute anoxia have been ruled out, the other causes of metabolic acidosis can be effectively treated by intravenous infusions of sodium bicarbonate in quantities sufficient to restore the blood pH to normal (see Case 32, p. 198). Since action must be prompt to avoid fatality, final diagnosis can await determination of blood lactate and other acids after treatment has been instituted.

Sustained *respiratory alkalosis* has five important causes among disorders producing the picture of metabolic stupor or coma: salicylism, hepatic coma, pulmonary disease, sepsis, and psychogenic hyperventilation. As is true with metabolic acidosis, these usually can be at least partially separated by clinical examination and simple laboratory measures.

Salicylate poisoning causes a combined respiratory alkalosis and metabolic acidosis that lowers the serum bicarbonate disproportionately to the degree of serum pH elevation. Salicylism should be suspected in a stuporous hyperpneic adult if the serum pH is normal or alkaline, and the serum bicarbonate is between 10 and 14 mEq. per L. Salicylism in children lowers serum bicarbonate still more and produces serum acidosis. The diagnosis of severe salicylism is supported by the purple color produced by adding ferric chloride to boiled urine and confirmed by finding a serum salicylate level in excess of 40 mg. per 100 cc.

Hepatic coma producing respiratory alkalosis rarely depresses the serum bicarbonate below 16 mEq. per L., and the diagnosis usually is betrayed by other signs of liver dysfunction. The associated clinical abnormalities of liver disease are sometimes minimal, particularly with fulminating acute yellow atrophy or when gastrointestinal hemorrhage precipitates coma in a chronic cirrhotic. Liver function tests must be relied upon in such instances.

Gram-negative sepsis is always associated with hyperventilation, probably a direct central effect of the endotoxin.[519a] Early in the course of the illness, the acid-base defect is that of a pure respiratory alkalosis ($HCO_3 > 15$ mEq. per L.), but later lactic acid accumulates and the stuporous patient usually presents a combined acid-base defect of respiratory alkalosis and metabolic acidosis ($HCO_3 < 15$ mEq. per L.). Fever and hypotension usually accompany the neurological signs and suggest the diagnosis.

Respiratory alkalosis due to pulmonary congestion, fibrosis, or pneumonia rarely depresses the serum bicarbonate significantly. This diagnosis should be considered in hypoxic, hyperpneic subjects in coma who have normal or slightly lowered serum bicarbonate levels and no evidence of liver disease. Psychogenic hyperventilation does not cause coma but may cause delirium and may be present as an additional symptom in a patient with psychogenic "coma."

HYPOVENTILATION. In an unconscious patient, hypoventilation means either respiratory compensation for metabolic alkalosis[569] or respiratory depression with consequent acidosis. The differential diagnosis is outlined in Table 9. In metabolic alkalosis the arterial blood pH is elevated ($>$ 7.45) as is the serum bicarbonate (> 35 mEq. per L.). In untreated respiratory acidosis with coma, the serum pH is low (< 7.35), and the serum bicarbonate is either normal or high, depending on treatment and how rapidly the respiratory failure has developed. The $Paco_2$ is always elevated in respiratory acidosis (usually > 55 mm. Hg) and often elevated because of respiratory compensation in metabolic alkalosis. In respiratory acidosis, the CSF pH is always low if artificial respiration has not been used.[70, 456] The arterial Pco_2 is elevated in both metabolic alkalosis and respiratory acidosis, but is rarely higher than 50 mm. Hg in alkalosis and almost invariably rises considerably higher than this when respiratory acidosis causes stupor or coma. In both disorders, the oxygen tension is reduced. The foregoing explains why an estimation of serum bicarbonate alone fails accurately to subdivide patients who hypoventilate except that a normal bicarbonate level is consistent with untreated respiratory acidosis but not with metabolic alkalosis.

Metabolic alkalosis results from either excessive ingestion of alkali or excessive loss of acid via gastrointestinal and renal routes. To find the specific cause often requires exhaustive laboratory analyses, but delirium and obtundation due to metabolic alkalosis are rarely severe and never life threatening so that time exists for careful diagnostic considerations.

Respiratory acidosis is a more pressing problem, caused by either severe pulmonary or neuromuscular disease (peripheral respiratory failure) or by depression of the respiratory center (central respiratory failure). Both causes induce hypoxia as well as CO_2 retention. Chest examinations almost always can differentiate neuromuscular from pulmonary disease and the presence of tachypnea distinguishes pulmonary or peripheral neuromuscular failure from central failure with its irregular or slow respiratory patterns. Severe respiratory acidosis of any origin is best treated by artificial respiration.

Pupils

Among patients in deep coma, the state of the pupils becomes the single most important criterion that clinically distinguishes between metabolic and structural disease. Preserved pupillary light reflexes despite concomitant respiratory depression, caloric unresponsiveness, decerebrate rigidity, or motor flaccidity suggest metabolic coma. Conversely, if asphyxia or glutethimide ingestion can be ruled out, the absence of pupillary light reflexes strongly implies that the disease is structural rather than metabolic.

Pupils canot be considered conclusively nonreactive to a light stimulus unless care has been taken to examine them with magnification and a very bright light. Ciliospinal reflexes are less reliable than the light reflexes but, like them, are usually preserved in metabolic coma even when motor and respiratory signs signify lower brainstem dysfunction.

Ocular Motility

The eyes usually rove randomly with mild metabolic coma and come to rest in the forward position as coma deepens. Although almost any eye position or random movement can be observed transiently when brainstem function is changing rapidly, a maintained conjugate lateral deviation or dysconjugate positioning of the eyes at rest suggests structural disease. Conjugate downward gaze can occur in metabolic as well as in structural disease and by itself is not helpful in differential diagnosis.

Case 23. A 63-year-old woman with severe hepatic cirrhosis and a portacaval shunt was found in coma. She groaned spontaneously but otherwise was unresponsive. Her respirations were 18 per minute and deep. The pupillary diameters were 4 mm. on the right and 3 mm. on the left, and both reacted to light. Her eyes were deviated conjugately downward and slightly to the right. The doll's-head maneuver elicited conjugate eye movement in all directions. Her muscles were flaccid, but her stretch reflexes were brisk and more active on the right with bilateral extensor plantar responses. No decorticate or decerebrate responses could be elicited. Her arterial blood pH was 7.58, and her $Paco_2$ was 21 mm. Hg.

Two days later she awoke, at which time her eye movements were normal. Four days later she again drifted into coma, this time with the eyes in the physiological position and with sluggish but full oculocephalic responses. She died on the sixth hospital day, with severe hepatic cirrhosis. No structural CNS lesion was found at autopsy.

Comment: This patient exhibited conjugate deviation of the eyes downward and to the right that lasted 24 hours and initially suggested a deep, right-sided cerebral hemispheric mass lesion. The return of gaze to normal with awakening and nonrepetition of the downward deviation when coma recurred ruled out a structural lesion. At autopsy, no intrinsic cerebral pathological lesion was found to explain the abnormal eye movements. We have subsequently observed transient downward deviation of the eyes in several other patients in metabolic coma.

Since reflex eye movements are particularly sensitive to depressant drugs, cold caloric stimulation often provides valuable information about the depth of coma in patients with metabolic disease. The ocular response to passive head movement is less reliable than the caloric test since absence of doll's-head eye movements may imply purposeful inhibition of the reflex and does not dependably distinguish psychogenic unresponsiveness from brainstem depression. Cold caloric stimulation produces tonic conjugate deviation toward the irrigated ear in patients in light coma and little or no response in those in deep coma. If caloric stimulation evokes nystagmus, cerebral connections are intact and the impairment of consciousness is either very mild and not metabolic or the "coma" is psychogenic. Finally, if caloric stimulation repeatedly produces dysconjugate eye movements, structural brainstem disease should be suspected (but see Chapter 1).

Case 24. A 20-year-old girl became unresponsive while riding in the back seat of her parents' car. There was no history of previous illness, but her parents stated that she had severe emotional problems. On examination, her vital signs and general physical examination were normal. She appeared to be asleep when left alone, with quiet shallow respiration and no spontaneous movements. Her pupils were 3 mm. and reactive. Oculocephalic responses were absent. She lay motionless to noxious stimuli but appeared to resist passive elevation of her eyelids. Cold caloric testing elicited tonic deviation of the eyes with no nystagmus. She awoke the next morning and admitted ingesting both phenobarbital and meprobamate to frighten her mother.

Comment: The coma in this patient initially appeared light or even simulated. However, tonic deviation of the eyes in response to cold caloric irrigation signified that normal cerebral effects were in abeyance and indicated that her unresponsiveness was the result of organic cerebral dysfunction.

Motor Activity

Patients with metabolic brain disease generally present two types of motor abnormalities: (1) nonspecific disorders of strength, tone, and reflexes, as well as focal or generalized seizures, (2) certain characteristic adventitious movements that are almost diagnostic of metabolic brain disease.

"Nonspecific" Motor Abnormalities

Diffuse motor abnormalities are frequent in metabolic coma and reflect the degree and distribution of central nervous system depression (Chapter 1). Paratonia, snouting, and prehensile sucking and grasp reflexes frequently go hand in hand with early mental changes, especially with dementia, and may also be elicited in patients in light coma. With increasing brainstem depression, decorticate and decerebrate rigidity and flaccidity appear. The rigid states are sometimes asymmetrical.

Case 25. A 60-year-old man was found in the street, stuporous, with an odor of wine on his breath. No other history was obtainable. His blood pressure was 120/80 mm. Hg, pulse rate 100 per minute, respirations 26 per minute and deep. His neck was supple. There was fetor hepaticus, and the skin was jaundiced. The liver was palpably enlarged. He responded to noxious stimuli only by groaning. There was no response to visual threat. His left pupil was 5 mm. and right pupil, 3 mm., and both reacted to light. The eyes diverged at rest, but passive head movement elicited full conjugate ocular movements. The corneal reflexes were decreased but present bilaterally. There was a left facial droop. The gag reflex was present. He did not move spontaneously but grimaced and demonstrated decerebrate responses to noxious stimuli. The limb muscles were symmetrically rigid, and stretch reflexes were hyperactive. The plantar responses were extensor. The lumbar spinal fluid pressure was 120 mm. and the CSF contained 30 mg. of protein per 100 cc. and one cell. Skull x-ray films were normal. The serum bicarbonate was 16 mEq. per L., chloride 104 mEq. per L., sodium 147 mEq. per L., and potassium 3.9 mEq. per L. Liver function studies were grossly abnormal.

The following morning he responded appropriately to noxious stimulation. Hyperventilation had decreased, and the decerebrate responses had disappeared. Diffuse rigidity, increased deep tendon reflexes, and bilateral extensor plantar responses remained. Improvement was rapid, and by the fourth hospital day he was awake and had normal findings on neurological examination. However, on the seventh hospital day his blood pressure declined and his jaundice increased. He became hypotensive on the ninth hospital day and died. The general autopsy disclosed severe hepatic cirrhosis. An examination of the brain revealed old infarcts of the posterior second and third frontal convolutions on the left and of the left inferior cerebellum. There were no other lesions.

Comment: In this patient, the signs of liver disease suggested the diagnosis of hepatic coma. At first, however, anisocoria and decerebrate rigidity hinted at a supratentorial mass lesion such as a subdural hematoma. The normal pupillary and doll's-eyes reactions favored metabolic disease and the subsequent absence of signs of rostral-caudal deterioration supported that diagnosis.

Focal weakness is surprisingly common with metabolic brain disease. Our series includes five patients in whom hypoglycemia produced transient hemiplegia, four patients with hepatic coma who were transiently hemiplegic, and several patients with uremia or hyponatremia who had focal weakness of supranuclear origin. Others have reported similar findings.[335, 387, 435]

Case 26. A 37-year-old man had been diabetic for 8 years. He received 35 units of protamine zinc insulin each morning in addition to 5 units of regular insulin when he believed he needed it. One week before admission, he lost consciousness transiently upon arising, and when he awoke, he had a left hemiparesis, which disappeared within seconds. The evening before admission the patient had received 35 units of protamine zinc and 5 units of regular insulin. He awoke at 6 A.M., on the floor, soiled with feces. His entire left side was numb and paralyzed. His pulse was 80 per minute, respirations 12, and blood pressure 130/80 mm. Hg. The general physical examination was unremarkable. He was lethargic but oriented. His speech was slurred. There was supranuclear left facial paralysis and left flaccid hemiplegia with weakness of the tongue, the trapezius, and the sternocleidomastoid muscles. There was a left extensor plantar response but no sensory impairment. The blood sugar was 31 mg. per 100 cc. His EEG was normal with no slow wave focus. He was given 25 gm. of glucose intravenously and recovered fully in 3 minutes.

Comment: Cerebral infarction initially seemed to be the most likely diagnosis. However, the patient was a little more drowsy than expected with an uncomplicated stroke unless the infarct were massive. The fact that his attack might have begun with unconsciousness made his physicians suspect hypoglycemia. Although the history of a previous similar episode was compatible with the natural history of an attack of carotid artery insufficiency, unconsciousness does not ordinarily occur with hemispheral ischemic attacks and probably that episode also represented hypoglycemia. Of our other four patients with hypoglycemic hemiplegia, three were children and all have been unconscious. The hemiplegia cleared rapidly in all after treatment.

Patients with metabolic brain disease often have both focal and generalized convulsions, particularly the latter, which are indistinguishable from the seizures of structural brain disease. When focal seizures occur, the focus tends to shift from attack to attack. Migratory seizures are especially common and hard to control in uremia.

Motor Abnormalities Characteristic of Metabolic Coma

Tremor, asterixis, and multifocal myoclonus are prominent manifestations of metabolic brain disease, especially of the secondary metabolic encephalopathies, but are rarely seen with focal structural lesions unless these latter have a toxic-infectious component.

TREMOR. The tremor of metabolic encephalopathy is coarse and irregular and has a rate of 8 to 10 per second. Usually these tremors are absent at rest and when present are most evident in the fingers of the outstretched hands. Severe tremors may spread to the face, tongue, and lower extremities, and they frequently interfere with purposive movements in agitated patients such as those with delirium tremens. The physiological mechanism responsible for this type of tremor is unknown. It is not seen in patients with unilateral hemispheral or focal brainstem lesions.

ASTERIXIS. First described by Adams and Foley[4] in patients with hepatic coma, asterixis is now recognized to accompany a wide variety of metabolic brain diseases.[103, 326] (See Case 10, page 108, for an example of asterixis accompanying subdural empyema.) Asterixis is a sudden palmar flapping movement of the hands at the wrists. It is most easily elicited in lethargic but awake patients by directing them to hold their arms outstretched with hands dorsiflexed at the wrist and fingers extended and abducted. In its incipiency, asterixis comprises a slight irregular tremor of the fingers beginning after a latent period of 2 to 30 seconds. Leavitt and Tyler[326] have described the two separate components of this tremulousness. One is an irregular oscillation of the fingers, usually in the anterior-posterior direction but with a rotary component at the wrist. The second consists of random movements of the fingers at the metacarpal-phalangeal joints. This second pattern becomes more and more marked as the patient holds his wrist dorsiflexed until finally the fingers lead the hand into a sudden downward jerk followed by a slower return to the original dorsiflexed position. Both hands are affected, but asynchronously, and as the abnormal movement intensifies it spreads to the feet, tongue, and face. Indeed, with severe metabolic tremors it sometimes becomes difficult to distinguish between intense asterixis and myoclonus.

Asterixis is generally seen in awake but lethargic patients and generally disappears with the advent of stupor or coma, although occasionally one can evoke the arrhythmic contraction in such subjects by passively dorsiflexing the wrist.

Electromyograms recorded during asterixis show a brief absence of muscular activity during the downward jerk, followed by a sudden muscular compensatory contraction, much like the sudden bobbing of the head that normally accompanies drowsiness. The sudden electrical silence is unexplained and not accompanied by EEG changes.[4, 326]

MULTIFOCAL MYOCLONUS. This consists of sudden, nonrhythmic, nonpatterned gross twitching involving parts of muscles or groups of muscles first in one part of the body, then another, and particularly affecting the facial and proximal musculature. It most commonly accompanies uremic and CO_2 encephalopathy. Multifocal myoclonus always signifies severe metabolic disturbances and usually is confined to patients in stupor or coma. Its physiology is unknown and the motor twitchings are not reflected by a specific EEG abnormality.

Differential Diagnosis

Distinction between Metabolic and Psychogenic Unresponsiveness

In awake patients, differences in the mental state, the EEG, the motor signs, and, occasionally, the breathing pattern distinguish metabolic from psychiatric disease.

Most conscious patients with metabolic brain disease are confused, and many are disoriented, especially for time. Their abstract thinking is defective; they cannot concentrate well and cannot easily retain new information.

162

Early during the illness, the outstretched dorsiflexed hands show irregular tremulousness and, frequently, asterixis. Snouting, sucking, and grasp reflexes are seen. The EEG is generally slow. Posthyperventilation apnea may be elicited and there may be hypoventilation or hyperventilation, depending on the specific metabolic illness. By contrast, awake patients with psychogenic illness, if they will cooperate, are not disoriented and can retain new information. They lack abnormal reflexes or adventitious movements, although they may have irregular tremor, and they have normal EEG frequencies. Ventilatory patterns, with the exception of psychogenic hyperventilation, are normal.

Unresponsive patients with metabolic disease have even slower activity in their EEG's than responsive patients with metabolic disease, and caloric stimulation elicits either tonic deviation of the eyes or, if the patient is deeply comatose, no response. Psychogenically unresponsive patients have normal EEG's and a normal response to caloric irrigation, with nystagmus having a quick phase away from the side of ice water irrigation; there is little or no tonic deviation of the eyes (see Chapter 5).

Distinction between Coma of Metabolic and Structural Origin

Motor and EEG changes provide the most important distinctions between metabolic brain disease and gross structural disease when patients are merely obtunded or lethargic. Most patients with metabolic brain disease have diffuse abnormal motor signs, tremor, myoclonus, and, especially, asterixis. The EEG is diffusely, but not focally, slow. The patient with gross structural disease, on the other hand, generally has abnormal focal motor signs and lacks asterixis. The EEG may be slow, but in addition, with supratentorial lesions, a focal abnormality will usually be present.

Finally, metabolic and structural brain diseases are distinguished from each other by combinations of signs and their evolution. Comatose patients with metabolic brain disease usually suffer from partial dysfunction affecting many levels of the neuraxis simultaneously yet concurrently retain the integrity of other functions originating at the same levels. The orderly rostral-caudal deterioration that is characteristic of supratentorial mass lesions does not occur in metabolic brain disease, nor is the anatomical defect regionally restricted as it is with subtentorial damage.

DIAGNOSIS OF SPECIFIC CAUSES OF METABOLIC COMA

Three criteria have determined which illnesses are discussed in this section. These are that the disorders (1) commonly cause coma, (2) are reversible if treated promptly, but potentially lethal otherwise, so that sound clinical judgment must govern the brief time available to make a diagnosis and institute treatment, (3) have certain neurological signs that are either characteristic or strongly suggest the diagnosis.

163

General Considerations

The differential diagnosis of metabolic coma is not always easy. The history often is unobtainable and the neurological examination in many instances suggests only that the cause of coma is metabolic without identifying the specific etiology. Thus, laboratory examinations and x-ray contrast studies may ultimately be required to make a final diagnosis. But when the patient is acutely and severely ill, and time is short, the major treatable causes of acute metabolic coma (which are few) must be considered systematically. In obscure cases, it is remarkable how often an accurate clue is derived from careful observation of the respiratory pattern accompanied, when indicated, by analysis of blood pH and serum bicarbonate, determination of blood sugar, and lumbar puncture.

Because hypoglycemic coma is frequent, dangerous, and often clinically obscure, it is well in any instance of undiagnosed stupor or coma to first draw blood for sugar analysis, then give 25 gm. of glucose intravenously. The injection can do no harm and is enough to protect the brain against hypoglycemia until the results of blood sugar examination are available.

Primary Metabolic Encephalopathy

The primary encephalopathies only rarely progress so rapidly that they first present themselves as problems in the diagnosis of coma. However, the three mentioned here tend to produce unconsciousness sufficiently early in their course that they may be confused with other conditions described in this book. The other primary metabolic encephalopathies usually cause coma late and only after a period of profound dementia has led to the appropriate diagnosis.

Jakob-Creutzfeldt Disease

Jakob-Creutzfeldt disease is a subacute disorder involving mainly the gray matter of the cerebral cortex. Histological examination discloses widespread neuronal degeneration in the neocortex and cerebellum as well as marked astrocytic gliosis. Neurons of the basal ganglia, brainstem, and hippocampus are often spared.[289] The disease appears to be caused by a slow virus infection[277] and can be transmitted to chimpanzees by cerebral inoculation of brain tissue from affected patients.[204] Virus-like particles have been observed in brain biopsy material from such patients.[576]

Clinically, the illness usually affects middle-aged adults, causing dementia, which progresses over a period of weeks to severe obtundation, stupor, and finally unresponsiveness. The motor system suffers disproportionately, and early in the disease there is diffuse paratonic rigidity with decorticate posturing and extensor plantar responses developing later. Early in the course, myoclonus appears in response to startle; later the myoclonus occurs spontaneously. There also may be generalized convulsions. The EEG is characteristic, consisting of a flat almost isoelectric background with superimposed synchronous periodic sharp waves.[402] The cerebrospinal fluid examination is usually normal. In the final stage of the disease, all spontaneous movements cease, and the patients remain in coma until they die of intercurrent infection.

The appearance of subacute dementia with myoclonic twitches in a middle-aged or elderly patient without systemic disease is diagnostic. Although there is a tendency to mistake the early symptoms for an involutional depression, the organic nature of the disorder rapidly becomes apparent. A similar picture is produced only by severe metabolic diseases (e.g., hepatic encephalopathy) or CNS syphilis (general paresis). However, these latter illnesses have characteristic chemical and laboratory signs and lack the typical EEG of Jakob-Creutzfeldt disease.

Schilder's Disease (Diffuse Sclerosis)

This is a subacute or acute disorder of white matter that primarily affects children or young adults, sometimes causing coma after an illness lasting only days or weeks. The brain contains large, often symmetrical, demyelinated areas in the hemispheres, usually sparing both the subcortical arcuate fibers and the white matter of the brainstem. Axis cylinders are destroyed almost to the same extent as the myelin sheath. Inflammatory cells and fat-filled macrophages are abundant around blood vessels. The cause of Schilder's disease is unknown. Pathologically, some of the cases in young adults are indistinguishable from acute multiple sclerosis, and in these older individuals it sometimes is called "acute diffuse sclerosis." Cumings[113] has found large increases in the hexosamine content of white matter of patients affected with this disorder, suggesting an inflammatory or reactive component to the illness that presumably differentiates it from other demyelinating disorders such as multiple sclerosis.

Schilder's disease begins with either an acute or insidious onset of symptoms indicating cerebral involvement. There is progressive dementia finally leading to coma. Generalized convulsions are common in children, less so in adults. Abnormal motor signs are always present, and focal motor signs (e.g., hemiparesis) are frequent. Language defects include aphasia or cerebral mutism. Cortical visual defects are one of the most prominent features and usually begin with hemianopsia. Later in the course most patients become blind, often retaining normal pupillary responses because the pregeniculate optic pathways are spared. The end stage of the disease, like that of Jakob-Creutzfeldt, is one of decorticate responses and coma.

The diagnosis can only be suspected clinically. Direct cerebral biopsy is required to make the diagnosis during life since there are no less drastic reliable laboratory tests. Because cerebral edema occasionally leads to increased intracranial pressure in these patients, a mistaken diagnosis of brain tumor may be made. Usually, however, attention to the course of the illness and the prominent visual impairment will suggest the correct diagnosis.

Marchiafava-Bignami Disease (Degeneration of the Corpus Callosum)

A rare disorder of white matter, this illness affects principally men of Italian extraction who are heavy drinkers of red wine. The essential lesion is demyelination of the corpus callosum that extends into the adjacent hemispheres and may simultaneously involve the optic tracts and middle cerebellar peduncles. Axis cylinders may be either destroyed or preserved. The process spares the brainstem and the cortical neurons, but since the patients are all chronic alcoholics with poor nutrition, it is likely that dysfunction in the nervous system extends considerably beyond the demyelinated areas. The etiological agent was originally believed to be a toxic factor in Italian wine, but since the disease occurs in Italian men (and occasionally those of other ethnic groups) who drink other alcoholic beverages, nutritional deficiency in patients genetically predisposed to the process seems a more likely explanation.[550]

The malady begins with delirium, which is rapidly followed by convulsions, widespread tremor, and rigidity. Patients decline into coma and usually die within a few weeks of onset. A single patient has recently been described who spontaneously recovered from his illness only to die of liver disease several years later.[330] The diagnosis can be suspected clinically but confirmed only at autopsy.

Secondary Metabolic Encephalopathy

Ischemia and Anoxia

Hypoxia of the brain almost always arises as part of a larger problem in oxygen supply, either because the ambient pressure falls or systemic abnormalities in the organism interrupt its delivery to the tissues. Barcroft[24] classified anoxia into anoxic, anemic, stagnant, and histotoxic types, the last being due to chemical interference with the tissue utilization of oxygen such as occurs when cyanide blocks the cytochrome system. Anoxic anoxia implies a *reduced arterial partial pressure* of oxygen; anemic anoxia, a *reduced carrying capacity* by the blood; and stagnant anoxia would today more appropriately be designated *ischemia,* since circulatory failure in the tissue never yields hypoxia alone. Though they can be caused by different conditions and diseases, all three categories share equally the potential for depriving brain tissue of its critical oxygen supply, the main differences between the anoxic, anemic, and ischemic forms lying on the arterial side. All three forms of anoxia also share the common effect of producing *cerebral venous hypoxia,* which is the best guide in vivo to estimate the partial pressure of the gas in the tissue.[515]

166

In *anoxic anoxia,* insufficient oxygen reaches the blood so that both the arterial oxygen content and tension are low. This situation results either from a low oxygen tension in the environment (e.g., high altitude or displacement of oxygen by an inert gas such as nitrogen) or from an inability of oxygen to reach and cross the alveolar capillary membrane (pulmonary disease). With mild or moderate hypoxia the cerebral blood flow increases to maintain the cerebral oxygen delivery, and no symptoms occur. However, the cerebral blood flow can only increase to about twice normal, and when the increase is insufficient to compensate for the degree of hypoxia the $CMRO_2$ begins to fall and symptoms of cerebral hypoxia occur.

In *anemic anoxia,* sufficient oxygen reaches the blood but the amount of hemoglobin available to bind and transport it is decreased. Under such circumstances, the blood oxygen content is decreased even though the physical tension of the gas in the blood is normal. Either low hemoglobin content (anemia) or chemical changes in hemoglobin that interfere with oxygen binding (e.g., carbon monoxide poisoning, methemoglobinemia) can be responsible. Coma occurs if the oxygen content drops so low that the brain's metabolic needs are unmet even by an increased cerebral blood flow. The lowered blood viscosity that occurs in anemia makes it somewhat easier for the cerebral blood flow to increase than in carbon monoxide poisoning.

In *ischemic anoxia,* the blood itself carries sufficient oxygen, but the cerebral blood flow is insufficient to supply cerebral tissues; diseases that greatly reduce the cardiac output, such as myocardial infarction, arrhythmia, shock, vasovagal syncope, or diseases that greatly increase the cerebral vascular resistance by arterial occlusion or spasm (hypertensive encephalopathy) are the usual causes.

The development of neurological signs in most patients with ischemia or hypoxia depends more on the severity and duration of the process than on its specific cause. Ischemia (vascular failure) is generally more dangerous than hypoxia alone because potentially toxic products of cerebral metabolism are not removed.

The clinical categories of ischemic and hypoxic brain damage can be subdivided into acute, chronic, and multifocal:

ACUTE DIFFUSE ISCHEMIA OR HYPOXIA occurs with cardiac arrest, syncopal episodes, inhalation of an inert gas or carbon monoxide, or acute pulmonary embolism. In all instances, it is likely that ischemia, rather than anoxemia alone, produces the major brain injury. Immediately, however, consciousness is lost rapidly, within 6 seconds after the cerebral circulation stops[479] or oxygen is no longer supplied. Fleeting light-headedness, loss of voluntary eye movements, and blindness sometimes precede unconsciousness. Generalized convulsions, pupillary dilatation, and bilateral extensor plantar responses quickly follow if anoxia is complete.

167

If tissue oxygenation is restored immediately, consciousness returns in seconds or minutes without sequelae, but if the oxygen deprivation lasts longer than 1 or 2 minutes, or if it is superimposed upon preexisting cerebral vascular disease, then stupor, confusion, and signs of motor dysfunction may persist for several hours or permanently. Under clinical circumstances, total ischemic anoxia lasting longer than 4 minutes kills brain cells with the neurons of the cerebral cortex (especially the hippocampus) and cerebellum (the Purkinje cells) dying first.[592] Severe diffuse ischemic anoxia lasting 10 minutes or more destroys the brain.[591] Experimentally, at least, much evidence indicates that the initial mechanism of anoxia's rapidly lethal effect on the brain may lie in the inability of the heart and the cerebral vascular bed to recover from severe ischemia or oxygen lack. This can be brought out by comparing the effects of experimental anoxia on the retina and the brain. The retina, being flat, can be oxygenated in an in vitro bath at 37° C. without a blood supply. Such a preparation will usually recover its action potential with reoxygenation of the bath after 20 minutes of total anoxia, which is much longer than the brain can tolerate an arrested circulation.[11] The big differences are that after 4 minutes of severe anoxia the heart fails irreversibly in most mammals,[491] and after a similar duration of absence of blood flow in the brain, the glial cells begin to swell so that they compress the capillaries, which prevents the reflow of blood through the previously ischemic zone.[355] If one makes meticulous efforts to maintain the circulation in experimental animals, the brain can fully recover from as long as 30 minutes of very severe hypoxemia with arterial P_{O_2} tensions of 20 mm. Hg or less.[219, 486] These recent laboratory findings suggest that guaranteeing the systemic circulation offers the strongest chance of effectively treating or preventing hypoxic brain damage.

Clinically, acute, short-lived hypoxic episodes are sometimes difficult to distinguish in retrospect from epilepsy, since convulsions mark both illnesses. Generally speaking, fits due to hypoxia are briefer, less intense, primarily tonic[199] and occur singly, whereas grand mal epileptic attacks usually last 3 to 5 minutes, are tonic and clonic, and tend to recur.

Laboratory tests sometimes help to implicate hypoxia as the cause of coma and should be used in doubtful cases. The problem here is that the neurological effects of a brief exposure to hypoxia can long outlast any changes in the blood gases or detectable residual concentrations of carbon monoxide hemoglobin. The electrocardiograph may suggest that ischemic hypoxia was the cause of coma if the record discloses cardiac arrhythmia, complete heart block, or changes consistent with acute myocardial infarction. However, these changes must be interpreted with caution since subarachnoid hemorrhages or encephalitis can induce somewhat similar electrocardiographic abnormalities[368, 535] (see Case 36, page 213).

The prognosis for recovery cannot be accurately judged immediately following removal from hypoxia. Some patients recover completely even though they fail to awaken fully for days after the exposure while others arouse promptly only to relapse and die a fortnight later (see below). Generally speaking, subjects who demonstrate intact brainstem function when removed from hypoxia, as manifested by normal pupillary light and ciliospinal responses, intact doll's-eye movements, and oculovestibular responses, have a good outlook for recovery of consciousness and perhaps their total faculties. The absence of any of these normal functions is serious, and pupils that are persistently fixed to light stimulation following hypoxia imply a hopeless outlook.

Pulmonary embolism is an important and little recognized cause of acute generalized cerebral anoxia. The mechanism of cerebral ischemia is probably decreased cerebral blood flow resulting from the fall in cardiac output that accompanies pulmonary embolization.[213] Whether the decreased cardiac output is itself simply a result of the obstruction of right heart outflow or whether humoral and reflex factors play a role is unclear.[252] The incidence of neurological symptoms resulting from pulmonary embolus varies, but mental changes occur in approximately 60 per cent of patients,[315] and neurological changes represent the major clinical finding in approximately 5 per cent of cases.[182] The clinical symptoms are usually those of abrupt, diffuse cerebral ischemia. The patient suddenly loses consciousness, either while exerting himself[429] or while at rest. There may be seizure activity coincident with syncope.[182] If the patient recovers consciousness by the time the physician sees him, he may be confused, tachypneic, and anxious, or the physical and neurological examinations may be normal. However, if the embolus has been large enough to cause a profound fall in cardiac output and more prolonged unconsciousness, the typical clinical manifestations of pulmonary embolus, including systemic hypotension, tachypnea, and hypoxia, are usually present in addition to the evidence of diffuse cerebral dysfunction. Focal neurological signs are sometimes prominent. Fred, Willerson, and Alexander[182] reported four patients in whom the presenting signs of pulmonary embolization were predominantly neurological. One had syncopal attacks, two developed focal neurological signs without changes in consciousness, and the fourth was stuporous with focal neurological signs. At autopsy every patient showed evidence of cerebral neuronal hypoxia, but none had evidence of focal infarction or paradoxical cerebral embolization[201] (see Chapter 2). The diagnosis of pulmonary infarction should be considered in any patient who suddenly faints, develops acute confusion or loses consciousness without an obvious reason. Virtually all patients complain of dyspnea, either at rest or on exercise,[487, 556] and most will be tachypneic when examined with arterial blood gases typical of intrapulmonary shunting with a decreased Po_2 (less than 80 mm. Hg) and a decreased Pco_2.[556] The blood gas determinations and lung scan are the most sensitive tests for screening, and if either is normal, acute pulmonary embolism is essentially excluded. The most frequent incorrect diagnosis is acute myocardial infarction, a disease in which brief syncopal attacks are comparatively rare.

SUBACUTE OR CHRONIC DIFFUSE HYPOXIA occurs with severe anemia, myocardial infarction, congestive heart failure, and pulmonary disease. Any of these conditions can produce metabolic stupor or coma, but the clinical picture tends to be nonspecific. Judgment slips away early, and confusion, disorientation, and lethargy emerge. More profound ischemia or hypoxia provokes periodic breathing, diffuse reflex changes, and small but reactive pupils. Ultimately, progressive hypoxia precipitates multifocal myoclonus, decorticate rigidity, and, occasionally, focal neurological signs in the form of monoplegia or hemiplegia. Such severe neurological changes usually ensue only after a period of cerebral underperfusion, or when the arterial Po_2 values have fallen to the range of 20 to 30 mm. Hg.

Patients in stupor or coma from subacute or chronic hypoxia usually come to medical attention with the provoking cause still evident so that physical abnormalities or direct laboratory evidence for the suspected cause can be obtained. Differential diagnosis requires attention to the following details. The cerebral blood flow never falls as the result of cardiac failure unless the cardiac output drops profoundly,[150] so that one should obtain evidence for severe degrees of congestive heart failure or cardiac arrhythmias in order to assign the cause of coma to cardiac causes alone. Similarly, blood oxygen tensions below 40 mm. Hg are required for hypoxia to produce cerebral symptoms. Anemia cannot be incriminated as a cause of delirium or coma unless the blood oxygen–carrying capacity is reduced by more than half.

Encephalopathy is seldom caused by a change in one of these functions, and it most often results from a combination of several. This may help explain why silent myocardial infarcts readily produce metabolic encephalopathy in moderately anemic elderly subjects with cerebral atherosclerosis even when the reduction in cardiac output is barely sufficient to precipitate overt heart failure.

MULTIFOCAL CEREBRAL ISCHEMIA OR ANOXIA occurs in hypertensive encephalopathy, where it presumably originates from focal vasoconstriction in cerebral vessels similar to that readily observed directly in the retina in this disorder. Similar ischemic insults of the brain are produced by widespread small vessel occlusion, which can result from: (1) increased viscosity of the blood (e.g., in polycythemia, cryoglobulinemia, macroglobulinemia, or sickle cell anemia), (2) multivascular in situ clotting (disseminated intravascular coagulation), (3) multiple small emboli arising in the heart (subacute bacterial endocarditis, nonbacterial thrombotic endocarditis), or from the effects of mechanical pump oxygenators substituting for the heart (the cardiopulmonary bypass syndrome), (4) fat embolism, (5) the parasitemia of cerebral malaria or, (6) as a direct disease of cerebral vessels, as in disseminated lupus erythematosus, periarteritis nodosa, or

170

generalized arteriosclerosis. In all of the above abnormalities, except perhaps arteriosclerosis in which coma is uncommon, there is a similar neurological picture consisting of delirium, stupor, or coma frequently combined with generalized or focal seizures and transient or fleeting multifocal neurological signs. In this combination of progressive diffuse plus focal neurological signs, the clinical picture differs from that of most metabolic encephalopathies and even from the other anoxic encephalopathies, which usually present more abruptly with diffuse and symmetrical neurological pictures. The disorders that most frequently cause coma are discussed in the following paragraphs.

Hypertensive encephalopathy can be a difficult diagnosis, but the importance of treating it correctly makes it a significant one. Typically the patients are moderately or severely hypertensive and have suffered a recent abrupt rise in blood pressure. The thing that often makes diagnosis difficult is that many deviate from this rule, and the blood pressure sometimes drops to near normal soon after a severe attack. Most patients with hypertensive encephalopathy have both retinal artery spasm and papilloretinal edema, and the majority have retinal exudates as well. The attacks can take several forms. One consists of progressive delirium and stupor with focal seizures. Another, and perhaps the most common, includes generalized or focal convulsions combined with headache, vomiting, and multifocal neurological weakness or cortical blindness. Typically the neurological signs last minutes, hours, or days, then disappear, leaving little or no residua. The spinal fluid pressure tends to be elevated over 180 mm. and sometimes rises as high as 300 to 400 mm. of CSF. The CSF protein is usually elevated, often ranging between 60 and 280 mg. per 100 cc.

Stupor or coma due to hypertensive encephalopathy can resemble that seen with uremia, brain tumor, or the recurrent transient ischemic attacks of cerebral vascular disease. Clinical judgment is important in diagnosis since laboratory tests sometimes fail to be diagnostic, particularly when uremia and hypertension coexist. Generally speaking, a BUN over 100 mg. per 100 cc. favors uremia as the diagnosis. Brain tumor seldom gives the kind of multifocal, bilateral, and transient cerebral attacks that characterize hypertensive disease. The transient ischemic attacks of vascular disease of the large cervical vessels usually differ by producing more stereotyped and short-lived episodes than hypertensive attacks. In addition, in ischemic cerebral vascular disease the blood pressure is rarely as high as with hypertensive encephalopathy, and the patients rarely have severe hypertensive eyeground changes.

Disseminated intravascular coagulation is a clinical-pathological entity that is not bound to a single illness but can be triggered by several; McKay has called it an intermediary mechanism of disease.[366] In the disorder there is free thrombin activity within the circulation that causes platelet aggregation and fibrin formation. The disorder may be associated with bleeding, but more frequently fibrin deposits itself in arterioles, venules, and capillaries to cause widespread ischemia of the organs involved. The pathological entities that commonly lead to disseminated intravascular coagulation are sepsis with the release of bacterial endotoxin,[32] malignancy,[131] and unknown causes often arising in the setting of no other diseases (thrombotic thrombocytopenic purpura).[13] Several authors believe that disseminated intravascular coagulation may play a role in entities such as fat embolism, cerebral malaria, and hypertensive encephalopathy.

McKay[366] has described the clinical and pathological picture. The symptoms of the disorder are primarily cerebral. This is probably because other organs, not having area-specific functions, can tolerate a greater volume of multifocal ischemia without presenting clinical abnormalities. Patients may complain of headache and difficulty in concentrating as well as a variety of fleeting and minor neurological symptoms including vertigo, visual blurring, and speech difficulty. The major neurological signs are those of diffuse cerebral dysfunction beginning with confusion and disorientation and leading in some instances to stupor and coma. Many of the patients who are delirious or stuporous have at the same time fleeting and changing neurological signs including visual field defects, generalized or focal seizures, and hemiparesis. Bleeding phenomena are common, including petechiae in the skin or optic fundi, purpura, and, occasionally, subdural or intracerebral hemorrhages.[366] A diagnosis is usually established by examination of coagulation factors in the blood. The platelet count is low and the prothrombin time elevated. Hypofibrinogenemia is usually present, and products split from fibrin can often be identified in the blood.

Cerebral malaria is a well-recognized complication of infection of Plasmodium falciparum and is usually the cause of death in that disease. Cerebral malaria was well recognized in World War II and in various series had a mortality of 5 to 48 per cent, usually depending on how severe the cerebral complications were when treatment was undertaken. The disease has become important again in this country because of the number of cases of malaria in American troops in South Vietnam. Daroff and associates[123] report 19 cases of cerebral malaria seen in a 10-month period during which 1200 cases of malaria were treated. There were no deaths. Smitskamp and Wolthuis[529] reported 10 deaths from cerebral malaria in 140 patients with malignant tertian malaria treated between 1956 and 1967. Cerebral malaria usually begins after the systemic disease is well under way, and thus all of Daroff's patients were in the hospital being evaluated and treated for malaria at the time when cerebral symptoms began. The most common neurological abnormality is a disturbance of consciousness ranging from acute confusion to lethargy, stupor, and, occasionally, frank coma. Focal neurological signs were encountered in only one of Daroff's 19 cases and that was a transient, unilateral hyperreflexia and hemisensory disturbance. Other series report a high incidence of focal neurological signs.[173] Granted that one thinks of it, the diagnosis is not difficult since the patients are all systemically ill with high fevers, and thick smears of the blood always contain abundant numbers of Plasmodium falciparum. The spinal fluid is usually under increased pressure but is otherwise normal. However, occasional patients have been reported with CSF pleocytosis, a protein increase, or both.

The pathogenesis of the cerebral ischemia is not entirely clear. Plugging of cerebral vessels by parasite-infected erythrocytes combined with endothelial proliferation has been described by several authors. In addition to the occluded vessels, there are frequently perivascular hemorrhages. Maigraith[354] has suggested that anoxia from decreased oxygen-carrying capacity of the infected erythrocytes is the primary process, which then leads to endothelial proliferation and plugging of vessels. Devakul, Harinasuta, and Reid[130] suggested that disseminated intravascular coagulation may be important as they noted a fall in plasma fibrinogen in two patients with severe cerebral malaria.

Fat embolism is a common pathological entity that affects as many as 24 per cent of patients dying after trauma.[484] Pathologically, small vessels, particularly those in lungs and brain, are occluded by lipid particles and at times by fibrin clots. Fat embolism has also been described occasionally in patients with pancreatitis, acute fatty necrosis of the liver, and sickle cell anemia. There is some dispute as to the origin of the fat that plugs small vessels. Some authors[484] believe that the material originates from the traumatized area, particularly bones, and finds its way to the lungs and then the systemic circulation. Others[502] believe that the emboli originate from plasma proteins and that the fibrin that plugs the vessels is probably a manifestation of disseminated intravascular coagulation.

Two clinical syndromes arise from fat embolus. The first, or pulmonary syndrome, is a result of multiple pulmonary microemboli that lead to progressive hypoxia with resulting tachypnea and hypocarbia. The hypoxia can be initially corrected by oxygen, but if emboli occlude enough alveolar capillaries, the patient may eventually develop respiratory failure. The second, or cerebral syndrome, is characterized by confusion, lethargy, stupor, or coma. Characteristically, the symptoms are not present immediately following the traumatic injury, but after a period of several hours to as long as 2 or 3 days the patients become lethargic and, in fulminant instances, comatose. The body temperature usually rises to 100 to 103° F., and the heart rate quickens. Most patients are tachypneic from pulmonary emboli, but even when obvious respiratory abnormalities are not present, blood gases usually reveal a depressed Po_2 and Pco_2. Accompanying the diffuse neurological signs of stupor and coma are a variety of focal signs including focal seizures, hemiparesis, or conjugate deviation of the eyes. The diagnosis can be extremely difficult to establish in mild to moderately severe cases. In severe or fulminating instances, a characteristic petechial rash develops on the second or third day after injury and is generally restricted to the neck, shoulders, and upper part of the anterior thorax. Biopsy of the petechiae reveals lipid emboli in small vessels. Similar petechiae may be seen in the eye grounds. The spinal fluid is normal. The prognosis with supportive care is good, and patients who survive an acute episode usually recover without significant neurological residua.

Open heart surgery with its attendant use of a cardiopulmonary bypass machine produces neurological damage in as many as half of the patients operated on.[568] The mechanism of neurological dysfunction appears to be plugging of multiple small vessels by platelet thrombi and other debris produced by the pump oxygenator.[58] At least in experimental animals, placing a filter in line with the pump oxygenator to remove the microdebris prevents the decrease in cerebral metabolism that otherwise occurs and significantly decreases the mortality from the use of this machine. In patients, there is a significant mortality, and among those who die, multiple large and small ischemic infarcts can be identified in the brain. Clinically, neurological dysfunction may occur either immediately or be delayed, but in either instance the likelihood and severity of postoperative neurological dysfunction increases directly in proportion to the length of time the patient receives cardiopulmonary bypass and to the age of the patient. The symptoms are similar to those of the other multifocal ischemic entities described above and include delirium, stupor, and coma, with or without focal dysfunction. In some of the patients, cutaneous petechial hemorrhages reminiscent of those occurring in fat emboli appear on the second or third day after surgery. If patients survive the acute episode, they usually make a fairly complete recovery, although Tufo, Ostfeld, and Shekelle identified signs of cerebral damage at discharge from the hospital in 15 per cent of the survivors.[568]

Endocarditis, whether arising from a chronic infection of the cardiac valves (subacute bacterial endocarditis) or de novo in a previously normal individual or in one suffering from a malignant disease (nonbacterial thrombotic endocarditis–marantic endocarditis), can trigger widespread embolic ischemia and infarction of the brain. The most common clinical picture in both types is that of an acute focal stroke, but in some instances, particularly in fulminating cases, smaller and more widespread emboli produce a clinical picture of a diffuse encephalopathy with or without focal signs. Jones, Siekert, and Geraci[281] describe the neurological manifestations of bacterial endocarditis. Twenty-one of their 110 patients developed severe "toxic encephalopathy," and these symptoms were the initial or presenting manifestations of endocarditis in 9 patients. An additional 44 patients had focal neurological signs and these were the initial manifestations of endocarditis in 17. Accurate diagnosis comes more easily when subacute bacterial endocarditis causes the cerebral symptoms, for such patients usually have signs of underlying heart disease and are usually

174

febrile and anemic with changing cardiac murmurs. The CSF may contain white cells and increased protein, fortifying one's suspicion of septic embolization. The diagnosis is more elusive in nonbacterial thrombotic endocarditis, for such patients can have the same cerebral picture, but cardiac abnormalities are usually minimal or absent.[69] The following case report illustrates the typical combination of diffuse and focal signs that characterize this group of disorders.

Case 27. A 55-year-old man developed a mass in the right buttock diagnosed as metastatic carcinoma 2 weeks prior to his admission to Memorial Hospital. Except for the mass, his physical examination was normal, as was a blood count, urinalysis, liver function tests, and blood electrolyte determinations. An enlargement of the left hilum was apparent on the chest x-ray film. The drainage from the buttock grew enterococci. In the hospital, he was treated with cyclophosphamide and radiation as well as antibiotics. The mass did not respond and produced progressively more pain, which required large doses of narcotics to control. Approximately 40 days after his admission, he became increasingly lethargic, a symptom at first attributed to narcotics. However, on the forty-third day he was noted to be stuporous with a stiff neck. His respirations were 36 per minute, the right pupil was 7 mm. and the left 4 mm., but both were reactive. The optic fundi were normal. He had a full range of roving eye movements. There was a depressed left corneal response accompanied by a left facial paresis, and a left hemiparesis and hemisensory defect. The stretch reflexes were hyperactive on the left and both plantar responses were extensor. A lumbar puncture revealed an opening pressure of 135 mm. CSF, 1 mononuclear cell, no red cells, a protein content of 40 mg. per 100 ml. and glucose of 70 mg. per 100 ml. A carotid arteriogram demonstrated occlusion of the right middle cerebral artery 2 cm. beyond the bifurcation. The remaining vessels looked normal. A hematological search for disseminated intravascular coagulation revealed no abnormalities except for a platelet count of 16,000. He remained in coma and gradually became hypotensive and azotemic. He died 5 days after the stupor began.

At autopsy the tumor turned out to be a malignant melanoma apparently arising in the buttocks and involving the regional lymph nodes, subcutaneous tissue, and peritoneal surfaces. The aortic and mitral valves were covered with nonbacterial vegetations, and emboli were identified in intramyocardial vessels, producing myocardial necrosis, as well as in cerebral vessels, producing infarction in the distributions of the right middle cerebral artery, the right posterior cerebral artery, and the left posterior inferior cerebellar artery. There were renal infarcts bilaterally and splenic infarcts as well.

SEQUELAE OF HYPOXIA. After recovery from an acute hypoxic insult, delayed *postanoxic encephalopathy* with coma sometimes occurs. The onset can be as long as 7 to 21 days after the initial hypoxia.[449] This serious sequel to hypoxia is not rare, as we have observed 14 such instances. The clinical picture includes an initial hypoxic insult that usually is sufficiently severe that patients are in deep coma when first found but awaken within 24 to 48 hours. Occasionally relapse occurs after a small hypoxic insult that is sufficient only to daze the patient and not to cause full unconsciousness. In either event, nearly all patients resume full activity within 4 or 5 days after the initial insult and then enjoy a clear and seemingly normal interval of 2 to 21 days. Then, abruptly, patients become irritable, apathetic, and confused. Some are agitated or develop mania. Walking changes to a halting shuffle, and diffuse spasticity or rigidity appears. The deterioration may progress to coma or death or may arrest itself at any point. A few patients have a second recovery period that leads to full health.

Delayed coma after hypoxia has been reported most often after carbon monoxide or asphyxial gas poisoning, but cases are known in which surgical anesthesia, hypoglycemia, or cardiac arrest has provided the antecedent insult. The neurological changes are at first often mistaken for a psychiatric disorder or even a subdural hematoma because of the lucid interval. Mental status examination clarifies the first of these errors, and the diffuse distribution of the neurological changes, the lack of headache, and the absence of rostral-caudal deterioration should eliminate the second.

The exact cause of delayed postanoxic encephalopathy is unknown. Pathologically, the brain contains diffuse, severe, and bilateral demyelination of the cerebral hemispheres with sparing of the immediate subcortical connecting fibers and of the brainstem. The basal ganglia are sometimes infarcted, but the nerve cells of the cerebral hemispheres and the brainstem remain mostly intact. The selective nature of these changes has led some workers to speculate that cerebral edema is the initial pathogenic step, while others have postulated an enzymic or even an autoimmune injury. No direct evidence supports any of these speculations.

The diagnosis of coma due to postanoxic encephalopathy is made from the history of the initial insult and by recognizing the characteristic signs and symptoms of metabolic coma. There is no specific treatment, but bed rest for patients with acute hypoxia may prevent the complication (see Case 1, page 16).

Hypoglycemia

Hypoglycemia is one of the most common and serious causes of metabolic coma[598] and capable of almost limitless combinations of signs and symptoms. Our own series includes 56 patients with severe hypoglycemic coma. Forty-nine were receiving insulin for the treatment of diabetes, two had pancreatic adenomas, and one had a huge retroperitoneal sarcoma. Of four patients who were alcoholics, two had chronic liver disease. Hypoglycemia in the latter type of patient is now recognized to result from a depletion of liver glycogen stores and impaired gluconeogenesis coupled with fasting.[180] Twelve of these cases were diagnosed incorrectly at first (Table 10), illustrating how often hypoglycemic encephalopathy is overlooked or mistaken for other conditions.

Pathologically, hypoglycemia directs its main damage at the cerebral hemispheres producing laminar or pseudolaminar necrosis in fatal cases but largely sparing the brainstem. The acute picture of metabolic encephalopathy due to hypoglycemia usually presents in one of four forms: (1) As a delirium manifested primarily by mental changes with either quiet and sleepy confusion or wild mania. (2) As coma accompanied by signs of multifocal brainstem dysfunction, including central neurogenic hyperventi-

Table 10. Transient neurological disorders caused by hypoglycemia

Patient	Signs and Symptoms	Original Diagnosis	Blood Sugar	Time Required to Recover to Normal after Care Given
E.L. ♂ 37	Excessive drowsiness and somnolence while driving, at work, etc.	Narcolepsy	18	8 hours
G.H. ♂ 39	Recurrent manic attacks, assaultive	Functional psychosis	9	6 hours
R.B. ♂ 44	Stuporous, irrational, no initial response to glucose	Acute psychotic reaction	58	6 hours
R.N. ♂ 42	Reckless driving, dysarthria, ataxia, amnesia	Acute intoxication	28	Immediate
S.B. ♀ 52	Extensor hypertonus, bilateral Babinski, coma	Basilar artery thrombosis	29	2 hours
C.P. ♂ 64	Coma of unknown origin	Basilar artery thrombosis	33	Immediate
J.B. ♀ 65	Deep coma with recurrent tetanic spasms	Basilar artery thrombosis	16	7 days
P.D. ♂ 28	Coma, hyperventilation, decerebrate rigidity	Subarachnoid hemorrhage	20	Immediate
J.H. ♂ 34	Coma, hyperventilation, stertorous respiration	Acute pulmonary edema	10	Died
F.S. ♂ 37	Left hemiparesis (conscious)	Cerebral infarction	31	Immediate
R.Q. ♂ 12	Recurrent generalized convulsions	Epilepsy	32	Immediate
M.C. ♀ 39	Status epilepticus with CSF pleocytosis	Acute meningitis	21	Immediate

lation and decerebrate spasms. In this form, pupillary light reactions, as well as oculocephalic and oculovestibular responses, are usually preserved to suggest that the underlying disorder is metabolic. The patients sometimes have shivering-like diffuse muscle activity and many are hypothermic (33 to 35° C.). (3) As a stroke-like illness characterized by focal neurological signs with or without accompanying coma. Montgomery and Pinner[387] have stressed this picture of transient focal hypoglycemic encephalopathy and an example is described as Case 26 on page 161. The pathological physiology of such focal signs in metabolic brain disease is not clear. Meyer and Portnoy[378] suggested that in the conditions of hypoglycemia, hypoxia, and hypotension, focal paralysis results from nutritional deprivation of an area already threatened by a borderline vascular supply. This may be true experimentally, but in man permanent motor paralysis is rare, and the weakness tends to shift from one side to another during different episodes of metabolic worsening. This kind of shifting deficit as well as the fact that focal neurological signs also occur in children in coma with severe hypoglycemia are against explaining localized neurological deficits in hypoglycemia as being due to cerebral vascular disease. (4) As an epileptic attack with single or multiple generalized convulsions and postictal coma. Many hypoglycemic patients convulse as the blood sugar level drops, and some have seizures as their only manifestation of hypoglycemia, leading to an erroneous diagnosis of epilepsy.

Neither the history nor the physical examination always distinguishes hypoglycemia from other causes of metabolic coma, although an important clinical point is (as is true also in hepatic coma) that the pupillary and oculovestibular reflex pathways are almost always spared. The great danger of this chameleon-like quality is that the longer hypoglycemia lasts, the more likely it is to produce irreversible neuronal loss. This may be the reason that more diabetics treated with insulin have EEG abnormalities than those treated with diet alone.[260] Insidious and progressive dementia is by no means rare among zealously controlled diabetics who often suffer recurrent minor hypoglycemia. Prolonged and irreversible coma also can result from severe hypoglycemia, as was illustrated by the following patient.

Case 28. A 58-year-old female was admitted in an unresponsive state. A history was not obtainable on admission, but the family later related that she recently had been nervous, depressed, and afraid of being alone. She had had an episode of unresponsiveness for which she was hospitalized several years earlier and from which she had recovered spontaneously after 2 days. The previous episode was believed, but never proved, to have been psychogenic.

Her general physical examination was essentially normal, as were her vital signs. She lay quietly in bed, unresponsive to speech but able to move all extremities when stimulated noxiously. The pupils were equal and reactive. Muscle tonus and strength appeared good, and the stretch reflexes were equal and active bilaterally. The plantar responses were flexor. Urinalysis revealed a 4+ sugar reaction and a 1+ test for acetone (she was not previously known to have been diabetic). A diagnosis of diabetic coma was made, and she was given 50 units of regular insulin intravenously and 50 units subcutaneously. Ninety minutes later her urine sugar was still 4+, and 100 additional units of regular insulin were given intravenously. Forty-five minutes later she had a generalized convulsion, and 50 cc. of 50 per cent dextrose were given intravenously. The seizure stopped, but she remained in deep coma with decerebrate motor responses. She had constricted but equal and reactive pupils, hyperactive deep tendon reflexes, and bilateral extensor plantar responses.

The following day she became less rigid and opened her eyes spontaneously, but otherwise paid no attention to her environment. At this time an EEG recorded background activity of 4 cps interspersed with frequent bursts of 1 to 3 cps activity. By the nitrous oxide technique,[299] the cerebral oxygen uptake was measured to be 1.1 cc. per 100 gm. brain per minute (normal 3.3 cc. per 100 gm. per minute). Three days later she was awake but she remained confused, disoriented, mildly lethargic, and unable to solve simple problems. Her EEG contained 4 to 6 cps waves interspersed with bursts of 2 to 4 cps activity. Her cerebral metabolic oxygen uptake was 2.2 cc. per 100 gm. brain per minute. Two days later (5 days after admission) she was more alert but still confused and disoriented. The cerebral oxygen uptake had increased to 2.6 cc. per 100 gm. brain per minute.

Ten days following admission she was oriented to person and place and could identify the correct year but not the month. She could add small numbers but was often wrong on problems of simple multiplication. She was unable to do serial 7's. She could read some words and a few sentences and was able to write simple sentences. At that time her cerebral metabolic oxygen uptake was 3.0 cc. per 100 gm. brain per minute. Her EEG contained 6 to 7 cps activity with interspersed bursts of 2 to 4 cps. Three months later, her dementia was unchanged. The cerebral oxygen uptake was again 3.0 cc. per 100 gm. brain per minute. Her mild diabetes did not require insulin or other hypoglycemic medications.

Comment: This woman's tragedy teaches several important lessons. The first is the importance of accurate clinical and laboratory diagnosis. An initial failure to recognize correctly what was almost certainly psychogenic unresponsiveness (oculovestibular tests were not performed) led to mild diabetes being incorrectly diagnosed as acidotic coma and treated with large amounts of insulin. Although never completely proved, all the circumstances indicated that disastrously severe hypoglycemia ensued, from which her brain never completely recovered. A second important point is that when hypoglycemia is profound or prolonged, glucose injections may not immediately restore brain function even though they raise the blood sugar level. This makes it imperative to obtain blood for sugar analysis *before* giving glucose to suspected hypoglycemics. Otherwise, all chance of accurate diagnosis may escape. Finally, the cerebral metabolic data from this patient illustrate that profound, chronic changes in mental function can be associated with only minimal reductions in total cerebral metabolism. After her acute illness had passed, she was left with the mentality of a 6-year-old, but her cerebral oxygen consumption returned to the lower limits of normal.

Cofactor Deficiency

Deficiency of one or more of the B vitamins is frequently the cause of delirium, dementia, and possibly stupor, but only thiamine deficiency is likely to be considered in the differential diagnosis of coma.[579]

Thiamine deficiency produces Wernicke's disease, a symptom complex due to neuronal and vascular damage of the gray matter and blood vessels surrounding the third ventricle, aqueduct, and fourth ventricle.[579] Why the lesions have such a focal distribution is not altogether understood, since, with deficiency, thiamine disappears from all brain areas at about the same rate.[137] However, a thiamine-dependent enzyme, transketolase, loses its activity in the pontine tegmentum more rapidly than in other areas,[138] and it is presumed that a focal effect such as this explains the restricted pathological changes.

The cause of thiamine deficiency is absence of the vitamin from the diet, and the most frequent reason is that patients have substituted alcohol for vitamin-containing foods. As would be expected with lesions involving the diencephalic and periaqueductal structures, the patients are obtunded, confused, and often have a striking failure of memory. They are rarely comatose.[356] These symptoms are common to many disorders, however, and can be attributed to Wernicke's disease only when accompanied by nystagmus and oculomotor paralysis, and when reversed by thiamine treatment. In very advanced cases, involvement of oculomotor muscles may be sufficient to produce not only complete external ophthalmoplegia but fixed, dilated pupils.[356] Most patients, in addition to eye signs, also suffer from ataxia, dysarthria, and mild peripheral neuropathy. Many have a curious universal indifference to noxious stimulation, and autonomic insufficiency is so common that orthostatic hypotension and shock are constant threats.[47] The hypotension of Wernicke's disease appears to result from a combination of neural lesions and depleted blood volume and is probably the most common cause of death in this illness.

Liver Disease

Cerebral dysfunction occurs either when liver function fails or when the liver is bypassed so that the portal circulation shunts intestinal venous drainage directly into the systemic circulation. Morphological changes are few in the brains of most patients with encephalopathy due to chronic liver disease except for an increase in large, Alzheimer type II astrocytes.[4] However, a very few patients in addition to having episodic hepatic coma also suffer a progressive mental, cerebellar, and extrapyramidal deterioration; the brains of such individuals contain zones of pseudolaminar necrosis, small cavitations, nerve cell loss in the basal ganglia and cerebellum, and glycogen-staining inclusions in the enlarged astrocytes.[577]

Many possible toxic agents or deficiencies have been suggested as potential causes for hepatic coma, but none successfully explains all instances of the condition. An elevated blood and brain ammonia level, which results from the products of intestinal digestion bypassing the urea-synthesizing mechanisms of the liver, has most often been incriminated as the agent at fault. Ammonia is unquestionably toxic to the brain since children with

180

inherited defects in urea synthesis develop severe cerebral degeneration producing stupor and coma in association with raised blood ammonia levels.[68] Furthermore, experimental hyperammonemia induces astrocytic abnormalities resembling those of hepatic encephalopathy.[84] However, a shortcoming of the ammonia theory is that ammonia levels are sometimes normal in comatose patients with liver failure, and it may be that several different abnormal substances can induce the neurological abnormality.[124] Geiger[202] suggested from animal experiments that encephalopathy results when the liver fails to supply uridine and cytidine to the brain. It is doubtful if this applies to the clinical problem since feeding these pyrimidines or purines or amino acids is without evident value for most patients with hepatic coma. Recently it has been suggested that abnormal neurotransmitters that could be synthesized in the gut by bacterial action on proteins, but no longer are detoxified by the bypassed or diseased liver, could account for the neurological abnormality of hepatic coma.[164] The theory results partly from the apparent improvement brought about in a few patients by the empirical treatment with levodopa. Whether or not this suggestion turns out to have merit, there do appear to be toxic stuffs in the cerebrospinal fluid of patients with hepatic coma. Such fluid perfused into the cerebral ventricles of either cats or rats induces an encephalopathy in the animal that cannot be reproduced by perfusing equal amounts of a normal person's CSF even when ammonia or glutamine is added in concentrations equal to those found in patients with hepatic coma.[59, 444]

The immediate pathogenesis of hepatic coma depends on the underlying cause. Many patients with severe liver disease develop encephalopathy as an inexorable step in progressive hepatic failure, and no sudden load or stress need be imposed. Patients with portal-systemic shunts, however, can have almost normal parenchymal liver function as judged by standard laboratory tests, yet develop hepatic encephalopathy when increased loads of nitrogenous substances are suddenly presented to their circulations, such as with gastrointestinal bleeding, infections, or high protein diets. These latter factors also can precipitate hepatic coma in patients with liver disease, as can ingestion of sedative drugs (mechanism unknown) or acetazolamide, which increases the ammonia concentration in renal blood[194] and also increases the brain CO_2 tension; either mechanism could be toxic.[454]

The clinical picture of hepatic encephalopathy is fairly consistent, but its onset often is difficult to define exactly. The incipient mental symptoms usually consist of a quiet, apathetic delirium, which either persists for several days or rapidly evolves into profound coma. Less often, in perhaps 10 to 20 per cent of the cases, the earliest symptoms are of a boisterous delirium verging on mania, an onset suggesting rapidly progressive liver disease such as acute yellow atrophy. Neither type of delirium is specific, as was illustrated by one of our patients with chronic cirrhosis who suffered two episodes of hepatic coma spaced 2 weeks apart. The first began with an agitated delirium; the second, with quiet obtundation. It was impossible to distinguish between the two attacks by biochemical changes or rate of evolution. Respiratory changes are a hallmark of severe liver disease. Hyperventilation, as judged by low arterial Pco_2 levels, occurs at all depths of coma and usually becomes clinically obvious as patients become deeply comatose. This almost invariable hyperventilation was illustrated by our own series of 30 patients: All had serum alkalosis and all but three had low Pco_2 values. These three exceptions had concomitant metabolic alkalosis, correction of which was followed by hyperventilation and respiratory alkalosis. Although some authors[392] have reported instances of metabolic acidosis, particularly in terminal patients, the implication is that encephalopathy unaccompanied by either respiratory or metabolic alkalosis is not hepatic in origin.

Moderately obtunded patients sometimes have lateral gaze nystagmus. Tonic conjugate downward or down and lateral ocular deviation has marked the onset of coma in several of our patients, and we have once observed reversible, vertical skew deviation during an episode of hepatic coma. Peripheral oculomotor paralyses are rare in hepatic coma unless patients have concomitant Wernicke's disease and, in fact, easily elicited brisk and conjugate oculocephalic and oculovestibular responses are generally a striking finding. The pupils are usually small but react to light. Asterixis is characteristic and frequently involves the muscles of the feet, tongue, and jaw as well as the hands. Patients with mild to moderate encephalopathy are usually found to have bilateral gegenhalten. Decorticate and decerebrate postural responses, muscle spasticity, and bilateral extensor plantar responses frequently accompany deeper coma. Focal neurological signs can appear in patients with deep coma and indeed were encountered in five of our unconscious patients. Four of these had hemiparesis, and in two the focal weakness shifted from side to side during the illness. The incidence of convulsions in hepatic coma varies in different series. Only one of our patients convulsed, but Adams and Foley[4] reported seizures in a third of their subjects. It is possible that the higher incidence in the Boston series may be related to alcohol withdrawal, but this is conjectural.

Hepatic coma is rarely a difficult diagnosis to make in patients who suffer from severe chronic liver disease and who gradually lose consciousness, displaying the obvious stigmata of jaundice, spider angiomata, fetor hepaticus, and enlarged livers and spleens. The diagnosis can be more difficult in patients whose coma is precipitated by an exogenous factor and who have either mild unsuspected liver disease or portal-systemic shunts. In this situation hepatic coma can be suspected by finding clinical evidence of metabolic encephalopathy combined with respiratory alkalosis and brisk oculocephalic reflexes, and the diagnosis is strengthened by identifying a portal-systemic shunt, plus an elevated serum ammonia level. The blood sugar should be measured in patients with severe liver disease since diminished liver glycogen stores may induce hypoglycemia and complicate hepatic coma. The spinal fluid is usually clear, free of cells, and has a normal protein content. It is rare to detect bilirubin in the CSF unless patients have serum bilirubin levels of at least 4 to 6 mg. per 100 cc. and chronic parenchymal liver failure as well. The EEG undergoes progressive slowing in hepatic coma, with slow activity beginning symmetrically in the frontal leads and spreading posteriorly as unconsciousness deepens. The changes are not specific or particularly helpful in differential diagnosis.

In differential diagnosis, mild hepatic encephalopathy is sometimes confused with psychiatric disturbances or acute alcoholism. Comatose patients in whom hepatic coma has developed rapidly often have motor signs that at first suggest structural disease of the brainstem, and they are sometimes mistakenly believed to have subdural hematoma or basilar artery thrombosis. In hepatic coma pupillary and caloric responses are normal, there is hyperventilation, and signs of rostral-caudal deterioration are absent, all of which rule out subdural hematoma. Subtentorial structural disease is ruled out by the normal pupillary and caloric responses as well as the fluctuating and inconstant quality of motor signs.

Renal Disease

Uremic encephalopathy is the metabolic encephalopathy of renal failure. Aside from cerebral edema, which may be more a manifestation of accompanying hypertensive encephalopathy than of the kidney disease, neuropathological changes are absent and the exact cause of the cerebral symptoms is unknown, since they often correlate poorly with the blood urea nitrogen or other serum biochemical or electrolyte abnormalities. The neurological symptoms of uremia are nearly always reversed by hemodialysis so that a dialyzable toxin of small molecular size is presumably at fault. Many have regarded urea as the likely offender, but this is probably not the case since urea infusions will not reproduce the symptoms, and hemodialysis will reverse clinical uremia even when the blood urea level is not lowered.[373] Since systemic acidosis develops so often in uremia, it was at one time postulated that acidosis of the brain might underlie the uremic syndrome. However, this is not the case since analysis of the cerebrospinal fluid from uremic patients almost always discloses a normal pH.[456] In experimental animals, Record and his co-workers[465] could accelerate some of the signs of uremic encephalopathy by infusing phenolic acids, but the levels required were much higher than one finds in the blood of uremic patients. Cerebral energy reserves remain normal in experimental uremia,[570] but the brain's permeability to sugars and to electrolytes is altered,[172] reflecting an abnormality in membrane function that may include a change in ionic pumping.

The clinical picture is nonspecific. Like most other metabolic encephalopathies, uremic encephalopathy, particularly when it develops rapidly, can produce a florid delirium marked by noisy agitation, delusions, and hallucinations. More often, however, progressive dull confusion with inappropriate behavior blends slowly into stupor or coma accompanied characteristically by respiratory changes, focal neurological signs, and convulsions. Untreated patients with uremic encephalopathy all have serum acidosis and associated hyperpnea. Without these, the diagnosis can hardly be entertained. (In treated patients, the presence or absence of acidosis has little effect on the cerebral symptoms.) Pupillary and oculomotor functions are seldom disturbed in uremia, certainly not in any diagnostic way. On the other hand, motor changes are rarely absent. Patients with chronic renal disease are weak, and as uremia evolves many of them develop intense asterixis as well as so much multifocal myoclonus that the muscles can appear to fasciculate. Tetany is frequent. Stretch reflex asymmetries are common, as are focal neurological weaknesses: 10 of our 45 patients with uremia had hemipareses that frequently cleared rapidly after hemodialysis or shifted from side to side during the course of the illness. Convulsions are distressingly common; either focal or generalized, they occurred in 15 of our patients and in 5 of the 13 reported by Locke, Merrill, and Tyler.[335] In our patients at least, there was little evidence that water intoxication caused the fits, and several examples occurred in patients who were free of serious hypertension.

Laboratory determinations tell one only that patients have uremia, but do not delineate this as the cause of coma. Renal failure is accompanied by complex biochemical, osmotic, and vascular abnormalities, and the degree of azotemia varies widely in patients with equally serious symptoms. One of our patients, a child with nephritis, had severe delirium and stupor despite a BUN of only 48 mg. per 100 cc. Other patients were free of cerebral symptoms with BUN values over 200 mg. per 100 cc. Uremia also causes aseptic meningitis, accompanied by stiff neck with as many as 250 lymphocytes and polymorphonuclear leukocytes per cu. mm. in the cerebrospinal fluid.[351] The spinal fluid pressure is abnormally elevated to over 160 to 180 mm. in some patients, a finding which has sometimes been taken to reflect cerebral edema. EEG slowing correlates with increasing degrees of azotemia, but many patients with slow records have little or no accompanying mental changes.[224] The electrophysiological changes are nonspecific and of no help in diagnosis.

In differential diagnosis, uremia must be distinguished from other causes of acute metabolic acidosis, from acute water intoxication, and from hypertensive encephalopathy.

Distinction from other causes of metabolic acidosis is straightforward if a laboratory is available. Among the severe acidoses causing the triad of coma, hyperpnea, and a low serum bicarbonate (uremia, diabetes, lactic acidosis, ingestion of exogenous poisons), only uremia is likely to cause

184

multifocal myoclonus, tetany, and generalized convulsions, and the others do not cause azotemia during their early stages.

Water intoxication is common in uremia and can be exceedingly difficult to diagnose or rule out as a cause of symptoms. Patients with azotemia are nearly always thirsty, and they have multiple electrolyte abnormalities. Excessive water ingestion, inappropriate fluid therapy, and hemodialysis (see below) all potentially reduce the serum osmolality and thereby induce or accentuate delirium and convulsions. The presence of water intoxication is confirmed by measuring a low serum osmolality (less than 260 mOsm. per L.) but it can be suspected when the serum sodium concentration falls below 120 mEq. per L.

Far and away the greatest problem in differential diagnosis, however, is to separate the symptoms of uremia from those of hypertensive encephalopathy, since both azotemia and advanced hypertension often plague the same patient. Each condition can cause seizures, focal neurological signs, increased intracranial pressure, and delirium or stupor. The following points may help to differentiate: Uremia seldom fluctuates so rapidly or causes such fleeting neurological signs as does hypertensive encephalopathy, and uremia rarely causes papilledema, cortical blindness, aphasia, or an increase in the spinal fluid protein content, whereas hypertensive encephalopathy produces all of these. Finally, despite occasional exceptions, uremia *usually* is associated with a very high BUN and hypertensive encephalopathy *usually* is associated with either a sustained very high blood pressure (diastolic pressure of 120 mm. Hg or greater) or a recently elevated blood pressure.

The following patient was diagnosed as having hypertensive encephalopathy because his symptoms suggested that particular disease and because his stupor had increased after recent hemodialysis. Because his blood pressure had not recently risen, however, it was impossible to be certain of the diagnosis until antihypertensive agents alleviated his neurological signs.

Case 29. A 45-year-old man with severe renal disease was being hemodialyzed twice weekly. He had once been in coma from uremia, but after dialysis had awakened and become alert with a normal neurological examination. However, his BUN remained near 100 mg. per 100 cc., and he was hypertensive. Thirty-six hours following routine dialysis, he had three generalized convulsions and he remained lethargic afterward. He was arousable but confused, disoriented, and blind. His pupils were 5 mm. in diameter and reacted to light, and there was a full range of extraocular movements on the doll's-head maneuver. His optic discs were not edematous, but there was such intense constriction of the retinal arterioles that the veins of the optic fundi were not visibly filled. He did not have focal motor weakness but had gegenhalten and hyperactive stretch reflexes in his extremities with bilateral extensor plantar responses. His blood pressure had not changed from its average level of 200/120 mm. Hg, nor had his BUN or electrolytes changed. The cerebral spinal fluid pressure in the lateral recumbent position was 90 mm. There were no red or white cells in the spinal fluid, and the protein was 50 mg. per 100 cc. His blood pressure was lowered to 180/90 mm. Hg with intravenous administration of methyldopate hydrochloride. Within 72 hours he became awake and rational; the blindness disappeared, the arteries of his eyegrounds became less constricted, and the veins were visible again.

Uremia is now frequently treated by hemodialysis, a development that sometimes adds to the neurological complexity of the syndrome. Neurological recovery does not always immediately follow effective dialysis, and patients often continue temporarily in coma or stupor. Indeed, one of our own patients remained comatose for 5 days after his blood nitrogen and electrolytes returned to normal. Such a delayed recovery did not imply permanent brain damage, however, for this man, like others with similar but less protracted delays, now enjoys normal neurological function. Dialysis itself may even contribute to encephalopathy if it too rapidly clears the blood urea. The mechanism is as follows: The blood-brain barrier is only slowly permeable to urea, but equilibrium eventually occurs so that in uremia the slowly acquired and persistent azotemia is reflected by high brain urea levels.[304] A rapid lowering of the blood urea by hemodialysis is not paralleled by an equally rapid reduction of brain urea. As a result, during dialysis the brain becomes hyperosmolar relative to blood, and water may shift suddenly from the extracerebral space to the brain.[520] Water intoxication with its own encephalopathy results (page 199) but can be prevented by slower dialysis or by introducing other agents such as fructose into the dialysis bath to maintain the blood osmolality.[295]

Pulmonary Disease

Hypoventilation due to advanced lung failure or other causes leads to severe encephalopathy or coma. Unless profound hypoxia occurs, permanent changes in the brain are lacking and the encephalopathy is fully reversible. Carbon dioxide retention, serum acidosis, and hypoxia, each has had its proponents as the principal cause for the cerebral symptoms. Serum acidosis per se is probably not an important factor, however, since alkali infusions fail to improve the neurological status of these patients. Also, although hypoxia may potentiate the illness, it is unlikely that it is the sole cause of the cerebral symptoms since patients with congestive heart failure tolerate equal degrees of hypoxemia with no encephalopathy. Sieker and Hickam[514] pointed out that of all the variables, the degree of carbon dioxide retention correlates most closely with the neurological symptoms, but cerebral symptoms also depend in part on the duration of the condition and on associated abnormalities such as the intensity of hypoxemia, heart failure, or infection. For example, some subjects with chronic hypercarbia have no cerebral symptoms despite $Paco_2$ levels of 55 to 60 mm. Hg, whereas others become stuporous in the face of a recent rise in $Paco_2$ to the same level. A factor explaining these discrepancies may be the existence of better brain buffering in states of chronic CO_2 retention as opposed to acute retention. Posner, Swanson, and Plum[456] recently found in patients with pulmonary insufficiency a good correlation between the intensity of neurological symptoms and the severity of carbon dioxide–induced acidosis in the spinal fluid. Their findings suggest that whether or not a neurological defect accompanies CO_2 retention depends at least partly on whether concomitant intracellular acidosis develops in the brain.

The symptoms of pulmonary encephalopathy are similar regardless of the cause of the respiratory decompensation. Among 37 patients with CO_2 narcosis in our own series, 29 had emphysema, 3 had hypoventilation due to obesity, and 5 had hypoventilation secondary to neuromuscular disease or depression of brainstem respiratory mechanisms.

The clinical picture of pulmonary encephalopathy includes dull diffuse headache accompanied by slowly developing drowsiness, stupor, or coma. The encephalopathy usually begins insidiously as pulmonary function fails, but coma occasionally begins abruptly if infection or sedative drugs precipitate rapid pulmonary decompensation. All patients with respiratory failure hypoventilate, as determined by elevated blood Pco_2 levels, and most of them are cyanotic as well. Those with obstructive emphysema usually wheeze, gasp, and puff with all too obviously increased efforts, but those with hypoventilation due to obesity or diseases of the nervous system breathe quietly, shallowly, and often irregularly. The pupils are small and briskly reactive to light unless hypoxia is profound. The ocular movements are usually normal. A striking phenomenon found in perhaps 10 per cent of patients with severe pulmonary insufficiency is distended ophthalmic veins and papilledema, reflecting increased intracranial pressure associated with the chronic hypercarbia and hypoxia. Signs of motor dysfunction tend to be less prominent in pulmonary encephalopathy than in other metabolic comas. Seizures are comparatively rare. Asterixis and multifocal myoclonus, on the other hand, are almost the rule and sometimes the myoclonus is so prominent that the subject grossly quivers and shakes. Friedreich described paramyoclonus multiplex[190] in a subject with chronic pulmonary disease, and this may have been the earliest, unknowing description of these metabolic neuromuscular changes. The muscles show moderately increased tonus, but the stretch reflexes are more often depressed than hyperactive. The plantar responses are usually extensor.

The diagnosis of hypoxic-hypercarbic encephalopathy is not difficult when patients have obvious pulmonary or cardiopulmonary failure and gradually develop obtundation, tremor, and twitching. A greater problem is presented when patients with previously compensated, but marginal, pulmonary function suddenly become hypoxic and hypercapnic because of an infection or excess sedation. Such patients may be erroneously suspected of having sedative poisoning or other causes of coma, but as in the following example, blood gas measurements make the diagnosis.

Case 30. A 60-year-old woman with severe chronic pulmonary disease went to a physician complaining of nervousness and insomnia. An examination disclosed no change in her pulmonary function, and she was given 100 mg. of pentobarbital to help her sleep. Her daughter found her unconscious the following morning and brought her to the hospital. She was comatose but withdrew appropriately from noxious stimuli. She was cyanotic, and her respirations were labored at 40 per minute. Her pupils were 3 mm. in diameter and reacted to light. There was a full range of extraocular movements on passive head turning. No evidence of asterixis or multifocal myoclonus was encountered, and her extremities were flaccid with slightly depressed tendon reflexes and bilateral extensor plantar responses. The arterial blood pH was 7.17; the $Paco_2$ was 70 mm. Hg; the serum bicarbonate was 25 mEq. per L., and the Pao_2 was 40 mm. Hg. She received a tracheostomy and finally artificial ventilation with a respirator for several days before she awakened and was able by her own efforts to maintain her arterial $Paco_2$ at its normal level of 45 mm. Hg.

Comment: This is not an unusual history. It is likely that the increased nervousness and insomnia were symptoms of increasing respiratory difficulty. The sedative hastened the impending decompensation and induced severe respiratory insufficiency as sleep stilled voluntary respiratory efforts. The rapidity with which she raised her $Paco_2$ from normal to a level of 70 mm. Hg is indicated by her normal serum bicarbonate, there having been no time for the renal compensation that usually accompanies respiratory acidosis.

Austen, Carmichael, and Adams[18] emphasized that in patients in whom CO_2 slowly accumulates, the complaints of insidiously appearing headache, somnolence, and confusion may occasionally attract more attention than the more direct signs of respiratory failure. If the subject also has increased intracranial pressure, papilledema, and bilateral extensor plantar responses, it is easy to see how the physician can at first reach the diagnosis of brain tumor or some other equally inappropriate conclusion. The important differential features are that in CO_2 retention focal signs are rare, blood gases are *always* abnormal, and the encephalopathy usually improves promptly if artificial ventilation is effectively administered. (After severe and protracted narcosis occasional patients can remain stuporous for several days after the blood gases are returned to normal, yet still recover. However, this sequence is rare.)

Two associated conditions are closely related to CO_2 narcosis and often accentuate its neurological effects. One is hypoxemia and the other is metabolic alkalosis, which often emerges as the result of treatment. Hypoxia accompanying CO_2 retention must be treated, because oxygen lack is immediately dangerous both to heart and brain. But administering inhaled oxygen often depresses the breathing of patients with severe CO_2 retention, making carbon dioxide levels climb even higher. In such patients it can be concluded that the previous hypoxemia stimulated respiration considerably through carotid body and aortic chemoreceptors; removal of the stimulus by oxygen therapy eliminates these drives, reduces ventilation, and intensifies hypercapnia. This potential sequence has made some physicians reluctant to give oxygen to patients with severe pulmonary disease. An

188

effective solution is to give low concentrations of oxygen (25 per cent) in air while observing the patient closely. If respiration declines and CO_2 retention occurs even with this minimal increase in oxygen tensions, oxygen therapy should be combined with artificial ventilation.

Renal bicarbonate excretion is relatively slow. As a result, correction of CO_2 narcosis by artificial respiration sometimes induces severe metabolic alkalosis if the carbon dioxide tension is returned quickly to normal in the face of a high serum bicarbonate level. Although metabolic alkalosis is usually asymptomatic, Rotheram, Safar, and Robin[481] recently reported five patients with pulmonary emphysema treated vigorously by artificial ventilation in whom metabolic alkalosis was associated with serious neurological symptoms. These patients, after initially recovering from CO_2 narcosis, developed severe alkalosis and again became obtunded. They developed multifocal myoclonus, had severe convulsions, and three died. Two patients regained consciousness after blood CO_2 levels were raised again by deliberately reducing the level of ventilation. We have observed a similar sequence of events in deeply comatose patients treated vigorously with artificial ventilation, but have found it difficult to conclude that alkalosis and not hypoxia was at fault. What seems likely is that too sudden hypocapnia induces cerebral vasoconstriction, which more than counterbalances the beneficial effects of raising the blood oxygen tension. Rotheram and his colleagues believe that the P_{CO_2} should be lowered gradually during treatment of respiratory acidosis to allow renal compensation to take place and prevent severe metabolic alkalosis. This is a reasonable approach so long as hypoxemia is prevented.

Endocrine Disease

Either Addison's disease or hypothyroidism occasionally can present as undiagnosed coma. Hyperparathyroidism and hypoparathyroidism can do the same but are discussed with abnormalities of electrolyte metabolism on page 202.

ADDISON'S DISEASE. The pathogenesis of the encephalopathy of Addison's disease probably involves several factors. The disease always produces hyponatremia and hyperkalemia, and often hypoglycemia as well. Hypotension is the rule, and, if severe, this alone can cause cerebral symptoms from ischemia. However, cortisone appears to have important effects on cerebral metabolism[605] and also decreases the free amino acid content of the brain. No matter what treatment is given, encephalopathy does not completely clear in addisonian patients unless cortisone is supplied.

A large percentage of untreated and undertreated patients with Addison's disease are mildly delirious.[155] Stupor and coma, however, usually appear only during addisonian crises. Changes in consciousness, respiration, pupils, and ocular movements are not different from those of other types of quiet metabolic coma. Motor signs, however, are helpful. Patients with addisonian crisis have flaccid weakness and either hypoactive or absent deep tendon reflexes, probably resulting from hyperkalemia; many of them suffer from generalized convulsions, which have been attributed to hyponatremia and water intoxication. Papilledema is occasionally present and presumably results from brain swelling due to steroid lack.[269, 585]

The neurological signs of addisonian coma are only rarely sufficiently distinctive to be diagnostic, although the combination of metabolic coma, absence of deep tendon reflexes, and papilledema should suggest adrenal insufficiency. Pigmented skin and hypotension are helpful supplementary signs and, when combined with a low serum sodium and a high serum potassium level, are almost unequivocal. The definitive diagnosis of adrenal insufficiency is made by the direct measurement of low blood or urine cortisol levels.

The main error in differential diagnosis of Addison's disease is to regard the hyponatremia, hyperkalemia, or hypoglycemia as the primary cause of the metabolic coma rather than as due to underlying adrenal insufficiency. This error can be avoided only by considering Addison's disease as a potential cause of metabolic coma and by heeding the other general physical signs and laboratory values. Hypotension and hyperkalemia, for example, rarely combine together in other diseases causing hyponatremia or hypoglycemia.

THYROID DYSFUNCTION. Both hyperthyroidism and hypothyroidism interfere with normal cerebral function, but exactly how the symptoms are produced is unclear. Thyroid hormone increases oxygen consumption in most tissues, but no consistent effect on the adult brain has been found.[25] Thyroxine administration increases the metabolic rate of cerebral cortex of experimental animals from birth to early adulthood, although not at full maturity.[159] Data in intact humans with thyroid disease are inconsistent. Gottstein[215] has reported that patients with hyperthyroidism demonstrate an increased cerebral blood flow and increased oxygen uptake over normal subjects, whereas patients with hypothyroidism undergo decreases in these parameters. The cerebral respiratory quotients in both groups of patients remained normal. Others[415] have found decreases in the cerebral blood flow in myxedema and increases in hyperthyroidism, but no changes in the cerebral oxygen uptake, and have related the changes in cerebral circulation to overall hemodynamic alterations rather than changes in brain metabolism. Sokoloff[530] has suggested that the principal effect of thyroid hormone is on protein metabolism but that the effects are restricted to the immature brain. Whatever the metabolic cause, symptoms of cerebral dysfunction are prominent in thyroid disease. In adult myxedema, thyroid replacement or correction of thyroid excess usually restores all neurological signs of adult disease to normal, but in infantile hypothyroidism normality is rarely achieved unless the defect is almost immediately recognized and corrected.

Hypothyroidism. Coma is a rare but frequently fatal complication of myxedema; of approximately 77 patients reported in the literature between 1911 and 1961, two thirds died.[179] The onset of myxedema coma is usually acute or subacute and occurs with infection or other stress in an untreated hypothyroid patient. Many authors have commented on the appearance of "suspended animation" in these profoundly hypometabolic patients. Characteristically, the patients are hypothermic with body temperatures between 87 and 91° F. They appear to hypoventilate and, indeed, usually have elevated blood Pco_2 values and mild anoxemia.

The diagnosis of myxedema in a patient in coma is suggested by cutaneous or subcutaneous stigmata of hypothyroidism plus a low body temperature and the finding of pseudomyotonic stretch reflexes. The diagnosis can be confirmed definitively only by thyroid function tests, but since myxedema coma is rapidly fatal, treatment with intravenous administration of tri-iodothyronine should begin once the clinical diagnosis has been made. Laboratory confirmation can come later.

The conditions most often confused with myxedema coma are those that often complicate it. The chief diagnostic error is to regard part of the picture as the whole cause of the encephalopathy. Carbon dioxide narcosis may be suspected if hypoventilation and CO_2 retention are present, but Pco_2 values are rarely above 50 to 55 mm. Hg in hypothyroidism, and hypothermia is not part of CO_2 narcosis. Severe hyponatremia is often present in severe myxedema, probably the result of inappropriate ADH secretion, and is the cause of seizures that occasionally occur. Gastrointestinal bleeding and shock also can complicate severe myxedema and divert attention from hypothyroidism as a cause of coma. Hypothermia, which is probably the most dramatic sign, should always suggest hypothyroidism but may also occur in other metabolic encephalopathies, especially hypoglycemia, depressant drug poisoning, and brainstem infarcts.

Thyrotoxicosis usually presents signs of increased central nervous system activity, i.e., anxiety, tremor, or hyperkinetic behavior. Rarely, in "thyroid storm," this can progress to confusion, stupor, or coma. The disorder usually develops in a patient with preexisting thyrotoxicosis, often partially treated, who develops precipitating factors such as an infection from a surgical procedure. The early clinical picture is dominated by signs of hypermetabolism. Fever is invariably present, profuse sweating occurs, there is marked tachycardia, and there may be signs of pulmonary edema and congestive heart failure. A more difficult problem is so-called apathetic thyrotoxicosis.[560] Such patients are usually elderly and present with neurological signs of depression and apathy. If untreated, the clinical symptoms progress to delirium and finally to stupor and coma. Nothing distinctive marks the neurological picture. Hypermetabolism is not clinically prominent, nor can one observe the eye signs generally associated with thyrotoxicosis. However, almost all of the patients show evidence of severe weight loss and

191

have cardiovascular symptoms, particularly atrial fibrillation and congestive heart failure. Many have signs of a moderately severe proximal myopathy. The diagnosis is established by obtaining tests of thyroid hyperfunction, and the neurological signs are reversed by antithyroid treatment.

DIABETES. Patients with diabetes mellitus can develop cerebral dysfunction leading to stupor or coma in several ways: (1) *Hypoglycemia* in patients with diabetes usually results from the use of insulin or an oral hypoglycemic agent, although spontaneous attacks of hypoglycemia[498] can characterize the early phase of diabetes. The neurological signs of hypoglycemia are discussed in a preceding section. (2) *Diabetic ketoacidosis* usually develops acutely or subacutely in a patient with relatively severe diabetes who neglects to take hypoglycemic agents or in whom an acute infection supervenes. Most of the patients are awake and alert when admitted to the hospital, often despite severe systemic acidosis with serum pH values below 7.0.[455] Some patients, however, are stuporous or comatose, and since their serum pH values are no lower than those of the awake patients, mechanisms of coma other than systemic acidosis have been proposed: Posner and Plum[455] suggested that the neurological changes in diabetic ketoacidosis could be a direct effect of acidosis on the nervous system. They observed that patients with severe systemic acidosis who were awake and alert maintained cerebral spinal fluid pH levels near normal, but the comatose patients had a low pH in the cerebral spinal fluid (see Metabolic Acidosis). They suggested that neurological changes in diabetic ketoacidosis occur when the mechanisms that usually protect central nervous system pH against changes in systemic pH fail. However, others have reported obtunded patients with normal spinal fluid pH.[417] A direct neurotoxic effect of keto-acids has been suggested,[474] but it requires much higher levels of these agents to produce neurological changes in experimental animals than ever emerge spontaneously in patients with diabetic ketoacidosis. Several authors have suggested that the hyperosmolality produced by hyperglycemia also may contribute to the neurological abnormalities of diabetic ketoacidosis just as hyperosmolality without ketoacidosis can produce neurological signs (see below). Finally, hyperglycemia leads to the accumulation in the central nervous system of metabolic products of glucose such as sorbital, fructose, and inositol. Prockop[458] has suggested that accumulation of these substances might interfere with normal cerebral metabolism. The diagnosis of diabetic ketoacidosis in a comatose patient is easily made because of the striking clinical finding of hyperventilation (deep respirations at 24 to 30 per minute), which leads the physician to the laboratory findings of metabolic acidosis and serum ketonemia (see Table 9). (3) *Diabetic lactic acidosis* usually occurs in patients receiving oral hypoglycemic agents, particularly phenformin, but has also been reported in patients not being treated for diabetes.[419] The mechanism of excess lactate production is unknown. Clinical signs and symptoms are the same as those of diabetic ketoacidosis or any other severe metabolic acidosis except that patients with lactic acidosis are more likely to be hypotensive or in shock. Lactic acidosis in diabetics is distinguished from diabetic ketoacidosis by the absence of high levels of ketone bodies in the serum. (4) *Nonketotic hyperosmolar coma.* This disorder, which appears to be an increasingly common cause of coma in diabetic patients, is discussed under Hyperosmolar States on page 201.

The complications described above produce their neurological symptoms before treatment is instituted, and neurological signs are usually reversed by therapy. Occasional patients with diabetic ketoacidosis, however, who are awake and alert on admission to the hospital become stuporous or comatose during the course of their treatment; some die. Posner and Plum[455] suggested that the mechanism of worsening during the treatment is related to a shift of pH in the nervous system from normal to acidotic (see p. 203, Metabolic Acidosis, for mechanism). Prockop[458] suggested that the accumulation of polyols (sorbitol, fructose, inositol) in the nervous system from hyperglycemia produces an osmolar gradient when the serum hyperglycemia is corrected. If so, water shift from the serum into the brain would produce cerebral edema, neurological dysfunction and, potentially, herniation and death. Too rapid correction of chemical abnormalities in diabetic ketoacidosis is contraindicated.

Encephalopathy Due to Remote Carcinoma

Carcinoma produces encephalopathy in several ways other than by metastases to the brain: (1) *Large retroperitoneal sarcomatous tumors* can cause severe hypoglycemia, perhaps by secretion of an insulin-like material. Although an attack of hypoglycemia may be the presenting symptom, the abdominal mass usually is easily palpable. (2) *Carcinomas* of the lung as well as certain other tumors (e.g., pancreas, ovary, prostate) *secrete an ACTH-like hormone* capable of causing Cushing's syndrome[466] with severe metabolic alkalosis, compensatory hypoventilation, and stupor. We have cared for one such patient who was severely obtunded, confused, and hypoventilating, and who had asterixis and bilateral extensor plantar responses.[456] (3) *"Limbic encephalitis"* is an uncommon effect of cancer, especially oat cell carcinoma of the lung, which is characterized by changes in affect, loss of recent memory, and progressive dementia, but usually not by stupor or coma. Clinical and pathological changes have been reviewed by Corsellis, Goldberg, and Norton.[105] The pathological changes include neuronal degeneration and inflammatory-like round cell infiltration in the brain, primarily in the temporal lobes, without evidence of invasion of the nervous system by cancer. The cellular changes suggest that a virus may cause the disorder. Other patients with carcinoma and associated dementia or toxic delirium (but not stupor or coma) have been reported in whom there were either no discernible pathological changes in the brain[87] or degenerative lesions were in the cerebellum[53] or thalamus.[122] (4) *Progressive multifocal leukoencephalopathy* complicates neoplastic diseases, particularly the lymphomas. The process induces in the cerebral hemispheres widespread subcortical demyelination, which Richardson[471] proposed was due to viral invasion of the nervous system. Electron microscopic studies,[607] and more recently tissue culture evidence,[422] support his view and implicate a virus of the papova[422] or of the SV40 type.[592a]

Clinically, multifocal leukoencephalopathy usually begins with confusion and disorientation and progresses over 2 to 7 months to culminate in coma and finally death. In addition to dementia, focal neurological signs are prominent and include aphasia, homonymous hemianopsia, and hemiplegia or quadriplegia. Generally, the cerebral hemispheres are most prominently involved, but sometimes brainstem foci produce ataxia and signs of cranial nerve dysfunction. The EEG is generally diffusely slow and may have focal abnormalities. The disease should be suspected in patients with carcinoma or a granulomatous disease, especially Hodgkin's disease, lymphosarcoma, or leukemia, who rapidly develop dementia or other neurological signs unaccompanied by evidence of focal cerebral or meningeal masses.

Exogenous Poisons

SEDATIVE AND PSYCHOTROPIC DRUGS. Psychotropic drugs such as marijuana, mescaline, and LSD may produce profound behavioral disturbances as well as severe delirium, but are rarely responsible for stupor or coma and so are not discussed in detail here. Suicide attempts with depressant drugs are responsible for the largest single group of patients who are brought to general hospitals in a coma of unknown cause. Not only is the problem appallingly frequent, but accurate histories are often all but impossible to obtain because of misguided efforts by friends and families to conceal the facts. For these reasons, an accurate diagnosis leans heavily upon the physical findings. Chemical analyses for sedatives are difficult, and laboratory confirmation of the clinical diagnosis usually is available in most hospitals only after the information is no longer useful in guiding treatment.

Sedatives such as barbiturate, glutethimide, meprobamate, phenothiazine, bromide, and alcohol can all produce coma if enough is taken. The mechanism of action of these drugs depends partly on their structure and partly on the dose. The barbiturates, for example, appear to act by interrupting synaptic transmission when taken in moderate amounts,[324] but larger doses interfere with cerebral oxidative enzymes and directly depress cellular metabolism.[459] None of the sedatives permanently damages neuronal function, making prompt diagnosis and effective treatment particularly important. If patients poisoned with depressant drugs survive long enough to reach the hospital, they should recover without physical sequelae provided that they receive adequate support of circulation and respiration and are protected against the complications of coma.[450]

Fairly consistent clinical findings attend stupor or coma with depressant drugs, and individual drugs usually produce only minor clinical differences. Almost all these agents depress vestibular and cerebellar function as readily as cerebral cortical function, so that nystagmus, ataxia, and dysarthria accompany or even precede the first overt signs of impaired consciousness. Larger amounts of drug produce coma, and in this quantity all of the agents depress brainstem autonomic responses. Respiration tends to be depressed at least as much as and sometimes more than somatic motor function. Except when glutethimide is the poison, or exceptionally huge doses well over the fatal threshold have been ingested, the pupils are small and reactive and ciliospinal reflexes are preserved. The oculocephalic movements are depressed or absent, and the oculovestibular responses to cold caloric testing are depressed and may be lost altogether in deep coma due to depressant drugs. The patients are usually flaccid with stretch reflexes that are diminished or absent. This typical picture is not always seen, especially if coma develops rapidly after ingestion of a fast-acting *barbiturate* such as secobarbital or pentobarbital. Then, respiratory depression may ensue almost as rapidly as does unconsciousness; signs in the motor system may initially evolve as if function were being depressed in a rostral-caudal fashion, with a brief appearance of hyperreflexia and even clonus and extensor plantar responses. Failure to recognize this short-lived (it rarely lasts more than 30 to 45 minutes) phase as due to depressant drugs can be fatal if the respiration is not supported. The identifying clue to the metabolic basis of the changes is that the pupillary reflexes are preserved and the motor signs are symmetrical. Virtually nothing else except brainstem hemorrhage (with bloody spinal fluid) or acute hypoglycemia can cause such rapid progress.

Chemical analyses are usually required to sort out which drug has been taken, but there are a few clinical hints that suggest a particular agent: acne, headache, and severe delirium, but rarely coma, are characteristic of bromidism. *Alcoholic stupor* can be a difficult diagnosis because so many patients who are unconscious for other reasons (head trauma, drug ingestion, as examples) will have the odor of "alcohol" (actually due to impurities in the liquor) on the breath. The patient in alcoholic stupor (blood level 250 to 300 mg. per 100 ml.) usually has a flushed face, a rapid pulse, and a low blood pressure and body temperature, all resulting from the vasodilatative effects of alcohol.[256] As the coma deepens (blood level of 300 to 400 mg. per 100 ml.), the patient becomes pale and quiet, and the pupils may dilate and become sluggishly reactive. With deeper depression, respiration fails. The depth of alcoholic stupor or coma may be deceptive when judged clinically. Repetitive stimulation during examinations in the emergency room often arouses the patient to the point where he requires little to remain awake, only to have him lapse into a deep coma with respiratory failure when left alone in bed. Alcohol is frequently taken in conjunction with barbiturates or other psychotropic drugs in a suicide attempt, and in these instances its action appears to be synergistic to that of the other depressant drugs. Under such circumstances of double ingestion, blood levels are no longer reliable in predicting the course, and sudden episodes of respiratory failure or cardiac arrhythmias are more frequent than in patients who have taken only a barbiturate. *Heroin overdosage* is an increasingly common problem facing not only hospitals located in ghetto neighborhoods but also those drawing from middle class districts.[341, 539] The drugs can be taken either by injection or sniffing. Overdosage with narcotics may occur from suicide attempts or, more commonly, when an addict or neophyte misjudges the amount or the quality of the heroin he is injecting or sniffing. Characteristic signs of opiate coma include pinpoint pupils that generally contract to a bright light and dilate rapidly if a narcotic antagonist is given. Respiratory abnormalities are prominent and result either from direct narcotic depression of the brainstem or from pulmonary edema, which is a frequent complication of heroin overdosage and is of uncertain pathogenesis. Of 14 patients comatose from narcotic poisoning reported by Steinberg and Karliner,[539] 4 were apneic and 6 had respiratory depression. One patient had slow, gasping respirations. Four patients were dyspneic and tachypneic and had clinical and x-ray findings suggesting pulmonary edema. Although opiates can produce hypothermia, by the time such patients reach the hospital they frequently have pneumonia so that their temperatures may be normal or elevated. The absence of needle marks does not rule out narcotic overdosage; in one series,[539] 4 of 11 patients comatose from heroin became so after their first injection. *Glutethimide* (Doriden) and *meprobamate* cause a peculiar state in which patients may be initially comatose with absence of responses to noxious stimuli and absence of oculocephalic responses, but if vigorous repetitive stimuli are delivered, such as repeated head turning or repeated supraorbital compression, the subjects may regain oculocephalic responses or even arouse, only to relapse into deep coma when the stimuli are withdrawn. *Anticholinergic drugs* (scopolamine, atropine) rarely cause coma but rather cause a severe dissociative delirium accompanied by fixed, dilated pupils.

The neurological examination by itself cannot categorically rule out other causes of metabolic brain disease, and the definitive diagnosis of coma due to depressant drug poisoning depends upon an accurate history or toxicological analysis of the blood or urine. The most common diagnostic error is to mistake deep coma from sedative poisoning for the coma of brainstem infarction. The initial distinction between these two conditions may be difficult, but small, reactive pupils, absence of caloric responses, failure to respond to noxious stimuli, absence of stretch reflexes, and muscular flaccidity suggest a profound metabolic disorder. Persisting decerebrate responses, hyperactive stretch reflexes, spasticity, dysconjugate eye movements to caloric tests, and unreactive pupils are more likely with

196

brainstem destruction. If both pupillary light reflexes and ciliospinal responses are present, deep coma is metabolic in origin. If both the pupillary reactions and the ciliospinal reflexes are lost, deep coma can be due to glutethimide, but in this instance muscular flaccidity, relatively good blood pressure control, and a lack of grossly irregular breathing are more consistent with metabolic than low brainstem disease.

Although this monograph has not focused on treatment, an exception must be made in this section, for ineffective care of patients with drug depression becomes itself a cause of coma. Patients poisoned by sedative drugs should not die if they once reach the hospital. The lethal dose of barbiturates is seven times the dose required to depress respiration to apnea and twice the dose required to produce severe hypotension.[325] It follows that if respiration and blood pressure are maintained and pulmonary complications are avoided, coma can persist for remarkably long periods and yet be followed by survival and normal function.

Case 31. A 73-year-old woman ingested 7.5 gm. of phenobarbital in a suicide attempt. She was found unconscious some hours later and brought to the hospital. She became apneic in the emergency room where an endotracheal tube and, later, a tracheostomy tube were inserted, and she was placed in a body respirator. The blood pressure was maintained with intravenous vasopressor agents. Her blood barbiturate level was 30 mg. per 100 cc. On the second and third hospital days, hemodialysis lowered the blood barbiturate level to 12.5 mg. per 100 cc., but the patient bled, and the dialysis was discontinued. However, after the dialysis she breathed spontaneously and vasopressors were no longer required. Nevertheless, she remained unresponsive to noxious stimuli, with absence of oculocephalic and stretch reflexes, and this state continued until, after 13 days of coma, she opened her eyes and withdrew appropriately from noxious stimuli. By 3 days later she was awake and in full possession of her mental faculties. Formal psychological tests 2 weeks later revealed no evidence for serious intellectual deterioration.

Comment: Phenobarbital is the only sedative capable of producing such prolonged unconsciousness, which is why this patient had hemodialysis. In patients poisoned with short-acting barbiturates or glutethimide, both we and others report lower mortalities with conventional treatment and diuretics[394, 450] than with hemodialysis.[343, 353]

DRUGS CAUSING METABOLIC ACIDOSIS. Three exogenous poisons cause metabolic acidosis: methyl alcohol, ethylene glycol, and paraldehyde. Methyl alcohol is metabolized to formic acid and perhaps other acid products. Ethylene glycol breaks down in the body to oxalic and other acids. Partially decomposed paraldehyde breaks down into acetic acid. These drugs are mainly ingested by chronic alcoholics or occasionally on a "dare" or by mistake. All of them produce rapidly progressing and severe acidosis, which threatens life if not treated immediately.

The clinical picture of metabolic acidosis ranges from no cerebral symptoms to delirium in a patient who appears severely ill. Coma is rare until just before death. Marked hyperpnea is invariable and the most important

197

clinical diagnostic feature. Other neurological signs are similar to those of many other rapidly advancing metabolic brain disorders. A distinctive feature of many patients who have ingested methyl alcohol is blindness with hyperemic optic discs. Methanol poisoning also causes pancreatitis and abdominal pain. However, these individual distinctions are not the most important diagnostic features: What is imperative is to recognize this general category of acute metabolic acidosis so that treatment can begin immediately with intravenous administration of sodium bicarbonate solution before coma and death ensue.

Case 32. A 39-year-old man had been intermittently drinking denatured alcohol for 10 days. He was admitted complaining that for several hours his vision was blurred and he was short of breath. He was alert, oriented, and coherent but restless. His blood pressure was 130/100 mm. Hg; his pulse was 130 per minute, and his respirations were 40 per minute, regular and deep. The only other abnormal physical findings were 20/40 vision, engorged left retinal veins with pink optic discs, and sluggishly reactive pupils, 5 mm. in diameter. His serum bicarbonate level was 5 mEq. per L., and his arterial pH was 7.16. An intravenous infusion was begun immediately and 540 mEq. of sodium bicarbonate was infused during the next 4 hours. By that time his arterial pH had risen to 7.47 and his serum bicarbonate to 13.9 mEq. per L. He was still hyperventilating but less restless. The infusion was continued at a slower rate for 20 hours to a total of 740 mEq. of bicarbonate. He recovered completely.

Comment: This patient had profound acidosis, as was reflected by the requirement of 540 mEq. of sodium bicarbonate to raise his serum bicarbonate from 5 to 13 mEq. per L. Even larger amounts have been required by other acidotic patients. The acidosis can be lethal with alarming rapidity: One of our patients walked into the hospital, complaining of blurred vision. He admitted drinking "a lot" of methyl alcohol and was hyperventilating. During the 10 minutes that it took to transfer him to a ward he lost consciousness. By the time an intravenous infusion could be started, his breathing and heart had stopped. No bicarbonate could be detected in a serum sample drawn simultaneously with death.

Abnormalities of Ionic or Acid-Base Environment of the CNS

Abnormalities of Osmolality. The term osmolality refers to the number of solute particles dissolved in a solvent and is usually expressed as milliosmoles per kilogram of solvent (mOsm./kg.). Osmolality can either be measured directly on the serum by the freezing point depression method or, for clinical purposes, calculated from the concentrations of sodium, glucose, and urea in the serum. The formula below gives a rough but clinically useful approximation of the serum osmolality:

$$\text{mOsm./kg.} = 2\ (\text{Na} + \text{K}) + \frac{\text{glucose}}{18} + \frac{\text{BUN}}{2.8}$$

Sodium and potassium are expressed in mEq. per L., and the divisors convert glucose and BUN, expressed in milligrams per 100 ml., to mEq. per L. Normal serum osmolality is 290 ± 5 mOsm./kg. The exact mechanism of neurological symptoms produced by hyperosmolality and hypo-osmolality is unclear, but hypo-osmolality leads to an increased cellular water content and tissue swelling, and hyperosmolality, to cerebral shrinkage. Since the brain has protective mechanisms against osmolar shifts,[244] abrupt changes in serum osmolality are likely to produce more neurological symptoms than slow changes, and thus no precise clear level at which symptoms develop can be given. However, osmolalities below about 260 mEq. per L. or above about 330 mEq. per L. are likely to produce cerebral symptoms. In addition, cerebral symptoms can be produced by sudden shifts of osmolality toward normal when an illness has produced a sustained shift of osmolality away from normal. This is particularly true when hyperosmolality is rapidly corrected, leading to a sudden shift of water into the brain, producing cerebral edema and attendant neurological complications.

HYPO-OSMOLAR STATES. Hyponatremia or "water intoxication" is a comparatively frequent cause of delirium, obtundation, and coma. As an example, initially unsuspected water intoxication was the cause of coma in 6 patients at The New York Hospital in a single 12-month period.

Hyponatremia means that body water is increased relative to solute. Symptoms result from water excess in the brain, hence the name water intoxication. The pathogenesis is thought to be related to altered excitability of the neural membrane. The membrane potential is influenced by the ratio of sodium outside to sodium inside the cell, and, more importantly, by the ratio of potassium outside to potassium inside the cell. Dilution of body compartments by water causes a greater absolute decrease in the extracellular sodium than in the less concentrated intracellular sodium and, conversely, a greater absolute decrease in the intracellular potassium than in the extracellular potassium. The sodium change affects the membrane little, but the potassium alteration decreases the membrane potential[210] and thereby increases neuronal excitability. It is doubtful that this dilutional change in itself alters the membrane potential sufficiently to cause the observed convulsions. During hyponatremic episodes there may be concomitant shifts of sodium into and potassium out of neurons[131a, 604] that accentuate the increased excitability and produce the neurological symptoms.

Several clinical conditions cause hyponatremia severe enough to induce delirium or coma. One is compulsive water drinking, a phenomenon reported in schizophrenic patients, or in alcoholics who suddenly develop a huge thirst to quell symptoms of gastritis.[547] The exact quantity of water required to cause water intoxication is not known, but some normal individuals tolerate 10 L. of water a day.[223] A second condition is acute water intoxication, which follows hemodialysis when the serum urea is suddenly lowered. Because urea diffuses slowly across the blood-brain barrier, brain urea remains high, causing hypertonicity of the CNS and a sudden shift of water into the brain. A third condition leading to water intoxication is the inappropriate secretion of antidiuretic hormone (ADH), originally described by Schwartz and coworkers[495] as a phenomenon in patients with bronchogenic carcinoma. Inappropriate ADH secretion is also found in patients with a variety of neurological diseases[209] and as a spontaneous phenomenon in patients with no known underlying disease.[221] The sustained output of ADH impairs free water clearance by the kidney and leads to water retention and an expanded extracellular volume. The expanded volume, in turn, causes decreased aldosterone output, which leads to urinary salt loss. Both the water retention and the salt loss contribute to hyponatremia. A fourth category is acute dilutional hyponatremia, a condition that often follows loss of salt-containing body fluids (e.g., by vomiting, diarrhea) and replacement with water. Subjects retain the water in order to maintain adequate extracellular fluid volumes and the serum sodium accordingly decreases. A fifth and frequent mechanism of hyponatremia is diuretic induced; this may follow the excessive use of any diuretic agent but is particularly frequent among elderly patients taking chlorothiazide, many of whom also develop hypokalemia. Finally, hyponatremia accompanies myxedema, adrenal insufficiency, and severe renal disease and can accentuate the symptoms of each of these potential causes of encephalopathy.

Coma in conditions causing water intoxication is rare except postictally; most patients with slowly developing or only moderately severe hyponatremia are delirious. They have asterixis and, often, multifocal myoclonus. Profound (serum sodium 95 to 110 mEq. per L.) and rapidly developing water intoxication commonly induces generalized convulsions that of themselves can be so severe that they are followed by prolonged coma and permanent brain damage.

Case 33. A 33-year-old schoolteacher was admitted to the hospital in coma. She had been working regularly until 2 days prior to admission when she stayed home with nausea and vomiting. Two hours before admission she was dysarthric when speaking on the telephone. Later she was found by friends on the floor, unconscious and cyanotic. She had three generalized convulsions and was brought to the hospital. Her blood pressure was 130/80 mm. Hg, her pulse 140 per minute, her respirations 24 per minute and regular, and her body temperature 38.7° C. She did not respond to noxious stimulation. Her eyes deviated conjugately to the left at rest but turned conjugately to the right with passive head turning. Her pupils were 6 mm. on the right, 5 mm. on the left, and they briskly constricted to light stimulation. Both corneal reflexes were present. Her arms, hands, and fingers were flexed with plastic rigidity and irregular athetoid movements. Her legs and feet were rigidly extended. There were bilateral extensor plantar responses. She had three more convulsions that began in the right hand and then rapidly became generalized.

Despite extensive investigations and tests for metabolic aberrations or poisons, the only abnormalities found in this woman were of acute water intoxication. Her serum values were as follows: sodium 98 mEq. per L., potassium 3.4 mEq. per L., osmolality 214 mOsm. per L. (normal = 290 ± 5). The BUN was 10 mg. per 100 cc.

Water restriction and infusion of 5 per cent NaCl rapidly returned the electrolyte values to normal. After several days she opened her eyes, grimaced when pinched, and moved all extremities. Her muscles remained rigid, however, especially on the right side, and she continued to have bilateral extensor plantar responses. She had no further seizures. Six months later she remained severely demented and unable to care for herself.

Comment: The etiology of this patient's hyponatremia was never established, but acute, idiopathic inappropriate ADH secretion[221] was suspected. It is likely that the severe and frequent seizures caused permanent anoxic brain damage.

A milder metabolic encephalopathy that rarely causes coma or seizures but frequently causes stupor occurs in elderly patients receiving chlorothiazide therapy. This common cause of metabolic brain disease most often affects patients with diffuse cerebral vascular disease, perhaps because their incipient brain dysfunction makes them more sensitive to mild metabolic imbalances. The delirium is probably only partially due to the hyponatremia. Hypokalemia, alkalosis, and extracellular fluid volume depletion often are also present and contribute to the neurological symptoms.

Hyponatremia has no unique signs or symptoms to suggest it in preference to other metabolic abnormalities but should be suspected in patients who suddenly develop an unexplained encephalopathy or seizures, particularly if they are receiving diuretics, have carcinoma of the lung or have neurological disease. The diagnosis is possible if the serum sodium level is below 120 mEq. per L. and highly likely when the sodium is below 100 to 110 mEq. per L.

HYPEROSMOLAR STATES. Severe water depletion producing *hypernatremia* occurs in children with severe diarrhea and, occasionally, in adults with diabetes insipidus. It also occurs in comatose patients who receive tube feedings containing a high solute content. In the first two conditions, free water losses exceed oral replacements, and in the third, insufficient free water is administered. The encephalopathy itself usually produces symptoms of delirium rather than coma and should be thought of in the comatose patient receiving tube feedings when signs of clinical worsening occur. Perhaps the chief danger of hypernatremia in children is to treat it too zealously with water, thereby inducing hyponatremia and seizures.

A syndrome of hyperosmolality due to *hyperglycemia* ("hyperglycemic nonketotic diabetic coma") is encountered in diabetics[203, 346] or in nondiabetic patients after severe burns.[476] In both instances the patients have intense hyperglycemia with blood sugar values ranging from 400 to 2000 mg. or more per 100 cc. but without ketonemia, ketonuria, or acidosis. The elevated blood sugar is probably not paralleled by a high brain sugar level.[202] Thus it is postulated that water shifts from the brain to the hyperosmolar plasma. The hyperglycemia also precipitates osmotic diuresis, which leads to dehydration and, if severe, to shock. In diabetics, the illness usually occurs in the elderly and untreated. Clinically, the patients are in stupor or frank metabolic coma, often with a history of severe polydipsia and polyuria. Seizures are common and often focal. Postictally there may be transient focal neurological signs. Symptoms are usually reversed by insulin and rehydration.

201

CALCIUM. Both high and low serum calcium values can be associated with neurological abnormalities.

Hypercalcemia. An elevated serum calcium level may be due to hyperparathyroidism, immobilization, or Beck's sarcoid. Hypercalcemia is a common and important complication of cancer, resulting from either metastatic lesions that demineralize the bones or as a remote effect of cancer on the endocrine system.[393] The clinical symptoms of hypercalcemia include anorexia, nausea, and frequently vomiting, intense thirst, polyuria, polydipsia, and often muscle weakness. Its neurological import is that hypercalcemia often presents with neurological symptoms, including mild diffuse encephalopathy with headache, rather than with evidence of systemic disease. Delusions and changes in the affect can be prominent; many patients with hypercalcemia have been initially treated for a psychiatric disorder until a blood calcium level was measured. With severe hypercalcemia, stupor and finally coma occur. Generalized and focal seizures are rare but have been reported.[236] Hypercalcemia should be suspected in a delirious patient who has a history of renal calculi, recent immobilization,[442] cancer, or evidence of another systemic disease known to cause the condition. Lacking evidence for these prodromata, it is still sometimes rewarding to obtain a serum calcium determination in patients with unexplained delirium.

Hypocalcemia is caused by hypoparathyroidism (often occurring late and unsuspected after thyroidectomy), occasionally by uremia, or, rarely, by an idiopathic disorder of calcium metabolism. The cardinal manifestations are neuromuscular irritability and tetany, but these may be absent when hypocalcemia develops insidiously, and hypocalcemic patients sometimes present with only a mild diffuse encephalopathy. Convulsions are common, but sustained coma is rare. Papilledema has been reported, associated with an increased intracranial pressure. This pseudotumor cerebri apparently is a direct effect of the metabolic abnormality.[218]

Hypocalcemia is commonly misdiagnosed as mental retardation, dementia, or epilepsy, and occasionally as brain tumor. Hypocalcemia should be suspected if the patient has cataracts, and the correct diagnosis is often inferred from observing calcification in the basal ganglia on skull roentgenographs.

DISORDERS OF SYSTEMIC ACID-BASE BALANCE. Systemic acidosis and alkalosis frequently accompany metabolic coma, and the attendant respiratory changes often give important clues about the causes of coma (see p. 152 and Table 9). However, of the four disorders of systemic acid-base balance, namely, respiratory and metabolic acidosis, respiratory and metabolic alkalosis, only respiratory acidosis produces stupor or coma with regularity, and perhaps even then the associated hypoxia is as important as is acidosis in producing the neurological abnormality. Even profound metabolic acidosis, the most immediately medically dangerous of the acid-base disorders, only rarely produces coma. Severe metabolic alkalosis is usually associated with delirium or, at most, obtundation but not coma, while respiratory alkalosis as such causes no more than lightheadedness and confusion. Therefore, if patients with acid-base disorders other than respiratory acidosis or severe and protracted metabolic acidosis are in coma, it is unlikely that the acid-base disturbance by itself is responsible. What is more likely in such instances is that the metabolic defect that is interfering with brain function is also responsible for the acid-base disturbance (e.g. uremia, hepatic encephalopathy or circulatory depression leading to lactic acidosis).

One of the reasons that disorders of systemic acid-base balance do not often interfere with brain function is that physiological mechanisms protect the acid-base balance of the brain (as reflected by the pH of its extracellular fluid, the CSF) against even large changes in the serum pH. This protection, which involves respiratory compensation, the establishment of ionic gradients, and a change in the cerebral blood flow, works particularly well in metabolic acidosis largely through effective respiratory compensation. It is less completely effective in protecting the brain against systemic abnormalities of metabolic alkalosis and respiratory alkalosis and is largely ineffective in respiratory acidosis because this condition directly eliminates the respiratory protective mechanism against the acid-base change. Posner and Plum[455] suggested that measurement of CSF pH correlates better with clinical symptoms in patients with acid-base disorders than does measurement of the serum pH. In their studies, it appeared that in patients with severe metabolic acidosis, coma developed only when compensatory mechanisms failed and the brain became acidotic along with the serum acidosis.

Acidosis exerts profound biochemical,[549] morphological,[100] and physiological[548] effects on nervous tissue. The exact mechanism by which changes in pH interfere with neuronal function is unclear, although both acidosis and anoxia lower the pH of the cell and may thereby interfere with its energy mechanism.[516] Clinically, severe *respiratory acidosis* produces stupor or coma, the degree of which is closely related to the pH of the spinal fluid[455] and the degree of hypoxemia (see section on pulmonary disease, p. 186). Patients with pure *metabolic acidosis* (i.e., diabetic acidosis, spontaneous lactic acidosis, ammonium chloride intoxication, methyl alcohol poisoning) usually initially have a normal pH in the CSF and are awake and alert despite a lowering of the serum pH, which may fall below 7.00 units.[455] Late in their course, coma has been reported in some such patients in whom only the chemical abnormality appeared sufficient to explain the neurological deterioration; the pH of the CSF was not reported in these instances, nor was their cardiovascular condition continuously monitored.[470, 566] In patients in coma due to diabetic acidosis whom we have studied, the pH of the lumbar CSF was abnormally low at the time their mental impairment was maximal.

Severe metabolic acidosis has a dangerously depressing influence on the cardiovascular system[14] and must be promptly reversed by giving bicarbonate-containing solutions. During the reversal, as the serum bicarbonate is raised rapidly, the Pco_2 in the serum rises. The charged bicarbonate ion does not diffuse readily across the blood-brain barrier into the cerebral extracellular space, but the CO_2 molecule does, which increases the concentration of carbonic acid and lowers the pH of the CSF. Thus, the correction of metabolic acidosis, although raising the serum pH, can paradoxically lower the extracellular pH of the brain. During this period, transient neurological depression may appear, but this is neither profound nor dangerous and does not outweigh the requirement for prompt correction of serum acidosis.

Alkalosis produces only mild encephalopathy. Acute *respiratory alkalosis* constricts the cerebral arterioles and decreases the cerebral blood flow. With the reduction of blood flow, lactic acid production by the brain increases, and there may be mild encephalopathy with confusion and slow waves in the EEG. However, the decrease in CBF is transient, and it is doubtful that prolonged respiratory alkalosis significantly interferes with cerebral function except perhaps in rare instances in which too vigorous and prolonged hyperventilation is used to overcorrect preexisting respiratory acidosis.[481] It follows that when respiratory alkalosis coexists with stupor or coma, one should search for the underlying cause, such as sepsis, hepatic coma, or cardiopulmonary hypoxemia, rather than looking to the hypocapnia to explain the neurological changes. Profound *metabolic alkalosis* produces a blunted confusional state rather than stupor or coma. The mechanism by which alkalosis interferes with cerebral function is unknown, although such patients undergo a large change in pH of the CSF toward the alkaline side. Respiratory mechanisms via hypoventilation only partially compensate for the metabolic alkalosis, but this does lower the arterial Po_2, often to levels of approximately 50 mm. Hg.[569] This significant hypoxemia probably contributes, at least partially, to the mental symptoms in metabolic alkalosis.

Central Nervous System Infection

MENINGITIS. Acute leptomeningeal infections frequently cause coma, mainly via mechanisms that impair cerebral metabolism. Meningeal infections are often accompanied by considerable cerebral edema. This directly contributes to the encephalopathy and may be so great that the swollen hemispheres herniate into the tentorial notch or the cerebellar tonsils impact themselves in the foramen magnum.[135] A more direct metabolic effect is that bacterial invaders cause severe meningeal vasculitis, which induces diffuse or focal ischemia of the underlying brain and can even lead to focal areas of necrosis. It also has been suggested that the invading organisms and their toxins directly interfere with cerebral metabolism by competing for nutrients and inhibiting vital enzyme reactions. Finally, the fluid therapy employed for these patients carries a potential risk of inducing acute water intoxication unless carefully regulated.[414] These considerations, as well as the close resemblance of the signs and symptoms of meningitis to other metabolic diseases, led us to include meningeal infections in this section.

The meningeal infections that produce coma are principally those caused by the acute pyogenic organisms, particularly meningococcus, pneumococcus, Haemophilus influenzae, and streptococcus, although the low resistance of the central nervous system means that organisms that otherwise have little pathogenicity occasionally cause acute meningitis. Meningococcal and H. influenzae infections frequently produce meningitis as their initial effect; pneumococcal and streptococcal meningitis, on the other hand, arise secondarily to infection elsewhere in the body in about half the cases.

The clinical appearance of acute meningitis is one of an acute metabolic encephalopathy with drowsiness or stupor accompanied by the toxic symptoms of chills, fever, tachycardia, and tachypnea. Most patients have either a headache or a history of it and stiff neck. Polymorphonuclear leukocytes are usually present in the CSF (or at least heavy bacterial counts plus hypoglycorrhachia) by the time the patient reaches the hospital. Patients with meningococcal infection may have the cutaneous stigmata of spotted fever, and those with other bacterial infections often have a suppurative source in the lung, a paranasal sinus, or the middle ear. If meningitis follows its usual evolution, it produces respiratory, ocular, and motor signs that generally resemble those of several other metabolic comas. In addition, however, there is a high incidence of focal neurological signs resulting postictally and from localized cerebral ischemia. Both focal and generalized convulsions are common, particularly when pneumococci and streptococci are the invading organisms.

In the diagnosis of meningitis, the presence of acute headache, fever, nuchal rigidity, and somnolence combined with a CSF containing polymorphonuclear leukocytes and a low sugar content hardly allows an alternative. However, there are special circumstances in which either life-threatening coma complicates the course of meningitis or the diagnosis is difficult to separate from other causes of insidiously developing coma. Williams, Swanson, and Chapman[597] emphasized a fulminating course in children who, during the first few hours of illness, suddenly developed signs of acute transtentorial rostral-caudal herniation superimposed on the initially characteristic signs of H. influenzae meningitis. The complication was attributed to severe edema of the brain. Clinically, such children rapidly lose consciousness and develop hyperpnea disproportionate to the degree of fever. The pupils dilate, at first moderately and then widely, then fix, and the child develops decerebrate motor signs. Urea, mannitol, or other hyperosmotic agents, if used properly, can prevent or reverse the full development of these ominous changes that are otherwise rapidly fatal. Dodge and Swartz[135] warn that lumbar puncture must be undertaken cautiously in patients with acute meningitis so as to minimize risks of enhancing temporal lobe or cerebellar herniation; they advise using no. 20 to 22 spinal needles and removing fluid slowly.

In elderly patients, bacterial meningitis sometimes presents as stupor or coma in which there may be focal neurological signs but little evidence of severe systemic illness or stiff neck. Such patients can be regarded incorrectly as having suffered a stroke, but this error is readily avoided by accurate spinal fluid examinations. Accurate spinal fluid examinations also avoid another potential error in the diagnosis of meningitis, namely, that of erroneously making a diagnosis of subarachnoid hemorrhage simply because the blood of a traumatic lumbar puncture obscures the elevated spinal fluid white cell count. With acute, intrinsic bleeding, there is approximately 1 white cell to each 1000 red cells in the CSF. Ratios higher than this should be investigated immediately with supplementary Gram stains and measurement of sugar contents.

Patients are occasionally observed who develop the encephalopathy of meningitis before white cells appear in the lumbar spinal fluid. The series of Carpenter and Petersdorf[78] includes several such cases, and the following is an example from our own series.

Case 34. A 28-year-old man complained of mild diurnal temperature elevation for several days with intermittent sore throat, chills, and malaise. He had no muscle or joint complaints or cough, but his chest felt tight. He saw his physician, who found him to be warm and to appear acutely ill, but he lacked significant abnormalities on examination except that his pharynx and ear canals were reddened. A diagnosis of influenza was made, but the next afternoon he had difficulty thinking clearly and was admitted to the hospital.

His blood pressure was 90/70 mm. Hg, pulse 120 per minute, respirations 20 per minute, and body temperature 38.6° C. He was acutely ill, restless, and unable to sustain his attention to cooperate fully in the examination. No rash, petechiae, or wheals were seen. There was slight nuchal rigidity and some mild spasm of the back and hamstring muscles. The remainder of the physical and the neurological examination was normal. The white blood count was 18,000 per cu. mm. with a shift to the left. Urinalysis was normal. A lumbar puncture was performed with the patient in the lateral recumbent position; the opening pressure was 210 mm., the closing pressure was 170 mm., and the clear CSF contained 1 red cell and no white cells. The next morning the protein was reported as 80 mg. per 100 cc., the sugar as 0.

That evening at 9 o'clock his temperature had declined to 38° C., and he was seemingly improved. Two hours later he had a chill followed by severe headache, and he became slightly irrational. The body temperature was 37.6° C. There was an increase in the nuchal rigidity and in the hamstring and back-muscle spasm. The white blood count had increased to 23,000 per cu. mm. Shortly before 1:30 A.M. he became delirious and then comatose with irregular respiration. The pupils were equal and reactive; the optic fundi were normal; the deep tendon reflexes were equal and active throughout. The left plantar response was extensor; the right was equivocal. Because of the high white count, fever, and coma, administration of large doses of antibiotics was started, but the diagnosis was uncertain.

The next morning the spinal fluid and throat cultures that had been obtained the evening before were found to contain Neisseria meningitidis and a lumbar puncture now revealed purulent spinal fluid containing 6000 white cells per cu. mm. under a high pressure with high protein and low sugar contents. His treatment with penicillin and sulfadiazine continued, and he recovered without sequelae.

Comment: The error in diagnosis in this patient was that the original spinal fluid sample was not examined microscopically. Bacteria can often be seen on a Gram stain of centrifuged spinal fluid of a patient with meningitis even when cells have not yet increased. If meningitis or other CNS infection is strongly suspected and no cells are found in an initial examination, the lumbar puncture should be repeated in 4 hours.

ENCEPHALITIS. Viruses, bacteria, rickettsiae, protozoa, and worms can all invade brain parenchyma. Only viruses and bacteria invade the brain acutely and diffusely enough to cause coma and to demand attention in the diagnosis of unconscious patients. Bacterial encephalitis has been considered above as part of meningitis. Viral encephalitis is discussed in this section and cerebral allergic responses to systemic viral infections in the next.

Viruses produce neurological signs by invading the neurons themselves where they compete for substrate and they interfere with the cell's metabolism. Viruses also evoke intense inflammatory and immunological responses in the adjacent brain parenchyma. If the virus destroys the neuron, a glial scar remains. If the neuron survives, it may nonetheless be marked with an inclusion body characteristic of a viral invader. In addition, focal cerebral ischemia may result from viral injury to adjacent blood vessels. Finally, cerebral swelling is common in viral encephalitis and sometimes is so intense that it acts like an expanding supratentorial mass lesion and produces the typical syndrome of rostral-caudal deterioration.[3]

Although a number of viruses cause human encephalitis, only four types of viral encephalitis in the United States are both common and produce coma: eastern equine, western equine, St. Louis, and herpes simplex encephalitis. The cerebral pathology of each of these illnesses has individually distinctive features, but in all there is extensive neuronal damage in the cerebral hemispheres accompanied by perivascular invasion with inflammatory cells and proliferation of microglia with formation of frequent glial nodules. The vascular endothelium often swells and proliferates. Areas of focal cortical necrosis as well as subcortical demyelination and necrosis are common. In herpes simplex encephalitis, diapedesis of red cells is sufficient to produce petechiae or frank hemorrhage in the areas of necrosis. Cowdry type A inclusion bodies in neurons and glial cells are a distinctive feature of this last illness, as is a remarkable predilection by the virus for the gray matter of the medial temporal lobe as well as other limbic structures in the insula, cingulate gyrus, and inferior frontal lobe.

Clinically, viral encephalitis begins with headache, drowsiness, and fever and progresses acutely or subacutely to produce stupor or coma, usually with nuchal rigidity. This early stage may be fulminating, and in some

207

instances only a few hours sees a transition from full health to stupor. Agitated delirium may precede coma and is especially common in herpes simplex encephalitis. Generalized convulsions are common with eastern equine and herpes simplex encephalitis but rare with western equine and St. Louis encephalitis. Focal motor signs frequently accompany the coma, and tremor commonly complements the agitated delirium of herpes encephalitis. Laboratory examinations are only moderately helpful and sometimes are even misleading. The cerebral spinal fluid pressure is usually increased (180 to 400 mm. of CSF), and the white cell count is almost invariably elevated (10 to 1000 cells per cu. mm., mostly mononuclear) although two of Drachman and Adams' patients[136] with herpes simplex encephalitis had normal cell counts early in the course of their illness. Pleocytosis appeared later in both. Up to 500 red cells per cu. mm. are common. The CSF protein content usually is elevated, values up to 870 mg. per 100 cc. having been reported. The CSF sugar is usually normal but occasionally depressed.[1a]

The clinical diagnosis of epidemic viral encephalitis (the equine and St. Louis varieties) is rarely a problem once an outbreak has started, being easily made in patients who develop headache, fever, nuchal rigidity, and pleocytosis. Indeed, care must be taken during an epidemic not to make a diagnosis of encephalitis when faced with other neurological illnesses or injuries causing coma. Herpes simplex encephalitis is a more difficult problem because it is sporadic and not epidemic. It has a subacute onset in which headache and fever can be overshadowed by inappropriate behavior, agitation, tremor, and memory loss. This picture can be misinterpreted as being due to delirium tremens or drug intoxication unless the spinal fluid is examined for white cells and the presence of fever is heeded appropriately. Herpes simplex encephalitis progresses to produce coma, focal motor signs, and seizures. Sometimes, as in the following case, severe hemispheral brain swelling produces transtentorial herniation and death.

Case 35. A 32-year-old children's nurse was admitted to the hospital in coma. She had felt vaguely unwell 5 days before admission and then developed occipital headache and vomiting. Two days before admission a physician carefully examined her but found only a temperature of 103° F. and a normal blood count. She remained alone for the next 48 hours and was found unconscious in her room just before admission.

Examination showed an unresponsive white female with her head and eyes deviated to the right. She had small ecchymoses over the left eye, left hip, and knee. Her neck was moderately stiff. The right pupil was slightly larger than the left; both reacted to light, and the oculocephalic reflex was intact. The corneal reflex was bilaterally sluggish, and the gag reflex was intact. Her extremities were flaccid, the stretch reflexes were 3+, and the plantar responses were flexor. In the emergency room she had a generalized convulsion associated with deviation of the head and the eyes to the left. The lumbar puncture pressure was 130 mm. of CSF. There were 550 mononuclear cells and 643 red blood cells per cu. mm. The CSF sugar was 65 and the protein was 54 mg. per 100 cc. Skull x-ray findings were normal. A right carotid arteriogram showed marked elevation of the sylvian vessels with only minimal deviation of the midline structures. Burr holes were placed; no subdural blood was found. A ventriculogram showed the third ventricle curved to the right. The EEG contained 1 to 2 cps high amplitude slow waves appearing regularly every 3 to 5 seconds from a background of almost complete electrical silence. Low amplitude 10 to 12 cps sharp wave bursts of gradually increasing voltage began over either frontal area and occurred every 1 to 2 minutes; they lasted 20 to 40 seconds and were associated with seizure activity.

Her seizures were partially controlled with anticonvulsants and she received 20 million units of penicillin and 3 gm. of chloramphenicol per day. Her condition gradually deteriorated, and on the eighth hospital day she developed midposition fixed pupils with absence of oculovestibular responses and diabetes insipidus with a serum osmolality of 313 mOsm. per L. and urine specific gravity of 1.005. Eight days after admission, lumbar puncture yielded a serosanguineous fluid with 26,000 RBC and 2200 mononuclear cells. The protein was 210 mg. per 100 cc. Examination of the serum for complement-fixing antibodies to herpes simplex virus at the onset of hospitalization disclosed no response at a 1:4 dilution, but a positive response at a 1:32 dilution was obtained just prior to death. She died 10 days after admission, having been maintained with artificial respiration and pressor agents for 48 hours.

At autopsy the herpes simplex virus was cultured from the cerebral cortex. The leptomeninges were congested, and the brain was swollen and soft with bilateral deep tentorial grooving along the hippocampal uncus. The diencephalon was displaced an estimated 8 to 10 mm. caudally through the tentorial notch. On cut section the medial and anterior temporal lobes as well as the insula were bilaterally necrotic, hemorrhagic, and soft. Linear and oval hemorrhages were found in the thalamus bilaterally and extended down the central portion of the brainstem as far as the pons. Hemorrhages were also found in the cerebellum, and there was a small, intact arteriovenous malformation in the right sylvian fissure. There were meningeal infiltrations of predominantly lymphocytes, some plasma cells, and polymorphonuclear leukocytes. The perivascular spaces were also infiltrated in places extending to the subcortical white matter. In some areas the entire cortex was necrotic with shrunken and eosinophilic nerve cells. Numerous areas of extravasated red blood cells were present in the cortex, basal ganglia, and upper brainstem. Marked microglial proliferation and astrocytic hyperplasia were present. Cowdry type A intranuclear inclusion bodies were present primarily in the oligodendroglia, but were also seen in astroglia, small neurons, and occasional capillary endothelial cells.

Comment: This patient's history, findings, and course were characteristic of herpes simplex encephalitis. In her, as in others with this disease, the tendency for the virus to cause focal and asymmetrical temporal lobe edema and necrosis created focal signs prompting mistaken suspicions of subdural hematoma or brain tumor. The latter error is frequently reinforced in such cases by arteriographic evidence of temporal lobe enlargement secondary to edema, and compounded by evidence secured from a radioactive brain scan showing a focal breakdown of the blood-brain barrier such as also occurs with neoplasms. A history, however, of 5 to 7 days or less of headache, fever, confusion and other signs of bilateral cerebral dysfunction along with pleocytosis is incompatible with either subdural hematoma or operable neoplasm and obviates the need for surgery and emergency contrast studies. More careful attention to the signs of impending transtentorial herniation and early treatment with dehydrating agents might have delayed or prevented this patient's death.

Postinfectious CNS Disorders

ENCEPHALOMYELITIS. Parainfections, disseminated encephalomyelitis and acute hemorrhagic leukoencephalopathy are terms applied to distinct but related clinical and pathological disorders, both of which probably are caused by an allergic response of the brain to a viral systemic invader. Similar clinical and pathological disorders can be produced in experimental animals by injection of brain extracts mixed with appropriate adjuvants; here, as in man, the presence of hemorrhagic changes appears to signify a hyperacute form of disseminated encephalomyelitis.[331]

In parainfectious disseminated encephalomyelitis the brain and spinal cord contain multiple perivascular zones of demyelination in which axis cylinders may be either spared or destroyed. There are usually intense perivascular cuffs of inflammatory cells. Clinically, the illness occasionally arises spontaneously but usually it follows by several days a known or presumed viral infection, frequently an exanthem (e.g., rubella, varicella) but occasionally a banal upper respiratory infection. The onset is usually rapid with headache, a return of fever, and delirium, stupor, or coma. Nuchal rigidity may be present. Both focal and generalized convulsions are common, as are focal motor signs such as hemiplegia or paraplegia.

Often careful examination discloses evidence for disseminated focal CNS dysfunction in the form of optic neuritis, conjugate and dysconjugate eye movement abnormalities, and sensory losses distributed differently from motor weaknesses In 80 per cent of the cases, the CSF cell count is elevated, usually to less than 500 lymphocytes. The CSF protein may be slightly increased, but the sugar is normal. In about one out of five patients, the CSF is entirely normal. The diagnosis of acute disseminated encephalomyelitis is suspected when a patient becomes neurologically ill following a systemic viral infection. Evidence of widespread or multifocal nervous system involvement and of mild lymphocytic meningitis supports the diagnosis.

ACUTE HEMORRHAGIC LEUKOENCEPHALOPATHY. This disorder is marked pathologically by an inflammation and demyelination similar to disseminated encephalomyelitis plus widespread hemorrhagic lesions in the cerebral white matter, which vary in diameter from microscopic to several centimeters and which are accompanied by focal necrosis and edema. The perivascular infiltrations frequently contain many neutrophils, and there is often perivascular fibrinous impregnation. The clinical course is as violent as the pathological response. The illness may follow a banal viral infection, but often no such history is obtained. The illness begins abruptly with headache, fever, nausea, and vomiting. The patients rapidly lapse into coma with high fever but little or no nuchal rigidity. Convulsions and focal neurological signs, especially hemiparesis, are common. Focal cerebral hemorrhages and edema may produce both the clinical and arteriographic signs of a supratentorial mass lesion.[107] The CSF is usually under increased pressure and contains from 10 to 500 mononuclear cells, and up to 1000 RBC per cu. mm. The CSF protein may be elevated to 100 to 300 mg. per 100 cc. or more.

As a rule, the only problem presented by disseminated and hemorrhagic encephalomyelitis in the differential diagnosis of coma is to distinguish these from the viral encephalopathies. If the history of a typical antecedent illness is lacking, and no encephalitis epidemic is at hand, confident differentiation must await the results of paired serum antibody titer determinations or tissue examination. As a general rule, patients with viral encephalitis tend to be more severely ill and to have higher fevers for longer times than patients with disseminated encephalomyelitis, with the exception of the hemorrhagic variety. Neither infectious nor parainfectious encephalitis much resembles in its course coma due to supratentorial mass lesions per se, and neither group produces symptoms and signs simulating subtentorial destructive lesions. Acute bacterial endocarditis sometimes produces a multifocal encephalopathy accompanied by coma, fever, and pleocytosis; here diagnosis is assisted by the presence of changing cardiac murmurs, by finding emboli in other organs, and by identifying septicemia in blood cultures.

Subarachnoid Hemorrhage

Clinical usage has adopted the term subarachnoid hemorrhage to describe intracranial bleeding in which the majority of the blood is ejected into the subarachnoid space rather than into the parenchyma of the brain, the latter being termed cerebral hemorrhage. Most subarachnoid hemorrhages originate from the rupture of an intracranial aneurysm, arising at the junction of two or more arteries at the base of the brain, but in a few cases parenchymal hypertensive hemorrhage ruptures out from the substance of the brain to produce major subarachnoid bleeding.

Coma in subarachnoid hemorrhage has several potential mechanisms. Acutely, the sudden ejection of blood under high pressure into the subarachnoid space must suddenly raise the intracranial pressure and distort intracranial structures in a manner akin to acute concussion. Subsequently, arterial spasm induced by the noxious effects of blood may well be responsible for diffuse ischemia of the brain. Sudden masses of blood ejected into either the anterior or posterior fossa readily induce transtentorial herniation. Finally, a rapidly developing communicating hydrocephalus is almost the rule after acute subarachnoid hemorrhage, presumably because blood components deposit themselves around the foramina of the fourth ventricle as well as in the basal cisterns and along the large venous sinuses, in all of which places they interfere with the free diffusion and absorption of the cerebrospinal fluid. It is possible that subarachnoid blood or its products also directly interfere with cerebral metabolism, since blood products profoundly irritate the meninges to produce chemical meningitis.[261] Many patients with subarachnoid bleeding have impaired brain function despite the lack of any evidence of either vasospasm or focal brain destruction, and it is this picture that we attribute to the metabolic effects of blood in the subarachnoid space and that prompts us to include the condition primarily with the metabolic encephalopathies.

In the clinical picture of subarachnoid hemorrhage, signs of metabolic coma commonly coexist with focal signs of cerebral dysfunction, making clinical localization of the ruptured aneurysm a notoriously inaccurate exercise. Almost all the patients have headache at onset, but hemogenic chemical meningitis requires several hours to develop and produce its symptoms so that neck stiffness is often absent during the first hours after bleeding, particularly in unconscious patients. In patients in coma, respiratory, ocular, and motor signs may be those of either metabolic coma or of rostral-caudal deterioration of brain function, depending on the distribution and evolution of the primary hemorrhage. Thus, as is true with meningitis, a change in breathing from eupnea to hyperventilation can herald the onset of midbrain compression due to transtentorial compression. A dilated pupil or total third nerve palsy may be more difficult to interpret, but usually implies that the aneurysm is on the ipsilateral carotid or posterior communicating artery, and has either directly compressed or bled into the oculomotor nerve. Less often, oculomotor paralysis is due to transtentorial herniation. The decision as to which process is responsible must be based on the remainder of the clinical findings. Focal motor signs and focal or generalized seizures are common. Focal motor signs that occur early in the period after bleeding are sometimes due to hemorrhage into the cerebral substance and sometimes apparently are due to ischemia from severe vasospasm. In either case, the resulting hemiparesis is more often contralateral to the aneurysm but can be ipsilateral, depending on where the major vasospasm lies. Focal motor signs occurring later in the illness are usually due to cerebral infarction and are not always in the distribution of the artery that contained the ruptured aneurysm.[111]

The acute intracranial hypertension that hemorrhage induces may produce papilledema and retinal hemorrhages within hours.[423] Subacute and chronic intracranial hypertension due to communicating hydrocephalus can start within hours of the ictus, prolonging coma or even leading to gradually developing dementia and stupor after an initial posthemorrhage improvement.[177] Such a mechanism is the usual explanation for the delirium and obtundation that characteristically start 3 to 4 days after bleeding.

The diagnosis of subarachnoid hemorrhage only rarely gives difficulty. One such occasion is when a bloody spinal fluid is erroneously attributed to a traumatic tap, and another is when the initial symptoms are less than the clinician expects for so dangerous an illness so that no lumbar puncture is performed at all. The first error is minimized by centrifuging bloody spinal fluid: Intrinsic bleeding discolors the supernatant fluid with oxyhemoglobin within 2 hours, whereas fresh trauma does not. The second error is avoided by recognizing the neurological meaning of certain symptoms and by an awareness that intracranial bleeding damages the cardiovascular system so as to produce potentially misleading EKG changes. The following patient illustrates these principles:

Case 36. A 44-year-old man was admitted to the hospital at 11 A.M. At 10:30 A.M. he had been climbing stairs when he suddenly fell unconscious, not striking his head. He awoke after several minutes, mildly confused and complaining of a generalized headache. By the time he arrived at the hospital, he was clearheaded and felt well. His pulse was 76 per minute, his blood pressure was 108/76 mm. Hg. An electrocardiogram showed a sinus rhythm with a 3:2 sinoauricular block and complete atrioventricular (AV) dissociation with a nodal escape rhythm at 52 per minute. He became lethargic during the examination and gradually lapsed into coma, which was at first attributed to acute myocardial infarction.

Forty minutes later, his blood pressure was 160/90 mm. Hg. He was unconscious and breathed irregularly at about 30 per minute. He moved his left arm spontaneously, but no other movement was seen. His right pupil was larger than the left and reacted sluggishly to light. Corneal reflexes could not be elicited. Bilateral papilledema with some hemorrhages around the disc was noted. His neck was supple. He was thought to have mild cardiac enlargement and gallop rhythm.

Twenty minutes later the patient awoke. Five minutes later he again lost consciousness, this time permanently. An electrocardiogram showed a normal sinus rhythm with ST elevation and T wave inversion in lead AVL. The changes were believed consistent with an early anterolateral myocardial infarction or ischemia. Ten minutes later his electrocardiogram showed a sinus arrhythmia, changing in 15 minutes to complete AV dissociation with a nodal rhythm of 50 per minute, then to ventricular tachycardia followed by supraventricular tachycardia. The ST and T wave abnormalities persisted.

He was seen by a neurological consultant shortly after he lapsed into coma for the final time. He had bilateral decerebrate responses to noxious stimuli. The pupils were small, briskly reactive, and equal. Bilateral oculovestibular responses were present but depressed. Bilateral diffuse hypertonus was found in the extremities along with extensor plantar responses. A lumbar puncture revealed grossly bloody spinal fluid under a pressure of 400 mm. and with a hematocrit of 23 per cent and pink discoloration of the supernatant fluid. An hour later the patient's pupils were found in midposition and were fixed to light with absence of oculovestibular responses. Hypertonus of the extremities gradually changed into flaccidity. Respiration ceased, and, following a brief period of artificial ventilation, he died. The autopsy disclosed a massive subarachnoid hemorrhage from rupture of an aneurysm of the anterior communicating artery.

Comment: Despite the patient's complaint of headache, and unconsciousness, it was several hours before his physicians realized that his coma was not the result of myocardial infarction. The important distinction is that, although mild encephalopathy is fairly common from the decreased cardiac output of myocardial infarction, coma is rare and probably occurs only in patients having a cardiac arrest. Subarachnoid hemorrhage often causes

213

electrocardiographic abnormalities,[229, 535] some of which mimic closely the abnormalities that accompany a myocardial infarction. The finding emphasizes the importance of diagnostic lumbar punctures in patients in coma.

Epilepsy

Epilepsy is characterized by intense cerebral neuronal activity followed by postictal metabolic cerebral depression of varying degrees and duration. Postictal coma ranges in intensity from complete unresponsiveness to stupor; protracted deep unresponsiveness lasting more than 15 to 30 minutes suggests that the seizure was caused by an underlying structural lesion. Postictal patients in coma usually are hyperpneic until the lactic acidosis produced by the muscular exercise of the seizure clears; pupillary light reflexes are intact and oculovestibular responses active; the motor system usually is unremarkable except for extensor plantar responses in about half. Postictal coma rarely produces problems in its differential diagnosis because the patient usually quickly awakens to give his history. The problem the physician most frequently faces is retrospective: Was a past, unobserved episode of unconsciousness due to epilepsy or to syncope? This differential diagnostic problem is a point that Engle[154] has pertinently discussed. However, there are three instances in which coma associated with seizures can be sufficiently prolonged to present diagnostic problems.

The first instance is status epilepticus, a series of generalized convulsions occurring at intervals so closely spaced (i.e., every few minutes) that consciousness is not regained between. This state strikes about 10 per cent of patients with untreated or inadequately treated epilepsy[328] and often follows the abrupt withdrawal of anticonvulsants. Status epilepticus is a serious medical emergency since the cumulative systemic and cerebral anoxia induced by repeated generalized seizures can produce irreversible brain damage or death[253, 453] (see Case 33, page 200); its diagnosis is readily made when repeated convulsions punctuate a state of otherwise nonspecific coma.

A second instance of prolonged coma, stupor, or delirium frequently follows seizures occurring in elderly patients who have either scars from past cerebral infarction, cerebral vascular insufficiency, or mild to moderate senile cerebral degeneration with dementia. The enormous cerebral metabolic demand imposed by a seizure or seizures,[102] plus the usual complication of severe systemic hypoxia during the attack, often is sufficient in these patients to compromise the viability of already borderline cerebral function and produce several hours of postictal coma followed by several days of delirium. As a rule, such patients ultimately recover most of their preseizure cerebral function, but each attack risks damaging more and more brain, making effective prevention and prompt treatment particularly important.

The third instance of sustained coma associated with seizures occurs when the unconsciousness is not simply postictal but is an integral result of a cerebral disease that also causes seizures. Many underlying destructive and metabolic cerebral disorders produce both seizures and coma and must be differentiated by other signs, symptoms, and laboratory studies. However, if one takes previously healthy patients in our own series, single or serial convulsions were followed by sustained unconsciousness only when caused by acute encephalitis or encephalomyelitis or acute hyponatremia. It is an axiom of treatment that convulsions should be stopped as promptly as possible since both the seizures themselves and the systemic hypoxemia that accompanies them are sources of potentially serious brain damage.

Disorders of Temperature Regulation

Both hyperthermia and hypothermia interfere with cerebral metabolism, producing diffuse neurological signs including delirium, stupor, and coma.

Hypothermia results from a variety of illnesses including disorders of the hypothalamus,[508] myxedema, hypopituitarism, and exposure. A low body temperature may accompany metabolic coma, particularly hypoglycemia and drug-induced coma, especially that resulting from barbiturate overdose, phenothiazine overdose, or alcoholism. With decreasing body temperature, cerebral metabolic needs decrease and thus cerebral blood flow and oxygen consumption fall. In the absence of any underlying disease that may be producing both coma and hypothermia, there is a rough correlation between the body temperature and cerebral oxygen uptake and the state of consciousness. Rosin and Exton-Smith[477] observed that patients with body temperatures above 32.2° C. were fully conscious unless there was some other metabolic reason for stupor and coma, whereas all of the patients whose body temperatures were below that temperature had at least clouding of consciousness, whatever the primary clinical condition. Duguid, Simpson, and Stowers[143] observed that no patients with body temperatures below 26° C. were conscious, whereas 8 of their 16 patients with temperatures between that level and 31° C. were awake and alert. Clinically, accidental hypothermia (i.e., hypothermia in the absence of any predisposing causes) is a disease mainly of elderly people exposed to moderately cold environment. It occurs in the winter months, and most of the reports have come from England, although a recent report describes 10 patients from Texas.[564] Hypothermic patients are often found unconscious in a cold environment, although fully a third have been in their beds rather than out in the street. The patients who are unconscious are strikingly pale, have a "pliable consistency of subcutaneous tissue," and may have the appearance of myxedema even though that disease is not present. The body feels cold to the touch even in protected areas such as the perineum. Respirations are slow and shallow and McNicol and Smith[370] reported arterial blood gases showing hypoxia, with CO_2 retention in 2 of their 15 cases. Neurologically, hypothermic patients usually have generalized muscular rigidity with occasional fascicular twitchings over the shoulders and trunk, but true shivering is absent. The deep tendon reflexes are usually present and may be hyper-

215

active but can have a delayed relaxation phase resembling that of myxedema. The pupils are constricted and reportedly may not respond to light. One makes the diagnosis by recording the body temperature and ruling out precipitating causes other than exposure. Since most clinical thermometers do not register below 35° C. (95° F.), simple perusal of the chart recording temperatures taken by the nursing staff may not reveal the true severity of the hypothermia, and the perceptive physician must measure the temperature with a thermometer that records sufficiently low readings. Hypothermia carries a high mortality. Only one of six patients with temperatures below 26° C. in Duguid's series recovered consciousness. However, those who do recover rarely suffer residual neurological changes. Pathological changes in the brains of patients who die include perivascular hemorrhages in the region of the third ventricle with chromatolysis of ganglion cells. Multifocal infarcts have been described in several viscera, including brain, and probably reflect the cardiovascular collapse that complicates severe hypothermia.

Hyperthermia sufficient to produce stupor or coma generally occurs only with *heat stroke*.[214, 512] There are several metabolic studies on the effects of heat on the nervous system. Nemoto and Frankel[403] reported an increase in the cerebral metabolic rate at temperatures between 38 and 42° C., but at 43° C. cerebral metabolic uptake was decreased. However, the cerebral anaerobic index (reflecting an increased lactate production) did not increase with elevated temperature, and the authors concluded that the failure of cerebral metabolism resulted from a limited supply of nucleotides required in cerebral glucose transport rather than from cerebral hypoxia. Meyer and Handa[377] reported decreases in cerebral oxygen metabolism and slowing of the EEG at temperatures above 42° C. These experimental studies correlate well with clinical studies, which consistently find that body temperatures of the order of 42° C. or 43° C. are required to produce coma, although lower temperatures may be associated with delirium.[146] Heat stroke occurs both in young people who exercise unduly in heat to which they are unacclimatized[485] and in older people (who presumably possess less plastic adaptive mechanisms) during the summer's first hot spell. It is a particular threat in patients taking anticholinergic drugs, which interfere with heat dissipation through sweating. Clinically, patients with heat stroke are in coma with hot, dry skin. The pupils are usually small and reactive; caloric responses are present except terminally, and the skeletal muscles are usually diffusely hypertonic. The diagnosis is made by recording a body temperature in excess of 42° C. Unlike patients with coma due to hypothermia, many who survive heat stroke are left with permanent neurological residua. Of 47 patients reported by Salem[485] suffering from heat stroke, 6 died and 4 developed serious complications. One remained quadriparetic with cerebellar ataxia, two were demented, one with cerebellar signs, and a final patient had a right hemiparesis.

216

Chapter 5

Psychogenic Unresponsiveness

Just as patriotism is the last (Samuel Johnson[279]) or the first (Ambrose Bierce[44]) refuge of a scoundrel, hysteria is a diagnostic haven to which uncertain physicians all too often repair when signs and symptoms seem anatomically or physiologically senseless. That the diagnosis of hysteria often tells more about the physician's lack of knowledge than the patient's disease has been amply documented. In Slater's series,[523] almost half of a group of 61 patients diagnosed as suffering hysteria were eventually found to have organic disease that explained their symptoms. Thus, the diagnosis of psychogenic unresponsiveness must be approached with the greatest care.[233] If after a meticulous neurological examination of a patient with suspected psychogenic unresponsiveness there is any question, a careful search for other causes of coma is obligatory.

Psychogenic unresponsiveness sustained for more than a few minutes is uncommon; it was the final diagnosis in only 4 of our original 386 patients (Table 1), and we have encountered only 4 further patients, 2 with catatonic stupor, during the past 5 years. However, hysteria was initially suspected in several patients before an organic cause for coma was ferreted out. The diagnosis of psychogenic unresponsiveness is made by demonstrating that both the cerebral hemispheres and the brainstem reticular formation can be made to function in a physiologically normal way even though the patient will seemingly not respond to his environment. Hysterical patients usually lie with their eyes closed, not attending to their surroundings. The respiratory rate and depth are invariably eupneic or tachypneic and the pupils are equal and reactive. (But beware of the malingerer who may sometimes self-instill mydriatics.) Oculocephalic responses may or may not be present, but caloric testing invariably produces nystagmus rather than tonic deviation of the eyes. There is often active resistance to opening of the eyelids, and they usually close rapidly when they are released. The slow steady closure of passively opened eyelids that occurs in many comatose patients cannot be mimicked voluntarily. Similarly, roving eye movements are absent since they also cannot be mimicked voluntarily.[169] Hysterical patients usually offer no resistance to passive movements of the extremities although normal tone is present, and if an extremity is moved suddenly momentary resistance may be felt. The deep tendon reflexes are usually normal, but they can be voluntarily suppressed and thus may be absent. Superficial abdominal reflexes are usually present, and plantar responses are invariably absent or flexor. The EEG is that of an awake patient rather than one in coma.

Case 37. A 26-year-old nurse with a history of generalized convulsions was admitted to a hospital after a night of alcoholic drinking followed by severe generalized convulsions. She had been given 50 per cent glucose and 500 mg. sodium amobarbital intravenously. Upon admission she was reportedly unresponsive to verbal command, but when noxious stimuli were administered she withdrew, repetitively thrust her extremities in both flexion and extension, and on one occasion spat at the examiner. Her respira-

218

tions were normal. The remainder of the general physical and neurological examinations was normal. She was given 10 mg. diazepam intravenously and 500 mg. Dilantin intravenously in two doses 3 hours apart. Eight hours later, because she was still unresponsive, a neurological consultation was requested. She lay quietly in bed, unresponsive to verbal commands and not withdrawing from noxious stimuli. Her respirations were normal; her eyelids resisted opening actively, and when they were opened, closed rapidly. The eyes did not move spontaneously; the doll's-eye responses were absent; the pupils were 3 mm. and reactive, and her extremities were flaccid with normal deep tendon reflexes, normal superficial abdominal reflexes, and flexor plantar responses. Twenty cc. of ice water was irrigated against the left tympanum, and nystagmus with a quick component to the right was produced. The examiner indicated to a colleague that the production of nystagmus indicated that she was conscious and that an EEG would establish the fact that she was conscious. She immediately "awoke." Her speech was dysarthric and she was unsteady on her feet when she got out of bed. An EEG was marked by low and medium voltage fast activity in all leads with some 8 cps alpha activity and intermittent 6 to 7 cps activity, a record suggesting sedation due to drugs. She recovered full alertness later in the day and was discharged a day later with her neurological examination being entirely normal. An EEG done at a subsequent time showed background alpha activity of 8 to 10 cps with a moderate amount of fast activity and little or no 5 to 7 cps slow activity.

This patient illustrates a common problem in differentiating "organic" and psychogenic unresponsiveness. She had been sedated and had a mild metabolic encephalopathy, but the preponderance of her signs was a result of psychogenic unresponsiveness. The presence of nystagmus on oculovestibular stimulation and an EEG that was only mildly slowed without other signs of neurological abnormality effectively ruled out organic coma.

Catatonic stupor is often more difficult to differentiate from "organic" unresponsiveness than is hysteria or malingering as outlined in the paragraphs above. There are several reasons for this difficulty. Patients with catatonic stupor give the appearance of being obtunded or semistuporous rather than comatose, a state compatible with normal pupillary and oculovestibular function even when the obtundation is structural in origin. Catatonic stupor is accompanied by a variety of autonomic and endocrine abnormalities that give the patient a particularly organic look. The EEG may be abnormal in states of both catatonic stupor and catatonic excitement. A clinical picture indistinguishable from catatonic stupor can be produced by structural disease of the brain in patients both with[31] and without preceding psychiatric dysfunction. All of these difficulties in differentiating catatonic from organic stupor arise because catatonic schizophrenia, particularly the periodic recurrent type, is probably a metabolic rather than a purely psychogenic disease as hysteria appears to be.

Catatonic schizophrenia is a disease of young people and frequently has an acute onset often preceded by an emotionally upsetting experience. Patients are thus likely to be brought to emergency rooms of general hospitals "stuporous" or "delirious" without a preceding history of psychiatric illness. The patient in catatonic stupor appears unresponsive to his environment, but usually maintains consciousness and cognitive functions, as attested to not only by a normal neurological examination at the time he is seen but by the fact that when he recovers he is often (but not always) able to recall all of the events that took place during the "stuporous" state. The patient in catatonic "stupor" usually lies with his eyes open, apparently unseeing. His skin is pale, frequently marred by acne, and has an oily or greasy appearance.[206] His pulse is rapid, usually between 90 and 120, and he may be hypertensive. Respirations are normal or rapid. His temperature is often elevated 1.0 to 1.5° C. above normal. The patient usually does not move spontaneously, and appears to be unaware of his surroundings. He may not blink to visual threat, although optokinetic responses are usually present. The pupils are dilated, and there is frequently alternating aniso-coria. They are, however, reactive to light. (Fixed, dilated pupils have been occasionally reported,[584] ostensibly as a result of excessive sympathetic stimulation; we have not observed such a phenomenon and wonder whether mydriatics had been self-instilled.) Some patients hold their eyes tightly closed and will not permit passive eye opening. Doll's-eye movements are absent, and caloric testing produces ocular nystagmus rather than tonic deviation. There is usually increased salivation, the patient either allowing the saliva to drool from his mouth or to accumulate in the back of the pharynx without being swallowed. Such subjects may be incontinent of urine or feces or, on the contrary, retain urine, requiring catheterization. Their extremities may be relaxed but are more commonly held in a rigid position and are resistant to passive movement. Choreiform jerks of the extremities and grimaces are common. Some catatonic patients will maintain for prolonged periods the posture into which the limbs are passively placed by the examiner (catalepsy). The reflexes are usually present, and there are no pathological reflexes.

The EEG is frequently abnormal in catatonia. Harding and associates[230] have reviewed the literature concerning the EEG and periodic psychotic states and have reported extensive EEG recordings in three patients with periodic catatonic stupor. In most patients with periodic catatonia, the onset of either catatonic excitement or stupor is accompanied by an increase in the frequency of the alpha rhythm with a decrease in its amplitude and the total amount of alpha activity present in the record. There is usually an increased amount of theta activity and an increased amount of low to moderate voltage fast activity. A few patients have been reported in whom delta activity in the 2 to 3 cps range was described. However, the record in catatonia most often resembles that of a low voltage, fast, normal record more than that of a comatose patient. At least one patient reported with prominent delta activity during catatonic stupor had become stuporous following a thyroidectomy and the degree of thyroid function was never fully evaluated.[587]

220

Unlike the stuporous or comatose patient with structural or the usual metabolic disease, a patient in catatonic stupor can frequently be aroused from that state by the intravenous injection of a barbiturate. The patient usually awakens immediately and may be lucid for a short period, only to relapse into "stupor" when the barbiturate wears off.

A more difficult clinical problem lies in distinguishing the patient with an acute delirium from one with a behavioral disorder such as mania or catatonic excitement. Both may be wildly agitated and combative, and such behavior may make it impossible to test for orientation and alertness. Hallucinatory activity may be either on an organic or a psychogenic basis, and the segmental neurological examination, insofar as it can be tested, may be normal in both groups of patients. Such behavior occasionally occurs in patients with functional disorders but arises even more frequently in those with an organic delirium such as accompanies acute decompensating liver disease, acute encephalitis, acute intoxication with psychotropic drugs, and withdrawal from alcohol or barbiturates. Although the passage of time usually resolves the problems, often the only immediately distinguishing feature is the EEG. In patients with hepatic encephalopathy, encephalitis, or alcohol- or barbiturate-induced delirium, slow EEG activity predominates, and during the withdrawal state from alcohol or barbiturates low voltage fast activity is the dominant rhythm. Patients with psychogenic behavioral disturbances usually have normal EEG's, but the presence of a normal EEG does not rule out an overdose of psychotropic drugs. In many instances, an immediate distinction between organic and psychogenic delirium cannot be made, and patients must be hospitalized for observation while a meticulous search for a metabolic cause of the delirium is made.

Chapter 6

Prognosis in Coma and the Diagnosis of Brain Death

Advances in medicine have made obsolete the traditional clinical definition of death, i.e., cessation of heartbeat. Cardiac resuscitative measures can salvage patients after periods of asystole lasting up to several minutes. Cardiopulmonary bypass machines permit cessation of the heartbeat for several hours with full recovery, and artificial appliances promise in the future to keep patients alive, without a normal heartbeat, for extended periods. The situation is even more striking with respiratory failure. Where formerly respiratory depression equaled death within minutes, now artificial respirators can maintain oxygen exchange indefinitely. These advances have permitted many patients with formerly lethal cardiac and pulmonary diseases to return to full and useful lives, but they have made cessation of heartbeat no longer an adequate definition of death and have switched the emphasis to cessation of brain function.[149] Three considerations make revisions in our concept of both death and irreversible coma important to the clinical neurologist: (1) Transplant programs require healthy peripheral organs for success and demand that criteria be available that define brain death with absolute certainty at a time when transplantable organs are still functioning. (2) Even if there were no transplant program, the ability of modern medicine to keep patients in the vegetative state for extended periods with antibiotics, artificial respirators, and vasoconstrictors demands consideration of when the brain is dead. Both patients and families insist upon death with dignity,[600] and efforts by physicians to needlessly extend a vegetative existence in a patient, while they do not harm the already dead individual, often emotionally ravage the families and discredit the profession. On the other side of the coin, the recuperative powers of the brain can seem astounding to the uninitiated, and individual patients whom uninformed physicians might give up for dead sometimes make full and complete recoveries. It is even more important to know when to fight for life than to be willing to diagnose brain death. (3) Intensive care facilities are limited and expensive. Their best use demands that patients likely to benefit from such intensive care be identified and selected and that these units not be overloaded with patients who can never recover cerebral function.

Mainly to the neurologist falls the difficult task of deciding whether further medical effort will fail to produce anything beyond vegetative existence and, conversely, when even a tiny chance remains that major medical efforts may yield an alive and sentient individual. The following sections explore some of the pathological physiology, biochemistry, and clinical signs upon which these decisions can be based. A distinction is made in this chapter between cerebral death and irreversible coma based on the following definitions:

Cerebral death occurs when brain damage is irreversible and so severe that the brain can no longer maintain internal homeostasis, i.e., normal respiratory or cardiovascular function or both. Although mechanical means may preserve peripheral organs for a time, a patient who is brain dead will, despite the most meticulous care, develop failure of the circulation after a few days or, rarely, after several weeks,[313] and the heartbeat will cease. That the brain has been dead for some time prior to the cessation of heartbeat is attested to by the fact that the organ is invariably autolyzed when examined postmortem (see below).

Irreversible coma occurs when brain damage is permanent and sufficiently severe that the individual is thereafter unable to maintain external home-ostasis (i.e., is unable to respond appropriately in any major way to the environment) although the brain may maintain internal homeostasis (i.e., respiration, circulation, and heartbeat). Unlike brain death, in which both the cerebral hemispheres and the brainstem undergo autolysis, the pathology of irreversible coma is often limited to the hemispheres or to focal areas of the brainstem, with laminar necrosis of the cerebral cortex, demyelination of the subcortical white matter, or focal infarctions of the brainstem reticular formation being the cause (see page 17). Such irreversible coma must be clearly differentiated from the de-efferented state (see page 24).

It should be noted that not all agree with the above definitions. Morison[388] has suggested that death is a *process* rather than an *event* and cannot, therefore, be determined as occurring at a particular moment. Moreover, he suggests that since life and death are abstract concepts, they are difficult, if not impossible, to define in concrete terms. However, in medical terms, this quandary is similar to that concerning the very definition of con-sciousness and coma; there may be no satisfactory definition of conscious-ness, but the physician can, by appropriate examination, determine if a patient is comatose or dead. In this regard, Kass[288] has distinguished be-tween the meaning of an abstract concept such as death and the operations used to determine and measure it. He has suggested that the latter (opera-tional definition) be referred to as "criteria for determining that death has occurred" rather than a definition of death. It is in that sense that the definitions and criteria noted above are given.

BASIC MECHANISMS

Many directly applied physical and chemical agents can injure the brain, but ultimately all lethal injuries probably exert their effect by producing tissue anoxia or its equivalent, thereby blocking cerebral energy production by the mitochondria. Nervous tissue is normally in a constant "high energy" state in which the oxidative metabolism of glucose generates a constant supply of ATP and phosphocreatine to maintain the membrane potentials, transmit impulses, and synthesize protoplasm. When the mechanisms that sustain these energy reserves go awry, ATP and phosphocreatine levels are depleted, membranes lose their pumping mechanisms, the cells swell[572]

225

and, at some point, the neuron loses its capacity to recover. The exact mechanism by which the neuron becomes permanently damaged is not known, although histochemical evidence suggests that oxidative enzymes themselves are destroyed.[347] The precise lethal point of no return is also unknown in molecular terms, and one must generally turn to larger and cruder physiological models when trying to find out just when and why the nervous system dies. As will be seen, such evidence is often neither very different from nor more extensive than that gained clinically at the bedside, for it indicates that the nervous system can harmlessly suspend its activity almost indefinitely when metabolically depressed or cooled but quickly dies when it loses its functional activity in the presence of anoxia or loss of substrate.

Anesthesia

The brain can be depressed to essentially functionless levels by anesthetic depressant drugs yet lose none of its capacity for total recovery when the anesthetic disappears. Lavenson, Swanson, and Plum[325] found that it required seven times as much barbiturate anesthesia to depress irreversibly the peripheral circulation as it did to stop the breathing. The electroencephalogram first becomes intermittently isoelectric at about the same level of anesthesia as is required to silence the respiratory centers and completely isoelectric at approximately three to four times that anesthetic dose. Despite such severe depressions, Bird, working in our laboratory, was able to restore experimental animals to full functional activity after periods of up to 6 hours of isoelectric EEG flattening provided he gave careful attention to mechanical artificial ventilation and other details of nursing care.

Chemically, anesthesia depresses the function of the brain but keeps it in a high energy state, poised for the resumption of normal function. Nilsson and Siesjö[410–412] anesthetized well-ventilated rats with various concentrations of halothane, nitrous oxide, and barbiturates. In all instances concentrations of ATP and phosphocreatine remained high at control levels, and the normal lactate-pyruvate ratios were maintained, indicating that no tissue hypoxia had occurred. By implication, the brain was in a state of primed, energy-rich, suspended animation and was neither damaged nor impaired for future functional activity. Shanes[507] has suggested that anesthetics physically "stabilize membranes," thus decreasing nerve conduction. Others[85, 573] have demonstrated inhibition of synaptic transmission. In either event, electrical activity of the nervous system would be reduced, the need for high energy phosphates decreased, and an energy-rich state the result.

Clinical experience with anesthesia well confirms the implications of the animal studies. Provided meticulous attention is given to the details of artificial respiration, to the support of circulation, and to preventing the complications of coma, patients usually survive self-induced anesthesia

226

by barbiturates and other drugs even when coma is so deep that artificial respiration must be provided for several days and the blood pressure supported for a week or more by pressor agents. Nor does any apparent or measurable impairment of brain function follow such flirtations with death, provided no severe systemic anoxia has occurred (e.g., by a complicating cardiac arrest). With such deep anesthesia all clinical and most physiological measures can indicate the absence of any brain function without implying irreversible damage. Evidence for any residual activity in central respiratory, pupillary, oculovestibular, and motor functions can be altogether lacking in deep barbiturate-induced coma, and the electroencephalogram can record electrocerebral silence for 24 hours or more yet total neurological recovery can follow.[48]

Anoxia

It is likely that even very brief periods of anoxia, perhaps as short as 2 minutes or less, can produce focal damage to the nervous system, but it is harder to determine how much anoxia is required to produce total irreversible injury of the brain and exactly how anoxia produces its damage. Some of the cellular mechanisms were alluded to on page 168, but it can be reemphasized that some evidence indicates that vascular tissue and not the neurons themselves provides the neurological Achilles heel to anoxia within the brain. When Ames and Gurian[11] exposed retinal ganglion cells to various periods of anoxia in vitro, using a technique that eliminated the tissue's dependence on its blood supply, the optic nerve action potential recovered almost to its control level after as much as 20 minutes of exposure to pure nitrogen. Similarly, Van Harreveld and Tachibana[572] demonstrated that the neuron retained the capacity to expel chloride after 20 to 72 minutes of anoxia. However, when Ames and colleagues[12, 89, 312] exposed the brains of rabbits to ischemic anoxia by temporarily occluding the cerebral vessels, irreversible brain injury and death followed after 5 to 7 minutes of vascular occlusion, and after 15 minutes of such ischemia much of the brain could no longer be re-perfused by blood. In these latter animals, widespread glial swelling had compressed the cerebral capillaries, and this plus an unusual intravascular "bleb" formation apparently caused extensive multifocal and confluent obstruction of the cerebral capillaries.

Clinical observations trying to determine how long anoxia must last to produce brain death seldom can control the necessary variables to give an accurate answer. For this reason, claims of recovery after unduly long anoxic exposure must be regarded cautiously. Many animal studies of the question have also provided equivocal results, either because it was not certain that the cerebral circulation had been totally occluded (this being a difficult feat in most experimental species) or because myocardial anoxia or hypotension was not eliminated, producing an uncontrolled element of postanoxic circulatory impairment. Kramer and Tuynman[314] circumvented

227

the latter limitation by raising the intracranial pressure to exceed the blood pressure and thereby arrest the cerebral circulation. With the heart protected by antihypertensive agents, such animals survived 1 to 4 minutes of total cerebral ischemia without any behavioral or EEG sequelae whatsoever. (No histological studies were reported.) The animals underwent only partial or delayed neurological recovery after 4 to 15 minutes of interrupted circulation, but those exposed to 20 minutes of ischemic anoxia invariably developed a permanent and complete loss of the brain's functional and electrical activity.

The recovery in these experiments of several animals after up to 15 minutes of absolute ischemic anoxia is considerably longer than has been reported in many other somewhat similar studies and undoubtedly represents a normothermic maximum due to the well-protected condition of the cardiovascular system. Recovery of at least some cerebral neurophysiological activity after even longer periods of anoxia—up to 30 to 60 minutes—has been reported by Hossmann and Olsson[247] in specially perfused animals; it is uncertain whether this observation can be applied to clinical situations.

CLINICAL CRITERIA

Cerebral Death

Since Mollaret and Goulon[386] first courageously examined the question in 1959, many workers have concerned themselves with trying to establish criteria that accurately and unequivocally predict that the brain is dead or about to die no matter what therapeutic measures one undertakes. Several committees and reviewers have examined appropriate clinical and electrographic criteria for cerebral death based on a retrospective analysis of patients who died.[275, 301, 385] The most widely known definition is that of the Ad Hoc Committe of the Harvard Medical School to examine the definition of brain death.[30] Those criteria, as well as slightly differing ones devised for selecting patients for the transplant program at Memorial Hospital for Cancer and Allied Diseases and in use at all the Cornell-affiliated hospitals, are outlined in Table 11 and discussed in detail below. In essence, there is general agreement that cerebral death has occurred when there is no discernible evidence for either cerebral hemispheral function or function of the brainstem vital centers for an extended period, and when it is clearly evident that the abnormality of cerebral function is the result of structural and not of metabolic disease. The examination for cerebral death includes attention to cerebral hemisphere function, brainstem function, and laboratory signs, the most commonly used of which is the electroencephalogram.

Irreversible Loss of Cerebral Hemispheral Function

All observers agree that there must be total unawareness to externally applied stimuli and that even the most noxious stimulus must evoke no

Table 11. Clinical criteria for diagnosis of brain death

Harvard Medical School Ad Hoc Committee

  1. Unreceptivity and unresponsivity—no response to externally applied stimuli
  2. No movements or breathing—1-hour observation, 3 minutes off respirator if P_{CO_2} normal at start
  3. No reflexes
  4. Flat electroencephalogram—tested twice 24 hours apart, 10–20 minute record 5–10 $\mu V/mm$.
  5. No hypothermia (temperature $< 32.2°$ C.) or CNS-depressant drugs

Memorial Hospital for Cancer and Allied Diseases

  1. Nature and duration of coma
      a. No drugs or hypothermia
      b. Structural disease or clearly known irreversible metabolic cause
      c. 12-hour observation
  2. Absence of cortical function
      a. No behavioral or reflex response to noxious stimuli above foramen magnum level
      b. Electroencephalogram isoelectric for 60 minutes at 5–10 $\mu V/cm$.
  3. Absence of brainstem function
      a. Fixed pupils
      b. No oculovestibular responses
      c. Apnea—unresponsive to CO_2
      d. Circulation may be intact
      e. Purely spinal reflexes may be retained

---

vocal or other purposeful response. The Harvard criteria demand that no reflex activity be present whatsoever, but our own experience and that of others[29] suggests that spinal neuronal activity, including stretch reflexes and primitive responses to noxious stimuli, can sometimes persist in cerebrally dead patients up to the time that the heart stops. The absence of cerebral hemisphere function can also be attested to by EEG recordings, the criteria for which are described below. How long cerebral hemisphere function must be absent is controversial. The Harvard criteria require a 24-hour period under observation. Many patients with severe head injuries who meet all other criteria for cerebral death do not maintain cardiac function for 24 hours despite the use of vasopressor drugs. Thus, when the presence of structural damage is obvious and severe (e.g., head injuries), we have concluded that a 12-hour period of examination is sufficient to determine cerebral death.

Examination of cerebral hemisphere function in the comatose patient is the least useful of all the predictive criteria since many fully reversible structural illnesses can temporarily produce a failure to respond to noxious stimuli. The crucial criteria of brain death are those that clinically denote absence of brainstem function and that by laboratory examination denote total absence of cerebral hemisphere function, i.e., the electroencephalogram.

Brainstem Function

Respiration. Spontaneous respiration must be absent, and most patients when examined will be maintained with an artificial respirator. Ability of the brainstem to respond to metabolic stimulation can be tested by turning off the respirator. If the Pco_2 is within normal range and the patient had been breathing room air for 10 minutes prior to the trial, 1 or 2 minutes without artificial respiration should produce a CO_2 tension high enough to near-maximally stimulate the respiratory centers. If blood gas determinations are not easily available, respiratory function may be tested by the technique of apneic oxygenation. With this technique, the patient is respired with 100 per cent oxygen for a period of 10 to 20 minutes and then the respirator is disconnected and oxygen is delivered through a catheter to the trachea at a rate of about 6 liters per minute. The oxygen tension in the alveoli under such circumstances remains sufficiently high that diffusion of oxygen across the alveolar membrane will maintain the arterial blood at adequate oxygen tensions.[192] This allows the Pco_2 to rise without any danger of further hypoxia, and the apneic patient may be safely observed for periods of 7 to 10 minutes.

Pupils. The pupils must be nonreactive. The Harvard criteria require that the pupils be dilated as well as fixed, but midposition fixed pupils are as good a sign, or better, of failure of brainstem function, as the examination of patients in any morgue will attest. The pupils should be tested with a bright light and the physician should be certain that mydriatric agents have not been used.

Ocular movements. Failure of brainstem function should be attested to by the failure to find any ocular responses to head turning and caloric irrigation of the ears with ice water.

Motor movements. The Harvard criteria also demand that there be no motor or reflex movements, including absence of corneal responses, no postural activity including decerebrate rigidity, and no stretch reflexes in the extremities. Physiological considerations make this an unnecessary criterion if all of the other criteria are met, since spinal reflex activity, both in response to noxious stimuli and tendon stretch, often persists in animals whose brains have been destroyed above the spinal or low medullary level and can be found in the spinal cord of man following high cord transection. A variety of peculiar, possibly medullospinal, motor movements can appear and persist for prolonged periods during artificial animation in patients otherwise cerebrally dead, as the following case illustrates.

Case 38. A 47-year-old woman developed a sudden, severe, diffuse headache. Her blood pressure was 180/80 mm. Hg and pulse 64 per minute, with occasional premature ventricular contractions. There were occasional spontaneous movements of the right side; the left side did not move and was flaccid. The respirations were 24 per minute, regular and deep. There was no response to visual threat. The pupils were small (3 mm.), equal, and reactive. There were full doll's-eye responses both horizontally and vertically. She

230

had intact gag and ciliospinal reflexes. Deep tendon reflexes were brisk bilaterally with absence of ankle and knee jerks and extensor plantar responses. By 5 hours later there was no response to any stimuli. Both pupils were midposition and fixed; the doll's-eye responses were absent. The plantar responses were absent, and the blood pressure had fallen below 70 mm. Hg. Shortly thereafter she required full respiratory maintenance. By the next day the examination revealed no response to noxious stimuli, the pupils were fixed at 6 mm. without light response, and there was no oculovestibular response to ice water calorics. She was unable to breathe even after being removed from the respirator and diffusion respired with oxgen for 10 minutes. The electroencephalogram was isoelectric, the blood pressure 160/90 mm. Hg, pulse 84 per minute, and the body temperature was 36.5° C. It was noted for the first time that if her neck were flexed or laterally rotated there was a sudden jerking flexion of both shoulders and extension of the arms at the elbows. The movement lasted less than 1 second but could be elicited each time the neck was manipulated. Later that day, other neurological signs being unchanged, one could still produce movement of the arms with neck flexion. There was also occasional movement of the neck toward extension when it was passively flexed, again as a sudden jerk. The movement varied from moment to moment with neck motion, at times one arm taking a decerebrate-like posture and the other a decorticate-like posture, and at times taking the reverse positions. When the neck was laterally rotated, however, the right arm assumed a decerebrate posture with no movement of the legs. Biceps stretch reflexes were now present bilaterally, but no other reflexes could be elicited. The movements and the remainder of the neurological examination persisted unchanged until the next day when the blood pressure progressively failed and her heart stopped.

Autopsy revealed a fresh subarachnoid hemorrhage located at the base of the brain on the right side, emanating from a ruptured berry aneurysm just beyond the first bifurcation of the right middle cerebral artery. The brain was severely edematous, and there was transtentorial herniation, more severe on the right, with compression of the brainstem by the herniated uncus. There was also cerebellar tonsillar herniation. Coronal sections revealed rupture of the hemorrhage into the cerebrum on the right side, extending into the white matter adjacent to the basal ganglia. There were no gross lesions in the brainstem other than distortion and pressure by the cone, but microscopically severe anoxic changes were present in neurons throughout the brainstem.

Laboratory Tests

The clinical diagnosis of brain death is generally neither difficult nor likely to err if one follows explicitly the criteria outlined above. However, the diagnosis carries a heavy responsibility and some medical centers have found it useful to develop laboratory tests to supplement the clinical criteria.

Electroencephalogram. The EEG is particularly helpful in the evaluation of absence of cerebral hemisphere function, and probably imperative to provide objective, verifiable support to clinical appraisals when organ transplantation is being considered. (In less legally demanding situations, however, it is doubtful that the experienced physician needs the EEG to tell him when the brain is dead.) All the evidence indicates that an isoelectric EEG for a period of 12 to 24 hours in a patient who is neither hypothermic nor has ingested depressant drugs means that no mental recovery is possible and usually means that the brain is already dead.

Silverman and associates[519] have recently reported a survey of 2650 isoelectric EEG's of up to 24 hours' duration. Only three from patients in this group, each in coma due to overdose of central nervous system depressant drugs, recovered cerebral function. However, several ostensibly isoelectric tracings were discarded because of faulty technique. The Silverman group has published the technical requirements necessary to establish electrocerebral silence (Table 12). It does appear that prolonged vegetative existence is occasionally possible in the presence of a postanoxic isoelectric EEG, as Brierley and co-workers[61] and Ingvar, Cronqvist, and Granholm[258] have reported. As mentioned earlier, after depressive drug poisoning, total loss of cerebral hemisphere function and isoelectric EEG's have been observed for as long as 50 hours with full clinical recovery.[48]

Table 12. Silverman committee recommendations for recording of EEG's in diagnosing brain death[519]

1. A minimum of 8 scalp electrodes and ear lobe reference electrodes must be employed to cover the major brain areas and be sure absence of EEG activity is not focal.
2. Interelectrode resistances should be under 10,000 ohms but over 100 ohms.
3. If an isoelectric tracing is recorded, each electrode of the montage should be gently touched to create an artifact potential.
4. Interelectrode linkages should be set at at least 10 cm.
5. The sensitivity should be increased to 3.5 and to 2.5 microvolts per mm. during part of the recording.
6. Time constants of 0.3 and 0.4 second should be used during part of the recording.
7. Monitoring devices are recommended to evaluate artifacts emanating from ECG, artificial animation machine, etc.
8. Tests for clinical and electrical reactivity to intense noxious and light stimuli should be applied.
9. Recording time should last at least 30 minutes.
10. Two isoelectric records 24 hours apart should be obtained. (This is recognized as a conservative recommendation and is presently being evaluated further.)

Cerebral circulation. Several laboratories have reported various techniques of examining the cerebral circulation in patients with severe structural brain disease who were thought to be dead. The rationale is that brain death would seem evident if absence of the cerebral circulation could be demonstrated. Physiologically, two events produce failure of the cerebral circulation. The first is probably rare but may sometimes acutely follow severe head injuries and includes a massive increase in intracranial pressure that finally equals the arteriolar and capillary perfusion pressure, at which point cerebral circulation ceases and the EEG becomes flat. Such changes have been demonstrated in the experimental animal by Cushing,[117] Langfitt and associates[323] and many others. The second, and probably more common, is the "no reflow phenomenon" of intravascular obstruction previously discussed (page 227). The pathological consequence of both events is the so-called respirator brain, a soft and necrotic organ that has autolyzed at body temperature when the respiratory and cardiovascular systems are kept functioning for many hours or days after brain circulation has ceased.[301, 313]

Cerebral circulation has been tested in several ways in patients with severe structural damage who are presumably dead or overwhelmingly damaged. Several investigators have done cerebral arteriography in patients who were believed to be dead and found no filling of the carotid circulation.[234] Angiographic nonfilling, however, can be due to artifacts of technique and sometimes has occurred for unexplained reasons in nonfatal neurological cases,[457] making this technique undependable for estimating cerebral viability. Goodman, Mishkin, and Dyken[211] studied cerebral perfusion by isotope angiography. Fifteen millicuries of sodium pertechnetate Tc^{99m} were injected as a bolus in the antecubital vein and emissions from the head were counted with a gamma camera with films being taken every 3 seconds for 24 seconds. This technique demonstrates both arteries and veins in the normal state. In three patients believed to be cerebrally dead, no filling of the vessels was found, and all were found to have soft necrotic brains at autopsy. If the appropriate equipment is available, this technique is simple and can easily be repeated at intervals to satisfy oneself that the circulation is absent for an extended period. Lobstein, Mantz, and Mack[334] have examined the arm to retina circulation time by injection of fluorescein and retinal photography in six patients believed to be cerebrally dead. They found extreme prolongation of the circulation time in five of their patients, varying from 29 seconds to 2 minutes. They suggest that prolonged circulation time from arm to retina may be confirmatory evidence for cerebral death, but the number of patients is small and the findings need confirmation.

Brain biopsy. Brain biopsy or direct surgical inspection also has been suggested to diagnose cerebral death. However, unless the surgeon drills holes over multiple areas of the cerebrum and brainstem it is hardly likely that either he or the pathologist can examine enough brain ante mortem in clinically equivocal cases to conclude that the remainder is dead as well.

Irreversible Coma

A far greater number of patients than those with brain death are those who are in coma immediately after an injury or an anoxic episode but who retain a fragment of neurological function such as reactive pupils or corneal reflex responses. It is extremely important for the neurologist to know whether he can identify within this group those who are irreversibly comatose and those who will recover. One wants to direct the resources of intensive care facilities and personnel to caring for patients who have a chance of recovery, yet physicians shrink from providing such meticulous

233

and intensive care if it will create no more than a human shell that survives in a hopeless vegetative state for months or years, cruelly burdening hospitals and families. Unfortunately, prognosis is often a very uncertain thing in such severely damaged patients in whom a fragment of brainstem function remains. Very little direct data are available to guide one's judgments, and we can only cite some inexact variables that weight the scales.

1. *Age.* The young brain has an intrinsic plasticity that helps it to recover from injuries that often are fatal to older patients. Whether this is because the young brain possesses more neurons or because it is able to establish connections between uninjured neuronal areas that are not yet fully committed in their development is unknown. Conversely, with advancing age serious structural injury to the brain is associated with a poorer prognosis. Thus, almost no matter what the acute neurological signs in traumatic coma, one can hold out hope for most children that they will recover to the point of sentient functioning, whereas few patients older than age 50 fully recover after severe brain injuries producing coma.

2. *Nature of the lesion.* As discussed below, the outcome after anoxic-ischemic lesions is more difficult to predict than the outcome from trauma, particularly as time passes after the insult. No reasonable predictions can be made in patients who suffer prolonged, nonanoxic metabolic coma since even elderly patients may survive and recover neurological function after many days of barbiturate-induced unconsciousness (page 197).

3. *Extent and course of neurological lesion.* The more extensive and severe a traumatic or anoxic injury, the less likely is the brain to recover, and, similarly, the longer the signs of severe injury last, the worse is the outlook. Prognosis is affected adversely by accompanying systemic illnesses such as atherosclerosis and liver disease and by complications that superimpose anoxemia, infection, or thromboembolism on the neurological problem. However, aside from these generalities, almost no one has made serially the close clinical observations on patients with coma that are needed to provide truly reliable guides for prognosis. Clinicians generally have found that signs of even very extensive brainstem injury, including fixed pupils, absence of oculovestibular responses, motor decerebration, or flaccidity and apnea, can be recovered from if they last for only a few minutes after the injury, but the forecast becomes less encouraging as each succeeding hour passes. However, as long as one can observe neurological improvement, at first from one day to the next and later from one week to the next, no physician can predict exactly how far recovery will go. Within these limits, the examination of certain functions may be particularly helpful.

a. *Pupils.* Bilateral fixed pupils from brainstem trauma or anoxic ischemia are a poor sign, and if the pupils remain unreactive for more than 12 to 24 hours, the likelihood of neurological recovery is small. As always with the examination of the pupils, it is important to be certain that they have not been fixed by drugs or prior ocular disease. Absence of oculovestib-

234

ular reflexes and inadequate spontaneous respiration are other signs of brainstem paralysis associated with a poor prognosis, but how often patients recover neurologically after losing these functions is undocumented.

b. *Motor signs.* Patients who remain unconscious and demonstrate decorticate or decerebrate posturing for more than a week are unlikely to recover full normal cerebral function if they are in the older age group. Children often recover from decorticate rigidity lasting as long as several weeks following an injury or an anoxic episode.

c. *Duration of unconsciousness.* As indicated below, duration of unconsciousness together with age provides the best guide for prognosis after head injury. It is not known whether similar considerations hold for anoxic-ischemic brain lesions or metabolic disease, although isolated examples of recovery after prolonged coma[332] suggest that guidelines may be difficult to establish.

d. *Cerebral blood flow and metabolism.* Three groups have examined these functions trying to assess their predictive value for patients in coma. Shalit and co-workers[506] studied nine patients with serious mechanical or vascular brain damage soon after injury. Neither a normal cerebral blood flow nor a relatively high initial brain oxygen uptake ($CMRO_2$) guaranteed neurological recovery. However, patients having a $CMRO_2$ of less than 30 per cent of normal had almost no remaining clinical function at the time of study and all subsequently died. Broderson and his group[64] performed similar studies on 26 patients with severe coma, 7 of whom fulfilled the clinical and EEG criteria of brain death. All the patients whose clinical examinations already indicated brain death had cerebral blood flow (CBF) values less than 10 per cent and $CMRO_2$ values less than 6 per cent of normal, which, combined with the radioisotope techniques employed, implied essentially no brain circulation or metabolism. In less badly damaged subjects, the Danish workers could not identify a critical $CMRO_2$ value below which recovery was impossible and found that in severe barbiturate poisoning, for example, $CMRO_2$ could fall to 20 per cent of normal yet be compatible with full recovery. According to Ingvar, Cronqvist, and Granholm,[258] at least some patients who have been chronically in coma for months or years have extremely low CBF values of 20 to 40 per cent of normal. It is not known whether such low values early after injury predict an irreversible lesion.

e. *Electroencephalogram.* Several authors have attempted to use the electroencephalogram to predict whether patients unconscious from anoxic brain disease will regain consciousness or will fail to survive. Hockaday and associates[242] were able to predict survival in the group of patients resuscitated after cardiac arrest with an 80 per cent reliability using EEG criteria alone. Pampiglione and Hardin[426] achieved approximately the same success rate in children. More recently, Binnie and colleagues[45] examined the EEG's of 93 patients resuscitated after cardiac arrest. Using EEG's taken

235

within 30 minutes to 7 days following resuscitation, and establishing criteria derived from analysis of 41 patients with uncomplicated head injury and a reliably established outcome, they were able to predict correctly either death or recovery in 92 of the 93 records, a confidence level of 99.8 per cent. Their criteria were established by visual inspection and have not yet been published. No such complete study has been carried out in patients unconscious from head injuries, but Bergamasco, Bergamini, and Doriguzzi[36] have suggested that the presence of sleep patterns in unconscious patients following head injury is a good prognostic sign, whereas all of their patients with continuous biphasic or monophasic electrical activity in all-night recordings died.

CLINICAL CONDITIONS

This section is brief because only a few careful and quantified observations have correlated the outcome of patients in coma with the extent of their initial injury as judged by neurological signs. We have already stressed that any patient with depressant drug poisoning who survives to reach the hospital is potentially salvageable and should recover completely if full treatment can be effectively applied. Purportively "grave signs" are well known with other metabolic diseases producing coma, but they usually reflect the observers' personal experience rather than dispassionate measurement and rarely can be relied upon as predictors of outcome. A similar lack of verified observations shrouds our knowledge about the early course of most patients in coma from anoxic or anemic anoxia. Only with head injuries and acute cardiac arrest does enough information exist to provide any guide at all, and this is presented in the paragraphs that follow.

Head Trauma

Severe head injury carries a high mortality, most of which follows within hours or days of the accident. According to Carlsson, von Essen, and Löfgren,[76] 96 per cent of primary deaths from head injury occur within 48 hours, and Heiskanen[234] obtained only a moderately lower figure (54 per cent). Most of these early deaths result from unsalvageably severe circulatory or brainstem damage, and, while there is some evidence that the acute deaths can be reduced by meticulous pulmonary care or hyperventilation therapy,[212] these measures appear mainly to defer the time of death or to increase the number of severely damaged survivors rather than to improve brain recovery.

Within the first 48 hours after head trauma, no yet-published clinical study provides sufficient information to tell which, if any, signs of neurological dysfunction unequivocally predict outcome so that, except for diagnosing brain death, clinical predictions should be deferred until after that time. Vapalahti and Troupp[574] have suggested that hyperventilation with respiratory alkalosis, hyperthermia, Cheyne-Stokes respiration, and extensor rigidity (in adults), when present, predict vegetative survival rather than full recovery. But some patients with each of these signs recovered, making the criteria not entirely reliable. Measurement of intraventricular pressure[574] during the first 48 hours was also helpful since most patients with pressure greater than 60 mm. Hg (780 mm. CSF) died and most of those with pressures less than 30 mm. Hg survived. In each group, however, were some patients who recovered, some who achieved only vegetative survival, and some who died. If one waits 48 hours, however, one encounters few, if any, surviving patients in whom fixed pupils or absence of respiratory control can be attributed directly to brainstem injury, so that the presence of these signs after 48 hours suggests that useful recovery will not occur. (Fixed pupils due to optic or oculomotor nerve lesions as well as respiratory insufficiency due to peripheral complications lack prognostic meaning.)

After 48 hours the two factors that bear most heavily on predicting the outcome are age and duration of unconsciousness.[76] The duration of post-traumatic amnesia also correlates with mental restitution but can only be determined in retrospect. No matter what the age, permanent unresponsiveness is not common after head injury and occurred, for example, in only 5 of Carlsson's 325 initially comatose survivors, but Vapalahti and Troupp reported that 13 of 50 severely brain injured patients survived in a comatose state for at least 1 month and some were alive but unconscious at 1 year. Mental incapacity to return to a previous social and economic level was more frequent, although even this can be surprisingly small.[382]

Most patients who are less than 20 years old and survive 48 hours after a head injury recover neurologically and mentally regardless of the severity and duration of coma. Coma tends to be less long-lasting in these young people, but effective restitution can follow even protracted unresponsiveness lasting as long as several months.[76] In patients over the age of 20 years, both increasing age and a longer duration of coma adversely affect the outlook for a normal neurological and mental function. This is illustrated by Figure 24 and underlined by the observation that fewer than half of the patients over 50 years of age return to work after traumatic coma lasting more than 24 hours.[76, 382]

No reported clinical studies have examined patients after post-traumatic coma regularly and systematically enough to know whether any early signs will unequivocally predict that permanent unconsciousness or permanent mindlessness will follow. Vapalahti and Troupp's study,[574] which includes 50 patients, suggests that most patients who hyperventilate and have temperatures above 39°C. and extensor rigidity will not fully recover.

We believe that clinical signs pointing to a dead brainstem provide at this time the only justification for stopping or reducing medical efforts during the first weeks after head trauma.

237

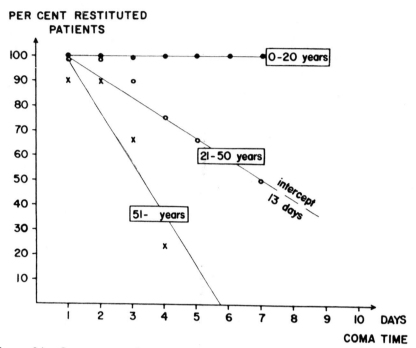

Figure 24. Percentage of patients who recovered full consciousness as a function of duration of coma. From Carlsson, C-A., von Essen, C., and Löfgren, J.: Factors affecting the clinical course of patients with severe head injuries. J. Neurosurg. 29:242-251, 1968. Reprinted by permission of the Journal of Neurosurgery.

Cardiac Arrest

Irreversible brain damage is relatively unusual among survivors of cardiac arrest; most such patients either die within a short time or recover without neurological residua. Alderete and co-workers[8] found that cardiac or respiratory arrest caused only 6 per cent of the deaths in their series of patients with clinical signs indicating brain death. Among 1710 patients with cardiac arrest reported by Stephenson,[540] 536 survived and 72 were available for long-term follow-up. Among the latter, 13 children under 10 years of age had permanent neurological deficits (3 had decerebrate coma and 8 suffered mental retardation).

The New York Hospital treats approximately 100 patients for cardiac arrest each year. Of the last 500 such patients, 16 per cent have survived for more than 4 weeks, among whom has been only one patient with prolonged, severe impairment of consciousness, combined with diffuse motor spasticity or the decerebrate state. However, several neurologically damaged patients were observed to have intact pupillary and oculocephalic reflexes as well as other preserved brainstem functions within a few hours after injury, yet never recovered fully. No patient survived in whom these brainstem functions were found to be absent for more than 72 hours after the cardiac arrest. These preliminary findings suggest that one can predict accurately enough which patients will die shortly following cardiac arrest, but they provide no reassurance that one can forecast accurately how much neurological function will return in patients in coma who are less than lethally damaged.

Bibliography

1. ABRAMSON, H. A. (ed.): *Problems of Consciousness.* Transactions of the First, Second, Third and Fourth Conferences. Josiah Macy, Jr., Foundation, New York, 1950–54.

1a. ABRAMSKY, O., CARMON, A., AND FELDMAN, S.: *Cerebrospinal fluid in acute necrotizing encephalitis. Hypochlorrhachia as a diagnostic aid.* J. Neurol. Sci. 14:183-187, 1971.

2. ADAMETZ, J. H.: *Rate of recovery of functioning in cats with rostral reticular lesions. An experimental study.* J. Neurosurg. 16:85-98, 1959.

3. ADAMS, R. D.: *Case 61–1964, case records of the Massachusetts General Hospital.* New Eng. J. Med. 271:1213-1320, 1964.

4. ADAMS, R. D., AND FOLEY, J. M.: *The neurological disorder associated with liver disease.* A. Res. Nerv. Ment. Dis., Proc. 32:198-237, 1953.

5. ADAMS, R. D., VICTOR, M., AND MANCALL, E. L.: *Central pontine myelinolysis. A hitherto undescribed disease occurring in alcoholic and malnourished patients.* Arch. Neurol. Psychiat. 81:154-172, 1959.

6. ADIE, W. J., AND CRITCHLEY, M.: *Forced grasping and groping.* Brain 50:142-170, 1927.

7. AKERT, K., KOELLA, W. P., AND HESS, R., JR.: *Sleep produced by electrical stimulation of the thalamus.* Amer. J. Physiol. 168:260-267, 1952.

8. ALDERETE, J. F., JERI, F. R., RICHARDSON, E. P., JR., SAMENT, S., SCHWAB, R. S., AND YOUNG, R. R.: *Irreversible coma: A clinical, electroencephalographic and neuropathological study.* Trans. Amer. Neurol. A. 93:16-20, 1968.

9. ALEMA, G., PERRIA, L., ROSADINI, G., ROSSI, G. F., AND FATTONI, J.: *Functional inactivation of the human brainstem related to level of consciousness. Intravertebral injection of barbiturate.* J. Neurosurg. 24:629-639, 1966.

10. ALTROCCHI, P. H., AND MENKES, J. H.: *Congenital ocular motor apraxia.* Brain 83:579-588, 1960.

11. AMES, A., III, AND GURIAN, B. S.: *Effects of glucose and oxygen deprivation on function of isolated mammalian retina.* J. Neurophysiol. 26:617-634, 1963.

12. AMES, A., III, WRIGHT, R. L., KOWADA, M., THURSTON, J. M., AND MAJNO, G.: *Cerebral ischemia. II. The no-reflow phenomenon.* Amer. J. Path. 52:437-454, 1968.

241

13. AMOROSI, E. L., AND ULTMANN, J. E.: *Thrombotic thrombocytopenic purpura: Report of 16 cases and review of the literature.* Medicine 45:139-159, 1966.

14. ANDERSEN, M. N., BORDER, J. R., AND MOURITZEN, C. V.: *Acidosis, catecholamines and cardiovascular dynamics: When does acidosis require correction?* Ann. Surg. 166:344-356, 1967.

15. ARDUINI, A., AND ARDUINI, M. G.: *Effects of drugs and metabolic alterations on brain stem arousal mechanism.* J. Pharmacol. Exp. Ther. 110:76-85, 1954.

16. ARING, C. D., AND TRUFANT, S. A.: *Effects of heavy metals on the central nervous system.* A. Res. Nerv. Ment. Dis., Proc. 32:463-474, 1953.

17. ATKINSON, E. A., FAIRBURN, B., AND HEATHFIELD, K. W. G.: *Intracranial venous thrombosis as complication of oral contraception.* Lancet 1:914-918, 1970.

18. AUSTEN, F. K., CARMICHAEL, M. W., AND ADAMS, R. D.: *Neurologic manifestations of chronic pulmonary insufficiency.* New Eng. J. Med. 257:579-590, 1957.

19. AUSTIN, J., MCAFEE, D., AND SHEARER, L.: *Metachromatic form of diffuse cerebral sclerosis.* Arch. Neurol. 12:447-455, 1965.

20. AZAMBUJA, N., LINDGREN, E., AND SJÖGREN, S. E.: *Tentorial herniations: I. Anatomy; II. Pneumography; III. Angiography.* Acta Radiol. 46:215-241, 1956.

21. BAILEY, P.: *Concerning the localization of consciousness.* Trans. Amer. Neurol. A. 80:1-12, 1955.

22. BAKER, N. H., AND MESSERT, B.: *Acute intermittent porphyria with central neurogenic hyperventilation.* Neurology 17:559-566, 1967.

23. BARBIZET, J.: *Yawning.* J. Neurol. Neurosurg. Psychiat. 21:203-209, 1958.

24. BARCROFT, R.: *The Respiratory Function of the Blood.* Cambridge University Press, Cambridge, 1925.

25. BARKER, S. B., AND KLITGAARD, H. M.: *Metabolism of tissues excised from thyroxine-injected rats.* Amer. J. Physiol. 170:81-86, 1952.

26. BARRIS, R. W., AND SCHUMAN, H. R.: *Bilateral anterior cingulate gyrus lesions. Syndrome of the anterior cingulate gyri.* Neurology 3:44-52, 1953.

27. BATINI, C., ET AL.: *Effects of complete pontine transections on the sleep-wakefulness rhythm: The mid-pontine pretrigeminal preparation.* Arch. Ital. Biol. 97:1-2, 1959.

28. BATSEL, H. L.: *Electroencephalographic synchronization and desynchronization in the chronic "cerveau isolé" of the dog.* Electroenceph. Clin. Neurophysiol. 12:421-430, 1960.

29. BECKER, D. P., ROBERT, C. M., JR., NELSON, J. R., AND STERN, W. E.: *An evaluation of the definition of cerebral death.* Neurology 20: 459-462, 1970.

30. BEECHER, H. K.: *A definition of irreversible coma: Report of the Ad Hoc Committee of the Harvard Medical School to examine the definition of brain death.* J.A.M.A. 205:85-88, 1968.

31. BELFER, M. L., AND D'AUTREMONT, C. C.: *Catatonia-like symptomatology: An interesting case.* Arch. Gen. Psychiat. 24:119-120, 1971.

32. BELLER, F. K.: *The role of endotoxin in disseminated intravascular coagulation.* Trans. 17th Ann. Symp. Blood, 1969, p. 125-149.

33. BENDER, M. B. (ed.): *The Oculomotor System.* Harper and Row, New York, 1964.

34. BENDER, M. B., AND SHANZER, S.: Oculomotor pathways defined by electric stimulation and lesions in the brainstem of monkey, in Bender, M. B. (ed.): *The Oculomotor System.* Harper and Row, New York, 1964.

35. BENNETT, I. L., JR., CARY, F. H., MITCHELL, G. L., AND COOPER, M. N.: *Acute methyl alcohol poisoning: A review based on experiences in an outbreak of 323 cases.* Medicine 32:431-463, 1953.

36. BERGAMASCO, B., BERGAMINI, L., AND DORIGUZZI, T.: *Clinical value of the sleep electroencephalographic patterns in post-traumatic coma.* Acta Neurol. Scand. 44:495-511, 1968.

37. BERGER, H.: *Ueber das Elektrenkephalogramm des Menschen.* Arch. Psychiat. Nervenkr. 87:527-570, 1929.

38. BERING, E. A., JR.: *Circulation of the cerebrospinal fluid. Demonstration of the choroid plexuses as the generator of the force for flow of fluid and ventricular enlargement.* J. Neurosurg. 19:405-413, 1962.

39. BICKFORD, R. G., AND BUTT, H. R.: *Hepatic coma: The electroencephalographic pattern.* J. Clin. Invest. 34:790-799, 1955.

40. BIEBER, I., AND FULTON, J. F.: *Relation of the cerebral cortex to the grasp reflex and to the postural and righting reflexes.* Arch. Neurol. Psychiat. 39:433-454, 1938.

41. BIELSCHOWSKY, A.: *Lectures on motor anomalies of the eyes.* Arch. Ophthal. 13:33-59, 1935.

42. BIELSCHOWSKY, A.: *Lectures on motor anomalies of the eyes. X. Supranuclear paralyses.* Amer. J. Ophthal. 22:603-613, 1939.

43. BIEMOND, A., AND DEJONG, J. M. B. V.: *On cervical nystagmus and related disorders.* Brain 92:437-458, 1969.

44. BIERCE, A.: *The Devil's Dictionary.* World Book Co., Yonkers, N. Y., 1948.

45. BINNIE, C. D., PRIOR, P. F., LLOYD, D. S. L., SCOTT, D. F., AND MARGERISON, J. H.: *Electroencephalographic prediction of fatal anoxic brain damage after resuscitation from cardiac arrest.* Brit. Med. J. 4:265-268, 1970.

46. BINNION, P. F., AND MCFARLAND, R. J.: *The relationship between cardiac massage and pupil size in cardiac arrest in dogs.* Cardiovasc. Res. 3:915-917, 1967.

243

47. BIRCHFIELD, R. I.: *Postural hypotension in Wernicke's disease.* Amer. J. Med. 36:404-414, 1964.

48. BIRD, T. D., AND PLUM, F.: *Recovery from barbiturate overdose coma with a prolonged isoelectric electroencephalogram.* Neurology 18: 456-460, 1968.

49. BITTENBENDER, J. B., AND QUADFASEL, F. A.: *Rigid and akinetic forms of Huntington's chorea.* Arch. Neurol. 7:275-288, 1962.

50. BLEGVAD, B.: *Caloric vestibular reaction in unconscious patients.* Arch. Otolaryngol. 75:506-514, 1962.

51. BORISON, H. L., AND WANG, S. C.: *Physiology and pharmacology of vomiting.* Pharmacol. Rev. 5:193-230, 1953.

52. BRAIN, R.: *The physiological basis of consciousness.* Brain 81:426-455, 1958.

53. BRAIN, W. R., AND WILKINSON, M.: *Subacute cerebellar degeneration associated with neoplasms.* Brain 88:465-478, 1965.

54. BRAZIER, M. A. B.: *The electrical activity of the nervous system.* Science 146:1423-1428, 1964.

55. BREMER, F.: *L'activité Cérébrale au Cours du Sommeil et de la Narcose.* Bull. Acad. Roy. Méd. Belg. 2:68-86, 1937.

56. BREMER, F.: *Some Problems in Neurophysiology.* University of London, Athlone Press, London, 1953.

57. BRENDLER, S. J., AND SELVERSTONE, B.: *Recovery from decerebration.* Brain 93:381-392, 1970.

58. BRENNAN, R. W., PATTERSON, R. H., JR., AND KESSLER, J.: *Cerebral blood flow and metabolism during cardiopulmonary bypass: Evidence of microembolic encephalopathy.* Neurology 21:665-672, 1971.

59. BRENNAN, R. W., AND PLUM, F.: *A cerebrospinal fluid transfer model for hepatic and uremic encephalopathy.* Trans. Amer. Neurol. A. 96:210-211, 1971.

60. BRICOLO, A., GENTILOMO, A., ROSADINI, G., AND ROSSI, G. F.: *Long-lasting post-traumatic unconsciousness. A study based on nocturnal EEG and polygraphic recording.* Acta Neurol. Scand. 44:512-532, 1968.

61. BRIERLEY, J. B., ADAMS, J. H., GRAHAM, D. I., AND SIMPSON, J. A.: *Neocortical death after cardiac arrest.* Lancet 2:560-565, 1971.

62. BRODAL, A.: *Anatomical points of view on the alleged morphological basis of consciousness.* Acta Neurochir. 12:166-186, 1965.

63. BRODAL, A., POMPEIANO, O., AND WALBERG, F.: *The Vestibular Nuclei and Their Connections, Anatomy and Functional Correlations.* Charles C Thomas, Springfield, Ill., 1962.

64. BRODERSON, P., HEILBRUN, P., PAULSON, O., OLESON, J., SKINHØJ, E., AND LASSEN, N. A.: *Cerebral blood flow and oxygen consumption in coma and brain death.* (in press).

65. BROWDER, J., AND MEYERS, R.: *Behavior of the systemic blood pressure, pulse rate and spinal fluid pressure associated with acute changes in intracranial pressure artificially produced.* Arch. Surg. 36:1-19, 1938.

66. BROWN, H. W., AND PLUM, F.: *The neurologic basis of Cheyne-Stokes respiration.* Amer. J. Med. 30:849-860, 1961.

67. BRUCHER, J. M.: *The frontal eye field of the monkey.* Int. J. Neurol. 5:262-281, 1966.

68. BRUTON, C. J., CORSELLIS, J. A. N., AND RUSSELL, A.: *Hereditary hyperammonemia.* Brain 93:423-434, 1970.

69. BRYAN, C. S.: *Nonbacterial thrombotic endocarditis with malignant tumors.* Amer. J. Med. 46:787-793, 1969.

70. BULGER, R. J., SCHRIER, R. W., AREND, W. P., AND SWANSON, A. G.: *Spinal-fluid acidosis and the diagnosis of pulmonary encephalopathy.* New Eng. J. Med. 274:433-437, 1966.

71. BURWELL, C. S., ROBIN, E. D., WHALEY, R. D., AND BICKELMANN, A. G.: *Extreme obesity associated with alveolar hypoventilation—a pickwickian syndrome.* Amer. J. Med. 21:811-818, 1956.

72. CADMAN, T. E., AND RORKE, L. B.: *Central pontine myelinolysis in childhood and adolescence.* Arch. Dis. Child. 44:342-350, 1969.

73. CAIRNS, H.: *Disturbances of consciousness with lesions of the brain stem and diencephalon.* Brain 75:109-146, 1952.

74. CAIRNS, H., OLDFIELD, R. C., PENNYBACKER, J. B., AND WHITTERIDGE, D.: *Akinetic mutism with an epidermoid cyst of the 3rd ventricle.* Brain 64:273-290, 1941.

75. CANNON, B. W.: *Acute vascular lesions of the brain stem. A complication of supratentorial space occupying lesions.* Arch. Neurol. Psychiat. 66:687-696, 1951.

76. CARLSSON, C-A., VON ESSEN, C., AND LÖFGREN, J.: *Factors affecting the clinical course of patients with severe head injuries. Part 1. Influence of biological factors. Part 2. Significance of posttraumatic coma.* J. Neurosurg. 29:242-251, 1968.

77. CARMEL, P. W.: *Sympathetic deficits following thalamotomy.* Arch. Neurol. 18:378-387, 1968.

78. CARPENTER, R. R., AND PETERSDORF, R. G.: *Clinical spectrum of bacterial meningitis.* Amer. J. Med. 33:262-275, 1962.

79. CARPENTER, S. J., McCARTHY, L. E., AND BORISON, H. L.: *Morphologic and functional effects of intracerebroventricular administration of autologous blood in cats.* Neurology 17:993-1002, 1967.

80. CARPENTER, W. B.: *Principles of Human Physiology.* Blanchard and Lea, Philadelphia, 1853.

81. CARTER, A. B.: *Cerebral Infarction.* Pergamon Press, Oxford, 1964.

82. CASTAIGNE, P., BUGE, A., CAMBIER, J., ESCOUROLLE, R., BRUNET, P. AND DEGOS, J. D.: *Démence thalamique d'origine vasculaire par ramollissement bilatéral, limité au territoire du pédicule rétro-mamillaire.* Rev. Neurol. 114:89-107, 1966.

83. CASTAIGNE, P., AND ESCOUROLLE, R.: *Etude topographique des lésions anatomiques dans les hypersomnies.* Rev. Neurol. 116:547-584, 1967.

84. CAVANAGH, J. B., AND KYU, M. H.: *Type II Alzheimer change experimentally produced in astrocytes in the rat.* J. Neurol. Sci. 12:63-75, 1971.

85. CHALAZONITIS, N.: *Effects of anesthetics on neural mechanisms. Selective actions of volatile anesthetics on synaptic transmission and autorhythmicity in single identifiable neurons.* Anesthesiology 28:111-123, 1967.

86. CHAPMAN, L. F., AND WOLFF, H. G.: *The cerebral hemispheres and the highest integrative functions of man.* Arch. Neurol. 1:357-424, 1959.

87. CHARATAN, F. B., AND BRIERLEY, J. B.: *Mental disorder associated with primary lung carcinoma.* Brit. Med. J. 1:765-768, 1956.

88. CHASE, T. N., MORETTI, L., AND PRENSKY, A. L.: *Clinical and electroencephalographic manifestations of vascular lesions of the pons.* Neurology 18:357-368, 1968.

89. CHIANG, J., KOWADA, M., AMES, A., III, WRIGHT, R. L., AND MAJNO, G.: *Cerebral ischemia. III. Vascular changes.* Amer. J. Path. 52:455-476, 1968.

90. CIEMBRONIEWICS, J. E.: *Subdural hematoma of the posterior fossa.* J. Neurosurg. 22:465-473, 1965.

91. CLARK, R. G., AND NORMAN, J. N.: *Metabolic alkalosis in pyloric stenosis.* Lancet 1:1244-1245, 1964.

92. CLEIN, L. J., AND BOLTON, C. F.: *Interhemispheric subdural hematoma: A case report.* J. Neurol. Neurosurg. Psychiat. 32:389-392, 1969.

93. CLEVELAND, J. C.: *Complete recovery after cardiac arrest for three hours.* New Eng. J. Med. 284:334-335, 1971.

94. CLITHEROW, N. R., FOWLER, A., AND SEDZIMER, C. B.: *Combined intracerebellar and posterior fossa subdural hematomas. Case report.* J. Neurosurg. 30:744-746, 1969.

95. COGAN, D. G.: *Ocular dysmetria: Flutter-like oscillations of the eyes, and opsoclonus.* Arch. Ophthal. 51:318-335, 1954.

96. COGAN, D. G.: *Neurology of the Ocular Muscles,* ed. 2. Charles C Thomas, Springfield, Ill., 1956.

97. COGAN, D. G., KUBIK, C. S., AND SMITH, W. L.: *Unilateral internuclear ophthalmoplegia: Report of eight clinical cases with one post-mortem study.* Arch. Ophthal. 44:783-796, 1950.

98. COHEN, B.: *Eye, head and body movements from semicircular canal nerve stimulation.* Neurology 15:270, 1965.

99. COHEN, B., SUZUKI, J. I., SHANZER, S., AND BENDER, M. B.: Semicircular canal control of eye movements, in Bender, M. B. (ed.): *The Oculomotor System.* Harper and Row, New York, 1964.

100. COHEN, M. M., AND HARTMANN, J. F.: Biochemical and ultrastructural correlates of cerebral cortex slices metabolizing in vitro, in Cohen, M. M., and Snider, R. S.: *Morphological and Biochemical Correlates of Neural Activity.* Harper and Row, New York, 1964, pp. 57-74.

101. COLLIER, J.: *The false localizing signs of intracranial tumors.* Brain 27:490-507, 1904.

102. COLLINS, R. C., POSNER, J. B., AND PLUM, F.: *Cerebral energy metabolism during electroshock seizures in mice.* Amer. J. Physiol. 218: 943-950, 1970.

103. CONN, H. O.: *Asterixis: Its occurrence in chronic pulmonary disease with a commentary on its general mechanism.* New Eng. J. Med. 259: 564-569, 1958.

104. COPE, C.: *The importance of oxygen in the treatment of cyanide poisoning.* J.A.M.A. 175:1061-1064, 1961.

105. CORSELLIS, J. A. N., GOLDBERG, G. J., AND NORTON, A. R.: *"Limbic encephalitis" and its association with carcinoma.* Brain 91:481-496, 1968.

106. COWAN, R. J., MAYNARD, C. D., AND LASSITER, K. R.: *Technetium-99m pertechnetate brain scans in the detection of subdural hematomas.* J. Neurosurg. 32:30-34, 1970.

107. COXE, W. S., AND LUSE, S. A.: *Acute hemorrhagic leukoencephalitis. A clinical and electron-microscopic report of 2 patients treated with surgical decompression.* J. Neurosurg. 20:584-596, 1963.

108. CRAVIOTO, H., SILBERMAN, J., AND FEIGIN, I.: *A clinical and pathologic study of akinetic mutism.* Neurology 10:10-21, 1960.

109. CRILL, W. E.: *Horner's syndrome secondary to deep cerebral lesions.* Neurology 16:325, 1966.

110. CRITCHLEY, M.: *The anterior cerebral artery and its syndromes.* Brain 53:120-165, 1930.

111. CROMPTON, M. R.: *Cerebral infarction following rupture of cerebral berry aneurysms.* Brain 87:263-280, 1964.

112. CROMPTON, M. R., TEARE, R. D., AND BOWEN, D. A. L.: *Prolonged coma after head injury.* Lancet 2:938-940, 1966.

113. CUMINGS, J. N.: Some biochemical considerations regarding different forms of demyelination, in Rose, A. J., and Pearson, C. M. (eds.): *Mechanisms of Demyelination.* McGraw-Hill Book Co., New York, 1963.

114. CUMINGS, J. N.: Cerebral lipid biochemistry in the demyelinations, in Cumings, J. N., and Kremer, M. (eds.): *Biochemical Aspects of Neurological Disorders,* 2nd ser. F. A. Davis Co. (Blackwell Scientific Publications), Philadelphia, 1965.

115. CUMINGS, J. N.: Trace elements in the brain in health and in neurological disease, in Ross, J. P. (ed.): *The Scientific Basis of Medicine—Annual Reviews.* Athlone Press, London, 1965.

116. CUSHING, H.: *Concerning a definite regulatory mechanism of the vasomotor centre which controls blood pressure during cerebral compression.* Bull. Hopkins Hosp. 12:290-292, 1901.

117. CUSHING, H.: *Some experimental and clinical observations concerning states of increased intracranial tension.* Amer. J. Med. Sci. 124:375-400, 1902.

118. CUSHING, H.: *The blood pressure reaction of acute cerebral compression, illustrated by cases of intracranial hemorrhage.* Amer. J. Med. Sci. 125:1017-1044, 1903.

119. CUSHING, H.: *Some aspects of the pathological physiology of intra-cranial tumors.* Bost. Med. Surg. J. 161:71-80, 1909.

120. DANDY, W. E.: *Changes in our conceptions of localization of certain functions in the brain.* Amer. J. Physiol. 93:643, 1930.

121. DANDY, W. E.: *The location of the conscious center in the brain—the corpus striatum.* Bull. Hopkins Hosp. 79:34-58, 1946.

122. DANIELS, A. C., CHOKROVERTY, S., AND BARRON, K. D.: *Thalamic degeneration, dementia, and seizures. Inappropriate ADH secretion associated with bronchogenic carcinoma.* Arch. Neurol. 21:15-24, 1969.

123. DAROFF, R. B., DELLER, J. J., JR., KASTL, A. J., JR., AND BLOCKER, W. W., JR.: *Cerebral malaria.* J.A.M.A. 202:679-682, 1967.

124. DASTUR, D. K., SESHADRI, R., AND TALAGERI, V. R.: *Liver-brain relationships in hepatic coma.* Arch. Intern. Med. 112:899-916, 1963.

125. DEJERINE, J.: *Sémiologie des Affections du Système Nerveux.* Masson et Cie, Paris, 1926.

126. DELAFRESNAYE, J. P., ET AL.: *Brain Mechanisms and Consciousness.* Blackwell Scientific Publications, Oxford, 1954.

127. DEMENT, W., AND KLEITMAN, N.: *Cyclic variations in EEG during sleep and their relation to eye movements, body motility and dreaming.* Electroenceph. Clin. Neurophysiol. 9:673-690, 1957.

128. DENNY-BROWN, D. E.: *The Basal Ganglia and Their Relation to Disorders of Movement.* Oxford University Press, London, 1962.

129. DENNY-BROWN, D. E., AND RUSSELL, W. R.: *Experimental cerebral concussion.* Brain 64:91-164, 1941.

130. DEVAKUL, K., HARINASUTA, T., AND REID, H. A.: *^{125}I-labelled fibrinogen in cerebral malaria.* Lancet 2:886-888, 1966.

131. DIDISHEIM, P., BOWIE, E. J., AND OWEN, C. A., JR.: *Intravascular coagulation-fibrinolysis (ICF) syndrome and malignancy: Historical review and report of two cases with metastatic carcinoid and with acute myelomonocytic leukemia.* Trans. 17th Ann. Symp. Blood, 1969, pp. 215-231.

131a. DILA, C. J., AND PAPPIUS, H. M.: *Cerebral water and electrolytes.* Arch. Neurol. 26:85-90, 1972.

132. DILL, L. V., AND ISENHOUR, C. E.: *Etiologic factors in experimentally produced pontile hemorrhages.* Arch. Neurol. Psychiat. 41:1146-1152, 1939.

133. DIMSDALE, H., AND LOGUE, V.: *Ruptured posterior fossa aneurysms and their surgical treatment.* J. Neurol. Neurosurg. Psychiat. 22:202-217, 1959.

134. DINSDALE, H. B.: *Spontaneous hemorrhage in the posterior fossa.* Arch. Neurol. 10:200-217, 1964.

135. DODGE, P. R., AND SWARTZ, M. N.: *Bacterial meningitis: II. Special neurologic problems, postmeningitic complications and clinico-pathological correlations.* New Eng. J. Med. 272:954-960, 1965.

136. DRACHMAN, D. A., AND ADAMS, R. D.: *Herpes simplex and acute inclusion-body encephalitis.* Arch. Neurol. 7:45-63, 1962.

137. DREYFUS, P. M.: *The quantitative histochemical distribution of thiamine in deficient rat brain.* J. Neurochem. 8:139-145, 1961.

138. DREYFUS, P. M.: *The regional distribution of transketolase in the normal and the thiamine deficient nervous system.* J. Neuropath. Exp. Neurol. 24:119-129, 1965.

139. DUCKER, T. B.: *Increased intracranial pressure and pulmonary edema. Part I. Clinical study of 11 patients.* J. Neurosurg. 28:112-117, 1968.

140. DUCKER, T. B., AND SIMMONS, R. L.: *Increased intracranial pressure and pulmonary edema. Part II. The hemodynamic response of dogs and monkeys to increased intracranial pressure.* J. Neurosurg. 28: 118-123, 1968.

141. DUCKER, T. B., SIMMONS, R. L., AND ANDERSON, R. W.: *Increased intracranial pressure and pulmonary edema. Part III. The effect of increased intracranial pressure on the cardiovascular hemodynamics of chimpanzees.* J. Neurosurg. 29:475-483, 1968.

142. DUFFY, G. P.: *Lumbar puncture in the presence of raised intracranial pressure.* Brit. Med. J. 1:407-409, 1969.

143. DUGUID, H., SIMPSON, R. G., AND STOWERS, J. M.: *Accidental hypothermia.* Lancet 2:1213-1219, 1961.

144. DUKE-ELDER, W. S.: *Text-Book of Ophthalmology.* C. V. Mosby Co., St. Louis, 1949, vol. 4, p. 4164.

145. DUVOISIN, R. C., AND YAHR, M. D.: *Posterior fossa aneurysms.* Neurology 15:231-241, 1965.

146. EBAUGH, F. G., BARNACLE, C. H., AND EWALT, J. R.: *Delirious episodes associated with artificial fever. A study of 200 cases.* Amer. J. Psychiat. 93:191-215, 1936.

147. ECCLES, J. C. (ed.): *Brain and Conscious Experience.* Springer Publishing Co., Inc., New York, 1966.

148. ECKER, A.: *Upward transtentorial herniation of the brainstem and cerebellum due to tumor of the posterior fossa.* J. Neurosurg. 5:51-61, 1948.

149. Editorial: *Determination of death.* Lancet 1:1092-1093, 1970.

150. EISENBERG, S., MADISON, L., AND SENSENBACH, W.: *Cerebral hemodynamic and metabolic studies in patients with congestive heart failure: II. Observations in confused subjects.* Circulation 21:704-709, 1960.

151. ELKINGTON, J. S.: Clinical manifestations of disorders of porphyrin metabolism, in Cumings, J. N., and Kremer, M. (eds.): *Biochemical Aspects of Neurological Disorders,* 1st ser. F. A. Davis Co. (Blackwell Scientific Publications), Philadelphia, 1959.

152. ELLIOTT, K. A. C., AND WOLFF, L. S.: Brain tissue respiration and glycolysis, in Elliott, K. A. C., Page, I. H., and Quastel, J. H. (eds.): *Neurochemistry; The Chemistry of Brain and Nerve,* ed. 2. Charles C Thomas, Springfield, Ill., 1962.

249

153. ELSCHNIG, A.: *Nystagmus retractorius ein cerebralis Herdsymptom.* Med. Klin. 9:8-11, 1913.

154. ENGLE, G. L.: *Fainting,* ed. 2. Charles C Thomas, Springfield, Ill., 1962.

155. ENGLE, G. L., AND MARGOLIN, S. G.: *Neuropsychiatric disturbances in Addison's disease and the role of impaired carbohydrate metabolism in production of abnormal cerebral function.* Arch. Neurol. Psychiat. 45:881-884, 1941.

156. ETHELBERG, S., AND JENSEN, V. A.: *Obscurations and further time related paroxysmal disorders in intracranial tumors.* Arch. Neurol. Psychiat. 68:130-149, 1952.

157. FARIS, A. A.: *Limbic system infarction. A report of two cases.* Neurology 19:91-96, 1969.

158. FAZEKAS, J. F., ALEXANDER, F. A. D., AND HIMWICH, H. E.: *Tolerance of newborn to anoxia.* Amer. J. Physiol. 134:281-287, 1941.

159. FAZEKAS, J. F., GRAVES, F. B., AND ALMAN, R. W.: *The influence of the thyroid on cerebral metabolism.* Endocrinology 48:169-174, 1951.

159a. FELDMAN, M. H.: *Physiological observations in a chronic case of locked-in syndrome.* Neurology 21:459-478, 1971.

160. FELDMAN, S. M., AND WALLER, H. J.: *Dissociation of electrocortical activation and behavioral arousal.* Nature 196:1320-1322, 1962.

161. FIELDS, W. S., RATINOV, G., WEIBEL, J., AND CAMPOS, R. J.: *Survival following basilar artery occlusion.* Arch. Neurol. 15:463-471, 1966.

162. FIESCHI, C., AGNOLI, A., BATTISTINI, N., BOZZAO, L., AND PRENCIPE, M.: *Derangement of regional cerebral blood flow and of its regulatory mechanisms in acute cerebrovascular lesions.* Neurology 18:1166-1179, 1968.

163. FINNEY, L. A., AND WALKER, A. E.: *Transtentorial Herniation.* Charles C Thomas, Springfield, Ill., 1962.

164. FISCHER, J. E., AND BALDESSARINI, R. J.: *False neurotransmitters and hepatic failure.* Lancet 2:75-80, 1971.

165. FISCHER, J. J.: *The Labyrinth-Physiology and Functional Tests.* Grune and Stratton, New York, 1956.

166. FISHER, C. M.: Clinical syndromes in cerebral arterial occlusion, in Fields, W. S. (ed.): *Pathogenesis and Treatment of Cerebrovascular Disease.* Charles C Thomas, Springfield, Ill., 1961, pp. 151-181.

167. FISHER, C. M.: *Ocular bobbing.* Arch. Neurol. 11:543-546, 1964.

168. FISHER, C. M.: *Some neuro-ophthalmological observations.* J. Neurol. Neurosurg. Psychiat. 30:383-392, 1967.

169. FISHER, C. M.: *The neurological examination of the comatose patient.* Acta Neurol. Scand. 45: Suppl. 36:1-56, 1969.

170. FISHMAN, R. A.: *Carrier transport of glucose between blood and cerebrospinal fluid.* Amer. J. Physiol. 206:836-844, 1964.

171. FISHMAN, R. A.: *Neurological aspects of magnesium metabolism.* Arch. Neurol. 12:562-569, 1965.

172. FISHMAN, R. A., AND RASKIN, N. H.: *Experimental uremic encephalopathy. Permeability and electrolyte metabolism of brain and other tissues.* Arch. Neurol. 17:10-21, 1967.

173. FITZ-HUGH, T., JR., PEPPER, D. S., AND HOPKINS, H. U.: *The cerebral form of malaria.* Bull. U.S. Army Medical Dept. 83:39-48, 1944.

174. FLUUR, E.: *Influences of semicircular ducts on extraocular muscles.* Acta Otolaryngol. Suppl. 149, 1959.

175. FOLEY, J. M., WATSON, C. W., AND ADAMS, R. D.: *Significance of electroencephalographic changes in hepatic coma.* Trans. Amer. Neurol. A. 75:161-164, 1950.

176. FOLTZ, E. L., AND SCHMIDT, R. P.: *The role of the reticular formation in the coma of head injury.* J. Neurosurg. 13:145-154, 1956.

177. FOLTZ, E. L., AND WARD, A. A., JR.: *Communicating hydrocephalus from subarachnoid bleeding.* J. Neurosurg. 13:546-566, 1956.

178. FORD, F. R., AND WALSH, F. B.: *Tonic deviations of the eyes produced by movements of the head.* Arch. Ophthal. 23:1274-1284, 1940.

179. FORESTER, C. F.: *Coma in myxedema.* Arch. Intern. Med. 111:734-743, 1963.

180. FRANKEL, N., COHEN, A. K., ARKY, R. A., AND FOSTER, A. E.: *Alcohol hypoglycemia: II. A postulated mechanism of action based on experiments with rat liver slices.* J. Clin. Endocr. 25:76-94, 1965.

181. FRASER, R. S., SPROULE, B. J., AND DVORKIN, J.: *Hypoventilation cyanosis and polycythemia in a thin man.* Canad. Med. A. J. 89:1178-1182, 1963.

182. FRED, H. L., WILLERSON, J. T., AND ALEXANDER, J. K.: *Neurological manifestations of pulmonary thromboembolism.* Arch. Intern. Med. 120:33-37, 1967.

183. FREDRICKSON, J. M., SCHWARZ, D., AND KORNHUBER, H. H.: *Convergence and interaction of vestibular and deep somatic afferents upon neurons in the vestibular nuclei of the cat.* Acta Otolaryngol. 61:168-188, 1966.

184. FREMONT-SMITH, F., AND PUTNAM, T. J.: *Value of lumbar puncture in diagnosis of suspected brain tumor.* J. Nerv. Ment. Dis. 76:261, 1932.

185. FRENCH, J. D.: *Brain lesions with prolonged unconsciousness.* Arch. Neurol. Psychiat. 68:727-740, 1952.

186. FRENCH, J. D.: The reticular formation, in Field, J., Magoun, H. W., and Hall, V. E. (eds.): *Handbook of Physiology.* Sect. 1, Neurophysiology. American Physiological Society, Washington, D. C., 1960, vol. 2, Chap. LII, pp. 1281-1305.

187. FRENCH, J. D., VERZEANO, M., AND MAGOUN, H. W.: *A neural basis of the anesthetic state.* Arch. Neurol. Psychiat. 69:519-529, 1953.

188. FRIEDE, R. L., AND ROESSMANN, U.: *The pathogenesis of secondary midbrain hemorrhages.* Neurology 16:1210-1216, 1966.

189. FRIEDMAN, E. A., GREENBURG, J. B., MERRILL, J. P., AND DAMMIN, G. J.: *Consequences of ethylene glycol poisoning.* Amer. J. Med. 32:891-902, 1962.

190. FRIEDREICH, N.: *Paramyoklonus multiplex.* Virchow Arch. Path. Anat. 86:421-430, 1881.

191. FRITZ, I. B.: *Factors influencing the rates of long-chain fatty acid oxidation and synthesis in mammalian systems.* Physiol. Rev. 41: 52-129, 1961.

192. FRUMIN, M. J., EPSTEIN, R. M., AND COHEN, G.: *Apneic oxygenation in man.* Anesthesiology 20:789-798, 1959.

193. FULTON, J. F., AND BAILEY, P.: *Tumors in the region of the third ventricle: their diagnosis and relation to pathological sleep.* J. Nerv. Ment. Dis. 69:1-25, 145-164, 261-277, 1929.

194. GABUZDA, G. J.: *Hepatic coma: Clinical considerations, pathogenesis, and management.* Advances Intern. Med. 11:11-41, 1963.

195. GALLAGHER, J. P., AND BROWDER, J.: *Extradural hematoma. Experience with 167 patients.* J. Neurosurg. 29:1-12, 1968.

196. GAMPER, E.: *Bau und leistungen eines menschlichen mittelhirnwesens (arhinencephalie mit encephalocele).* Z. ges Neurol. Psychiat. 102: 154-235, 1926.

197. GAMPER, E.: *Bau und leistungen eines menschlichen mittelhirnwesens (arhinencephalie mit encephalocele) zugleich ein beitrag zur teratologie und fasersytematik.* Z. ges Neurol. Psychiat. 104:49-120, 1926.

198. GARCIN, R., BERTRAND, I., KIPFER, M., GRUNER, J., AND PESTEL, M.: *Hémiballismus. Etude anatomo-clinique.* Rev. Neurol. 81:964-968, 1949.

199. GASTAUT, H., AND FISCHER-WILLIAMS, M.: The physiopathology of epileptic seizures, in Field, J., Magoun, H. W., and Hall, V. E. (eds.): *Handbook of Physiology.* Sect. I, Neurophysiology. American Physiological Society, Washington, D. C., 1959, vol. 1, Chap. 14, p. 329.

200. GAYET, M.: *Affection encéphalique (encéphalite diffuse probable).* Arch. Physiol. Norm. Path. 2e ser. 2:341-351, 1875.

201. GAZZANIGA, A. B., AND DALEN, J. E.: *Paradoxical embolism: Its pathophysiology and clinical recognition.* Ann. Surg. 171:137-142, 1970.

202. GEIGER, A.: *Correlation of brain metabolism and function by the use of a brain perfusion method in situ.* Physiol. Rev. 38:1-20, 1958.

203. GERICH, J. E., MARTIN, M. M., AND RECANT, L.: *Clinical and metabolic characteristics of hyperosmolar nonketotic coma.* Diabetes 20:228-238, 1971.

203a. GERNANDT, B. E.: *Response of mammalian vestibular neurons to horizontal rotation and caloric stimulation.* J. Neurophysiol. 12:173-184, 1949.

204. GIBBS, C. J., JR., GAJDUSEK, D. C., ASHER, D. M., ALPERS, M. P., BECK, E., DANIEL, P. M., AND MATTHEWS, W. B.: *Creutzfeldt-Jakob disease (spongiform encephalopathy): transmission to the chimpanzee.* Science 161:388-389, 1968.

205. GJERRIS, F., AND MELLEMGAARD, L.: *Transitory cortical blindness in head injury.* Acta Neurol. Scand. 45:623-631, 1969.

206. GJESSING, R., AND GJESSING, L.: *Some main trends in the clinical aspects of periodic catatonia.* Acta Psychiat. Scand. 37:1-13, 1961.

207. GLASS, A.: *Mental arithmetic and blocking of the occipital alpha rhythm.* Electroenceph. Clin. Neurophysiol. 16:595-603, 1964.

208. GOEBEL, H. H., KOMATSUZAKI, A., BENDER, M. B., AND COHEN, B.: *Lesions of the pontine tegmentum and conjugate gaze paralysis.* Arch. Neurol. 24:431-440, 1971.

209. GOLDBERG, M.: *Hyponatremia and the inappropriate secretion of antidiuretic hormone.* Amer. J. Med. 35:293-298, 1963.

210. GOLDMAN, D. E.: *Potential, impedance and rectification in membranes.* J. Gen. Physiol. 27:37-60, 1943.

211. GOODMAN, J. M., MISHKIN, F. S., AND DYKEN, M.: *Determination of brain death by isotope angiography.* J.A.M.A. 209:1869-1872, 1969.

212. GORDON, E.: Results of treatment with hyperventilation in patients with severe head injuries, in Ross Russell, R. W. (ed.) : *Brain and Blood Flow.* Pitman Publishing Co., London, 1970, pp. 365-369.

213. GORHAM, L. W.: *A study of pulmonary embolism. Part I.* Arch. Intern. Med. 108:8-22, 1961.

214. GOTTSCHALK, P. G., AND THOMAS, J. E.: *Heat Stroke.* Mayo Clinic Proc. 41:470-482, 1966.

215. GOTTSTEIN, U.: *Der hirnkreislauf bei hyperthyreose und myxödem.* Verh. dp. Ges inn Med. 70:921-924, 1964.

216. GOWERS, W. R.: *A Manual of Diseases of the Nervous System.* The Blakiston Co., Philadelphia, 1893.

217. GRAHAM, D. I., AND ADAMS, J. H.: *Ischemic brain damage in fatal head injuries.* Clin. Develop. Med. 39/40:34-40, 1971.

218. GRANT, D. K.: *Papilloedema and fits in hypoparathyroidism.* Quart. J. Med. N. S. 22:243-259, 1953.

219. GRAY, F. D., JR., AND HORNER, G. J.: *Survival following extreme hypoxemia.* J.A.M.A. 211:1815-1817, 1970.

220. GRIFFITH, J. F., AND DODGE, P. R.: *Transient blindness following head injury in children.* New Eng. J. Med. 278:648-651, 1968.

221. GRUMER, H. A., DERRYBERRY, W., DUBIN, A., AND WALDSTEIN, S. S.: *Idiopathic, episodic, inappropriate secretion of antidiuretic hormone.* Amer. J. Med. 32:954-963, 1962.

222. GURDJIAN, E. S., ET AL.: *Studies on experimental concussion.* Neurology 4:674-681, 1954.

223. HABENER, J. F., DASHE, A. M., AND SOLOMON, D. H.: *Response of normal subjects to prolonged high fluid intake.* J. Appl. Physiol. 19:134-136, 1964.

224. HAGSTAM, K. E.: *EEG frequency content related to chemical blood parameters in chronic uremia.* Scand. J. Urol. Nephrol. Suppl. 7, 1971.

225. HALDANE, J. S.: *A lecture on the symptoms, causes and prevention of anoxemia.* Brit. Med. J. 2:65-71, 1919.

253

226. HALSEY, J. H., AND DOWNIE, A. W.: *Decerebrate rigidity with preservation of consciousness.* J. Neurol. Neurosurg. Psychiat. 29:350-355, 1966.

227. HAMBY, W. B.: *Intracranial Aneurysms.* Charles C Thomas, Springfield, Ill., 1952.

228. HAMEROFF, S. B., GARCIA-MULLIN, R., AND ECKHOLDT, J.: *Ocular bobbing.* Arch. Ophthal. 82:774-780, 1969.

229. HAMMERMEISTER, K. E., AND REICHENBACH, D. D.: *QRS changes, pulmonary edema, and myocardial necrosis associated with subarachnoid hemorrhage.* Amer. Heart J. 78:94-100, 1969.

230. HARDING, G., JEAVONS, P. M., JENNER, F. A., DRUMMOND, P., SHERIDAN, M., AND HOWELLS, G. W.: *The electroencephalogram in three cases of periodic psychosis.* Electroenceph. Clin. Neurophysiol. 21:59-66, 1966.

231. HATCHER, M. A., JR., AND KLINTWORTH, G. K.: *The sylvian aqueduct syndrome. A clinicopathologic study.* Arch. Neurol. 15:215-222, 1966.

232. HAYWARD, J. N., AND BOSHELL, B. R.: *Paraldehyde intoxication with metabolic acidosis.* Amer. J. Med. 23:965-976, 1957.

233. HEAD, H.: *The diagnosis of hysteria.* Brit. Med. J. 1:827-829, 1922.

234. HEISKANEN, O.: *Cerebral circulatory arrest caused by acute increase of intracranial pressure.* Acta Neurol. Scand. (Suppl. 7) 40: 1964.

235. HENSON, R. A.: The demyelinations, in Cumings, J. N., and Kremer, M. (eds.): *Biochemical Aspects of Neurological Disorders,* 2nd ser. F. A. Davis Co. (Blackwell Scientific Publications), Philadelphia, 1965.

236. HERISHANU, Y., ABRAMSKY, O., AND LAVY, S.: *Focal neurological manifestations in hypercalcemia.* Eur. Neurol. 4:283-288, 1970.

237. HEUSNER, A. P.: *Yawning and associated phenomena.* Physiol. Rev. 26:156-168, 1946.

238. HILL, D., AND PARR, G. (ed.): *Electroencephalography—A Symposium on Its Various Aspects,* ed. 2. Macmillan Co., New York, 1963.

239. HIMWICH, H. E.: *Brain Metabolism and Cerebral Disorders.* Williams and Wilkins Co., Baltimore, 1951.

240. HITCHCOCK, E., AND ANDREADIS, A.: *Subdural empyema: A review of 29 cases.* J. Neurol. Neurosurg. Psychiat. 27:422-434, 1964.

241. HOAGLAND, H., ET AL.: *Effects of hypoglycemia and pentobarbital sodium on electrical activity of cerebral cortex and hypothalamus (dogs).* J. Neurophysiol. 2:276-288, 1939.

242. HOCKADAY, J. M., POTTS, F., EPSTEIN, E., BONAZZI, A., AND SCHWAB, R. S.: *Electroencephalographic changes in acute cerebral anoxia from cardiac or respiratory arrest.* Electroenceph. Clin. Neurophysiol. 18: 575-586, 1965.

243. HOLCOMB, B.: *Causes and diagnosis of various forms of coma.* J.A.M.A. 77:2112-2114, 1921.

244. HOLLIDAY, M. A., KALAYCI, M. N., AND HARRAH, J.: *Factors that limit brain volume changes in response to acute and sustained hyper- and hyponatremia.* J. Clin. Invest. 47:1916-1928, 1968.

245. HOLMES, G.: *Palsies of conjugate ocular movements.* Brit. J. Ophthal. 5:241-250, 1921.

246. HOLMES, G.: *The cerebral integration of the ocular movements.* Brit. Med. J. 2:107-112, 1938.

247. HOSSMAN, K-A., AND OLSSON, Y.: *Suppression and recovery of neuronal function in transient cerebral ischemia.* Brain Res. 22:313-325, 1970.

248. HOWELL, D. A.: *Upper brain-stem compression and foraminal impaction with intracranial space-occupying lesions and brain swelling.* Brain 82:525-550, 1959.

249. HOWELL, D. A.: *Longitudinal brain stem compression with buckling.* Arch. Neurol. 4:572-579, 1961.

249a. HOYT, W. F., AND DAROFF, R. B.: Supranuclear disorders of ocular control systems in man, in P. Bach-y-Rita, C. Collins, and J. E. Hyde (eds.) : *The Control of Eye Movements.* Academic Press, New York, 1971.

250. HUCKABEE, W. E.: *Abnormal resting blood lactate. I. The significance of hyperlactatemia in hospitalized patients.* Amer. J. Med. 30:833-839, 1961.

251. HUCKABEE, W. E.: *Abnormal resting blood lactate. II. Lactic acidosis.* Amer. J. Med. 30:840-848, 1961.

252. HUME, M., SEVITT, S., AND THOMAS, D. P.: *Venous Thrombosis and Pulmonary Embolism.* Harvard University Press, Cambridge, Massachusetts, 1970, pp. 252-278.

253. HUNTER, J., AND JASPER, H. H.: *Effects of thalamic stimulation in unanesthetized animals.* Electroenceph. Clin. Neurophysiol. 1:305-324, 1949.

254. HUNTER, R. A.: *Status epilepticus; history, incidence, and problems.* Epilepsia 1:162-188, 1959.

255. HUTCHINSON, J.: *Four lectures on compression of the brain.* Clin. Lect. Reps. London Hosp. 4:10-55, 1867.

256. IMRIE, J. A.: *Acute alcoholic poisoning.* Brit. Med. J. 2:428-430, 1955.

257. INGVAR, D., ET AL.: *Cerebral circulation and metabolism in a comatose patient.* Arch. Neurol. 11:13-21, 1964.

257a. INGVAR, D. H., AND BRUN, A.: Das Komplette apallische Syndrom. Arch. Psychiat. Nervenkr. (in press).

258. INGVAR, D. H., CRONQVIST, S., AND GRANHOLM, L.: *Cerebral blood flow in coma, apallic syndromes and akinetic mutism.* Proc. Internatl. CBF Symposium, London, 1970.

259. INGVAR, D. H., AND SOURANDER, P.: *Destruction of the reticular core of the brain stem. A patho-anatomical follow-up of a case of coma of three years' duration.* Arch. Neurol. 23:1-8, 1970.

260. IZZO, J. L., SCHUSTER, D. B., AND ENGEL, G. L.: *The electroencephalogram of patients with diabetes mellitus.* Diabetes 2:93-99, 1953.

261. JACKSON, I. J.: *Aseptic hemogenic meningitis.* Arch. Neurol. Psychiat. 62:572-589, 1949.

262. JACKSON, J. H.: *Selected Writings of John Hughlings Jackson* (Taylor, J. [ed.]) Basic Books, New York, 1958, 2 vol.

263. JACOB, J. C., ET AL.: *Electroencephalographic changes in chronic renal failure.* Neurology 15:419-429, 1965.

264. JAMIESON, K. G.: *Aneurysms of the vertebrobasilar system.* J. Neurosurg. 21:781-797, 1964.

265. JAMIESON, K. G., AND YELLAND, J. D. N.: *Extradural hematoma. Report of 167 cases.* J. Neurosurg. 29:13-23, 1968.

266. JAMPEL, R. S.: *Representation of the near-response on the cerebral cortex of the macaque.* Amer. J. Ophthal. 48:573-582, 1959.

267. JASPER, H. H., PROCTOR, L. D., KNIGHTON, R. S., NOSHAY, W. C., AND COSTELLO, R. T. (eds.): *Reticular Formation of the Brain.* Little, Brown and Co., Boston, 1958.

268. JASPER, H., AND VAN BUREN, J.: *Interrelationships between cortex and subcortical structures: Clinical electroencephalographic studies.* Electroenceph. Clin. Neurophysiol. Suppl. 4:168-202, 1953.

269. JEFFERSON, A.: *Clinical correlation between encephalopathy and papilloedema in Addison's disease.* J. Neurol. Neurosurg. Psychiat. 19:21-27, 1956.

270. JEFFERSON, G.: *The tentorial pressure cone.* Arch. Neurol. Psychiat. 40:857-876, 1938.

271. JEFFERSON, G.: *The nature of concussion.* Brit. Med. J. 1:1-15, 1944.

272. JEFFERSON, G., ET AL.: *Les etats de conscience en neurologie.* Premier Cong. Internatl. Soc. Neurol., Acta Med. Belg. 1957.

273. JELLINGER, K., AND SEITELBERGER, F.: *Protracted post-traumatic encephalopathy. Pathology, pathogenesis and clinical implications.* J. Neurol. Sci. 10:51-94, 1970.

273a. JENNETT, W. B., AND PLUM, F.: *The persistent vegetative state: A syndrome in search of a name.* Lancet 1:734-737, 1972.

274. JENNETT, W. B., AND STERN, W. E.: *Tentorial herniation; the midbrain and the pupil. Experimental studies in brain compression.* J. Neurosurg. 17:598-609, 1960.

275. JENSEN-JUUL, P.: *Criteria of Brain Death. Selection of Donors for Transplantation.* Munksgaard, Copenhagen, 1970.

276. JOHNSON, H. C., AND WALKER, A. E.: *The angiographic diagnosis of spontaneous thrombosis of the internal and common carotid arteries.* J. Neurosurg. 8:631-659, 1951.

277. JOHNSON, R. T., AND JOHNSON, K. P.: Slow and chronic virus infections of the nervous system, in Plum, F. (ed.): *Recent Advances in Neurology.* F. A. Davis Co., Philadelphia, 1969, pp. 33-78.

278. JOHNSON, R. T., AND YATES, P. O.: *Clinico-pathological aspects of pressure changes at the tentorium.* Acta Radiol. 46:242-249, 1956.

279. JOHNSON, S.: cited in, Boswell, J.: *Life of Johnson.*

280. JOHNSTON, I. H., JOHNSTON, J. A., AND JENNETT, B.: *Intracranial-pressure changes following head injury.* Lancet 2:433-436, 1970.

281. JONES, H. R., JR., SIEKERT, R. G., AND GERACI, J. E.: *Neurologic manifestations of bacterial endocarditis.* Ann. Intern. Med. 71:21-28, 1969.

282. JORDANOV, J., AND RUBEN, H.: *Reliability of pupillary changes as a clinical sign of hypoxia.* Lancet 2:915-917, 1967.

283. JOUVET, M.: Telencephalic and rhombencephalic sleep in the cat, in Wolstenholme, G. E. W., and O'Connor, M. (eds.): *The Nature of Sleep.* Little, Brown and Co., Boston, 1961, pp. 188-208.

284. JOUVET, M.: *Recherches sur les Structures Nerveuses et les Méchanismes Responsables des Differentes Phases du Sommeil Physiologique.* Arch. Ital. Biol. 100:125-206, 1962.

285. JOUVET, M.: *Biogenic amines and the states of sleep.* Science 163: 32-41, 1969.

286. KALBAG, R. M., AND WOOLF, A. L.: *Cerebral Venous Thrombosis.* Oxford University Press, London, 1967.

287. KAPP, J., AND PAULSON, G.: *Pupillary changes induced by circulatory arrest.* Neurology 16:225-229, 1966.

288. KASS, L. R.: *Death as an event: A commentary on Robert Morison.* Science 173:698-702, 1971.

289. KATZMAN, R., KAGAN, E. H., AND ZIMMERMAN, H. M.: *A case of Jakob-Creutzfeldt disease: I. Clinical pathological analysis.* J. Neuropath. Exp. Neurol. 20:78-94, 1961.

290. KAUFMANN, G. E., AND CLARK, K.: *Continuous simultaneous monitoring of intraventricular and cervical subarachnoid cerebrospinal fluid pressure to indicate development of cerebral or tonsillar herniation.* J. Neurosurg. 33:145-150, 1970.

291. KAVANAUGH, G. J., AND GOLDSTEIN, N. P.: *Acute idiopathic metencephalitis.* Proc. Staff Meet. Mayo Clin. 33:53-56, 1958.

292. KELLY, R.: *Colloid cysts of the third ventricle.* Brain 74:23-65, 1951.

293. KEMPER, T. L., AND ROMANUL, F. C. A.: *State resembling akinetic mutism in basilar artery occlusion.* Neurology 17:74-80, 1967.

294. KEMPINSKY, W. H.: *Experimental study of distant effects of acute focal brain injury.* Arch. Neurol. Psychiat. 79:376-389, 1958.

295. KENNEDY, A. C., ET AL.: *The pathogenesis and prevention of cerebral dysfunction during dialysis.* Lancet 1:790-793, 1964.

296. KERNOHAN, J. W., AND WOLTMAN, H. W.: *Incisura of the crus due to contralateral brain tumor.* Arch. Neurol. Psychiat. 21:274-287, 1929.

297. KERR, F. W. L., AND BROWN, J. A.: *Pupillomotor pathways in the spinal cord.* Arch. Neurol. 10:262-270, 1964.

298. KETY, S. S., EVARTS, E. V., AND WILLIAMS, H. L. (ed.): *Sleep and Altered States of Consciousness.* A. Res. Nerv. Ment. Dis., Proc., vol. 45, 1967.

257

299. KETY, S. S., AND SCHMIDT, C. F.: *The nitrous oxide method for the quantitative determination of cerebral blood flow in man; theory, procedure and normal values.* J. Clin. Invest. 27:476-483, 1948.

300. KILOH, L. G., AND OSSELTON, J. W:. *Clinical Electroencephalography.* Butterworth, London, 1961.

301. KIMURA, J., GERBER, H. W., AND McCORMICK, W. F.: *The isoelectric electroencephalogram. Significance in establishing death in patients maintained on mechanical respirators.* Arch. Intern. Med. 121:511-517, 1968.

302. KING, B. D., SOKOLOFF, L., AND WECHSLER, R. L.: *The effects of l-epinephrine and l-nor-epinephrine upon cerebral circulation and metabolism in man.* J. Clin. Invest. 31:273-279, 1952.

303. KLEE, A.: *Akinetic mutism: Review of the literature and report of a case.* J. Nerv. Ment. Dis. 133:536-553, 1961.

304. KLEEMAN, C. R., DAVSON, H., AND LEVIN, E.: *Urea transport in the central nervous system.* Amer. J. Physiol. 203:739-747, 1962.

305. KLEIST, K.: *Gegenhalten (motorischer negativismus) zwangreifen und thalamus opticus.* Monatsschr. Psychiat. Neurol. 65:317-396, 1927.

306. KLINTWORTH, K. G.: *The pathogenesis of secondary brainstem hemorrhages as studied in an experimental model.* Amer. J. Path. 47: 525-537, 1965.

307. KLINTWORTH, K. G.: *Paratentorial grooving of human brains with particular reference to transtentorial herniation and the pathogenesis of secondary brainstem hemorrhages.* Amer. J. Path. 53:391-399, 1968.

308. KOCHER, T.: *Hirnershutterung, Hirndruck und chirugische Eingriffe bei Hirnerkdankungen,* in *Nothnagel's Specialle Pathologie und Therapie.* A. Holder, Wien, 1901.

309. KOEBER, H.: *Trois observations de mouvements de rétraction de sulbe (Nystagmus retractorius).* Clinique Ophthal. p. 147, Abs. Jahresb. Ophthal. 34:683, 1903.

310. KOREIN, J., CRAVIOTO, H., AND LEICACH, M.: *Reevaluation of lumbar puncture. A study of 129 patients with papilledema or intracranial hypertension.* Neurology 9:290-297, 1959.

311. KOSARY, I. Z., GOLDHAMMER, Y., AND LERNER, M. A.: *Acute extradural hematoma of the posterior fossa.* J. Neurosurg. 24:1007-1012, 1966.

312. KOWADA, M., AMES, A., III, MAJNO, G., AND WRIGHT, R. L.: *Cerebral ischemia. I. An improved experimental method for study; cardiovascular effects and demonstration of an early vascular lesion in the rabbit.* J. Neurosurg. 28:150-157, 1968.

313. KRAMER, W.: *From reanimation to deanimation (intravital death of the brain during artificial respiration).* Acta Neurol. Scand. (Suppl. 4) 39:139-153, 1963.

314. KRAMER, W., AND TUYNMAN, J. A.: *Acute intracranial hypertension— an experimental investigation.* Brain Res. 6:686-705, 1967.

258

315. KRAUSE, S., AND SILVERBLATT, M.: *Pulmonary embolism: A review with emphasis on clinical and electrocardiographic diagnosis*. Arch. Intern. Med. 96:19-25, 1955.

316. KRAYENBÜHL, H. A.: *Cerebral venous and sinus thrombosis*. Clin. Neurosurg. 14:1-23, 1967.

317. KRAYENBÜHL, H., WYSS, O. A. M., AND YASARGIL, M. G.: *Bilateral thalamotomy and pallidotomy as treatment for bilateral parkinsonism*. J. Neurosurg. 18:429-444, 1961.

318. KRETSCHMER, E.: *Das apallische syndrom*. Z. ges Neurol. Psychiat. 169:576-579, 1940.

319. KUBIK, C. S., AND ADAMS, R. D.: *Subdural empyema*. Brain 66:18-42, 1943.

320. KUBIK, C. S., AND ADAMS, R. D.: *Occlusion of the basilar artery—a clinical and pathological study*. Brain 69:73-121, 1946.

321. LANGE, L. S., AND LASZLO, G.: *Cerebral tumor presenting with hyperventilation*. J. Neurol. Neurosurg. Psychiat. 28:317-319, 1965.

322. LANGFITT, T. W.: *Increased intracranial pressure*. Clin. Neurosurg. 16:436-471, 1969.

323. LANGFITT, T. W., TANNANBAUM, H. M., KASSELL, N. F., AND ZAREN, H.: *Acute intracranial hypertension, cerebral blood flow, and the EEG*. Electroenceph. Clin. Neurophysiol. 20:139-148, 1966.

324. LARRABEE, M. G., AND POSTERNAK, J. M.: *Selective action of anesthetics on synapses and axons in mammalian sympathetic ganglia*. J. Neurophysiol. 15:91-114, 1952.

325. LAVENSON, G. S., JR., PLUM, F., AND SWANSON, A. G.: *Physiological management compared with pharmacological and electrical stimulation in barbiturate poisoning*. J. Pharmacol. Exp. Ther. 122:271-280, 1958.

326. LEAVITT, S., AND TYLER, H. R.: *Studies in asterixis*. Arch. Neurol. 10:360-368, 1964.

327. LEHRICH, J. R., WINKLER, G. F., AND OJEMANN, R. G.: *Cerebellar infarction with brain stem compression. Diagnosis and surgical treatment*. Arch. Neurol. 22:490-498, 1970.

328. LENNOX, W. G.: *Epilepsy and Related Disorders*. Little, Brown and Co., Boston, 1960, Chap. 12.

329. LENNOX, W. G., GIBBS, F. A., AND GIBBS, E. L.: *The relationship in man of cerebral activity to blood flow and to blood constituents*. A. Res. Nerv. Ment. Dis., Proc. 18:277-297, 1938.

330. LEVENTHAL, C. M., BARINGER, J. R., ARNASON, B. G., AND FISHER, C. M.: *A case of Marchiafava-Bignami disease with clinical recovery*. Trans. Amer. Neurol. A. 90:87-91, 1965.

331. LEVINE, S., AND WENK, E. J.: *A hyperacute form of allergic encephalomyelitis*. Amer. J. Path. 47:61-88, 1965.

332. LEWIN, W.: Observations on prolonged unconsciousness after head injury, in Cumings, J. N., and Kremer, M. (eds.): *Biochemical Aspects of Neurological Disorders,* 2nd ser. F. A. Davis Co. (Blackwell Scientific Publications), Philadelphia, 1965, Chap. 11.

333. LINDSLEY, D. B.: Attention, consciousness, sleep and wakefulness, in Field, J., Magoun, H. W., and Hall, V. E. (eds.): *Handbook of Physiology.* Sect. I, Neurophysiology. American Physiological Society, Washington, D. C., 1960, vol. 3, Chap. 64.

334. LOBSTEIN, A., MANTZ, J. M., AND MACK, G.: *Circulation rétinienne, electrorétinogramme et coma dépassé.* Bibl. Ophthalmol. 76:237-241, 1968.

335. LOCKE, S., MERRILL, J. P., AND TYLER, H. R.: *Neurologic complications of acute uremia.* Arch. Intern. Med. 108:519-530, 1961.

336. LOEB, C.: *Electroencephalographic changes during the state of coma.* Electroenceph. Clin. Neurophysiol. 10:589-606, 1958.

337. LOEB, C., ROSADINI, G., AND POGGIO, G. F.: *Electroencephalograms during coma: Normal and borderline records in 5 patients.* Neurology 9:610-618, 1959.

338. LOGUE, V.: Posterior fossa aneurysms, in *Clinical Neurosurgery.* The Proceedings of the Congress of Neurological Surgeons. Williams and Wilkins Co., Baltimore, 1964, vol. 11, pp. 183-219.

339. LOGUE, V., AND MONCKTON, G.: *Posterior fossa angiomas.* Brain 77: 252-273, 1954.

340. LOOMIS, A. L., HARVEY, E. N., AND HOBART, G. A., III: *Distribution of disturbance patterns in the human electroencephalogram with special reference to sleep.* J. Neurophysiol. 1:413-430, 1938.

341. LOURIA, D. B., HENSLE, T., AND ROSE, J.: *The major medical complications of heroin addiction.* Ann. Intern. Med. 67:1-22, 1967.

342. LOURIE, H.: *Seesaw nystagmus.* Arch. Neurol. 9:531-533, 1963.

343. LUBASH, G. D., FERRARI, M. J., SCHERR, L., AND RUBIN, A. L.: *Sedative overdosage and the role of hemodialysis.* Arch. Intern. Med. 110:884-887, 1962.

344. LUBIC, L. G., AND MAROTTA, J. T.: *Brain tumor and lumbar puncture.* Arch. Neurol. Psychiat. 72:568-572, 1954.

345. LUNDBERG, N.: *Continuous recording and control of ventricular fluid pressure in neurological practice.* Acta Psychiat. Neurol. Scand. (Suppl. 149) 36: 1960.

346. MACCARIO, M., MESSIS, C. P., AND VASTOLA, E. F.: *Focal seizures as a manifestation of hyperglycemia without ketoacidosis: A report of 7 cases with review of the literature.* Neurology 15:195-206, 1965.

347. MACDONALD, M., AND SPECTOR, R. G.: *The influence of anoxia on respiratory enzymes in rat brain.* Brit. J. Exp. Path. 44:11-15, 1963.

348. MACEWEN, W.: *The pupil in its semeiological aspects.* Amer. J. Med. Sci. 94:123-146, 1887.

349. MACEWEN, W.: *Pyrogenic Infective Diseases of the Brain and Spinal Cord.* J. Maclehose and Sons, Glasgow, 1893.

350. MACKENZIE, I.: *The clinical presentation of the cerebral angioma.* Brain 76:184-214, 1953.

351. MADONICK, M. J., BERKE, K., AND SCHIFFER, I.: *Pleocytosis and meningeal signs in uremia.* Arch. Neurol. Psychiat. 64:431-436, 1950.

352. MAGOUN, H. W.: *The Waking Brain,* ed. 2. Charles C Thomas, Springfield, Ill., 1963.

353. MAHER, J. F., SCHREINER, G. E., AND WESTERVELT, F. B., JR.: *Acute glutethimide intoxication.* Amer. J. Med. 33:70-82, 1962.

354. MAIGRAITH, B. G.: *Pathological Processes in Malaria and Blackwater Fever.* Blackwell Scientific Publications, Oxford, 1948.

355. MAJNO, G., AMES, A., III, CHIANG, J., AND WRIGHT, R. L.: *No reflow after cerebral ischemia.* Lancet 2:569-570, 1967.

356. MANCALL, E. L., AND McENTEE, W. J.: *Alterations of the cerebellar cortex in nutritional encephalopathy.* Neurology 15:303-313, 1965.

357. MANGOLD, R., ET AL.: *Effects of sleep and lack of sleep on cerebral circulation and metabolism of normal young men.* J. Clin. Invest. 34:1092-1100, 1955.

358. MANNING, M. P., AND YU, P. N. G.: *Electrocardiographic changes in poliomyelitis.* Amer. J. Med. Sci. 222:658-662, 1951.

359. MARGOLIS, G., ODOM, G. L., WOODHALL, B., AND BLOOR, B. M.: *The role of small angiomatous malformations in the production of intracerebral hematomas.* J. Neurosurg. 8:564-575, 1951.

360. MARINESCO, G., AND DRAGANESCO, S.: *Contribution anatomo-clinique a l'étude du syndrome de Foerster.* L'Encéphale 24:685-699, 1929.

361. MARSHALL, W. J. S., JACKSON, J. L. F., AND LANGFITT, T. W.: *Brain swelling caused by trauma and arterial hypertension.* Arch. Neurol. 21:545-553, 1969.

362. MASSON, C. B.: *The dangers of diagnostic lumbar puncture in increased intracranial pressure due to brain tumor, with a review of 200 cases in which lumbar puncture was done.* A. Res. Nerv. Ment. Dis., Proc. 8:422, 1927.

363. MAUTHNER, L.: *Zur Pathologie und Physiologie des Schlafes nebst Bemerkungen über die "Nona."* Wien Klin. Wochenschr. 40:961, 1001, 1049, 1092, 1144, 1185; 1890.

364. McCORMICK, W. F., AND DANNEEL, C. M.: *Central pontine myelinolysis.* Arch. Intern. Med. 119:444-478, 1967.

365. McILWAIN, H.: Electrical pulses and the in vitro metabolism of cerebral tissue, in Elliott, K. A. C., Page, I. H., and Quastel, J. H. (eds.): *Neurochemistry: The Chemistry of Brain and Nerve,* ed. 2. Charles C Thomas, Springfield, Ill., 1962, Chap. 9.

366. McKAY, D. G.: *Disseminated Intravascular Coagulation: An Intermediary Mechanism of Disease.* Harper and Row, New York, 1965.

261

367. McKean, C. M., Schanberg, S. M., and Giarman, N. J.: *A mechanism of the indole defect in experimental phenylketonuria.* Science 137: 604-605, 1962.

368. McKissock, W., Richardson, A., and Walsh, L.: *Spontaneous cerebellar hemorrhage: A study of 34 consecutive cases treated surgically.* Brain 83:1-9, 1960.

369. McNealy, D. E., and Plum, F.: *Brainstem dysfunction with supratentorial mass lesions.* Arch. Neurol. 7:10-32, 1962.

370. McNicol, M. W., and Smith, R.: *Accidental hypothermia.* Brit. Med. J. 1:19-21, 1964.

371. Medical Research Council, Brain Injuries Committee: *A glossary of psychological terms commonly used in cases of head injury.* Medical Research Council War Memorandum #4, HMSO, London, 1941.

372. Meldrum, B. S., Papy, J. J., and Vigouroux, R. A.: *Intracarotid air embolism in the baboon.* Brain Res. 25:301-315, 1971.

373. Merrill, J. P., Legrain, M., and Hoigne, R.: *Observations on the role of urea in uremia.* Amer. J. Med. 14:519-520, 1953.

374. Merritt, H. H., and Aring, C. D.: *The differential diagnosis of cerebral vascular lesions.* A. Res. Nerv. Ment. Dis., Proc. 18:682-695, 1938.

375. Messert, B., Henke, T. K., and Langheim, W.: *Syndrome of akinetic mutism associated with obstructive hydrocephalus.* Neurology 16: 635-649, 1966.

376. Meyer, A.: *Herniation of the brain.* Arch. Neurol. Psychiat. 4: 387-400, 1920.

377. Meyer, J. S., and Handa, J.: *Cerebral blood flow and metabolism during experimental hyperthermia (fever).* Minn. Med. 50:37-44, 1967.

378. Meyer, J. S., and Portnoy, H. D.: *Localized cerebral hypoglycemia simulating stroke.* Neurology 8:601-614, 1958.

379. Meyers, R.: *Systemic, vascular and respiratory effects of experimentally induced alterations in intraventricular pressure.* J. Neuropath. Exp. Neurol. 1:241-264, 1942.

380. Meyers, R.: *Dandy's striatal theory of "The center of consciousness"; surgical evidence and logical analysis indicating its improbability.* Arch. Neurol. Psychiat. 65:659-671, 1951.

381. Migrino, S., and Frugoni, P.: *Significance of vestibulo-ocular reflex alterations in comatose patients after head injury.* Acta Neurochir. 16:321-322, 1967.

382. Miller, H., and Stern, G.: *The long-term prognosis of severe head injury.* Lancet 1:225-229, 1965.

383. Miller, J. D., Stanek, A., and Langfitt, T. W.: *Concepts of cerebral perfusion pressure and vascular compression during intracranial hypertension.* Prog. Brain Res. 35:411-432, 1972.

384. Mitchell, R. A., Loeschke, H. H., Massion, W. H., and Severinghaus, J. W.: *Respiratory responses mediated through superficial chemosensitive areas on the medulla.* J. Appl. Physiol. 18:523-533, 1963.

385. MOHANDAS, A., AND CHOU, S. N.: *Brain death. A clinical and pathological study.* J. Neurosurg. 35:211-218, 1971.

386. MOLLARET, P., AND GOULON, M.: *Le coma dépassé.* Rev. Neurol. 101:3-15, 1959.

387. MONTGOMERY, B. M., AND PINNER, C. A.: *Transient hypoglycemic hemiplegia.* Arch. Intern. Med. 114:680-684, 1964.

388. MORISON, R. S.: *Death: Process or event?* Science 173:694-698, 1971.

389. MORISON, R. S., AND DEMPSEY, E. W.: *A study of thalamo-cortical relations.* Amer. J. Physiol. 135:281-292, 1942.

390. MORUZZI, G.: *Active processes in the brain stem during sleep.* Harvey Lect. 58:233-297, 1963.

391. MORUZZI, G., AND MAGOUN, H. W.: *Brain stem reticular formation and activation of the EEG.* Electroenceph. Clin. Neurophysiol. 1: 455-473, 1949.

392. MULHAUSEN, R., EICHENHOLZ, A., AND BLUMENTALS, A: *Acid-base disturbances in patients with cirrhosis of the liver.* Medicine 46:185-189, 1967.

393. MYERS, W. P. L., TASHIMA, C. K., AND ROTHSCHILD, E. O.: *Endocrine syndromes associated with nonendocrine neoplasms.* Med. Clin. N. Amer. 50:763-778, 1966.

394. MYSCHETSKY, A., AND LASSEN, N. A.: *Urea-induced, osmotic diuresis and alkalization of urine in acute barbiturate intoxication.* J.A.M.A. 185:936-942, 1963.

395. NABARRO, J. D. N.: Clinical aspects of pituitary and adrenal disorders, in Cumings, J. N., and Kremer, M. (eds.): *Biochemical Aspects of Neurological Disorders,* 1st ser. F. A. Davis Co. (Blackwell Scientific Publications), Philadelphia, 1958.

396. NATHANSON, M.: Caloric response in barbiturate coma, in Bender, M. B. (ed.): *The Oculomotor System.* Harper and Row, New York, 1964, pp. 484-487.

397. NATHANSON, M., AND BERGMAN, P. S.: *Newer methods of evaluation of patients with altered states of consciousness.* Med. Clin. N. Amer. 42:701-710, 1958.

398. NEEDHAM, C. W., BERTRAND, G., AND MYLES, S. T.: *Multiple cranial nerve signs from supratentorial tumors.* J. Neurosurg. 33:178-183, 1970.

399. NELSON, D. A., AND RAY, C. D.: *Respiratory arrest from seizure discharges in limbic system. Report of cases.* Arch. Neurol. 19:199-207, 1968.

400. NELSON, J. R.: *The minimal ice water caloric test.* Neurology 19: 577-585, 1969.

401. NELSON, J. R., AND JOHNSTON, C. H.: *Ocular bobbing.* Arch. Neurol. 22:348-356, 1970.

402. NELSON, J. R., AND LEFFMAN, H.: *The human diffusely projecting system.* Arch. Neurol. 8:544-556, 1963.

263

403. NEMOTO, E. M., AND FRANKEL, H. M.: *Cerebral oxygenation and metabolism during progressive hyperthermia.* Amer. J. Physiol. 219: 1784-1788, 1970.

404. NETSKY, M. G., AND STROBOS, R. R. J.: *Neoplasms within the midbrain.* Arch. Neurol. Psychiat. 68:116-129, 1952.

405. NEUMANN, M. A.: *Pick's disease.* J. Neuropathol. Exp. Neurol. 8: 255-282, 1949.

406. NEUMANN, M. A., AND COHN, R.: *Incidence of Alzheimer's disease in a large mental hospital.* Arch. Neurol. Psychiat. 69:615-636, 1953.

407. NEWMAN, N., GAY, A. J., AND HEILBRUN, M. P.: *Disjugate ocular bobbing: Its relation to midbrain, pontine, and medullary function in a surviving patient.* Neurology 21:633-637, 1971.

408. NEWSOM DAVIS, J.: *An experimental study of hiccup.* Brain 93:861-872, 1970.

409. NIELSEN, J. M., AND JACOBS, L. L.: *Bilateral lesions of the anterior cingulate gyri.* Bull. Los Angeles Neurol. Soc. 16:231-234, 1951.

410. NILSSON, L.: *The influence of barbiturate anesthesia upon the energy state and upon acid-base parameters of the brain in arterial hypotension and in asphyxia.* Acta Neurol. Scand. 47:233-253, 1971.

411. NILSSON, L., AND SIESJÖ, B. K.: *The effect of anesthetics upon labile phosphates and upon extra- and intracellular lactate, pyruvate and bicarbonate concentrations in the rat brain.* Acta Physiol. Scand. 80:235-248, 1970.

412. NILSSON, L., AND SIESJÖ, B. K.: *The effect of deep halothane hypotension upon labile phosphates and upon extra- and intracellular lactate and pyruvate concentrations in the rat brain.* Acta Physiol. Scand. 81:508-516, 1971.

412a. NORDGREN, R. E., MARKESBERY, W. R., FUKUDA, K., AND REEVES, A. G.: *Seven cases of cerebral medullary disconnexion: The "locked-in syndrome."* Neurology 21:1140-1148, 1971.

413. NORMAN, R. M.: Lipid diseases of the brain, in Williams, D. (ed.): *Modern Trends in Neurology,* 3rd ser. Butterworth, Washington, D. C., 1962, Chap. 11, pp. 173-199.

414. NYHAN, W. L., AND COOKE, R. E.: *Symptomatic hyponatremia in acute infections of the central nervous system.* Pediatrics 18:604-613, 1956.

415. O'BRIEN, M. D., AND HARRIS, P. W. R.: *Cerebral-cortex perfusion-rates in myxoedema.* Lancet 1:1170-1172, 1968.

416. O'DOHERTY, D. S., AND GREEN, J. B.: *Diagnostic value of Horner's syndrome in thrombosis of the carotid artery.* Neurology 8:842-845, 1958.

417. OHMAN, J. L., JR., MARLISS, E. B., AOKI, T. T., MUNICHOODAPPA, C. S., KHANNA, V. V., AND KOZAK, G. P.: *The cerebrospinal fluid in diabetic ketoacidosis.* New Eng. J. Med. 284:283-290, 1971.

418. O'LEARY, J. L., AND COBEN, L. A.: *The reticular core-1957.* Physiol. Rev. 38:243-276, 1958.

419. OLIVA, P. B.: *Lactic acidosis.* Amer. J. Med. 48:209-225, 1970.

420. OPPENHEIM, H.: *Diseases of the Nervous System,* ed. 2. E. E. Mayer (trans.). J. B. Lippincott Co., Philadelphia, 1900.

421. OWEN, O. E., MORGAN, A. P., KEMP, H. G., SULLIVAN, J. M., HERRERA, M. G., AND CAHILL, G. F., JR.: *Brain metabolism during fasting.* J. Clin. Invest. 46:1589-1595, 1967.

422. PADGETT, B., WALKER, D. L., ZURHEIN, G., ECKROADE, R. J., AND DESSEL, B. H.: *Cultivation of papova-like virus from human brain with progressive multifocal leukoencephalopathy.* Lancet 1:1257-1260, 1971.

423. PAGANI, L. F.: *The rapid appearance of papilledema.* J. Neurosurg. 30:247-249, 1969.

424. PAILLAS, J. E., SEDAN, R., AND BONNEL, J.: *On the changes of consciousness produced by subtentorial lesions.* Acta Neurochir. 12: 315-388, 1965.

425. PALVOLGYI, R.: *Regional cerebral blood flow in patients with intracranial tumors.* J. Neurosurg. 31:149-163, 1969.

426. PAMPIGLIONE, G., AND HARDEN, A.: *Resuscitation after cardiocirculatory arrest.* Lancet 1:1261-1265, 1968.

427. PANT, S. S., BENTON, J. W., AND DODGE, P. R.: *Unilateral pupillary dilatation during and immediately following seizures.* Neurology 16: 837-840, 1966.

428. PAPPENHEIMER, J. R., FENCL, V., HEISEY, S. R., AND HELD, D.: *Role of cerebral fluids in control of respiration as studied in unanesthetized goats.* Amer. J. Physiol. 208:436-450, 1965.

429. PARMLEY, L. F., JR., SENIOR, R. M., MCKENNA, D. H., AND JOHNSTON, G. S.: *Clinically deceptive massive pulmonary embolism.* Chest 58: 15-23, 1970.

430. PASIK, P., AND PASIK, T.: Oculomotor functions in monkeys with lesions of the cerebrum and superior colliculi, in Bender, M. B. (ed.): *The Oculomotor System.* Harper and Row, New York, 1964, Chap. 3, pp. 40-80.

431. PASIK, P., PASIK, T., AND BENDER, M. B.: *The prectectal syndrome in monkeys. I. Disturbances of gaze and body posture. II. Spontaneous and induced nystagmus, and "lightning" eye movements.* Brain 92: 521-534; 871-884, 1969.

431a. PASIK, P., PASIK, T., AND SCHILDER, P.: *Extrageniculostriate vision in the monkey: Discrimination of luminous flux-equated figures.* Exp. Neurol. 24:421-437, 1969.

432. PAULSON, G., AND GOTTLIEB, G.: *Development reflexes: The reappearance of fetal and neonatal reflexes in aged patients.* Brain 91:37-52, 1968.

433. PAULSON, G., NASHOLD, B. S., AND MARGOLIS, G.: *Aneurysms of the vertebral artery.* Neurology 9:590-598, 1959.

434. PAULSON, O. B., LASSEN, N. A., AND SKINHØJ, E.: *Regional cerebral blood flow in apoplexy without arterial occlusion.* Neurology 20: 125-138, 1970.

435. PEARCE, J. M. S.: *Focal neurological syndromes in hepatic failure.* Postgrad. Med. J. 39:653-657, 1963.

436. PEARCE, L. A., ET AL.: *An ultrastructural and biochemical investigation of Lafora's disease.* Trans. Amer. Neurol. A. 90:102-106, 1965.

437. PEDERSEN, E.: *Studies on the central pathway of the flexion reflex in man and animal, and changes in the reflex threshold and the circulation after spinal transection.* Acta Psychiat. Neurol. Scand. Suppl. 88, 1954.

438. PENFIELD, W., AND JASPER, H.: *Epilepsy and the Functional Anatomy of the Human Brain.* Little, Brown and Co., Boston, 1954.

439. PENFIELD, W., AND MILNER, B.: *Memory deficit produced by bilateral lesions in the hippocampal zone.* Arch. Neurol. Psychiat. 79:475-497, 1958.

440. PEVEHOUSE, B. C., BLOOM, W. H., AND McKISSOCK, W.: *Ophthalmologic aspects of diagnosis and localization of subdural hematomas.* Neurology 10:1037-1041, 1960.

441. PICKLES, W.: *Acute focal edema of the brain in children in head injuries.* New Eng. J. Med. 240:92-95, 1949.

442. PLUM, F.: *Mineral metabolism following poliomyelitis.* Arch. Phys. Med. 42:348-362, 1961.

443. PLUM, F.: Neurological integration of behavioural and metabolic control of breathing, in Porter, R. (ed.): *Ciba Foundation Symposium on Breathing: Hering-Breuer Centenary Symposium.* Churchill, London, 1970, pp. 159-181.

444. PLUM, F.: The CSF in hepatic encephalopathy, in Polli, E. (ed.): *Neurochemistry of Hepatic Coma.* Karger, Basel, 1971. Exp. Biol. Med. 4:34-41, 1971.

445. PLUM, F.: *Brain swelling and edema in cerebral vascular disease.* Res. Publ. A. Res. Nerv. Ment. Dis. 41:318-348, 1966.

446. PLUM, F., AND ALVORD, E. C., JR.: *Apneustic breathing in man.* Arch. Neurol. 10:101-112, 1964.

447. PLUM, F., AND BRENNAN, R. W.: *Dissociation of autoregulation and chemical regulation in cerebral circulation following seizures.* Trans. Amer. Neurol. A. 95:27-30, 1970.

448. PLUM, F., BROWN, H. W., AND SNOEP, E.: *Neurologic significance of posthyperventilation apnea.* J.A.M.A. 181:1050-1055, 1962.

449. PLUM, F., POSNER, J. B., AND HAIN, R. F.: *Delayed neurological deterioration after anoxia.* Arch. Intern. Med. 110:18-25, 1962.

450. PLUM, F., AND SWANSON, A. G.: *Barbiturate poisoning treated by physiological methods.* J.A.M.A. 163:827-835, 1957.

451. PLUM, F., AND SWANSON, A. G.: *Abnormalities in the central regulation of respiration in acute and convalescent poliomyelitis.* Arch. Neurol. Psychiat. 80:267-285, 1958.

452. PLUM, F., AND SWANSON, A. G.: *Central neurogenic hyperventilation in man.* Arch. Neurol. Psychiat. 81:535-549, 1959.

453. PLUM, F., AND WASTERLAIN, C. G.: Cerebral and systemic anoxia with experimental seizures, in Brierley, J. B., and Meldrum, B. S. (eds.): *Brain Hypoxia*. Heinemann, London, 1971.

454. POSNER, J. B., AND PLUM, F.: *The toxic effects of carbon dioxide and acetazolamide in hepatic encephalopathy*. J. Clin. Invest. 39:1246-1258, 1960.

455. POSNER, J. B., AND PLUM, F.: *Spinal-fluid pH and neurologic symptoms in systemic acidosis*. New Eng. J. Med. 277:605-613, 1967.

456. POSNER, J. B., SWANSON, A. G., AND PLUM, F.: *Acid-base balance in cerebrospinal fluid*. Arch. Neurol. 12:479-496, 1965.

457. PRIBRAM, H. F. W.: *Angiographic appearances in acute intracranial hypertension*. Neurology 11:10-21, 1961.

458. PROCKOP, L. D.: *Hyperglycemia, polyol accumulation, and increased intracranial pressure*. Arch. Neurol. 25:126-140, 1971.

459. QUASTEL, J. H.: Effects of anesthetics, depressants, and tranquilizers on brain metabolism, in Elliott, K. A. C., Page, I. H., and Quastel, J. H. (eds.): *Neurochemistry: The Chemistry of Brain and Nerve*, ed. 2. Charles C Thomas, Springfield, Ill., 1962, Chap. 32.

460. RAFAELSEN, O. J.: *Action of insulin on carbohydrate uptake of iso- lated rat spinal cord*. J. Neurochem. 7:33-44, 1961.

461. RAMÓN-MOLINER, E., AND NAUTA, W. J. H.: *The isodendritic core of the brain stem*. J. Comp. Neurol. 126:311-336, 1966.

462. RANSON, S. W.: *Somnolence caused by hypothalamic lesions in the monkey*. Arch. Neurol. Psychiat. 41:1-23, 1939.

463. RAY, B. S., AND DUNBAR, H. S.: *Thrombosis of the dural venous sinuses as a cause of "pseudotumor cerebri."* Ann. Surg. 134:376-386, 1951.

464. RAY, B. S., HINSEY, J. C., AND GEOHEGAN, W. A.: *Observations on the distribution of the sympathetic nerves to the pupil and upper extremity as determined by stimulation of the anterior roots in man.* Ann. Surg. 118:647-655, 1943.

465. RECORD, N. B., PRICHARD, J. W., GALLAGHER, B. B., AND SELIGSON, D.: *Phenolic acids in experimental uremia. 1. Potential role of phenolic acids in the neurological manifestations of uremia.* Arch. Neurol. 21: 387-994, 1969.

466. REEM, G. H., AND VANAMEE, P.: *Electrolyte disturbances associated with cancer.* J. Chron. Dis. 16:737-755, 1963.

467. REEVES, A. G., AND POSNER, J. B.: *The ciliospinal response in man.* Neurology 19:1145-1152, 1969.

468. REICHARDT, M.: *Hirnstamm und Psychiatrie.* Monatsschr. Psychiat. Neurol. 68:470-506, 1928. (Translation in J. Nerv. Ment. Dis. 70: 390-396, 1929.)

469. REIGH, E. E., AND O'CONNELL, T. J.: *Extradural hematoma of the posterior fossa with concomitant supratentorial subdural hematoma.* J. Neurosurg. 19:359-364, 1962.

470. RELMAN, A. S., SHELBURNE, P. F., AND TALMAN, A.: *Profound acidosis resulting from excessive ammonium chloride in previously healthy subjects.* New Eng. J. Med. 264:848-852, 1961.

471. RICHARDSON, E. P., JR.: *Progressive multifocal leukoencephalopathy.* New Eng. J. Med. 265:815-823, 1961.

472. RICHARDSON, J. C., CHAMBERS, R. A., AND HEYWOOD, P. M.: *Encephalopathies of anoxia and hypoglycemia.* Arch. Neurol. 1:178-190, 1959.

473. ROMANO, J., AND ENGEL, G. L.: *Delirium: I. Electroencephalographic data.* Arch. Neurol. Psychiat. 51:356-377, 1944.

474. ROOT, H. F., AND LEECH, R.: *Diabetic coma and hyperglycemic stupor compared.* Med. Clin. N. Amer. 30:1115-1130, 1946.

475. ROSADINI, G., AND ROSSI, G. F.: *On the suggested cerebral dominance for consciousness.* Brain 90:101-112, 1967.

476. ROSENBERG, S. A., ET AL.: *The syndrome of dehydration, coma and severe hyperglycemia without ketosis in patients convalescing from burns.* New Eng. J. Med. 272:931-938, 1965.

477. ROSIN, A. J., AND EXTON-SMITH, A. N.: *Clinical features of accidental hypothermia, with some observations on thyroid function.* Brit. Med. J. 1:16-19, 1964.

478. ROSOMOFF, H. L.: *Method for simultaneous quantitative estimation of intracranial contents.* J. Appl. Physiol. 16:395-396, 1961.

479. ROSSEN, R., KABAT, H., AND ANDERSON, J. P.: *Acute arrest of cerebral circulation in man.* Arch. Neurol. Psychiat. 50:510-528, 1943.

480. ROSSI, G. F., AND ZANCHETTI, A.: *The brainstem reticular formation.* Arch. Ital. Biol. 95:199-235, 1957.

481. ROTHERMAN, E. B., JR., SAFAR, P., AND ROBIN, E. D.: *CNS disorder during mechanical ventilation in chronic pulmonary disease.* J.A.M.A. 189:993-996, 1964.

482. ROWE, G. G., ET AL.: *Study in man of cerebral blood flow and cerebral glucose, lactate and pyruvate metabolism before and after eating.* J. Clin. Invest. 38:2154-2158, 1959.

483. SAIFER, A.: The biochemistry of Tay-Sachs disease, in Volk, B. W. (ed.): *Tay-Sachs Disease.* Grune and Stratton, New York, 1964.

484. SALDEEN, T.: *Fat embolism and signs of intravascular coagulation in a posttraumatic autopsy material.* J. Trauma 10:273-286, 1970.

485. SALEM, S. N.: *Neurological complications of heat-stroke in Kuwait.* Ann. Trop. Med. Parasitol. 60:393-400, 1966.

486. SALFORD, L. G., BRIERLEY, J. B., PLUM, F., AND SIESJÖ, B. K.: *Histology and high energy substrates in rat brain after graded hypoxia.* Panminerva Med. 13:185, 1971.

487. SASAHARA, A. A., CANNILLA, J. E., MORSE, R. L., SIDD, J. J., AND TREMBLAY, G. M.: *Clinical and physiologic studies in pulmonary thromboembolism.* Amer. J. Cardiol. 20:10-20, 1967.

488. SCHEIBEL, A. B.: *On detailed connections of the medullary and pontine reticular formation.* Anat. Rec. 109:345-346, 1951.

489. SCHEINBERG, P., BOURNE, B., AND REINMUTH, O. M.: *Human cerebral lactate and pyruvate extraction.* Arch. Neurol. 12:246-251, 1965.

490. SCHEINKER, I. M.: *Transtentorial herniation of the brain stem; a characteristic clinicopathologic syndrome; pathogenesis of hemorrhages in the brain stem.* Arch. Neurol. Psychiat. 53:289-298, 1945.

491. SCHNEIDER, M.: Critical blood pressure in the cerebral circulation, in Schade, J. P., and McMenemey, W. H. (eds.): *Selective Vulnerability of the Brain in Hypoxaemia.* F. A. Davis Co. (Blackwell Scientific Publications), Philadelphia, 1963, pp. 7-20.

492. SCHUMACHER, G. A., AND WOLFF, H. G.: *Experimental studies on headache.* Arch. Neurol. Psychiat. 45:199-214, 1941.

493 SCHUTTA, H. S., KASSELL, N. F., AND LANGFITT, T. W.: *Brain swelling produced by injury and aggravated by arterial hypertension. A light and electron microscopic study.* Brain 91:281-294, 1968.

494. SCHWARTZ, G. A., AND ROSNER, A. A.: *Displacement and herniation of the hippocampal gyrus through the incisura tentorii; a clinicopathological study.* Arch. Neurol. Psychiat. 46:297-321, 1941.

495. SCHWARTZ, W. B., ET AL.: *Syndrome of renal sodium loss and hyponatremia probably resulting from inappropriate secretion of antidiuretic hormone.* Amer. J. Med. 23:529-542, 1957.

496. SCOVILLE, W. B., AND MILNER, B.: *Loss of recent memory after bilateral hippocampal lesions.* J. Neurol. Neurosurg. Psychiat. 20:11-21, 1957.

497. SEGARRA, J. M.: *Cerebral vascular disease and behavior. I. The syndrome of the mesencephalic artery (basilar artery bifurcation).* Arch. Neurol. 22:408-418, 1970.

498. SELTZER, H. S., FAJANS, S. S., AND CONN, J. W.: *Spontaneous hypoglycemia as an early manifestation of diabetes mellitus.* Diabetes 5:437-442, 1956.

499. SENCER, W.: *The lumbar puncture in the presence of papilledema.* J. Mt. Sinai Hosp. 23:808-815, 1956.

500. SERAFETINIDES, E. A., HOARE, R. D., AND DRIVER, M. V.: *Intracarotid sodium amylobarbitone and cerebral dominance for speech and consciousness.* Brain 88:107-130, 1965.

501. SEVERINGHAUS, J. W., MITCHELL, R. A., RICHARDSON, B. W., AND SINGER, M. M.: *Respiratory control at high altitude suggesting active transport regulation of CSF pH.* J. Appl. Physiol. 18:1155-1166, 1963.

502. SEVITT, S.: *Fat Embolism.* Butterworth, London, 1962.

503. SEYFFARTH, H., AND DENNY-BROWN, D.: *The grasp reflex and the instinctive grasp reaction.* Brain 71:109-183, 1948.

504. SHAFAR, J.: *The syndromes of the third neurone of the cervical sympathetic system.* Amer. J. Med. 40:97-109, 1966.

505. SHAHANI, B., BURROWS, P., AND WHITTY, C. W. M.: *The grasp reflex and perseveration.* Brain 93:181-192, 1970.

506. SHALIT, M. N., BELLER, A. J., FEINSOD, M., DRAPKIN, A. J., AND COTEV, C.: *The blood flow and oxygen consumption of the dying brain.* Neurology 20:740-748, 1970.

507. SHANES, A. M.: *Electrochemical aspects of physiological and pharmacological action in excitable cells.* Pharmacol. Rev. 10:59-274, 1958.

508. SHAPIRO, W. R., WILLIAMS, G. H., AND PLUM, F.: *Spontaneous recurrent hypothermia accompanying agenesis of the corpus callosum.* Brain 92:423-436, 1969.

509. SHAW, C. M., ALVORD, E. C., JR., AND BERRY, R. G. *Swelling of the brain following ischemic infarction with arterial occlusion.* Arch. Neurol. 1:161-177, 1959.

510. SHELDEN, W. D., PARKER, H. L., AND KERNOHAN, J. W.: *Occlusion of the aqueduct of Sylvius.* Arch. Neurol. Psychiat. 23:1183-1202, 1930.

511. SHERRINGTON, C. S.: *Cataleptoid reflexes in the monkey.* Proc. Roy. Soc. Lond. 60:411-414, 1897.

512. SHIBOLET, S., COLL, R., GILAT, T., AND SOHAR, E.: *Heatstroke: Its clinical picture and mechanism in 36 cases.* Quart. J. Med. 36: 525-548, 1967.

513. SHIMOJYO, S., SCHEINBERG, P., AND REINMUTH, O.: *Cerebral blood flow and metabolism in the Wernicke-Korsakoff syndrome.* J. Clin. Invest. 46:849-854, 1967.

514. SIEKER, H. O., AND HICKAM, J. B.: *Carbon dioxide intoxication.* Medicine 35:389-423, 1956.

515. SIESJÖ, B. K., AND PLUM, F.: Pathophysiology of anoxic brain damage, in Gaull, G. E. (ed.): *Biology of Brain Dysfunction.* Plenum Publishing Corp., New York, 1972.

516. SIESJÖ, B. K., AND PLUM, F.: *Cerebral energy metabolism in normoxia and in hypoxia.* Acta Anesthesiol. Scand. Suppl. 45:81-101, 1971.

517. SILVERMAN, D.: *Some observations on the EEG in hepatic coma.* Electroenceph. Clin. Neurophysiol. 14:53-59, 1962.

518. SILVERMAN, D.: *Retrospective study of the EEG in coma.* Electroenceph. Clin. Neurophysiol. 15:486-503, 1963.

519. SILVERMAN, D., MASLAND, R. L., SAUNDERS, M. G., AND SCHWAB, R. S.: *Irreversible coma associated with electrocerebral silence.* Neurology 20:525-533, 1970.

519a. SIMMONS, R. L., ET AL.: *The role of the central nervous system in septic shock: II. Hemodynamic, respiratory and metabolic effects of intracisternal or intraventricular endotoxin.* Ann. Surg. 167:158-167, 1968.

520. SITPRIJA, V., AND HOLMES, J. H.: *Preliminary observations of change in intracranial pressure and intraocular pressure during hemodialysis.* Trans. Amer. Soc. Artif. Inter. Organs 8:300-308, 1962.

521. SKINNER, J. E.: *Electrocortical desynchronization during functional blockade of the mesencephalic reticular formation.* Brain Res. 22: 254-258, 1970.

522. SKULTETY, F. M.: *Clinical and experimental aspects of akinetic mutism. Report of a case.* Arch. Neurol. 19:1-14, 1968.

523. SLATER, E.: *Diagnosis of "hysteria."* Brit. Med. J. 1:827-829, 1922.

524. SMALL, J. M., AND WOOLF, A. L.: *Fatal damage to the brain by epileptic convulsions after a trivial injury to the head.* J. Neurol. Neurosurg. Psychiat. 20:293-301, 1957.

525. SMITH, A. L., SATTERTHWAITE, H. S., AND SOKOLOFF, L.: *Induction of brain D(—)-β-hydroxybutyrate dehydrogenase activity by fasting.* Science 163:79-81, 1969.

526. SMITH, J. L., AND COGAN, D. G.: *Internuclear ophthalmoplegia; a review of fifty-eight cases.* Arch. Ophthal. 61:687-694, 1959.

527. SMITH, J. L., AND DAVID, N. J.: *Internuclear ophthalmoplegia. Two new clinical signs.* Neurology 14:307-309, 1964.

528. SMITH, J. L., DAVID, N. J., AND KLINTWORTH, G.: *Skew deviation.* Neurology 14:96-105, 1964.

529. SMITSKAMP, H., AND WOLTHUIS, F. H.: *New concepts in treatment of malignant tertian malaria with cerebral involvement.* Brit. Med. J. 1:714-716, 1971.

530. SOKOLOFF, L.: *Action of thyroid hormones and cerebral development.* Amer. J. Dis. Child. 114:498-506, 1967.

531. SOLOMON, P., AND ARING, C. D.: *Differential diagnosis in patients entering the hospital in coma.* J.A.M.A. 105:7-12, 1935.

532. SOUADJIAN, J. V., AND CAIN, J. C.: *Intractable hiccup. Etiologic factors in 220 cases.* Postgrad. Med. 43:72-77, 1968.

533. SPATZ, H., AND STROESCU, G. J.: *Zur Anatomie und Pathologie der äusseren Liquorräume des Gehirns. Die Zisternenvergvellung beim Hirntumor.* Nervenarzt 7:481-496, 1934.

534. SPIEGEL, E. A., WYCIS, H. T., ORCHINIK, C. W., AND FREED, H.: *The thalamus and temporal orientation.* Science 121:771-772, 1955.

535. SRIVASTAVA, S. C., AND ROBSON, A. O.: *Electrocardiographic abnormalities associated with subarachnoid hemorrhage.* Lancet 2:431-433, 1964.

536. STANLEY, J. A., AND BAISE, G. R.: *The swinging flashlight test to detect minimal optic neuropathy.* Arch. Ophthal. 80:769-771, 1968.

537. STEEGMAN, A. T.: *Primary pontile hemorrhage.* J. Nerv. Ment. Dis. 114:35-65, 1951.

538. STEELE, J. C., RICHARDSON, J. C., AND OLSZEWSKI, J.: *Progressive supranuclear palsy.* Arch. Neurol. 10:333-359, 1964.

539. STEINBERG, A. D., AND KARLINER, J. S.: *The clinical spectrum of heroin pulmonary edema.* Arch. Intern. Med. 122:122-127, 1968.

540. STEPHENSON, H. E., JR.: Cerebral anoxia and the neurologic sequelae after cardiac arrest, in *Cardiac Arrest and Resuscitation*, ed. 3. C. V. Mosby Co., St. Louis, 1969, pp. 455-473.

541. STRICH, S. J.: *Diffuse degeneration of cerebral white matter in severe dementia following head injury.* J. Neurol. Neurosurg. Psychiat. 19: 163-185, 1956.

542. STRICH, S. J.: The pathology of brain damage due to blunt head injuries, in Walker, A. E., Caveness, W. F., and Critchley, M. (eds.): *The Late Effects of Head Injury.* Charles C Thomas, Springfield, Ill., 1969.

543. SUNDERLAND, S.: *The tentorial notch and complications produced by herniations of the brain through that aperture.* Brit. J. Surg. 45:422-438, 1958.

544. SUNDERLAND, S., AND BRADLEY, K. C.: *Disturbances of oculomotor function accompanying extradural haemorrhage.* J. Neurol. Neurosurg. Psychiat. 16:35-46, 1953.

545. SUTTON, G. C., HONEY, M., AND GIBSON, R. V.: *Clinical diagnosis of acute massive pulmonary embolism.* Lancet 1:271-273, 1969.

546. SUZUKI, K., KATZMAN, R., AND KOREY, S. R.: *Chemical studies on Alzheimer's disease.* J. Neuropath. Exp. Neurol. 24:211-224, 1965.

547. SWANSON, A. G., AND ISERI, O. A.: *Acute encephalopathy due to water intoxication.* New Eng. J. Med. 258:831-834, 1958.

548. SWANSON, A. G., STAVNEY, L. S., AND PLUM, F.: *Effects of blood pH and carbon dioxide on cerebral electrical activity.* Neurology 8:787-792, 1958.

549. SWANSON, P. D.: *Acidosis and some metabolic properties of isolated cerebral tissues.* Arch. Neurol. 20:653-663, 1969.

550. SYMONDS, C. P.: The demyelinating diseases, in Cumings, J. N., and Kremer, M. (eds.): *Biochemical Aspects of Neurological Disorders,* 1st ser. F. A. Davis Co. (Blackwell Scientific Publications), Philadelphia, 1959, Chap. 4, pp. 46-56.

551. SYMONDS, C. P.: *Concussion and its sequelae.* Lancet 1:1-5, 1962.

552. SYMPOSIUM: *The Brain and Its Functions.* Blackwell Scientific Publications, Oxford, 1958.

553. SYMPOSIUM: *International symposium on the physiopathology of the states of consciousness.* Acta Neurochir. 12:161-378, 1965.

554. SZENTÁGOTHAI, J.: *The elementary vestibulo-ocular reflex arc.* J. Neurophysiol. 13:395-407, 1950.

555. SZENTÁGOTHAI, J.: Pathways and synaptic articulation patterns connecting vestibular receptors and oculomotor nuclei, in Bender, M. B. (ed.): *The Oculomotor System.* Harper and Row, New York, 1964, Chap. 8.

556. SZUCS, M. M., JR., BROOKS, H. L., GROSSMAN, W., BANAS, J. S., JR., MEISTER, S. G., DEXTER, L., AND DALEN, J. E.: *Diagnostic sensitivity of laboratory findings in acute pulmonary embolism.* Ann. Intern. Med. 74:161-166, 1971.

557. TEILMAN, N. K.: *Hemangiomas of the pons.* Arch. Neurol. Psychiat. 69:208-223, 1953.

558. TERZIAN, H.: *Behavioural and EEG effects of intracarotid sodium amytal injection.* Acta Neurochir. 12:230-239, 1965.

559. THEWS, G.: Implications to physiology and pathology of oxygen diffusion at the capillary level, in Schade, J. P., and McMenemey, W. H. (eds.): *Selective Vulnerability of the Brain to Hypoxaemia.* F. A. Davis Co. (Blackwell Scientific Publications), Philadelphia, 1963.

560. THOMAS, F. B., MAZZAFERRI, E. L., AND SKILLMAN, T. G.: *Apathetic thyrotoxicosis: A distinctive clinical and laboratory entity.* Ann. Intern. Med. 72:679-685, 1970.

561. THOMPSON, G. N.: *Cerebral area essential to consciousness.* Bull. Los Angeles Neurol. Soc. 16:311-334, 1951.

562. THOMPSON, H. S.: *Afferent pupillary defects. Pupillary findings associated with defects of the afferent arm of the pupillary light reflex arc.* Amer. J. Ophthal. 62:860-873, 1966.

563. THOMPSON, R. K., AND MALINA, S.: *Dynamic axial brainstem distortion as a mechanism explaining the cardiorespiratory changes in increased intracranial pressure.* J. Neurosurg. 16:664-675, 1959.

564. TOLMAN, K. G., AND COHEN, A.: *Accidental hypothermia.* Canad. Med. A. J. 103:1357-1361, 1970.

565. TOWER, D. B.: The neurochemical substrates of cerebral function and activity, in Harlow, H. F., and Woolsey, C. N. (eds.): *Biological and Biochemical Bases of Behavior.* University of Wisconsin Press, Madison, 1958, pp. 285-366.

566. TRANQUADA, R. E., GRANT, W. J., AND PETERSON, C. R.: *Lactic acidosis.* Arch. Intern. Med. 117:192-202, 1966.

567. TSCHUDY, D. P., ET AL.: *Acute intermittent porphyria; the first "overproduction disease" localized to a specific enzyme.* Proc. Nat. Acad. Sci. USA 53:841-847, 1965.

568. TUFO, H. M., OSTFELD, A. M., AND SHEKELLE, R.: *Central nervous system dysfunction following open-heart surgery.* J.A.M.A. 212:1333-1340, 1970.

569. TULLER, M. A., AND MEHDI, F.: *Compensatory hypoventilation and hypercapnia in primary metabolic alkalosis.* Amer. J. Med. 50:281-290, 1971.

570. VAN DEN NOORT, S., ECKEL, R. E., BRINE, K. L., AND HRDLICKA, J.: *Brain metabolism in experimental uremia.* Arch. Intern. Med. 126: 831-834, 1970.

571. VAN GEHUCHTEN, P.: *Le Méchanisme de la Mort dans Certains Cas de Tumeur Cérébrales.* Rev. Neurol. (Paris) 65:702, 1936.

572. VAN HARREVELD, A., AND TACHIBANA, S.: *Recovery of cerebral cortex from asphyxiation.* Amer. J. Physiol. 202:59-65, 1962.

573. VAN POZNAK, A.: *The effect of inhalation anesthetics on repetitive activity generated at motor nerve endings.* Anesthesiology 28:124-127, 1967.

574. VAPALAHTI, M., AND TROUPP, H.: *Prognosis for patients with severe brain injuries.* Brit. Med. J. 3:404-407, 1971.

575. VASTINE, J. H., AND KINNEY, K. K.: *The pineal shadow as an aid in the localization of brain tumors.* Amer. J. Roentgenol. 17:320-324, 1927.

576. VERNON, M. L., HORTA-BARBOSA, L., FUCCILLO, D. A., SEVER, J. L., BARINGER, J. R., AND BIRNBAUM, G.: *Virus-like particles and nucleo-protein-type filaments in brain tissue from two patients with Creutz-feldt-Jakob disease.* Lancet 1:964-967, 1970.

577. VICTOR, M., ADAMS, R. D., AND COLE, M.: *The acquired (non-Wilsonian) type of chronic hepatocerebral degeneration.* Medicine 44:345-396, 1965.

578. VICTOR, M., ANGEVINE, J. B., JR., MANCALL, E. L., AND FISCHER, C. M.: *Memory loss with lesions of hippocampal formation.* Arch. Neurol. 5:244-263, 1961.

579. VICTOR, M., ADAMS, R. D., AND COLLINS, G. H.: *The Wernicke-Korsakoff Syndrome.* F. A. Davis Co., Philadelphia, 1971.

580. VILLABLANCA, J.: *Electroencephalogram in the permanently isolated forebrain of the cat.* Science 133:44-46, 1962.

581. VINCENT, C., DAVID, M., AND THIEBAUT, F.: *Le Cône de Pression Temporal dans les Tumeurs des Hémisphères Cérébraux. Sa Symptomatologie; Sa Gravité; Les Traitments qu'il Convient de lui Opposer.* Rev. Neurol. 65:536-545, 1936.

582. VON ECONOMO, C.: *Encephalitis Lethargica: Its Sequelae and Treatment.* Newman, K. O. (trans.). Oxford University Press, London, 1931.

583. VON GLEES, P., AND BAILEY, R. A.: *Schichtung und fasergrösse des tractus spino-thalamicus des menschen.* Monatsschr. Psychiat. Neurol. 122:129-141, 1951.

584. VON WESTPHAL, A.: *Ueber ein im katatonischen stupor beobachtetes pupillenphänomen sowie bemerkungen über die pupillenstarre bei hysterie.* Deut. Med. Wochenschr. 33:1080-1086, 1907.

585. WALKER, A. E., AND ADAMKIEWICZ, J. J.: *Pseudotumor cerebri associated with prolonged corticosteroid therapy.* J.A.M.A. 188:779-784, 1964.

586. WALSH, F. B., AND HOYT, W. F.: *Clinical Neuro-ophthalmology,* ed. 3. Williams and Wilkins Co., Baltimore, 1969, vol. 1.

587. WALTER, W. G.: *Electro-encephalography in cases of mental disorder.* J. Ment. Sci. 88:110-121, 1942.

588. WALTER, W. G.: Intrinsic rhythms of the brain, in Field, J., Magoun, H. W., and Hall, V. E. (eds.): *Handbook of Physiology.* Sect. 1, Neurophysiology. American Physiological Society, Washington, D. C., 1959, vol. 1, pp. 279-298.

589. WARD, A. A., JR.: *Decerebrate rigidity.* J. Neurophysiol. 10:89-103, 1947.

590. WEICKHARDT, G. D., AND DAVIS, R. L.: *Solitary abscess of the brainstem.* Neurology 14:918-925, 1964.

591. WEINBERGER, L. M., GIBBON, M. H., AND GIBBON, J. H., JR.: *Temporary arrest of the circulation to the central nervous system: I. Physiologic effects.* Arch. Neurol. Psychiat. 43:615-634, 1940.

592. WEINBERGER, L. M., GIBBON, M. H., AND GIBBON, J. H., JR.: *Temporary arrest of the circulation to the central nervous system: II. Pathologic effects.* Arch. Neurol. Psychiat. 43:961-986, 1940.

592a. WEINER, L. P., ET AL.: *Virus related to SV40 in patients with progressive multifocal leukoencephalopathy.* New Eng. J. Med. 286:385-389, 1972.

593. WEINSTEIN, J. D., LANGFITT, T. W., BRUNO, L., FAVEN, H. A., AND JACKSON, J. L. F.: *Experimental study of patterns of brain distortion and ischemia produced by an intracranial mass.* J. Neurosurg. 28: 513-521, 1968.

594. WELLS, C. E.: *Cerebral embolism.* Arch. Neurol. Psychiat. 81:667-677, 1959.

595. WHITTY, C. W. M.: The neurologic basis of memory, in Williams, D. (ed.): *Modern Trends in Neurology,* 3rd ser. Butterworth, Washington, D. C., 1962, Chap. 16, pp. 314-335.

596. WHITTY, C. W. M., AND LEWIN, W.: *Vivid day-dreaming; an unusual form of confusion following anterior cingulectomy.* Brain 80:72-76, 1957.

597. WILLIAMS, C. P. S., SWANSON, A. G., AND CHAPMAN, J. T.: *Brain swelling with acute purulent meningitis.* Pediatrics 34:220-227, 1964.

598. WILLIAMS, R. H.: Hypoglycemosis, in Williams, R. H. (ed.): *Diabetes.* Paul B. Hoeber, New York, 1960, Chap. 46.

599. WILSON, S. A. K.: *Epileptic variants.* J. Neurol. Psychopath. 8: 223-240, 1928.

600. WOLFLE, D.: *Dying with dignity.* Science 168:1403, 1970.

601. WOLMAN, L.: *Ischaemic lesions in the brain-stem associated with raised supratentorial pressure.* Brain 76:364-377, 1953.

602. WOLSTENHOLME, G. E. W., AND O'CONNOR, M. (eds.): *The Nature of Sleep.* Little, Brown and Co., Boston, 1961.

603. WOOD, M. W., AND MURPHY, F.: *Obstructive hydrocephalus due to infarction of a cerebellar hemisphere.* J. Neurosurg. 30:260-263, 1969.

604. WOODBURY, D. M.: *Effect of acute hyponatremia on distribution of water and electrolytes in various tissues of rat.* Amer. J. Physiol. 185: 281-286, 1956.

605. WOODBURY, D. M.: *Relation between the adrenal cortex and the central nervous system.* Pharmacol. Rev. 10:275-357, 1958.

606. YAKOVLEV, P. I.: *Paraplegia in flexion of cerebral origin.* J. Neuropath. Exp. Neurol. 13:267-296, 1954.

607. ZU RHEIN, G. M., AND CHOU, S-M.: *Particles resembling papova viruses in human cerebral demyelinating disease.* Science 148:1477-1479, 1965.

Index

280